THE RELIGIOUS
AFFECTIONS

THE RELIGIOUS
AFFECTIONS

JONATHAN EDWARDS

THE BANNER OF TRUTH TRUST

THE BANNER OF TRUTH TRUST
3 Murrayfield Road, Edinburgh EH12 6EL
PO Box 621, Carlisle, Pennsylvania 17013, U.S.A.

*   *   *

First published 1746
First Banner of Truth edition 1961
Reprinted in paperback format 1986

ISBN 0 85151 485 5

Reprinted 1984

ISBN 0 85151 431 6

*   *   *

Printed in Great Britain by
Billing & Sons Ltd., Worcester

PUBLISHERS' NOTE

MANY editions of *The Religious Affections* have been published since the first edition of 1746, and there are some variations in punctuation between them. While this edition follows the text of the Worcester edition, the punctuation has been examined throughout and occasionally revised to aid the modern reader. A few minor amendments and corrections have been made in the text, which is unabridged. Where possible the footnote quotations from Puritan authors have been checked and the page references have been altered to later and more accessible editions of their works. Thus the page numbers of quotations from Thomas Shepard refer to the Boston, 1853, 3-volume edition of his Works (*The Sincere Convert* and *The Sound Believer* in Vol. I and *The Parable of the Ten Virgins* in Vol. II) and the page references of quotations from John Flavel are from the 6-volume, complete edition of his Works, London, 1820. If the present demand for Puritan literature continues these would be the editions of Shepard and Flavel most suited for re-publication.

CONTENTS

7

Part III

INTRODUCTION

By universal confession of the princeliest leaders in the world of thought, Jonathan Edwards must be included among those whose gifts are of the supremest sort.

His most famous books, on the intellectual and theological side, were the product of his latest years. *The Freedom of the Will, The Defence of the Doctrine of Original Sin, The Discussion of the Nature of True Virtue, The Treatise on God's Last End in the Creation,* were all written in the Stockbridge period of his life (1751-1758); and the majority of them were not published until after his earthly tasks were done, and his body had been laid to rest in the Princeton Churchyard. It was a polemical purpose which inspired these great works—the purpose of refuting Arminianism. But, in themselves, they are among the monumental books of history. They have the incorruptible quality, the asbestos element, in them. A latent fire pulses and quivers under the acute and victorious and remorseless argument, and there is that in their pages which will keep them vital and vitalising so long as men crave great thoughts to live and die with.

The Freedom of the Will is, as Isaac Taylor said, " a classic in metaphysics "; and, whether or no we admit its thesis that human liberty must live and move and have its being within the sphere of a divine determinism, it throws its spell over us. Mr. Lecky has condemned the treatise on Original Sin as " one of the most revolting books that have ever proceeded from the pen of man "; but, when a shallow optimism beguiles us with its enchantments, and when life is painted, in M. Renan's fashion, as an affectionate picnic and " a delightful excursion through reality," we need the Puritanism of Edwards to remind us that things are not so far removed from disaster and tragedy, and that there is a far-reaching and deep-seated alienation which separates man from God. It may be that, in his consideration of the nature of True Virtue, he sometimes makes over-exacting demands of our frail and storm-driven humanity; but he is himself one of the high men who died in the pursuit of great things, and, when he depicts the love of God as the first beginning and the last end of our thoughts and words and ways, he portrays his own motive and his own goal. And as for creation, Edwards tells us that it is the unveiling of the divine glory, the publishing of some of the syllables in the august and adorable and blessed Name of God, the writing out in legible characters of a little of His matchless and unfathomable perfection. This man always walks on the sublimest levels. To us, who look up to him from far beneath, he seems to have his proper place among the cherubim who know.

But sometimes he draws nearer still to the sacred Presence and the gracious Face. He takes rank among the seraphim who burn. That is the peerless society in which we find him when we read *The Religious Affections*.

It is an older book than those others. It was published in 1746, and before that, it had been preached in a series of sermons to his congregation in 1742 and 1743;—were they not a richly favoured people to listen to discourses which laid bare to them the mysteries of the Kingdom of Heaven? It was the Great Revival which gave birth to the book.

In the closing months of 1734, and all through 1735, when Edwards had been for some seven or eight years minister of his charge, the plenteous rains of the Holy Spirit began to fall on the souls he was so eager to instruct and bless. The town, he wrote, was "never so full of love, never so full of joy and yet so full of distress, as it was then." Whenever men and women met, and it mattered nothing whether they were old or young, the talk turned on divine and eternal things. There were meetings in private houses as well as in the church. A profound and universal concern about religion took possession of the place. And through it all Edwards moved, his heart filled with thankfulness, and his mind intent on scrutinising these goings of God in His sanctuary. He noted that, first, the awakened consciousness was plunged into depths of gloom and fear. It realised that there was awful danger impending. Its whole energies were strained and bent to escape from the wrath to come. Then he saw the troubled soul learning to acknowledge the sovereignty of God, and to leave itself implicitly in His hands, and to confess its need of the mediation of Christ. And, by and by, after many

confused strivings and many humbling discoveries, he beheld it
arriving at the happy harbour of salvation, the storm changed
into a calm at God's command and will. These were the blessed
sights he found on every side of him. He studied them, during
that strange and glorious year of 1735, with the keen mental
interest of the psychologist and the rejoicing gratitude of the
bond-servant of Jesus Christ.

Then, to his great grief, the splendid vision faded into the
light of common day. Worldliness and sin commenced to re-
assert themselves in Northampton. But, though the reign of
grace had declined, there were signs that ere long it might return.
For this Edwards waited and prayed and toiled; and God gave
him the desires of his heart. In 1740, the Revival came back,
like the reappearance of spring after a temporary and dishearten-
ing winter. This time it was destined to spread far beyond his
own parish, through New England first, and then over the sea
to Britain and the Continent of Europe. It became the wonderful spiritual quickening which we associate with the names of
Whitefield and Wesley, as well as with that of Edwards. It had
its blemishes and blunders, which its enemies magnified, and
which stirred poignant regrets in its warmest friends. There
were often alarming and disquieting bodily effects. There was
an idea, which soon became too prevalent, that God and Christ
and heaven and hell were revealed immediately to the soul; and
thus men disparaged the written Word and the Spirit's employ-
ment of it as His instrument. There were itinerant preachers
who pushed themselves forward, and who frequently were
very severe in their strictures on the Church's ordained
ministers. There was real danger that the settled order of
God's house would be overturned. These were mournful and
mysterious flaws, and Edwards lamented their presence and
wished to have them rectified. But about the work of God itself,
its genuineness, its depth, its marvellous effects, he had no manner of doubt. "Who that saw the state of things in New
England a few years ago," he asks, "would have thought that
in so little a time there would be such a change?" The conscience of the people had been roused into a new sensitiveness.
The young had laid aside their levity. The taverns were
deserted. The wealthy had relinquished their vanities. The
Bible was loved and pondered, and the Lord's Day was religi-

ously observed. Old quarrels were ended, and those who had been at variance were joining hands again in brotherliness and amity. Could these things be Satan's spurious counterfeit—his mirage which dazzled the eye and befooled the heart? Were they not God's superhuman and irrefutable reality?

In connection with the Awakening of 1735, Edwards wrote the *Narrative of Surprising Conversions;* in connection with the later movement of 1740 and the subsequent years, he gave to the world two books, *The Distinguishing Marks of a Work of the Spirit of God*, and the *Thoughts on the Revival.* Afterwards came the *Treatise Concerning the Religious Affections*. It represents his best and maturest conclusions on the great theme with which it deals.

Its style has often been stigmatised in no measured terms. And indeed we have little of the point and pathos and mother-wit of John Bunyan and Thomas Shepard, little of the sonorous eloquence of Howe, little of the Oriental fragrance of Rutherford. We are told that, in his later life, Edwards regretted that he had paid such small attention to graces of diction, and expressed himself as well aware of the persuasive virtue which lies in words fitly chosen. In his own writings it seems many a time as if he were thinking aloud, and were throwing out his thoughts just as they came to him, in all their ruggedness and all their richness, with no attempt to chisel them into shape and to give them perfection of form. And yet, if we read this book with any care, we shall find that, regarded simply in its literary aspect, it has many passages brimming over with tenderness, and many which move us by their massive strength of utterance, and some too that are melodious with a great organ music which must leave its echoes reverberating in our hearts. The indictment of the style of *The Affections* has been stated extravagantly and pressed too far.

There is an indubitable sadness in the tone of the book. The prevailing atmosphere is that of October rather than of May. It is as though, during the years which had elapsed since the passing of the Revival, Edwards had grown more and more alive to its faults and to the excesses which could be charged against it. He never lost his faith that the wind of the Spirit had been blowing, beneficently and conqueringly, over the valley of dry bones; but he was cut to the quick when he remembered the variety of false experiences, the hypocrisies, the degenerations, which accompanied the Awakening. In these pages he strives to leave behind him the accidents of time and place, the dis-illusionments of recent experience, the men and women from whom he had hoped great things which never came. He forgets the morning clouds which had looked so rosy in the early dawn but had vanished so quickly, and the rivers that had set out with volume and sparkle and ripple, only to lose themselves in the sand. He takes his ideal into his secret chamber, and con-siders it in the light of Scripture and of what the divine Spirit had taught his own soul. Thus *The Religious Affections* has no mere local and transient interest, as the presentment of a fleeting and disappointing episode in the history of the Church; it lives and will live as the portraiture of the men who are after God's heart.

Certain features in the portrait strike us especially. One of them is its caution and balance—the way in which the artist discriminates, and sifts, and sets this consideration over against that other, and gives to each its appropriate value and weight. And another is its completeness; when we have taken it all in, we recognise that here, beyond question, is the picture of the soul which under the tuition of divine grace has grown worthy of union with God Himself. Again, the book leaves with us, as few books do, the sense of the arduousness of the Christian life. "The righteous scarcely are saved," we feel when we are in the company of Jonathan Edwards. Such delusions may ensnare the heart as it climbs toward God's high heaven; such nets may entangle it; such principalities and powers are fighting against it —ah, there is no progress half so serious as this, there is no cam-paign against such fearful odds. If God were not for us and in us, we should be disgraced and slain before an hour had passed.

At times, as has been pointed out by more than one, Edwards seems too pure and sublimated and lofty. Is it the case, we ask, that "the first objective ground of gracious affections is the transcendently excellent and amiable character of divine things as they are in themselves, and not any conceived relation they bear to self, or self-interest"? May not gratitude to the God who has done great things for him be the earliest feeling of the young disciple, and delight in the stainlessness and grandeur of that God Himself only a subsequent experience, which comes after fellowship and intimacy with the Father and the Son and the Spirit?

And yet—and yet, *da mihi magistrum.* Not a day passed, Jerome tells us, in which Cyprian of Carthage did not address the command to his amanuensis, "Give me the master!" And then the amanuensis would take down some one of the treatises of Tertullian—Tertullian with his originality, his profundity, his force and fulness of thought, his speculation, his clear and convincing dialectic. Everyone of us who would grow in the grace and knowledge of the Lord Jesus Christ, everyone who would read aright his own heart, and would learn what God requires of him, must say of *The Religious Affections,* "Da mihi magistrum!" It savours of sacrilege to hint any criticism of a book which soars to such heights and which is so instinct with the wisdom that cometh from afar.

In these pages Jonathan Edwards has asserted for all time the inwardness and spirituality of true religion. It is far removed, he assures us, from a mechanical routine of duty; it is no cold and careful taskwork. They are greatly mistaken who imagine that it is something sacerdotal and sacramentarian. It is the outgoing towards Himself, in love and in life, of the soul which God has touched and which God inhabits. It is "the motion of a hidden fire," trembling in the breast, warming all the heart, consuming in its ardent flame the dross of our sins, cleansing and energising and transfiguring us until—miracle of miracles! —even we are heaven's fine and burnished gold.

We may fall just now immeasurably beneath the ideal which is painted in those sublime and searching chapters; but, if we are children in the household of the Lord, one thing is sure—we shall be smitten with the passion to reach it. And perhaps no one, on this side the New Jerusalem, has come nearer reaching it than the man who has delineated it here for us.

ALEXANDER SMELLIE
1898

THE AUTHOR'S PREFACE

THERE is no question whatsoever that is of greater importance to mankind, and that it more concerns every individual person to be well resolved in, than this: *What are the distinguishing qualifications of those that are in favour with God, and entitled to His eternal rewards?* Or, which comes to the same thing, What is *the nature of true religion?* *And wherein do lie the distinguishing notes of that virtue and holiness that is acceptable in the sight of God?* But though it be of such importance, and though we have clear and abundant light in the word of God to direct us in this matter, yet there is no one point wherein professing Christians do more differ one from another. It would be endless to reckon up the variety of opinions on this point, that divide the Christian world; making manifest the truth of that declaration of our Saviour, "Strait is the gate and narrow is the way, that leads to life, and few there be that find it."

The consideration of these things has long engaged me to attend to this matter, with the utmost diligence and care, and exactness of search and inquiry, that I have been capable of. It is a subject on which my mind has been peculiarly intent ever since I first entered on the study of divinity. But as to the success of my inquiries, it must be left to the judgment of the reader of the following treatise.

I am sensible it is much more difficult to judge impartially of that which is the subject of this discourse, in the midst of the dust and smoke of such a state of controversy as this land is now in about things of this nature. As it is more difficult to write impartially, so it is more difficult to read impartially. Many will probably be hurt in their spirits, to find so much that appertains to religious affection here condemned: and perhaps indignation and contempt will be excited in others by finding so much here justified and approved. And it may be, some will be ready to charge me with inconsistence with myself, in so much approving some things, and so much condemning others; as I have found this has always been objected to by some, ever since the begin-

15

ning of our late controversies about religion. It is a hard thing to be a hearty zealous friend of what has been good and glorious in the late extraordinary appearances, and to rejoice much in it; and at the same time to see the evil and pernicious tendency of what has been bad, and earnestly to oppose that. But yet, I am humbly but fully persuaded, we shall never be in the way of truth, nor go on in a way acceptable to God and tending to the advancement of Christ's kingdom, till we do so. There is indeed something very mysterious in it, that so much good, and so much bad, should be mixed together in the church of God; just as it is a mysterious thing which has puzzled and amazed many a good Christian, that there should be that which is so divine and precious, viz.: the saving grace of God, and the new and divine nature, dwelling with so much corruption, hypocrisy, and iniquity, in the heart of the same saint. Yet neither of these is more mysterious than real. And neither of them is a new or rare thing. It is no new thing, that much false religion should prevail, at a time of great reviving of true religion; and that at such a time multitudes of hypocrites should spring up among true saints. It was so in that great reformation, and revival of religion, that was in Josiah's time; as appears by Jer. iii. 10, and iv. 3, 4, and also by the great apostasy that there was in the land, so soon after his reign. So it was in that great outpouring of the Spirit upon the Jews, that was in the days of John the Baptist; as appears by the great apostasy of that people so soon after so general an awakening, and by the temporary religious comforts and joys of many: John v. 35, "Ye were willing for a season to rejoice in his light." So it was in those great commotions that were among the multitude, occasioned by the preaching of Jesus Christ; of the many that were then called, but few were chosen; of the multitude that were roused and affected by his preaching, and at one time or other appeared mightily engaged, full of admiration of Christ, and elevated with joy, but few were true disciples, that stood the shock of the great trials that came afterwards, and endured to the end. Many were like the stony ground, or thorny ground, and but few, comparatively, like the good ground. Of the whole heap that was gathered, great part was chaff, that the wind afterwards drove away; and the heap of wheat that was left was comparatively small; as appears abundantly by the history of the New Testament. So it was in that great outpouring of the Spirit that was in the apostles' days; as appears by Matt. xxiv. 10-13. Gal. iii. 1, and iv. 11, 15. Phil. ii. 21, and iii. 18, 19, and the two epistles to the Corinthians, and many other parts of the New Testament. And so it was in the great reformation from Popery. It appears plainly to have been in the visible church of God, in times of great reviving of religion from time to time, as it is with the fruit trees in the spring; there are a multitude of blossoms, all of which appear fair and beautiful, and there is a promising appearance of young fruits; but many of them are of short continuance; they soon fall off, and never come to maturity.

Not that it is to be supposed that it will always be so; for though there never will, in this world, be an entire purity, either in particular saints, in a perfect freedom from mixtures of corruption; or in the church of God, without any mixture of hypocrites with saints, and counterfeit religion, and false appearances of grace with true religion and real holiness: yet it is evident that there will come a time of much greater purity in the church of God, than has been in ages past; it is plain by these texts of Scripture, Isa. lii. 1. Joel iii. 17. Zech. xiv. 21 Psal. lxix, 32, 35, 36. Isa. iv. 3, 4, xxxv. 8, 10. Ezek. xx. 38. Psal. xxxvii. 9, 10, 22, 29. And one great reason of it will be that at that time God will give much greater light to his people, to distinguish between true religion and its counterfeits. Mal. iii. 3, " And he shall sit as a refiner and purifier of silver: and he shall purify the sons of Levi, and purge them as gold and silver, that they may offer to the Lord an offering in righteousness." With ver. 18, which is a continuation of the prophecy of the same happy times. " Then shall ye return, and discern between the righteous and the wicked, between him that serveth God, and him that serveth him not."

It is by the mixture of counterfeit religion with true, not discerned and distinguished, that the devil has had his greatest advantage against the cause and kingdom of Christ all along hitherto. It is by this means, principally, that he has prevailed against all revivings of religion that ever have been since the first founding of the Christian church. By this, he hurt the cause of Christianity in and after the apostolic age, much more than by all the persecutions of both Jews and heathens. The apostles, in all their epistles, show themselves much more concerned at the former mischief than the latter. By this, Satan prevailed against the Reformation, begun by Luther, Zwinglius and others, to put a stop to its progress, and bring it into disgrace, ten times more than by all those bloody, cruel, and before unheard-of persecutions of the Church of Rome. By this, principally, has he prevailed against revivals of religion, that have been in our nation since the Reformation. By this he prevailed against New England, to quench the love and spoil the joy of her espousals, about a hundred years ago. And I think I have had opportunity enough to see plainly that by this the devil has prevailed against the late great revival of religion in New England, so happy and promising in its beginning. Here, most evidently, has been the main advantage Satan has had against us; by this he has foiled us. It is by this means, that the daughter of Zion in this land now lies on the ground, in such piteous circumstances as we now behold her, with her garments rent, her face disfigured, her nakedness exposed, her limbs broken, and weltering in the blood of her own wounds, and in no wise able to arise; and this, so quickly after her late great joys and hopes: Lam. i. 17, "Zion spreadeth forth her hands, and there is none to comfort her: the Lord hath commanded concerning Jacob, that his adversaries shall be round about him." I have seen the devil prevail the same way against two great revivings of religion in this country. Satan goes on with mankind as he began with them. He prevailed against our first parents, and cast them out of paradise, and suddenly brought all their happiness and glory to an end, by appearing to be a friend to their happy paradisaic state, and pretending to advance it to higher degrees. So the same cunning serpent, that beguiled Eve through his subtilty, by perverting us from the simplicity that is in Christ, hath suddenly prevailed to deprive us of that fair prospect we had a little while ago, of a kind of paradisaic state of the church of God in New England.

After religion has revived in the church of God, and enemies appear, people that are engaged to defend its cause are commonly most exposed where they are least sensible of danger. While they are wholly intent upon the opposition that appears openly before them, to make head against that, and do neglect carefully to look all around them, the devil comes behind them, and gives a fatal stab unseen; and has opportunity to give a more home stroke, and wound the deeper, because he strikes at his leisure and according to his pleasure, being obstructed by no guard or resistance.

And so it is ever likely to be in the church, whenever religion revives remarkably, till we have learned well to distinguish between true and false religion, between saving affections and experiences, and those manifold fair shows and glistering appearances by which they are counterfeited; the consequences of which, when they are not distinguished, are often inexpressibly dreadful. By this means the devil gratifies himself, by bringing it to pass that that should be offered to God by multitudes, under a notion of a pleasing acceptable service to him, that is indeed above all things abominable to him. By this means he deceives great multitudes about the state of their souls, making them think they are something when they are nothing; and so eternally undoes them; and not only so, but establishes many in a strong confidence of their eminent holiness, who are in God's sight some of the vilest of hypocrites. By this means he many ways damps and wounds religion in the hearts of the saints, obscures and deforms it by corrupt mixtures, causes their religious affections woefully to degenerate, and sometimes for a considerable time to be like the manna that bred worms and stank; and dreadfully ensnares and confounds the minds of others of the saints, and brings them into great difficulties and temptations, and entangles them in a wilderness out of which they can by no means extricate themselves. By this means Satan mightily encourages the hearts of open enemies of religion, and strengthens their hands, and fills them with weapons, and makes strong their fortresses: when, at the same time, religion and the church of God lie exposed to them, as a city without walls. By this means he brings it to pass, that men work wickedness under a notion of doing God service, and so sin without restraint, yea with earnest forwardness and zeal, and with all their might. By this means he brings in even the friends of religion, insensibly to themselves, to do the work of enemies, by destroying religion in a far more effectual manner than open enemies can do, under a notion of advancing it. By this means the devil scatters the flock of Christ, and sets them one against another, and that with great heat of spirit, under a notion of zeal for God; and religion, by degrees, degenerates into vain jangling; and during the strife, Satan leads both parties far out of the right way, driving each to great extremes, one on the right hand and the other on the left, according as he finds they are most inclined, or most easily moved and swayed, till the right path in the middle is almost wholly neglected. And in the midst of this confusion, the devil has great opportunity to advance his own interest, and make it strong in ways innumerable, and get the government of all into his own hands, and work his own will. And by what is seen of the terrible consequences of this counterfeit religion, when not distinguished from true religion, God's people in general have their minds unhinged and unsettled in things of religion, and know not where to set their foot, or what to think or do; and many are brought into doubts, whether there be anything in religion; and heresy and infidelity and atheism greatly prevail.

Therefore it greatly concerns us to use our utmost endeavours clearly to discern, and have it well settled and established, wherein true religion does consist. Till this be done, it may be expected that great revivings of religion will be but of short continuance; till this be done, there is but little good to be expected of all our warm debates, in conversation and from the press, not knowing clearly and distinctly what we ought to contend for.

My design is to contribute my mite, and use my best (however feeble) endeavours to this end, in the ensuing treatise; wherein it must be noted that my design is somewhat diverse from the design of what I have formerly published, which was to show the *distinguishing marks of a work of the Spirit of God*, including both His common and saving operations; but what I aim at now, is to show the nature and signs of the *gracious operations* of God's Spirit, by which they are to be distinguished from all things whatsoever that the minds of men are the subjects of, which are not of a saving nature. If I have succeeded in this my aim in any tolerable measure, I hope it will tend to promote the interest of religion. And whether I have succeeded to bring any light to this subject or no, and however my attempts may be reproached in these captious and censorious times, I hope in the mercy of a gracious God for the acceptance of the sincerity of my endeavours; and hope also for the candour and prayers of the true followers of the meek and charitable Lamb of God.

Part I

CONCERNING THE NATURE OF THE AFFECTIONS, AND THEIR IMPORTANCE IN RELIGION

1 PETER I. 8

Whom having not seen, ye love; in whom, though now ye see him not, yet believing, ye rejoice with joy unspeakable and full of glory.

IN these words the apostle represents the state of the minds of the Christians he wrote to, under the persecutions they were then the subjects of. These persecutions are what he has respect to in the two preceding verses, when he speaks of *the trial of their faith,* and of *their being in heaviness through manifold temptations.*

Such trials are of threefold benefit to true religion. Hereby the truth of it is manifested, and it appears to be indeed true religion; they, above all other things, have a tendency to distinguish between true religion and false, and to cause the difference between them evidently to appear. Hence they are called by the name of *trials,* in the verse immediately preceding the text, and in innumerable other places; they try the faith and religion of professors, of what sort it is, as apparent gold is tried in the fire and manifested whether it be true gold or no. And the faith of true Christians being thus tried and proved to be true, is " found to praise and honour and glory" as in that preceding verse.

And then, these trials are of further benefit to true religion; they not only manifest the truth of it, but they make its genuine beauty and amiableness remarkably to appear. True virtue never appears so lovely as when it is most oppressed; and the divine excellency of real Christianity is never exhibited with such advantage as when under the greatest trials: then it is that true faith appears much more precious than gold, and upon this account is " found to praise and honour and glory."

And again, another benefit that such trials are of to true religion is that they purify and increase it. They not only manifest it to be true, but also tend to refine it, and deliver it from those mixtures of that which is false which encumber and impede it; that nothing may be left but that which is true. They tend to cause the amiableness of true religion to appear to the best advantage, as was before observed; and not only so, but they tend to increase its beauty by establishing and confirming it, and making it more lively and vigorous, and purifying it from those things that obscured its lustre and glory. As gold that is tried in the fire is purged from its alloy and all remainders of dross, and comes forth more solid and beautiful; so true faith being tried as gold is tried in the fire, becomes more precious, and thus also is " found unto praise and honour and glory." The apostle seems to have respect to each of these benefits that persecutions are of to true religion, in the verse preceding the text.

And in the text, the apostle observes how true religion operated in the Christians he wrote to, under their persecutions, whereby these benefits of persecution appeared in them; or what manner of operation of true religion, in them, it was, whereby their religion, under persecution, was manifested to be true religion, and eminently appeared in the genuine beauty and amiableness of true religion, and also appeared to be increased and purified, and so was like to be " found unto praise and honour and glory at the appearing of Jesus Christ." And there were two kinds of operation, or exercise of true religion, in them, under their sufferings, that the apostle takes notice of in the text, wherein these benefits appeared.

1. *Love to Christ:* " Whom having not yet seen, ye love. The world was ready to wonder what strange principle it was that influenced them to expose themselves to so great sufferings, to forsake the things that were seen, and renounce all that was dear and pleasant which was the object of sense. They seemed to the men of the world about them as though they were beside themselves, and to act as though they hated themselves; there was nothing in their view that could induce them thus to suffer, and support them under, and carry them through such trials. But although there was nothing that was seen, nothing that the world

saw, or that the Christians themselves ever saw with their bodily eyes, that thus influenced and supported them, yet they had a supernatural principle of love to something unseen; they loved Jesus Christ, for they saw Him spiritually whom the world saw not, and whom they themselves had never seen with bodily eyes.

2. *Joy in Christ.* Though their outward sufferings were very grievous, yet their inward spiritual joys were greater than their sufferings; and these supported them and enabled them to suffer with cheerfulness.

There are two things which the apostle takes notice of in the text concerning this joy. 1. The manner in which it rises, the way in which Christ, though unseen, is the foundation of it, viz., by faith; which is the evidence of things not seen: " In whom, though now ye see him not, yet believing, ye rejoice." 2. The nature of this joy; " unspeakable and full of glory." Unspeakable in the kind of it; very different from worldly joys, and carnal delights; of a vastly more pure, sublime, and heavenly nature, being something supernatural and truly divine and so ineffably excellent; the sublimity and exquisite sweetness of which there were no words to set forth. Unspeakable also in degree; it pleasing God to give them this holy joy with a liberal hand, and in large measure, in their state of persecution.

Their joy was full of glory. Although the joy was unspeakable, and no words were sufficient to describe it, yet something might be said of it, and no words more fit to represent its excellency than these, that it was *full of glory;* or, as it is in the original, *glorified joy.* In rejoicing with this joy, their minds were filled, as it were, with a glorious brightness, and their natures exalted and perfected. It was a most worthy, noble rejoicing, that did not corrupt and debase the mind, as many carnal joys do; but did greatly beautify and dignify it; it was a prelibation of the joy of heaven, that raised their minds to a degree of heavenly blessedness; it filled their minds with the light of God's glory, and made themselves to shine with some communication of that glory.

Hence the proposition or doctrine, that I would raise from these words, is this:

True Religion, in great part, consists in Holy Affections

We see that the apostle, in observing and remarking the operations and exercises of religion in the Christians he wrote to, wherein their religion appeared to be true and of the right kind when it had its greatest trial of what sort it was, being tried by persecution as gold is tried in the fire, and when their religion not only proved true, but was most pure, and cleansed from its dross and mixtures of that which was not true, and when religion appeared in them most in its genuine excellency and native beauty, and was found to praise, and honour, and glory; the apostle, I say, singles out the religious affections of *love* and *joy* that were then in exercise in them : these are the exercises of religion he takes notice of, wherein their religion did thus appear true and pure, and in its proper glory. Here I would,

1. Show what is intended by the affections.
2. Observe some things which make it evident, that a great part of true religion lies in the affections.

I. It may be inquired, what the affections of the mind are.

I answer : The affections are no other than the more vigorous and sensible exercises of the inclination and will of the soul.

God has endued the soul with two faculties : one is that by which it is capable of perception and speculation, or by which it discerns, and views, and judges of things; which is called the understanding. The other faculty is that by which the soul does not merely perceive and view things, but is some way inclined with respect to the things it views or considers; either is inclined *to* them, or is disinclined and averse *from* them; or is the faculty by which the soul does not behold things as an indifferent unaffected spectator, but either as liking or disliking, pleased or displeased, approving or rejecting. This faculty is called by various names; it is sometimes called the *inclination:* and, as it has respect to the actions that are determined and governed by it, is called the *will:* and the mind, with regard to the exercises of this faculty, is often called the *heart.*

The exercises of this faculty are of two sorts; either those by which the soul is carried out towards the things that are in view, in approving of them, being pleased with them, and inclined to them; or those in which the soul opposes the things that are in view, in disapproving of them, and in being displeased with them, averse from them, and rejecting them.

And as the exercises of the inclination and will of the soul are various in their kinds, so they are much more various in their degrees. There are some exercises of pleasedness or displeased-ness, inclination or disinclination, where the soul is carried but a little beyond a state of perfect indifference. And there are other degrees above this, wherein the approbation or dislike, pleasedness or aversion, are stronger, wherein we may rise higher and higher, till the soul comes to act vigorously and sensibly, and the actings of the soul are with that strength, that (through the laws of the union which the Creator has fixed between the soul and the body) the motion of the blood and animal spirits begins to be sensibly altered; whence oftentimes arises some bodily sensation, especi-ally about the heart and vitals, that are the fountain of the fluids of the body: from whence it comes to pass that the mind, with regard to the exercises of this faculty, perhaps in all nations and ages, is called the *heart*. And, it is to be noted that they are these more vigorous and sensible exercises of this faculty that are called the *affections*.

The will, and the affections of the soul, are not two faculties; the affections are not essentially distinct from the will, nor do they differ from the mere actings of the will, and inclination of the soul, but only in the liveliness and sensibleness of exercise.

It must be confessed, that language is here somewhat imper-fect, and the meaning of words in a considerable measure loose and unfixed, and not precisely limited by custom, which governs the use of language. In some sense, the affection of the soul differs nothing at all from the will and inclination, and the will never is in any exercise any further than it is affected; it is not moved out of a state of perfect indifference, any otherwise than as it is affected one way or other. But yet there are many act-ings of the will and inclination that are not so commonly called *affections:* in every thing we do, wherein we act voluntarily, there is an exercise of the will and inclination; it is our inclination that governs us in our actions; but all the actings of the inclination and will, in all our common actions of life, are not ordinarily called affections. Yet what are commonly called affections are not essentially different from them, but only in the degree and manner of exercise. In every act of the will whatsoever, the soul either likes or dislikes, is either inclined or disinclined to what is in view: these are not essentially different from those affections of love and hatred. That liking or inclination of the soul to a thing, if it be in a high degree, and be vigorous and lively, is the very same thing with the affection of love; and that disliking and disinclining if in a great degree, is the very same with hatred. In every act of the will for or towards something not present, the soul is in some degree inclined to that thing; and that inclination, if in a considerable degree, is the very same with the affection of desire. And in every degree of the act of the will, wherein the soul approves of something present, there is a degree of pleasedness; and that pleasedness, if it be in a considerable degree, is the very same with the affections of joy or delight. And if the will disapproves of what is present, the soul is in some degree displeased, and if that displeasedness be great, it is the very same with the affection of grief or sorrow.

Such seems to be our nature, and such the laws of the union of soul and body, that there never is in any case whatsoever, any lively and vigorous exercise of the will or inclination of the soul without some effect upon the body, in some alteration of the motion of its fluids, and especially of the animal spirits. And, on the other hand, from the same laws of the union of the soul and body, the constitution of the body and the motion of its fluids may promote the exercise of the affections. But yet it is not the body, but the mind only, that is the proper seat of the affections. The body of man is no more capable of being really the subject of love or hatred, joy or sorrow, fear or hope, than the body of a tree, or than the same body of man is capable of thinking and understanding. As it is the soul only that has ideas, so it is the soul only that is pleased or displeased with its ideas. As it is the soul only that thinks, so it is the soul only that loves or hates, rejoices or is grieved at what it thinks of. Nor are these motions of the animal spirits and fluids of the body anything properly belonging to the nature of the affections, though they always accompany them, in the present state; but are only effects or concomitants of the affections that are entirely distinct from the affections themselves, and no way essential to them; so that an unbodied spirit may be as capable of love and hatred, joy or sorrow, hope or fear, or other affections, as one that is united to a body.

The affections and passions are frequently spoken of as the same; and yet in the more common use of speech, there is in some respect a difference. Affection is a word that, in its ordinary signification, seems to be something more extensive than passion, being used for all vigorous lively actings of the will or inclination; but passion for those that are more sudden, and whose effects on the animal spirits are more violent, and the mind more overpowered, and less in its own command.

As all the exercises of the inclination and will are either in approving and liking, or disapproving and rejecting; so the affections are of two sorts; they are those by which the soul is carried out to what is in view, cleaving to it, or seeking it; or those by which it is averse from it, and opposes it.

Of the former sort are love, desire, hope, joy, gratitude, complacence. Of the latter kind are hatred, fear, anger, grief, and such like; which it is needless now to stand particularly to define.

And there are some affections wherein there is a composition of each of the aforementioned kinds of actings of the will; as in the affection of *pity*, there is something of the former kind towards the person suffering, and something of the latter towards what he suffers. And so in zeal, there is in it high approbation of some person or thing, together with vigorous opposition to what is conceived to be contrary to it.

There are other mixed affections that might be also mentioned, but I hasten to the second thing proposed, which was to observe some things that render it evident that true religion in great part consists in the affections.

Evidence that True Religion lies much in the Affections

1. What has already been said of the nature of the affections makes this evident, and may be sufficient without adding anything further, to put this matter out of doubt; for who will deny that true religion consists in a great measure in vigorous and lively actings of the inclination and will of the soul, or the fervent exercises of the heart?

That religion which God requires, and will accept, does not consist in weak, dull, and lifeless wishes, raising us but a little above a state of indifference: God, in His word, greatly insists upon it, that we be in good earnest, "fervent in spirit," and our hearts vigorously engaged in religion: Rom. xii. 11, "Be ye fervent in spirit, serving the Lord." Deut. x. 12, "And now, Israel, what doth the Lord thy God require of thee, but to fear the Lord thy God, to walk in all his ways, and to love him, and to serve the Lord thy God with all thy heart, and with all thy soul?" and chap. vi. 4, 5, "Hear, O Israel, the Lord our God is one Lord: And thou shalt love the Lord thy God with all thy heart, and with all thy might." It is such a fervent vigorous engagedness of the heart in religion that is the fruit of a real circumcision of the heart, or true regeneration, and that has the promises of life; Deut. xxx. 6, "And the Lord thy God will circumcise thine heart, and the heart of thy seed, to love the Lord thy God with all thy heart, and with all thy soul, that thou mayest live."

If we be not in good earnest in religion, and our wills and inclinations be not strongly exercised, we are nothing. The things of religion are so great, that there can be no suitableness in the exercises of our hearts to their nature and importance, unless they be lively and powerful. In nothing is vigour in the actings of our inclinations so requisite as in religion; and in nothing is lukewarmness so odious. True religion is evermore a powerful thing; and the power of it appears, in the first place in the inward exercises of it in the heart, where is the principal and original seat of it. Hence true religion is called the *power of godliness*, in distinction from the external appearances of it, that are the *form* of it, 2 Tim. iii. 5: "Having a form of godliness, but denying the power of it." The Spirit of God, in those that have sound and solid religion, is a spirit of powerful holy affection; and therefore God is said "to have given the Spirit of power, and of love, and of a sound mind," 2 Tim. i. 7. And such, when they receive the Spirit of God in his sanctifying and saving influences, are said to be "baptized with the Holy Ghost, and with fire," by reason of the power and fervour of those exercises the Spirit of God excites in their hearts, whereby their hearts, when grace is in exercise, may be said to "burn within them;" as is said of the disciples, Luke xxiv. 32.

The business of religion is from time to time compared to those exercises wherein men are wont to have their hearts and strength greatly exercised and engaged, such as running, wrestling or agonizing for a great prize or crown, and fighting with strong enemies that seek our lives, and warring as those that by violence take a city or kingdom.

And though true grace has various degrees, and there are some that are but babes in Christ, in whom the exercise of the inclination and will towards divine and heavenly things is comparatively weak; yet every one that has the power of godliness in his heart has his inclinations and heart exercised towards God and divine things, with such strength and vigour that these holy exercises do prevail in him above all carnal or natural affections, and are effectual to overcome them: for every true disciple of Christ "loves him above father or mother, wife and children, brethren and sisters, houses and lands: yea, than his own life." From hence it follows, that wherever true religion is, there are vigorous exercises of the inclination and will towards divine objects: but by what was said before, the vigorous, lively, and sensible exercises of the will, are no other than the affections of the soul.

2. The Author of the human nature has not only given affections to men, but has made them very much the spring of men's actions. As the affections do not only necessarily belong to the human nature, but are a very great part of it; so (inasmuch as by regeneration persons are renewed in the whole man, and sanctified throughout) holy affections do not only necessarily belong to true religion, but are a very great part of it. And as true religion is of a practical nature, and God hath so constituted the human nature that the affections are very much the spring of men's actions, this also shows that true religion must consist very much in the affections.

Such is man's nature that he is very inactive, any otherwise than he is influenced by some affection, either love or hatred, desire, hope, fear, or some other. These affections we see to be the springs that set men a-going, in all the affairs of life, and engage them in all their pursuits: these are the things that put men forward, and carry them along, in all their worldly business; and especially are men excited and animated by these in all affairs wherein they are earnestly engaged, and which they pursue with vigour. We see the world of mankind to be exceeding busy and active; and the affections of men are the springs of the motion. Take away all love and hatred, all hope and fear, all anger, zeal, and affectionate desire, and the world would be in a great measure motionless and dead; there would be no such thing as activity amongst mankind, or any earnest pursuit whatsoever. It is affection that engages the covetous man, and him that is greedy of worldly profits, in his pursuits; and it is by the affections that the ambitious man is put forward in his pursuit of worldly glory; and it is the affections also that actuate the voluptuous man in his pursuit of pleasure and sensual delights. The world continues, from age to age, in a continual commotion and agitation, in a pursuit of these things; but take away all affection, and the spring of all this motion would be gone, and the motion itself would cease. And as in worldly things worldly affections are very much the spring of men's motion and action; so in religious matters the spring of their actions is very much religious affection: he that has doctrinal knowledge and speculation only, without affection, never is engaged in the business of religion.

3. Nothing is more manifest in fact, than that the things of religion take hold of men's souls no further than they affect them. There are multitudes that often hear the word of God, and therein hear of those things that are infinitely great and important, and that most nearly concern them, and all that is heard seems to be wholly ineffectual upon them, and to make no alteration in their disposition or behaviour; and the reason is, they are not affected with what they hear. There are many that often hear of the glorious perfections of God, His almighty power and boundless wisdom, His infinite majesty, and that holiness of God, by which He is of purer eyes than to behold evil, and cannot look on iniquity, and the heavens are not pure in His sight, and of God's infinite goodness and mercy; they hear of the great works of God's wisdom, power and goodness, wherein there appear the admirable manifestations of these perfections; they hear particularly of the unspeakable love of God and Christ, and of the great things that Christ has done and suffered, and of the great things of another world, of eternal misery in bearing the fierceness and wrath of Almighty God, and of endless blessedness and glory in the presence of God, and the enjoyment of His dear love; they also hear the peremptory commands of God, and His gracious counsels and warnings, and the sweet invitations of the gospel; I say, they often hear these things and yet remain as they were before, with no sensible alteration in them, either in heart or practice, because they are not affected with what they hear; and ever will be so till they are affected.

I am bold to assert that there never was any considerable change wrought in the mind or conversation of any person, by anything of a religious nature that ever he read, heard or saw, that had not his affections moved. Never was a natural man engaged earnestly to seek his salvation; never were any such brought to cry after wisdom, and lift up their voice for understanding, and to wrestle with God in prayer for mercy; and never was one humbled and brought to the foot of God, from anything that ever he heard or imagined of his own unworthiness and deservings of God's displeasure; nor was ever one induced to fly for refuge unto Christ, while his heart remained unaffected. Nor was there ever a saint awakened out of a cold, lifeless frame, or recovered from a declining state in religion, and brought back from a lamentable departure from God, without having his heart affected. And in a word, there never was anything considerable brought to pass in the heart or life of any man living, by the things of religion, that had not his heart deeply affected by those things.

4. The holy Scriptures do everywhere place religion very much in the affection; such as fear, hope, love, hatred, desire, joy, sorrow, gratitude, compassion, and zeal.

The Scriptures place much of religion in godly fear; insomuch that it is often spoken of as the character of those that are truly religious persons, that they tremble at God's word, that they fear before Him, that their flesh trembles for fear of Him, and that they are afraid of His judgments, that His excellency makes them afraid, and His dread falls upon them, and the like: and a compellation commonly given the saints in Scripture, is "fearers of God," or "they that fear the Lord." And because the fear of God is a great part of true godliness, hence true godliness in general, is very commonly called by the name of *the fear of God;* as every one knows that knows anything of the Bible.

So hope in God and in the promises of His Word is often spoken of in the Scripture as a very considerable part of true religion. It is mentioned as one of the three great things of which religion consists, 1 Cor. xiii. 13. Hope in the Lord is also frequently mentioned as the character of the saints: Psal. cxlvi. 5, "Happy is he that hath the God of Jacob for his help, whose hope is in the Lord his God." Jer. xvii. 7, "Blessed is the man that trusteth in the Lord, and whose hope the Lord is." Psal. xxxi. 24, "Be of good courage, and He shall strength your heart, all ye that hope in the Lord." And the like in many other places. Religious fear and hope are, once and again, joined together, as jointly constituting the character of the true saints; Psal. xxxiii.

18, "Behold, the eye of the Lord is upon them that fear him, upon them that hope in his mercy." Psal. cxlvii. 11, "The Lord taketh pleasure in them that fear Him, in those that hope in his mercy." Hope is so great a part of true religion, that the apostle says, " We are saved by hope," Rom. viii. 24. And this is spoken of as the helmet of the Christian soldier. 1 Thess. v. 8, "And for a helmet, the *hope* of salvation;" and the sure and steadfast anchor of the soul, which preserves it from being cast away by the storms of this evil world. Heb. vi. 19, " Which hope we have as an anchor of the soul, both sure and steadfast, and which entereth into that within the vail." It is spoken of as a great fruit and benefit which true saints receive by Christ's resurrection: 1 Pet. i. 3, "Blessed be the God and Father of our Lord Jesus Christ, which according to his abundant mercy, hath begotten us again unto a lively hope by the resurrection of Jesus Christ from the dead."

The Scriptures place religion very much in the affection of *love,* in love to God and the Lord Jesus Christ, and love to the people of God, and to mankind. The texts in which this is manifest, both in the Old Testament and New, are innumerable. But of this more afterwards.

The contrary affection of *hatred* also, as having sin for its object, is spoken of in Scripture as no inconsiderable part of true religion. It is spoken of as that by which true religion may be known and distinguished; Prov. viii. 13, "The fear of the Lord is to hate evil." And accordingly the saints are called upon to give evidence of their sincerity by this; Psal. xcvii. 10, "Ye that love the Lord hate evil." And the Psalmist often mentions it as an evidence of his sincerity; Psal. ci. 2, 3, "I will walk within my house with a perfect heart. I will set no wicked thing before mine eyes; I hate the work of them that turn aside." Psal. cxix. 104, "I hate every false way." So ver. 128. Again, Psal. cxxxix. 21, " Do not I hate them, O Lord, that hate thee?"

So holy desire, exercised in longings, hungerings, and thirstings after God and holiness, is often mentioned in Scripture as an important part of true religion; Isa. xxvi. 8, "The desire of our soul is to thy name, and to the remembrance of thee." Psal. xxvii. 4, "One thing have I desired of the Lord, that will I seek after, that I may dwell in the house of the Lord all the days of my life, to behold the beauty of the Lord, and to inquire in his temple." Psal. xlii, 1, 2, "As the hart panteth after the water brooks, so panteth my soul after thee, O God; my soul thirsteth for God, for the living God: when shall I come and appear before God?" Psal. lxiii. 1, 2, "My soul thirsteth for thee, my flesh longeth for thee, in a dry and thirsty land, where no water is; to see thy power and thy glory, so as I have seen thee in the sanctuary." Psal. lxxxiv. 1, 2, "How amiable are thy tabernacles, O Lord of hosts! My soul longeth, yea, even fainteth for the courts of the Lord: my heart and my flesh crieth out for the living God." Psal. cxix. 20, "My soul breaketh for the longing that it hath unto thy judgments at all times." So Psal. lxxiii. 25, and cxliii. 6, 7, and cxxx. 6. Cant. iii. 1, 2. Such a holy desire and thirst of soul is mentioned, as one thing which renders or denotes a man truly blessed, in the beginning of Christ's sermon on the mount, Matt. v. 6: "Blessed are they that do hunger and thirst after righteousness; for they shall be filled." And this holy thirst is spoken of, as a great thing in the condition of a participation of the blessings of eternal life; Rev. xxi. 6, "I will give unto him that is athirst of the fountain of the water of life freely."

The Scriptures speak of holy joy as a great part of true religion. So it is represented in the text. And as an important part of religion, it is often exhorted to, and pressed, with great earnestness; Psal. xxxvii. 4, "Delight thyself in the Lord; and he shall give thee the desires of thine heart." Psal. xcvii. 12, "Rejoice in the Lord, ye righteous." So Psal. xxxiii. 1, "Rejoice in the Lord, O ye righteous." Matt. v. 12, "Rejoice, and be exceeding glad." Phil. iii. 1, "Finally, brethren, rejoice in the Lord." And chap. iv. 4, "Rejoice in the Lord alway; and again I say, Rejoice." 1 Thess. v. 16, "Rejoice evermore." Psal. cxlix, 2, "Let Israel rejoice in him that made him; let the children of Zion be joyful in their king." This is mentioned among the principal fruits of the Spirit of grace; Gal. v: 22, "The fruit of the Spirit is love," &c. The Psalmist mentions his holy joy as an evidence of his sincerity. Psal. cxix. 14, "I have rejoiced in the way of thy testimonies, as much as in all riches."

Religious sorrow, mourning, and brokenness of heart, are also frequently spoken of as a great part of true religion. These things are often mentioned as distinguishing qualities of the true saints, and a great part of their character; Matt. v. 4, "Blessed

are they that mourn; for they shall be comforted." Psal. xxxiv.
18, "The Lord is nigh unto them that are of a broken heart;
and saveth such as be of a contrite spirit." Isa. lxi. 1, 2, "The
Lord hath anointed me, to bind up the broken-hearted, to comfort all that mourn." This godly sorrow and brokenness of heart
is often spoken of, not only as a great thing in the distinguishing
character of the saints, but as that in them which is peculiarly
acceptable and pleasing to God; Psal. li. 17, "The sacrifices of
God are a broken spirit: a broken and a contrite heart, O God,
thou wilt not despise." Isa. lvii. 15, "Thus saith the high and
lofty One that inhabiteth eternity, whose name is Holy, I dwell
in the high and holy place; with him also that is of a contrite and
humble spirit, to revive the spirit of the humble, and to revive
the heart of the contrite ones." Chap. lxvi. 2, "To this man will
I look, even to him that is poor and of a contrite spirit."

Another affection often mentioned, as that in the exercise of
which much of true religion appears, is *gratitude;* especially as
exercised in thankfulness and praise to God. This being so much
spoken of in the book of Psalms, and other parts of the holy Scriptures, I need not mention particular texts.

Again, the holy Scriptures do frequently speak of compassion
or mercy, as a very great and essential thing in true religion; insomuch that good men are in Scripture denominated from hence;
and a merciful man and a good man are equivalent terms in
Scripture; Isa. lvii. 1, "The righteous perisheth, and no man
'ayeth it to heart; and merciful men are taken away." And the
Scripture chooses out this quality, as that by which, in a peculiar
manner, a righteous man is deciphered; Psal. xxxvii. 21, "The
righteous showeth mercy, and giveth;" and ver. 26, "He is ever
merciful, and lendeth." And Prov. xiv. 31, "He that honoureth
the Lord hath mercy on the poor." And Col. iii. 12, "Put ye on,
as the elect of God, holy and beloved, bowels of mercies," &c.
This is one of those great things by which those who are truly
blessed are described by our Saviour; Matt. v. 7, "Blessed are the
merciful, for they shall obtain mercy." And this Christ also
speaks of, as one of the weightier matters of the law; Matt. xxiii.
23, "Woe unto you, scribes and Pharisees, hypocrites, for ye pay
tithe of mint, and anise, and cummin, and have omitted the
weightier matters of the law, judgment, mercy, and faith." To
the like purpose is that, Mic. vi. 8, "He hath showed thee, O

man, what is good: and what doth the Lord require of thee, but
to do justly, and love mercy, and walk humbly with thy God?"
And also that, Hos. vi. 6, "For I desired mercy, and not sacrifice": which seems to have been a text much delighted in by
our Saviour, by his manner of citing it once and again, Matt.
ix. 13, and xii. 7.

Zeal is also spoken of, as a very essential part of the religion
of true saints. It is spoken of as a great thing Christ had in
view, in giving himself for our redemption; Tit. ii. 14, "Who
gave himself for us, that he might redeem us from all iniquity,
and purify unto himself a peculiar people, zealous of good
works." And this is spoken of as the great thing wanting in the
lukewarm Laodiceans, Rev. iii. 15, 16, 19.

I have mentioned but a few texts, out of an innumerable multitude, all over the Scripture, which place religion very much in
the affections. But what has been observed may be sufficient to
show that they who would deny that much of true religion lies
in the affections, and maintain the contrary, must throw away
what we have been wont to own for our Bible, and get some other
rule by which to judge of the nature of religion.

5. The Scriptures do represent true religion, as being summarily comprehended in love, the chief of the affections and
fountain of all other affections.

So our blessed Saviour represents the matter, in answer to the
lawyer who asked him which was the great commandment of
the law. Matt. xxii. 37-40: "Jesus said unto him, Thou shalt love
the Lord thy God with all thy heart, and with all thy soul, and
with all thy mind. This is the first and great commandment.
And the second is like unto it, Thou shalt love thy neighbour
as thyself. On these two commandments hang all the law and
the prophets." Which last words signify as much, as that these
two commandments comprehend all the duty prescribed, and the
religion taught in the law and the prophets. And the apostle
Paul does from time to time make the same representation of the
matter; as in Rom. xiii. 8, "He that loveth another, hath fulfilled
the law." And ver. 10, "Love is the fulfilling of the law." And
Gal. v. 14, "For all the law is fulfilled in one word, even in this,
Thou shalt love thy neighbour as thyself." So likewise in 1 Tim.
i. 5, "Now the end of the commandment is charity out of a pure
heart," &c. So the same apostle speaks of love as the greatest

thing in religion, and as the vitals, essence and soul of it; without which the greatest knowledge and gifts, and the most glaring profession, and every thing else which appertains to religion, are vain and worthless; and represents it as the fountain from whence proceeds all that is good, in 1 Cor. xiii. throughout; for that which is there rendered *charity*, in the original is ἀγάπη, the proper English of which is *love*.

Now, although it be true that the love thus spoken of includes the whole of a sincerely benevolent propensity of the soul towards God and man; yet it is evident from what has been before observed, that this propensity or inclination of the soul, when in sensible and vigorous exercise, becomes affection, and is no other than affectionate love. And surely it is such vigorous and fervent love which Christ speaks of as the sum of all religion, when he speaks of loving God with all our hearts, with all our souls, and with all our minds, and our neighbour as ourselves, as the sum of all that was taught and prescribed in the law and the prophets.

Indeed it cannot be supposed, when this affection of love is here, and in other Scriptures, spoken of as the sum of all religion, that hereby is meant the act, exclusive of the habit, or that the exercise of the understanding is excluded, which is implied in all reasonable affection. But it is doubtless true, and evident from these Scriptures, that the essence of all true religion lies in holy love; and that in this divine affection, and an habitual disposition to it, and that light which is the foundation of it, and those things which are the fruits of it, consists the whole of religion.

From hence it clearly and certainly appears, that great part of true religion consists in the affections. For love is not only one of the affections, but it is the first and chief of the affections, and the fountain of all the affections. From love arises hatred of those things which are contrary to what we love, or which oppose and thwart us in those things that we delight in : and from the various exercises of love and hatred, according to the circumstances of the objects of these affections, as present or absent, certain or uncertain, probable or improbable, arise all those other affections of desire, hope, fear, joy, grief, gratitude, anger, &c. From a vigorous, affectionate, and fervent love to God will necessarily arise other religious affections; hence will arise an intense hatred and abhorrence of sin, fear of sin, and a dread of God's displeasure, gratitude to God for his goodness, complacence and joy in

God when God is graciously and sensibly present, and grief when
He is absent, and a joyful hope when a future enjoyment of God
is expected, and fervent zeal for the glory of God. And in like
manner, from a fervent love to men will arise all other virtuous
affections towards men.

6. The religion of the most eminent saints we have an account
of in the Scripture consisted much in holy affections.

I shall take particular notice of three eminent saints, who have
expressed the frame and sentiments of their own hearts, and so
described their own religion, and the manner of their intercourse
with God, in the writings which they have left us that are a part
of the sacred canon.

The first instance I shall take notice of, is David, that " man
after God's own heart;" who has given us a lively portraiture of
his religion in the book of Psalms. Those holy songs of his he
has there left us are nothing else but the expressions and breathings of devout and holy affections; such as an humble and fervent
love to God, admiration of His glorious perfections and wonderful works, earnest desires, thirstings, and pantings of soul after
God, delight and joy in God, a sweet and melting gratitude to
God for His great goodness, a holy exultation and triumph of
soul in the favour, sufficiency, and faithfulness of God, his love
to and delight in the saints, the excellent of the earth, his great
delight in the Word and ordinances of God, his grief for his own
and others' sins, and his fervent zeal for God and against the
enemies of God and his church. And these expressions of holy
affection, which the psalms of David are everywhere full of, are
the more to our present purpose, because those psalms are not
only the expressions of the religion of so eminent a saint, that
God speaks of as so agreeable to His mind, but were also, by the
direction of the Holy Ghost, penned for the use of the church of
God in its public worship, not only in that age but in after ages;
as being fitted to express the religion of all saints, in all ages, as
well as the religion of the Psalmist. And it is moreover to be
observed, that David, in the book of Psalms, speaks not as a private person but as the Psalmist of Israel, as the subordinate head
of the church of God, and leader in their worship and praises;
and in many of the psalms speaks in the name of Christ, as per-
sonating Him in these breathings forth of holy affection; and in
many other psalms he speaks in the name of the church.

Another instance I shall observe, is the apostle Paul, who was in many respects, the chief of all the ministers of the New Testament; being, above all others, a chosen vessel unto Christ, to bear His name before the Gentiles, and made a chief instrument of propagating and establishing the Christian church in the world, and of distinctly revealing the glorious mysteries of the gospel, for the instruction of the church in all ages; and (as has not been improperly thought by some) the most eminent servant of Christ that ever lived, received to the highest rewards in the heavenly kingdom of his Master. By what is said of him in the Scripture, he appears to have been a person that was full of affection. And it is very manifest that the religion he expresses in his epistles consisted very much in holy affections. It appears by all his expressions of himself, that he was, in the course of his life, inflamed, actuated, and entirely swallowed up, by a most ardent love to his glorious Lord, esteeming all things as loss, for the excellency of the knowledge of Him, and esteeming them but dung that he might win Him. He represents himself as overpowered by this holy affection, and as it were compelled by it to go forward in his service through all difficulties and sufferings, 2 Cor. v. 14, 15. And his epistles are full of expressions of an overpowering affection towards the people of Christ. He speaks of his dear love to them, 2 Cor. xii. 19, Phil. iv. 1, 2 Tim. i. 2; of his "abundant love," 2 Cor. ii. 4; and of his "affectionate and tender love," as of a nurse towards her children, 1 Thess. ii. 7, 8: " But we were gentle among you, even as a nurse cherisheth her children; so, being affectionately desirous of you, we were willing to have imparted unto you, not the gospel of God only, but also our own souls, because ye were dear unto us." So also he speaks of his "bowels of love," Phil. i. 8, Philem. 7, 12, and 20. So he speaks of his " earnest care " for others, 2 Cor. viii. 16, and of his " bowels of pity, or mercy towards them," Phil ii. 1; and of his concern for others even to anguish of heart, 2 Cor. ii. 4: " For out of much affliction and anguish of heart, I wrote unto you with many tears; not that ye should be grieved, but that ye might know the love which I have more abundantly unto you." He speaks of the great conflict of his soul for them, Col. ii. 1. He speaks of great and continual grief that he had in his heart from compassion to the Jews, Rom. ix. 2. He speaks of " his mouth's being opened, and his heart enlarged " towards Christians, 2 Cor.

vi. 11: "O ye Corinthians, our mouth is open unto you, our heart is enlarged." He often speaks of his "affectionate and longing desires," 1 Thess. ii. 8, Rom. i. 11, Phil. i. 8, and chap. iv. 1, 2 Tim. i. 4. The same apostle is very often, in his epistles, expressing the affection of *joy*, 2 Cor. i. 12, and chap. vii. 7, 9, 16. Phil. i. 4, and chap. ii. 17, and chap. iii. 3. Col. i. 24. 1 Thess. iii. 9. He speaks of his "rejoicing with great joy," Phil. iv. 10, Philem. i. 7; of his "joying and rejoicing," Phil. ii. 17, "of his rejoicing exceedingly," 2 Cor. vii. 13, and of his being "filled with comfort, and being exceeding joyful," 2 Cor. vii. 4. He speaks of himself as "always rejoicing," 2 Cor. vi. 10. So he speaks of the triumphs of his soul, 2 Cor. ii. 14, and of "his glorying in tribulation," 2 Thess. i. 4, and Rom. v. 3. He also expresses the affection of *hope;* in Phil. i. 20, he speaks of his "earnest expectation, and his hope." He likewise expresses an affection of *godly jealousy*, 2 Cor. xi. 2, 3. And it appears by his whole history, after his conversion, in the Acts, and also by all his epistles, and the accounts he gives of himself there, that the affection of *zeal,* as having the cause of his Master and the interest and prosperity of His church for its object, was mighty in him, continually inflaming his heart, strongly engaging to those great and constant labours he went through, in instructing, exhorting, warning, and reproving others, "travailing in birth with them;" conflicting with those powerful and innumerable enemies who continually opposed him, wrestling with principalities and powers, not fighting as one who beats the air, running the race set before him, continually pressing forwards through all manner of difficulties and sufferings; so that others thought him quite beside himself. And how full he was of affection does further appear by his being so full of tears: in 2 Cor. ii. 4, he speaks of his "many tears;" and so Acts xx. 19; and of his "tears that he shed continually night and day," ver. 31.

Now any one who can consider these accounts given in the Scripture of this great apostle, and which he gives of himself, and yet not see that his religion consisted much in affection, must have a strange faculty of managing his eyes, to shut out the light which shines most full in his face.

The other instance I shall mention is of the apostle John, that beloved disciple, who was the nearest and dearest to his Master of any of the twelve, and was by Him admitted to the greatest privileges of any of them; being not only one of the three who were admitted to be present with Him in the mount at His trans-figuration, and at the raising of Jairus's daughter, and whom He took with Him when He was in His agony, and one of the three spoken of by the apostle Paul as the three main pillars of the Christian church; but was favoured above all in being admitted to lean on his Master's bosom at His last supper, and in being chosen by Christ as the disciple to whom He would reveal His wonderful dispensations towards His church to the end of time, as we have an account in the Book of Revelation, and to shut up the canon of the New Testament and of the whole Scripture; being preserved much longer than all the rest of the apostles, to set all things in order in the Christian church after their death.

It is evident by all his writings (as is generally observed by divines) that he was a person remarkably full of affection: his addresses to those whom he wrote to being inexpressibly tender and pathetical, breathing nothing but the most fervent love; as though he were all made up of sweet and holy affection. The proofs of which cannot be given without disadvantage, unless we should transcribe his whole writings.

7. He whom God sent into the world to be the Light of the world, and Head of the whole church, and the perfect example of true religion and virtue, for the imitation of all, the Shepherd whom the whole flock should follow wherever He goes, even the Lord Jesus Christ, was a Person who was remarkably of a tender and affectionate heart; and His virtue was expressed very much in the exercise of holy affections. He was the greatest instance of ardency, vigour and strength of love, to both God and man, that ever was. It was these affections which got the victory, in that mighty struggle and conflict of His affections, in His agonies, when "He prayed more earnestly, and offered strong crying and tears," and wrestled in tears and in blood. Such was the power of the exercises of His holy love that they were stronger than death, and in that great struggle overcame those strong exercises of the natural affections of fear and grief, when He was sore amazed, and His soul was exceeding sorrowful even unto death. And He also appeared to be full of affection in the course of His life. We read of His great zeal, fulfilling that in the 69th Psalm, "The zeal of thine house hath eaten me up," John ii. 17. We read of His grief for the sins of men, Mark iii. 5: "He looked round about on them with anger, being grieved for the hardness

of their hearts;" and His breaking forth in tears and exclamations from the consideration of the sin and misery of ungodly men, and on the sight of the city of Jerusalem which was full of such inhabitants, Luke xix. 41, 42: "And when he was come near, he beheld the city, and wept over it, saying, If thou hadst known, even thou, at least in this thy day, the things which belong unto thy peace! But now they are hid from thine eyes." With chap. xiii. 34, "O Jerusalem, Jerusalem, which killest the prophets, and stonest them that are sent unto thee; how often would I have gathered thy children together, as a hen doth gather her brood under her wings, and ye would not!" We read of Christ's earnest desire, Luke xxii. 15: "With desire I have desired to eat this passover with you before I suffer." We often read of the affection of pity or compassion in Christ, Matt. xv. 32, and xix. 34, Luke vii. 13, and of His "being moved with compassion," Matt. ix. 36, and xiv. 14, and Mark vi. 34. And how tender did His heart appear to be, on occasion of Mary's and Martha's mourning for their brother, and coming to Him with their complaints and tears! Their tears soon drew tears from His eyes; He was affected with their grief, and wept with them, though He knew their sorrow should so soon be turned into joy by their brother's being raised from the dead; see John xi. And how ineffably affectionate was that last and dying discourse which Jesus had with His eleven disciples the evening before He was crucified; when He told them He was going away, and foretold them the great difficulties and sufferings they should meet with in the world when He was gone; and comforted and counselled them as His dear little children; and bequeathed to them His Holy Spirit, and therein His peace and His comfort and joy, as it were in His last will and testament, in the 13th, 14th, 15th, and 16th chapters of John; and concluded the whole with that affectionate intercessory prayer for them and His whole church, in chap. xvii. Of all the discourses ever penned or uttered by the mouth of any man, this seems to be the most affectionate and affecting.

8. The religion of heaven consists very much in affection.

There is doubtless true religion in heaven, and true religion in its utmost purity and perfection. But according to the Scripture representation of the heavenly state, the religion of heaven consists chiefly in holy and mighty love and joy, and the expression of these in most fervent and exalted praises. So that the religion

of the saints in heaven consists in the same things with that religion of the saints on earth which is spoken of in our text, viz.,
love, and " joy unspeakable and full of glory." Now it would be
very foolish to pretend that, because the saints in heaven be not
united to flesh and blood, and have no animal fluids to be moved
(through the laws of union of soul and body) with those great
emotions of their souls, therefore their exceeding love and joy
are no affections. We are not speaking of the affections of the
body, but of the affections of the soul, the chief of which are *love*
and *joy*. When these are in the soul, whether that be in the body
or out of it, the soul is affected and moved. And when they are
in the soul in that strength in which they are in the saints in
heaven, the soul is mightily affected and moved, or, which is the
same thing, has great affections. It is true, we do not experimentally know what love and joy are in a soul out of a body, or
in a glorified body; *i.e.*, we have not had experience of love and
joy in a soul in these circumstances; but the saints on earth do
know what divine love and joy in the soul are, and they know
that love and joy are of the same kind with the love and joy
which are in heaven in separate souls there. The love and joy
of the saints on earth is the beginning and dawning of the light,
life, and blessedness of heaven, and is like their love and joy
there; or rather, the same in nature, though not the same with
it, or like to it, in degree and circumstances. This is evident by
many Scriptures, as Prov. iv. 18; John iv. 14, and chap. vi. 40, 47,
50, 51, 54, 58; 1 John iii. 15; 1 Cor. xiii. 8-12. It is unreasonable
therefore to suppose that the love and joy of the saints in heaven
not only differ in degree and circumstances from the holy love
and joy of the saints on earth, but is so entirely different in
nature, that they are no affections; and merely because they have
no blood and animal spirits to be set in motion by them, which
motion of the blood and animal spirits is not of the essence of
these affections in men on the earth, but the effect of them; although by their reaction they may make some circumstantial difference in the sensation of the mind. There is a sensation of the
mind which loves and rejoices, that is antecedent to any effects
on the fluids of the body; and this sensation of the mind, therefore, does not depend on these motions in the body, and so may
be in the soul without the body. And wherever there are the
exercises of love and joy, there is that sensation of the mind,

whether it be in the body or out; and that inward sensation, or kind of spiritual sense or feeling, and motion of the soul, is what is called affection: the soul when it thus feels (if I may say so), and is thus moved, is said to be affected, and especially when this inward sensation and motion are to a very high degree, as they are in the saints in heaven. If we can learn anything of the state of heaven from the Scripture, the love and joy that the saints have there is exceeding great and vigorous; impressing the heart with the strongest and most lively sensation of inexpressible sweetness, mightily moving, animating, and engaging them, making them like a flame of fire. And if such love and joy be not affections, then the word *affection* is of no use in language. Will any say that the saints in heaven, in beholding the face of their Father and the glory of their Redeemer, and contemplating His wonderful works, and particularly His laying down His life for them, have their hearts nothing moved and affected by all which they behold or consider?

Hence, therefore, the religion of heaven, consisting chiefly in holy love and joy, consists very much in affection; and therefore, undoubtedly, true religion consists very much in affection. The way to learn the true nature of anything is to go where that thing is to be found in its purity and perfection. If we would know the nature of true gold we must view it, not in the ore, but when it is refined. If we would learn what true religion is, we must go where there is true religion, and nothing but true religion, and in its highest perfection, without any defect or mixture. All who are truly religious are not of this world; they are strangers here and belong to heaven; they are born from above, heaven is their native country, and the nature which they receive by this heavenly birth, is a heavenly nature, they receive an anointing from above; that principle of true religion which is in them is a communication of the religion of heaven; their grace is the dawn of glory; and God fits them for that world by conforming them to it.

9. This appears from the nature and design of the ordinances and duties which God hath appointed, as means and expressions of true religion.

To instance in the duty of prayer: it is manifest we are not appointed in this duty to declare God's perfections, His majesty, holiness, goodness, and all-sufficiency, and our meanness, emptiness, dependence, and unworthiness, and our wants and desires, to inform God of these things, or to incline His heart, and prevail with Him to be willing to show us mercy; but suitably to affect our own hearts with the things we express, and so to prepare us to receive the blessings we ask. And such gestures and manner of external behaviour in the worship of God, which custom has made to be significations of humility and reverence, can be of no further use than as they have some tendency to affect our own hearts, or the hearts of others.

And the duty of singing praises to God seems to be appointed wholly to excite and express religious affections. No other reason can be assigned why we should express ourselves to God in verse rather than in prose, and do it with music, but only that such is our nature and frame that these things have a tendency to move our affections.

The same thing appears in the nature and design of the sacraments which God hath appointed. God, considering our frame, hath not only appointed that we should be told of the great things of the gospel, and of the redemption of Christ, and instructed in them by His Word; but also that they should be, as it were, exhibited to our view, in sensible representations in the sacraments, the more to affect us with them.

And the impressing divine things on the hearts and affections of men is evidently one great and main end for which God has ordained that His Word delivered in the holy Scriptures should be opened, applied, and set home upon men, in preaching. And therefore it does not answer the aim which God had in this institution, merely for men to have good commentaries and expositions on the Scripture, and other good books of divinity; because, although these may tend as well as preaching to give men a good doctrinal or speculative understanding of the things of the Word of God, yet they have not an equal tendency to impress them on men's hearts and affections. God hath appointed a particular and lively application of His Word to men in the preaching of it, as a fit means to affect sinners with the importance of the things of religion, and their own misery and necessity of a remedy, and the glory and sufficiency of a remedy provided; and to stir up the pure minds of the saints, and quicken their affections, by often bringing the great things of religion to their remembrance, and setting them before them in their proper colours, though they know them, and have been fully instructed in them already, 2 Pet. i. 12, 13. And, particularly, to promote those two affections in them which are spoken of in the text, love and joy, "Christ gave some, apostles; and some, prophets; and some, evangelists; and some, pastors and teachers; that the body of Christ might be edified in love," Eph. iv. 11, 12, 16. The apostle, in instructing and counselling Timothy concerning the work of the ministry, informs him that the great end of that word which a minister is to preach, is love or charity, 1 Tim. i. 3, 4, 5. And another affection which God has appointed preaching as a means to promote in the saints, is joy; and therefore ministers are called "helpers of their joy," 2 Cor. i. 24.

10. It is an evidence that true religion, or holiness of heart, lies very much in the affection of the heart, that the Scriptures place the sin of the heart very much in hardness of heart. This the Scriptures do everywhere. It was hardness of heart which excited grief and displeasures in Christ towards the Jews, Mark iii. 5: " He looked round about on them with anger, being grieved for the hardness of their hearts." It is from men's having such a heart as this, that they treasure up wrath for themselves: Rom. ii. 5, "After thy hardness and impenitent heart, treasurest up unto thyself wrath against the day of wrath, and revelation of the righteous judgment of God." The reason given why the house of Israel would not obey God, was, that they were hard-hearted: Ezekiel iii. 7, " But the house of Israel will not hearken unto thee; for they will not hearken unto me : for all the house of Israel are impudent and hard-hearted." The wickedness of that perverse rebellious generation in the wilderness, is ascribed to the hardness of their hearts: Psal. xcv. 7-10, "To-day, if ye will hear his voice, harden not your heart, as in the provocation, and as in the day of temptation in the wilderness; when your fathers tempted me, proved me, and saw my work : forty years long was I grieved with this generation, and said, It is a people that do err in their heart," &c. This is spoken of as what prevented Zedekiah's turning to the Lord: 2 Chron. xxxvi. 13, " He stiffened his neck, and hardened his heart from turning to the Lord God of Israel." This principle is spoken of as that from whence men are without the fear of God, and depart from God's ways: Isa. lxiii. 17, " O Lord, why hast thou made us to err from thy ways, and hardened our heart from thy fear?" And men's

rejecting Christ, and opposing Christianity, is laid to this principle: Acts xix. 9, "But when divers were hardened, and believed not, but spake evil of that way before the multitude." God's leaving men to the power of the sin and corruption of the heart is often expressed by God's hardening their hearts: Rom. ix. 18, "Therefore hath he mercy on whom he will have mercy, and whom he will he hardeneth." John xii. 40, "He hath blinded their minds, and hardened their hearts." And the apostle seems to speak of "an evil heart that departs from the living God," and "a hard heart," as the same thing: Heb. iii. 8, "Harden not your heart, as in the provocation," &c.; ver. 12, 13, "Take heed, brethren, lest there be in any of you an evil heart of unbelief, in departing from the living God: but exhort one another daily, while it is called to-day; lest any of you be hardened through the deceitfulness of sin." And that great work of God in conversion, which consists in delivering a person from the power of sin, and mortifying corruption, is expressed, once and again, by God's "taking away the heart of stone, and giving a heart of flesh," Ezek. xi. 19, and chap. xxxvi. 26.

Now by a hard heart is plainly meant an unaffected heart, or a heart not easy to be moved with virtuous affections, like a stone, insensible, stupid, unmoved, and hard to be impressed. Hence the hard heart is called a *stony heart,* and is opposed to a heart of flesh, that has feeling, and is sensibly touched and moved. We read in Scripture of a hard heart, and a tender heart; and doubtless we are to understand these, as contrary the one to the other. But what is a tender heart but a heart which is easily impressed with what ought to affect it? God commends Josiah, because his heart was tender; and it is evident by those things which are mentioned as expressions and evidences of this tenderness of heart, that by his heart being tender is meant, his heart being easily moved with religious and pious affection: 2 Kings xxii. 19, "Because thine heart was tender, and thou hast humbled thyself before the Lord, when thou heardest what I spake against this place, and against the inhabitants thereof, that they should become a desolation and a curse, and hast rent thy clothes, and wept before me, I also have heard thee, saith the Lord." And this is one thing wherein it is necessary we should "become as little children, in order to our entering into the kingdom of God," even that we should have our hearts tender, and easily affected and moved in spiritual and divine things, as little children have in other things.

It is very plain in some places, in the texts themselves, that by hardness of heart is meant a heart void of affection. So, to signify the ostrich's being without natural affection to her young, it is said, Job xxxix. 16, " She hardeneth her heart against her young ones, as though they were not her's." So a person having a heart unaffected in time of danger, is expressed by his hardening his heart: Prov. xxviii. 14, " Happy is the man that feareth alway; but he that hardeneth his heart shall fall into mischief."

Now, therefore, since it is so plain that by a hard heart, in Scripture, is meant a heart destitute of pious affections, and since also the Scriptures do so frequently place the sin and corruption of the heart in hardness of heart; it is evident that the grace and holiness of the heart, on the contrary, must, in a great measure, consist in its having pious affections, and being easily susceptive of such affection. Divines are generally agreed that sin radically and fundamentally consists in what is negative, or privative, having its root and foundation in a privation or want of holiness. And therefore undoubtedly, if it be so that sin does very much consist in hardness of heart, and so in the want of pious affections of heart, holiness does consist very much in those pious affections.

I am far from supposing that all affections do show a tender heart: hatred, anger, vainglory, and other selfish and self-exalting affections, may greatly prevail in the hardest heart. But yet it is evident that hardness of heart and tenderness of heart are expressions that relate to the affection of the heart, and denote the heart's being susceptible of, or shut up against, certain affections; of which I shall have occasion to speak more afterwards.

Upon the whole, I think it clearly and abundantly evident that true religion lies very much in the affections. Not that I think these arguments prove that religion in the hearts of the truly godly is ever in exact proportion to the degree of affection and present emotion of the mind: for undoubtedly there is much affection in the true saints which is not spiritual; their religious affections are often mixed; all is not from grace, but much from nature. And though the affections have not their seat in the body, yet the constitution of the body may very much contribute to the present emotion of the mind. And the degree of religion is rather to be judged of by the fixedness and strength of the habit that is exercised in affection, whereby holy affection is habitual, than by the degree of the present exercise; and the strength of that habit is not always in proportion to outward effects and manifestations, or inward effects in the hurry and vehemence and sudden changes of the course of the thoughts of the mind. But yet it is evident that religion consists so much in affection, as that without holy affection there is no true religion; and no light in the understanding is good which does not produce holy affection in the heart: no habit or principle in the heart is good which has no such exercise; and no external fruit is good which does not proceed from such exercises.

Inferences from the Doctrine

Having thus considered the evidence of the proposition laid down, I proceed to some inferences.

1. We may hence learn how great their error is who are for discarding all religious affections, as having nothing solid or substantial in them.

There seems to be too much of a disposition this way prevailing in this land at this time. Because many who, in the late extraordinary season, appeared to have great religious affections did not manifest a right temper of mind, and ran into many errors, in the time of their affection and the heat of their zeal; and because the high affections of many seem to be so soon come to nothing, and some who seemed to be mightily raised and swallowed up with joy and zeal, for a while, seem to have returned like the dog to his vomit; hence religious affections in general are grown out of credit with great numbers, as though true religion did not at all consist in them. Thus we easily and naturally run from one extreme to another. A little while ago we were in the other extreme; there was a prevalent disposition to look upon all high religious affections as eminent exercises of true grace, without much inquiring into the nature and source of those affections and the manner in which they arose: if persons did but appear to be indeed very much moved and raised, so as to be full of religious talk, and express themselves with great warmth and earnestness, and to be filled, or to be very full, as the phrases were; it was too much the manner, without further examination, to conclude such persons were full of the Spirit of God, and had eminent experience of His gracious influences. This was the extreme which was prevailing three or four years ago. But of late, instead of esteeming and admiring all religious affections without distinction, it is a thing much more prevalent to reject and discard all without distinction. Herein appears the subtilty of Satan. While he saw that affections were much in vogue, knowing the greater part of the land were not versed in such things, and had not had much experience of great religious affections to enable them to judge well of them, and distinguish between true and false; then he knew he could best play his game by sowing tares amongst the wheat, and mingling false affections with the works of God's Spirit: he knew this to be a likely way to delude and eternally ruin many souls, and greatly to wound religion in the saints, and entangle them in a dreadful wilderness, and by and by to bring all religion into disrepute.

But now, when the ill consequences of these false affections appear, and it is become very apparent that some of those emotions which made a glaring show and were by many greatly admired, were in reality nothing; the devil sees it to be for his interest to go another way to work, and to endeavour to his utmost to propagate and establish a persuasion that all affections and sensible emotions of the mind, in things of religion, are nothing at all to be regarded, but are rather to be avoided and carefully guarded against, as things of a pernicious tendency. This he knows is the way to bring all religion to a mere lifeless formality, and effectually shut out the power of godliness, and every thing which is spiritual, and to have all true Christianity turned out of doors. For although to true religion there must indeed be something else besides affection, yet true religion consists so much in the affections that there can be no true religion without them. He who has no religious affection is in a state of spiritual death, and is wholly destitute of the powerful, quickening, saving influences of the Spirit of God upon his heart. As there is no true religion where there is nothing else but affection, so there is no true religion where there is no religious affection. As, on the one hand, there must be light in the understanding as well as an affected fervent heart; where there is heat without light, there can be nothing divine or heavenly in that heart; so, on the other hand, where there is a kind of light without heat, a head stored with notions and speculations, with a cold and unaffected heart, there can be nothing divine in that light; that knowledge is no true spiritual knowledge of divine things. If the great things of religion are rightly understood, they will affect the heart. The reason why men are not affected by such infinitely great, important, glorious, and wonderful things, as they often hear and read of in the Word of God, is undoubtedly because they are blind; if they were not so, it would be impossible, and utterly inconsistent with human nature, that their hearts should be otherwise than strongly impressed, and greatly moved by such things.

This manner of slighting all religious affections is the way exceedingly to harden the hearts of men, and to encourage them in their stupidity and senselessness, and to keep them in a state of spiritual death as long as they live, and bring them at last to death eternal. The prevailing prejudice against religious affections at this day, in the land, is apparently of awful effect to harden the hearts of sinners, and damp the graces of many of the saints, and stun the life and power of religion, and preclude the effect of ordinances, and hold us down in a state of dulness and apathy. It undoubtedly causes many persons greatly to offend God, in entertaining mean and low thoughts of the extraordinary work He has lately wrought in this land.

And for persons to despise and cry down all religious affections is the way to shut all religion out of their own hearts, and to make thorough work in ruining their souls.

They who condemn high affections in others are certainly not likely to have high affections themselves. And let it be considered, that they who have but little religious affection have certainly but little religion. And they who condemn others for their religious affections, and have none themselves, have no religion.

There are false affections, and there are true. A man's having much affection, does not prove that he has any true religion: but if he has no affection, it proves that he has no true religion. The right way is not to reject all affections, nor to approve all; but to distinguish between affections, approving some and rejecting others; separating between the wheat and the chaff, the gold and the dross, the precious and the vile.

2. If it be so that true religion lies much in the affections, hence we may infer that such means are to be desired as have much of a tendency to move the affections. Such books, and such a way of preaching the word, and administering ordinances, and such

a way of worshipping God in prayer, and singing praises, is much to be desired, as have a tendency deeply to affect the hearts of those who attend these means.

Such a kind of means would formerly have been highly approved of, and applauded by the generality of the people of the land, as the most excellent and profitable, having the greatest tendency to promote the ends of the means of grace. But the prevailing taste seems of late strangely to be altered: that pathetical manner of praying and preaching which would formerly have been admired and extolled, and that for this reason, because it had such a tendency to move the affections, now, in great multitudes, immediately excites disgust, and moves no other affections than those of displeasure and contempt.

Perhaps, formerly the generality (at least of the common people) were in the extreme of looking too much to an affectionate address in public performances: but now a very great part of the people seem to have gone far into a contrary extreme. Indeed there may be such means as may have a great tendency to stir up the passions of weak and ignorant persons, and yet have no great tendency to benefit their souls: for though they may have a tendency to excite affections, they may have little or none to excite gracious affections, or any affections tending to grace. But undoubtedly, if the things of religion in the means used are treated according to their nature and exhibited truly, so as tends to convey just apprehensions and a right judgment of them, the more they have a tendency to move the affections the better.

3. If true religion lies much in the affections, hence we may learn what great cause we have to be ashamed and confounded before God, that we are no more affected with the great things of religion. It appears from what has been said that this arises from our having so little true religion.

God has given to mankind affections, for the same purpose which he has given all the faculties and principles of the human soul for, viz., that they might be subservient to man's chief end, and the great business for which God has created him, that is, the business of religion. And yet how common is it among mankind, that their affections are much more exercised and engaged in other matters than in religion! In things which concern men's worldly interest, their outward delights, their honour and reputation, and their natural relations, they have their desires eager, their appetites vehement, their love warm and affectionate, their zeal ardent; in these things their hearts are tender and sensible, easily moved, deeply impressed, much concerned, very sensibly affected, and greatly engaged; much depressed with grief at losses, and highly raised with joy at worldly successes and prosperity. But how insensible and unmoved are most men about the great things of another world! How dull are their affections! How heavy and hard their hearts in these matters! Here their love is cold, their desires languid, their zeal low, and their gratitude small. How they can sit and hear of the infinite height, and depth, and length, and breadth of the love of God in Christ Jesus, of His giving His infinitely dear Son, to be offered up a sacrifice for the sins of men, and of the unparalleled love of the innocent, and holy, and tender Lamb of God, manifested in His dying agonies, His bloody sweat, His loud and bitter cries, and bleeding heart, and all this for enemies, to redeem them from deserved, eternal burnings, and to bring to unspeakable and everlasting joy and glory—and yet be cold and heavy, insensible and regardless! Where are the exercises of our affections proper, if not here? What is it that does more require them? And what can be a fit occasion of their lively and vigorous exercise, if not such a one as this? Can anything be set in our view greater and more important? Anything more wonderful and surprising? Or more nearly concerning our interest? Can we suppose the wise Creator implanted such principles in the human nature as the affections, to be of use to us, and to be exercised on certain proper occasions, but to lie still on such an occasion as this? Can any Christian who believes the truth of these things entertain such thoughts?

If we ought ever to exercise our affections at all, then they ought to be exercised about those objects which are most worthy of them. But is there anything which Christians can find in heaven or earth so worthy to be the objects of their admiration and love, their earnest and longing desires, their hope, and their rejoicing, and their fervent zeal, as those things that are held forth to us in the gospel of Jesus Christ? In which not only are things declared most worthy to affect us, but they are exhibited in the most affecting manner. The glory and beauty of the blessed Jehovah, which is most worthy in itself to be the object of our admiration and love, is there exhibited in the most affecting manner that can be conceived of, as it appears shining in all its lustre in the face of an incarnate, infinitely loving, meek, compassionate, dying Redeemer. All the virtues of the Lamb of God, His humility, patience, meekness, submission, obedience, love and compassion, are exhibited to our view in a manner the most tending to move our affections of any that can be imagined; as they all had their greatest trial, and their highest exercise, and so their brightest manifestation, when He was in the most affecting circumstances; even when He was under His last sufferings, those unutterable and unparalleled sufferings He endured from his tender love and pity to us. There also the hateful nature of our sins is manifested in the most affecting manner possible: as we see the dreadful effects of them in what our Redeemer, who undertook to answer for us, suffered for them. And there we have the most affecting manifestation of God's hatred of sin, and His wrath and justice in punishing it; as we see His justice in the strictness and inflexibleness of it; and His wrath in its terribleness, in so dreadfully punishing our sins, in One who was infinitely dear to Him, and loving to us. So has God disposed things in the affair of our redemption, and in His glorious dispensations, revealed to us in the gospel, as though every thing were purposely contrived in such a manner as to have the greatest possible tendency to reach our hearts in the most tender part, and move our affections most sensibly and strongly. How great cause have we therefore to be humbled to the dust that we are no more affected!

Part II

SHOWING WHAT ARE NO CERTAIN SIGNS THAT RELIGIOUS AFFECTIONS ARE TRULY GRACIOUS, OR THAT THEY ARE NOT

IF any one, on the reading of what has been just now said, is ready to acquit himself and say, " I am not one of those who have no religious affections; I am often greatly moved with the consideration of the great things of religion," let him not content himself with this, that he has religious affections: for as we observed before, as we ought not to reject and condemn all affections as though true religion did not at all consist in affection; so, on the other hand, we ought not to approve of all, as though every one that was religiously affected had true grace, and was therein the subject of the saving influences of the Spirit of God. The right way is to distinguish among religious affections, between one sort and another. Therefore let us now endeavour to do this; and in order to do it, I would do two things.

I. I would mention some things which are no signs one way or the other, either that affections are such as true religion consists in, or that they are otherwise; that we may be guarded against judging of affections by false signs.

II. I would observe some things, wherein those affections which are spiritual and gracious differ from those which are not so, and may be distinguished and known.

FIRST, I would take notice of some things, which are no signs that affections are gracious, or that they are not.

I. *It is no sign one way or the other, that religious affections are very great, or raised very high.*

Some are ready to condemn all high affections: if persons appear to have their religious affections raised to an extraordinary pitch, they are prejudiced against them, and determine that they are delusions without further inquiry. But if it be, as has been proved, that true religion lies very much in religious affections,

54

then it follows that, if there be a great deal of true religion, there will be great religious affections; if true religion in the hearts of men be raised to a great height, divine and holy affections will be raised to a great height.

Love is an affection, but will any Christian say, men ought not to love God and Jesus Christ in a high degree? And will any say, we ought not to have a very great hatred of sin, and a very deep sorrow for it? Or that we ought not to exercise a high degree of gratitude to God for the mercies we receive of Him, and the great things He has done for the salvation of fallen men? Or that we should not have very great and strong desires after God and holiness? Is there any who will profess that his affections in religion are great enough, and will say, "I have no cause to be humbled, that I am no more affected with the things of religion than I am; I have no reason to be ashamed, that I have no greater exercises of love to God and sorrow for sin, and gratitude for the mercies which I have received?" Who is there that will bless God that he is affected enough with what he has read and heard of the wonderful love of God to worms and rebels, in giving His only begotten Son to die for them, and with the dying love of Christ; and will pray that he may not be affected with them in any higher degree, because high affections are improper and very unlovely in Christians, being enthusiastical, and ruinous to true religion.

Our text plainly speaks of great and high affections when it speaks of "rejoicing with joy unspeakable, and full of glory:" here the most superlative expressions are used which language will afford. And the Scriptures often require us to exercise very high affections: thus, in the first and great commandment of the law, there is an accumulation of expressions, as though words were wanting to express the degree in which we ought to love God: "Thou shalt love the Lord thy God with all thy heart, with all thy soul, with all thy mind, and with all thy strength." So the saints are called upon to exercise high degrees of joy: "Rejoice," says Christ to His disciples, "and be exceeding glad," Matt. v. 12. So it is said, Psalm lxviii. 3, "Let the righteous be glad: let them rejoice before God; yea, let them exceedingly rejoice." So in the same book of Psalms, the saints are often called upon to shout for joy; and in Luke vi. 23, to leap for joy. So they are abundantly called upon to exercise high degrees of gratitude for mercies, to "praise God with all their hearts, with hearts lifted up in the ways of the Lord, and their souls magnifying the Lord, singing his praises, talking of his wondrous works, declaring his doings, &c."

And we find the most eminent saints in Scripture often professing high affections. Thus the Psalmist speaks of his love, as if it were unspeakable; Psal. cxix. 97, "O how love I thy law!" So he expresses a great degree of hatred of sin, Psal. cxxxix. 21, 22: "Do not I hate them, O Lord, that hate thee? And am not I grieved with them that rise up against thee? I hate them with perfect hatred." He also expresses a high degree of sorrow for sin: he speaks of his sins "going over his head as a heavy burden that was too heavy for him: and of his roaring all the day, and his moisture being turned into the drought of summer," and his bones being as it were broken with sorrow. So he often expresses great degrees of spiritual desires, in a multitude of the strongest expressions which can be conceived of; such as "his longing, his soul's thirsting as a dry and thirsty land where no water is, his panting, his flesh and heart crying out, his soul's breaking for the longing it hath," &c. He expresses the exercises of great and extreme grief for the sins of others, Psal. cxix. 136, "Rivers of water run down mine eyes, because they keep not thy law." And verse 53, "Horror hath taken hold upon me, because of the wicked that forsake thy law." He expresses high exercises of joy, Psal. xxi. 1: "The king shall joy in thy strength, O Lord, and in thy salvation how greatly shall he rejoice." Psal. lxxi. 23, "My lips shall greatly rejoice when I sing unto thee." Psal. lxiii. 3, 4, 5, 6, 7, "Because thy lovingkindness is better than life, my lips shall praise thee. Thus will I bless thee while I live: I will lift up my hands in thy name. My soul shall be satisfied as with marrow and fatness; and my mouth shall praise thee with joyful lips; when I remember thee upon my bed, and meditate on thee in the night watches. Because thou hast been my help; therefore in the shadow of thy wings will I rejoice."

The Apostle Paul expresses high exercises of affection. Thus he expresses the exercises of pity and concern for others' good, even to anguish of heart; a great, fervent, and abundant love, and earnest and longing desires, and exceeding joy; and speaks of the exultation and triumphs of his soul, and his earnest expectation and hope, and his abundant tears, and the travails of his soul, in pity, grief, earnest desires, godly jealousy, and fervent zeal, in many places that have been cited already, and which therefore I need not repeat. John the Baptist expressed great joy, John iii. 29. Those blessed women that anointed the body of Jesus are represented as in a very high exercise of religious affection, on occasion of Christ's resurrection, Matt. xxviii. 8: "And they departed from the sepulchre with fear and great joy."

It is often foretold of the church of God in her future happy seasons here on earth, that they shall exceedingly rejoice: Psal. lxxxix. 15, 16, "They shall walk, O Lord, in the light of thy countenance. In thy name shall they rejoice all the day: and in thy righteousness shall they be exalted." Zech. ix. 9, "Rejoice greatly, O daughter of Zion; shout, O daughter of Jerusalem: behold, thy King cometh," &c. The same is represented in innumerable other places. And because high degrees of joy are the proper and genuine fruits of the gospel of Christ, therefore the angel calls this gospel, " good tidings of great joy, that should be to all people."

The saints and angels in heaven, that have religion in its highest perfection, are exceedingly affected with what they behold and contemplate of God's perfections and works. They are all as a pure heavenly flame of fire in their love, and in the greatness and strength of their joy and gratitude: their praises are represented, "as the voice of many waters and as the voice of a great thunder." Now the only reason why their affections are so much higher than the holy affections of saints on earth is, they see the things they are affected by more according to their truth, and have their affections more conformed to the nature of things. And therefore, if religious affections in men here below are but of the same nature and kind with theirs, the higher they are, and the nearer they are to theirs in degree, the better, because therein they will be so much the more conformed to truth, as theirs are.

From these things it certainly appears, that religious affections being in a very high degree is no evidence that they are not such as have the nature of true religion. Therefore they do greatly err who condemn persons as enthusiasts, merely because their affections are very high.

And on the other hand, it is no evidence that religious affections are of a spiritual and gracious nature, because they are great. It is very manifest by the Holy Scripture, our sure and infallible rule to judge of things of this nature, that there are religious affections which are very high that are not spiritual and saving. The Apostle Paul speaks of affections in the Galatians which had been exceedingly elevated, and which yet he manifestly speaks of as fearing that they were vain and had come to nothing: Gal. iv. 15, "Where is the blessedness you spoke of? For I bear you record, that if it had been possible, you would have plucked out your own eyes, and have given them to me." And in the 11th verse, he tells them, "he was afraid of them, lest he had bestowed upon them labour in vain." So the children of Israel were greatly affected with God's mercy to them when they had seen how wonderfully He wrought for them at the Red Sea, where they sang God's praise; though they soon forgat His works. So they were greatly affected again at mount Sinai when they saw the marvellous manifestations God made of Himself there; and seemed mightily engaged in their minds, and with great forwardness made answer, when God proposed His holy covenant to them, saying, "All that the Lord hath spoken will we do, and be obedient." But how soon was there an end to all this mighty forwardness and engagedness of affection! How quickly were they turned aside after other gods, rejoicing and shouting around their golden calf! So great multitudes who were affected with the miracle of raising Lazarus from the dead, were elevated to a high degree, and made a mighty ado when Jesus presently after entered into Jerusalem, exceedingly magnifying Christ, as though the ground were not good enough for the ass He rode to tread upon; and therefore cut branches off palm trees, and strewed them in the way; yea, pulled off their garments, and spread them in the way; and cried with loud voices, "Hosanna to the Son of David, blessed is he that cometh in the name of the Lord, hosanna in the highest," so as to make the whole city ring again, and put all into an uproar. We learn by the evangelist John that the reason why the people made this ado, was because they were affected with the miracle of raising Lazarus, John xii. 18. Here was a vast multitude crying "Hosanna" on this occasion, so that it gave occasion to the Pharisees to say, "Behold, the world has gone after him," John xii. 19, but Christ had at that time but few true disciples. And how quickly was this ado at an end! All of this nature is quelled and dead, when this Jesus stands bound, with a mock robe and a crown of thorns, to be derided, spit upon, scourged, condemned and executed. Indeed, there was a great and loud outcry concerning Him among the multitude then as well as before; but of a very different kind: it is not then, " Hosanna, hosanna," but " Crucify, crucify."

And it is the concurring voice of all orthodox divines, that there may be religious affections, which are raised to a very high degree, and yet there be nothing of true religion.*

II. *It is no sign that affections have the nature of true religion, or that they have not, that they have great effects on the body.*

All affections whatsoever have in some respect or degree an effect on the body. As was observed before, such is our nature, and such are the laws of union of soul and body, that the mind can have no lively or vigorous exercise without some effect upon the body. So subject is the body to the mind, and so much do its fluids, especially the animal spirits, attend the motions and exercises of the mind, that there cannot be so much as an intense thought, without an effect upon them. Yea, it is questionable whether an embodied soul ever so much as thinks one thought, or has any exercise at all, but that there is some corresponding motion or alteration of motion, in some degree, of the fluids in some part of the body. But universal experience shows that the exercise of the affections have in a special manner a tendency to some sensible effect upon the body. And if this be so, that the exercise of the affections has in a special manner a tenwell suppose, the greater those affections be, and the more vigorous their exercise (other circumstances being equal), the greater will be the effect on the body. Very great and strong exercises of the affections have great effects on the body. And therefore, seeing there are very great affections, both common and spiritual, it is not to be wondered at that great effects on the body should arise from both these kinds of affections. And consequently these effects are no signs that the affections they arise from are of one kind or the other.

Great effects on the body certainly are no sure evidences that affections are spiritual; for we see that such effects oftentimes arise from great affections about temporal things, and when religion is no way concerned in them. And if great affections about

* Mr. Stoddard observes, " That common affections are sometimes stronger than saving."—*Guide to Christ.*

secular things, that are purely natural, may have these effects, I know not by what rule we should determine that high affections about religious things, which arise in like manner from nature, cannot have the like effect.

Nor, on the other hand, do I know of any rule any have to determine that gracious and holy affections, when raised as high as any natural affections, and having equally strong and vigorous exercises, cannot have a great effect on the body. No such rule can be drawn from reason: I know of no reason why a being affected with a view of God's glory should not cause the body to faint, as well as being affected with a view of Solomon's glory. And no such rule has as yet been produced from the Scripture; none has ever been found in all the late controversies which have been about things of this nature. There is a great power in spiritual affections: we read of the power which worketh in Christians, and of the Spirit of God being in them as the Spirit of power, and of the effectual working of His power in them, Eph. iii. 7, 20; 2 Tim. i. 7. But man's nature is weak: flesh and blood are represented in Scripture as exceeding weak; and particularly with respect to its unfitness for great spiritual and heavenly operations and exercises, Matt. xxvi. 41, 1 Cor. xv. 43 and 50. The text we are upon speaks of "joy unspeakable, and full of glory." And who that considers what man's nature is, and what the nature of the affections is, can reasonably doubt but that such unutterable and glorious joys may be too great and mighty for weak dust and ashes, so as to be considerably overbearing to it? It is evident by the Scripture that true divine discoveries, or ideas of God's glory, when given in a great degree, have a tendency, by affecting the mind, to overbear the body; because the Scripture teaches us often that if these ideas or views should be given to such a degree as they are given in heaven, the weak frame of the body could not subsist under them, and that no man can, in that manner, see God and live. The knowledge which the saints have of God's beauty and glory in this world, and those holy affections that arise from it, are of the same nature and kind with what the saints are subjects of in heaven, differing only in degree and circumstances: what God gives them here is a foretaste of heavenly happiness, and an earnest of their future inheritance. And who shall limit God in His giving this earnest, or say He shall give so much of the inheritance, such a part of the future reward, as an earnest of the whole, and no more? And seeing God has taught us in His word that the whole reward is such that it would at once destroy the body, is it not too bold a thing for us so to set bounds to the sovereign God, as to say that, in giving the earnest of this reward in this world, He shall never give so much of it as in the least to diminish the strength of the body, when God has nowhere thus limited Himself?

The Psalmist, speaking of the vehement religious affections he had, speaks of an effect in his flesh or body, besides what was in his soul, expressly distinguishing one from the other, once and again: Psal. lxxxiv. 2, "My soul longeth, yea, even fainteth for the courts of the Lord: my heart and my flesh crieth out for the living God." Here is a plain distinction between the heart and the flesh, as being each affected. So Psal. lxiii. 1, "My soul thirsteth for thee, my flesh longeth for thee in a dry and thirsty land, where no water is." Here also is an evident designed distinction between the soul and the flesh.

The prophet Habakkuk speaks of his body's being overborne by a sense of the majesty of God, Hab. iii. 16: "When I heard, my belly trembled: my lips quivered at the voice: rottenness entered into my bones, and I trembled in myself." So the Psalmist speaks expressly of his flesh trembling, Psal. cxix. 120: "My flesh trembleth for fear of thee."

That such ideas of God's glory as are sometimes given in this world have a tendency to overbear the body is evident, because the Scripture gives us an account that this has sometimes actually been the effect of those external manifestations God has made of Himself to some of the saints, which were made to that end, viz., to give them an idea of God's majesty and glory. Such instances we have in the prophet Daniel, and the Apostle John. Daniel, giving an account of an external representation of the glory of Christ, says, Dan. x. 8, "And there remained no strength in me; for my comeliness was turned into corruption, and I retained no strength." And the Apostle John, giving an account of a like manifestation made to him, says, Rev. i. 17, "And when I saw him, I fell at his feet as dead." It is in vain to say here, these were only external manifestations or symbols of the glory of Christ, which these saints beheld: for though it be true that they were outward representations of Christ's glory, which they beheld with their bodily eyes; yet the end and use of these external symbols or representations was to give to these prophets an idea of the thing represented, and that was the true divine glory and majesty of Christ, which is His spiritual glory; they were made use of only as significations of this spiritual glory, and thus undoubtedly they received them, and improved them, and were affected by them. According to the end for which God intended these outward signs, they received by them a great and lively apprehension of the real glory and majesty of God's nature, which they were signs of; and thus were greatly affected, their souls swallowed up, and their bodies overborne. And I think they are very bold and daring who will say God cannot, or shall not, give the like clear and affecting ideas and apprehensions of the same real glory and majesty of His nature to any of His saints, without the intervention of any such external shadows of it.

Before I leave this head, I would further observe that it is plain the Scripture often makes use of bodily effects, to express the strength of holy and spiritual affections; such as trembling, groaning, being sick, crying out, panting, and fainting. Now if it be supposed that these are only figurative expressions, to represent the degree of affection; yet I hope all will allow that they are fit and suitable figures to represent the high degree of those spiritual affections which the Spirit of God makes use of them to represent; which I do not see how they would be, if those spiritual affections, let them be in never so high a degree, have no tendency to any such things; but that, on the contrary, they are the proper effects and sad tokens of false affections, and the delusion of the devil. I cannot think God would commonly make use of things which are very alien from spiritual affections, and are shrewd marks of the hand of Satan, and smell strong of the bottomless pit, as beautiful figures to represent the high degree of holy and heavenly affections.

III. *It is no sign that affections are truly gracious affections, or that they are not, that they cause those who have them to be fluent, fervent and abundant, in talking of the things of religion.*

There are many persons who, if they see this in others, are greatly prejudiced against them. Their being so full of talk is with them a sufficient ground to condemn them as Pharisees and ostentatious hypocrites. On the other hand, there are many who, if they see this effect in any, are very ignorantly and imprudently forward at once to determine that they are the true children of God, and are under the saving influences of His Spirit, and speak of it as a great evidence of a new creature; they say, "Such an one's mouth is now opened: he used to be slow to speak, but now he is full and free; he is free now to open his heart, and tell his experiences, and declare the praises of God; it comes from him as free as water from a fountain"; and the like. And especially they are captivated into a confident and undoubting persuasion that they are savingly wrought upon, if they are not only free and abundant but very affectionate and earnest in their talk.

This, however, is the fruit of but little judgment, a scanty and short experience, as events do abundantly show, and is a mistake persons often run into through their trusting to their own wisdom and discerning, and making their own notions their rule instead of the Holy Scripture. Though the Scripture be full of rules, both how we should judge of our own state, and also how we should be conducted in our opinion of others; yet we have nowhere any rule by which to judge ourselves or others to be in a good estate from any such effect: for this is but the religion of the mouth and of the tongue, and what is in the Scripture represented by the leaves of a tree, which, though the tree ought not to be without them, yet are nowhere given as an evidence of the goodness of the tree.

That persons are disposed to be abundant in talking of things of religion may be from a good cause, and it may be from a bad one. It may be because their hearts are very full of holy affections, "for out of the abundance of the heart the mouth speaketh": and it may be because persons' hearts are very full of religious affection which is not holy, for still " out of the abundance of the heart the mouth speaketh." It is very much the nature of the affections, of whatever kind they be, and whatever objects they are exercised about, if they are strong, to dispose persons to be very much in speaking of that which they are affected with: and not only to speak much but to speak very earnestly and fervently. And therefore persons talking abundantly and very fervently about the things of religion can be an evidence of no more than this, that they are very much affected with the things of religion; but this may be (as has been already shown) and there be no grace. That which men are greatly affected with, while the high affection lasts, they will be earnestly engaged about, and will be likely to show that earnestness in their talk and behaviour; as the greater part of the Jews, in all Judea and Galilee, did for a while, about John the Baptist's preaching and baptism, when they were willing for a season to rejoice in his light; a mighty ado was made, all over the land and among all sorts of persons, about this great prophet and his ministry. And so the multitude, in like manner, often manifested a great earnestness, a mighty engagedness of spirit, in every thing that was external, about Christ and His preaching and miracles, " being astonished at His doctrine, anon with joy receiving the Word " following Him sometimes night and day, leaving meat, drink, and sleep to hear Him : once following Him into the wilderness, fasting three days going to hear Him; sometimes crying Him up to the clouds, saying, " Never man spake like this man ! " being fervent and earnest in what they said. But what did these things come to in the greater part of them?

A person may be over-full of talk of his own experiences, commonly falling upon it everywhere and in all companies; and when it is so, it is rather a dark sign than a good one. As a tree that is over-full of leaves seldom bears much fruit; and as a cloud, though to appearance very pregnant and full of water, if it brings with it overmuch wind, seldom affords much rain to the dry and thirsty earth; which very thing the Holy Spirit is pleased several times to make use of, to represent a great show of religion with the mouth without answerable fruit in the life : Prov. xxv. 14, " Whoso boasteth himself of a false gift is like clouds and wind without rain." And the Apostle Jude, speaking of some in the primitive times that crept in unawares among the saints, and having a great show of religion, were for a while not suspected, " These are clouds (says he) without water, carried about of winds," Jude ver. 4 and 12. And the Apostle Peter, speaking of the same, says, 2 Pet. ii. 17, " These are clouds carried with a tempest."

False affections, if they are equally strong, are much more forward to declare themselves than true : because it is the nature of false religion to affect show and observation, as it was with the Pharisees.*

---

* That famous experimental divine, Mr. Shepard, says, " A Pharisee's trumpet shall be heard to the town's end, when simplicity walks through the town unseen. Hence a man will sometimes covertly com-

IV. *It is no sign that affections are gracious, or that they are otherwise, that persons did not make them themselves, or excite them of their own contrivance, and by their own strength.*

There are many in these days that condemn all affections which are excited in a way that the subjects of them can give no account of, as not seeming to be the fruit of any of their own endeavours, or the natural consequence of the faculties and principles of human nature, in such circumstances, and under such means, but to be from the influence of some extrinsic and supernatural power upon their minds. How greatly has the doctrine of the inward experience, or sensible perceiving of the immediate power and operation of the Spirit of God, been reproached and ridiculed by many of late! They say the manner of the Spirit of God is to co-operate in a silent, secret, and undiscernible way with the use of means, and our own endeavours; so that there is no distinguishing by sense between the influences of the Spirit of God and the natural operations of the faculties of our own minds.

And it is true, that for any to expect to receive the saving influences of the Spirit of God while they neglect a diligent improvement of the appointed means of grace, is unreasonable presumption. And to expect that the Spirit of God will savingly operate upon their minds without the Spirit's making use of means, as subservient to the effect, is enthusiastical. It is also undoubtedly true that the Spirit of God is very various in the manner and circumstances of His operations, and that sometimes He operates in a way more secret and gradual, and from smaller beginnings, than at others.

---

mend himself (and *myself* ever comes in), and tells you a long story of conversion; and a hundred to one if some lie or other slip not out with it. Why, the secret meaning is, *I pray admire me*, and *Pray think what a broken-hearted Christian am I." Parable of the Ten Virgins*, p. 284.

And holy Mr. Flavel says thus: " O reader, if thy heart were right with God, and thus didst not cheat thyself with a vain profession, thou wouldst have frequent business with God which thou wouldst be loth thy dearest friend, or the wife of thy bosom, should be privy to. *Non est religio, ubi omnia patent.* Religion doth not lie open to all, to the eyes of men. Observed duties maintain our credit; but secret duties maintain our life. It was the saying of a heathen, about his secret correspondence with his friend, *What need the world be acquainted with it?* Thou and I are theatre enough to each other. There are inclosed pleasures in religion which none but renewed spiritual souls do feelingly understand." *Flavel's Touchstone of Sincerity.* Works Vol. V, p. 520.

But if there be indeed a Power, entirely different from and beyond our power, or the power of all means and instruments, and above the power of nature, which is requisite in order to the production of saving grace in the heart, according to the general profession of the country, then certainly it is in no wise unreasonable to suppose that this effect should very frequently be produced after such a manner, as to make it very manifest, apparent, and sensible that it is so. If grace be indeed owing to the powerful and efficacious operation of an extrinsic agent, or divine efficient out of ourselves, why is it unreasonable to suppose it should seem to be so to them who are the subjects of it? Is it a strange thing that it should seem to be as it is? When grace in the heart indeed is not produced by our strength, nor is the effect of the natural power of our own faculties, or any means or instruments, but is properly the workmanship and production of the Spirit of the Almighty, is it a strange and unaccountable thing, that it should seem to them who are subjects of it agreeable to truth, and not right contrary to truth; so that if persons tell of effects that they are conscious of in their own minds, that seem to them not to be from the natural power or operation of their minds but from the supernatural power of some other agent, should it at once be looked upon as a sure evidence of their being under a delusion, because things seem to them to be as they are? For this is the objection which is made: it is looked upon as a clear evidence, that the apprehensions and affections that many persons have are not really from such a cause, because they seem to them to be from that cause. They declare that what they are conscious of seems to them evidently not to be from themselves, but from the mighty power of the Spirit of God; and others from hence condemn them, and determine what they experience is not from the Spirit of God, but from themselves, or from the devil. Thus unreasonably are multitudes treated at this day by their neighbours.

If it be indeed so, as the Scripture abundantly teaches, that grace in the soul is so the effect of God's power, that it is fitly compared to those effects which are farthest from being owing to any strength in the subject, such as a generation, or a being begotten, and resurrection, or a being raised from the dead, and creation, or a being brought out of nothing into being, and that it is an effect wherein the might power of God is greatly glorified, and the exceeding greatness of His power is manifested, Eph. i. 17-20; then what account can be given of it, that the Almighty, in so great a work of His power, should so carefully hide His power that the subjects of it should be able to discern nothing of it? Or what reason or revelation have any to determine that He does so? If we may judge by the Scripture, this is not agreeable to God's manner in His operations and dispensations; but on the contrary, it is God's manner, in the great works of His power and mercy which He works for His people, to order things so as to make His hand visible, and His power conspicuous, and men's dependence on Him most evident, that no flesh should glory in His presence, 1 Cor. i. 27-29, that God alone might be exalted, and that the excellency of the power might be of God and not of man, and that Christ's power might be manifested in our weakness, and none might say, mine own hand hath saved me. Isa. ii. 11-17, 2 Cor. iv. 7, 2 Cor. xii. 9, Judg. vii. 2. So it was in most of those temporal salvations which God wrought for Israel of old, which were types of the salvation of God's people from their spiritual enemies. So it was in the redemption of Israel from their Egyptian bondage; He redeemed them with a strong hand and an outstretched arm; and that His power might be the more conspicuous, He suffered Israel first to be brought into the most helpless and forlorn circumstances. So it was in the great redemption by Gideon; God would have his army diminished to a handful, and they without any other arms than trumpets and lamps and earthen pitchers. So it was in the deliverance of Israel from Goliath, by a stripling with a sling and a stone. So it was in that great work of God, His calling the Gentiles, and converting the heathen world after Christ's ascension, after that the world by wisdom knew not God, and all the endeavours of philosophers had proved in vain for many ages to reform the world, and it was by every thing become abundantly evident that the world was utterly helpless, by anything else but the mighty power of God. And so it was in most of the conversions of particular persons we have an account of in the history of the New Testament: they were not wrought on in that silent, secret, gradual, and insensible manner which is now insisted on; but with those manifest evidences of a supernatural power wonderfully and suddenly causing a great change, which in these days are looked upon as certain signs of delusion and enthusiasm.

The Apostle, in Eph. i. 18, 19, speaks of God's enlightening the minds of Christians, and so bringing them to believe in Christ, to the end that they might know the exceeding greatness of His power to them who believe. The words are, "The eyes of your understanding being enlightened; that ye may know what is the hope of his calling, and what the riches of the glory of his inheritance in the saints, and what is the exceeding greatness of his power to us-ward who believe, according to the working of his mighty power," &c. Now when the apostle speaks of their being thus the subjects of His power, in their enlightening and effectual calling, to the end that they might know what His mighty power was to them who believe, he can mean nothing else than, "that they might know by experience." But if the saints know this power by experience, then they feel it and discern it to be sensibly distinguishable from the natural operations of their own minds, which is not agreeable to a notion of God's operating so secretly and undiscernibly, that it cannot be known that they are the subjects of the influence of any extrinsic power at all, any otherwise than as they may argue it from Scripture assertions; which is a different thing from knowing it by experience.

So that it is very unreasonable and unscriptural to determine that affections are not from the gracious operations of God's Spirit, because they are sensibly not from the persons themselves that are the subjects of them.

On the other hand, it is no evidence that affections are gracious that they are not properly produced by those who are the subjects of them, or that they arise in their minds in a manner they cannot account for.

There are some who make this an argument in their own favour; when speaking of what they have experienced, they say, "I am sure I did not make it myself; it was a fruit of no contrivance or endeavour of mine; it came when I thought nothing of it; if I might have the world for it, I cannot make it again when I please." And hence they determine that what they have experienced must be from the mighty influence of the Spirit of God, and is of a saving nature; but very ignorantly, and without grounds. What they have been the subjects of may indeed not be from themselves directly, but may be from the operation of an invisible agent, some spirit besides their own: but it does not thence follow that it was from the Spirit of God. There are other spirits who have influence on the minds of men besides the Holy Ghost. We are directed not to believe every spirit, but to try the spirits whether they be of God. There are many false spirits, exceeding busy with men, who often transform themselves into angels of light, and do in many wonderful ways, with great subtlety and power, mimic the operations of the Spirit of God. And there are many of Satan's operations, which are very distinguishable from the voluntary exercises of men's own minds. They are so, in those dreadful and horrid suggestions and blasphemous injections with which he follows many persons; and in vain and fruitless frights and terrors which he is the author of. And the power of Satan may be as immediate and as evident in false comforts and joys, as in terrors and horrid suggestions; and oftentimes is so in fact. It is not in men's power to put themselves in such raptures, as the Anabaptists in Germany, and many other raving enthusiasts like them, have been the subjects of.

And besides, it is to be considered that persons may have those impressions on their minds, which may not be of their own producing, nor from an evil spirit, but from the Spirit of God, and yet not be from any saving but a common influence of the Spirit of God; and the subjects of such impressions may be of the number of those we read of, Heb. vi. 4, 5, " that are once enlightened, and taste of the heavenly gift, and are made partakers of the Holy Ghost, and taste the good word of God, and the powers of the world to come;" and yet may be wholly unacquainted with those " better things that accompany salvation," spoken of in ver. 9.

And where neither a good nor evil spirit has any immediate hand, persons, especially such as are of a weak and vapoury habit of body, and the brain weak and easily susceptive of impressions, may have strange apprehensions and imaginations, and strong affections attending them, unaccountably arising, which are not voluntarily produced by themselves. We see that such persons are liable to such impressions about temporal things; and there is equal reason why they should about spiritual things. As a person who is asleep has dreams that he is not the voluntary author of; so may such persons in like manner be the subjects of involuntary impressions when they are awake.

V. *It is no sign that religious affections are truly holy and spiritual, or that they are not, that they come with texts of Scripture, remarkably brought to the mind.*

It is no sign that affections are not gracious that they are occasioned by Scriptures so coming to mind; provided it be the Scripture itself, or the truth which the Scripture so brought contains and teaches, that is the foundation of the affection, and not merely, or mainly, the sudden and unusual manner of its coming to the mind.

But on the other hand, neither is it any sign that affections are gracious that they arise on occasion of Scriptures brought suddenly and wonderfully to the mind; whether those affections be fear or hope, joy or sorrow, or any other. Some seem to look upon this as a good evidence that their affections are saving, especially if the affections excited are hope or joy, or any other which are pleasing and delightful. They will mention it as an evidence that all is right, that their experience came with the Word, and will say, "There were such and such sweet promises brought to my mind: they came suddenly, as if they were spoken to me: I had no hand in bringing such a text to my own mind; I was not thinking of anything leading to it; it came all at once, so that I was surprised. I had not thought of it a long time before; I did not know at first that it was Scripture; I did not remember that ever I had read it." And it may be, they will add, "One Scripture came flowing in after another, and so texts all over the Bible, the most sweet and pleasant, and the most apt and suitable which could be devised; and filled me full as I could hold: I could not but stand and admire: the tears flowed; I was full of joy and could not doubt any longer." And thus they think they have undoubted evidence that their affections must be from God, and of the right kind, and their state good: but without any manner of grounds. How came they by any such rule, as that if any affections or experiences arise with promises, and comfortable texts of Scripture unaccountably brought to mind without their recollection, or if a great number of sweet texts follow one another in a chain, that this is a certain evidence their experiences are saving? Where is any such rule to be found in the Bible, the great and only sure directory in things of this nature?

What deceives many of the less understanding and considerate sort of people in this matter seems to be this; that the Scripture is the Word of God, and has nothing in it which is wrong, but is pure and perfect; and therefore those experiences which come from the Scripture must be right. But then it should be considered, affections may arise on occasion of the Scripture, and not properly come from the Scripture, as the genuine fruit of the Scripture and by a right use of it; but from an abuse of it. All that can be argued from the purity and perfection of the Word of God, with respect to experiences, is this, that those experiences which are agreeable to the Word of God are right, and cannot be otherwise; and not that those affections must be right which arise on occasion of the Word of God coming to the mind.

What evidence is there that the devil cannot bring texts of Scripture to the mind, and misapply them to deceive persons? There seems to be nothing in this which exceeds the power of Satan. It is no work of such mighty power to bring sounds or letters to persons' minds, that we have any reason to suppose nothing short of Omnipotence can be sufficient for it. If Satan has power to bring any words or sounds at all to persons' minds, he may have power to bring words contained in the Bible. There is no higher sort of power required in men to make the sounds which express the words of a text of Scripture, than to make the sounds which express the words of an idle story or song. And so the same power in Satan, which is sufficient to renew one of those kinds of sounds in the mind, is sufficient to renew the other: the different signification, which depends wholly on custom, alters not the case as to ability to make or revive the sounds or letters. Or will any suppose that texts or Scriptures are such sacred things that the devil durst not abuse them nor touch them? In this also they are mistaken. He who was bold enough to lay hold on Christ Himself, and carry Him hither and thither, into the wilderness and into a high mountain and to a pinnacle of the temple, is not afraid to touch the Scripture and abuse that for his own purpose; as he showed at the same time that he was so bold with Christ, he then brought one Scripture and another, to deceive and tempt him. And if Satan did presume, and was permitted to put Christ Himself in mind of texts of Scripture to tempt *Him*, what reason have we to determine that he dare not, or will not be permitted, to put wicked men in mind of texts of Scripture to tempt and deceive *them?* And if Satan may thus abuse one text of Scripture, so he may another. Its being a very excellent place of Scripture, a comfortable and precious promise, alters not the case as to his courage or ability. And if he can bring one comfortable text to the mind, so he may a thousand; and may choose out such Scriptures as tend most to serve his purpose; and may heap up Scripture promises, tending, according to the perverse application he makes of them, wonderfully to remove the rising doubts and to confirm the false joy and confidence of a poor deluded sinner.

We know that the devil's instruments, corrupt and heretical teachers, can and do pervert the Scripture to their own and others' damnation, 2 Pet. iii. 16. We see they have the free use of Scripture in every part of it: there is no text so precious and sacred but they are permitted to abuse it, to the eternal ruin of multitudes of souls; and there are no weapons they make use of with which they do more execution. And there is no manner of reason to determine that the devil is not permitted thus to use the Scripture, as well as his instruments. For when the latter do it, they do it as his instruments and servants, and through his instigation and influence: and doubtless he does the same he instigates others to do; the devil's servants do but follow their master, and do the same work that he does himself.

And as the devil can abuse the Scripture, to deceive and destroy men, so may men's own folly and corruptions as well. The sin which is in men acts like its father. Men's own hearts are deceitful like the devil, and use the same means to deceive.

So that it is evident that persons may have high affections of hope and joy, arising on occasion of texts of Scripture, yea, precious promises of Scripture coming suddenly and remarkably to their minds, as though they were spoken to them, yea, a great multitude of such texts following one another in a wonderful manner; and yet all this be no argument that these affections are divine, or that they are any other than the effects of Satan's delusions.

And I would further observe that persons may have raised and joyful affections, which may come with the Word of God, and not only so but from the Word, and those affections not be from Satan, nor yet properly from the corruptions of their own hearts, but from some influence of the Spirit of God with the Word, and yet have nothing of the nature of true and saving religion in them. Thus the stony ground hearers had great joy from the word; yea, which is represented as arising from the Word, as growth from a seed; and their affections had in their appearance a very great and exact resemblance with those represented by the growth on the good ground, the difference not appearing until it was discovered by the consequences in a time of trial: and yet there was no saving religion in these affections.*

VI. *It is no evidence that religious affections are saving, or that they are otherwise, that there is an appearance of love in them.*

There are no professing Christians who pretend that this is an argument against the truth and saving nature of religious affections. But, on the other hand, there are some who suppose it is a good evidence that affections are from the sanctifying and saving influences of the Holy Ghost. Their argument is that Satan cannot love, this affection being directly contrary to the devil whose very nature is enmity and malice. And it is true that nothing is more excellent, heavenly, and divine, than a spirit of true Christian love to God and men: it is more excellent than knowledge, or prophecy, or miracles, or speaking with the tongues of men and angels. It is the chief of the graces of God's Spirit, and the life, essence and sum of all true religion; and that by which we are most conformed to heaven, and most contrary to hell and the devil. But yet it is ill arguing from hence that there are no counterfeits of it. It may be observed that the more excellent anything is, the more will be the counterfeits of it. Thus there are many more counterfeits of silver and gold than of iron and copper: there are many false diamonds and rubies, but who goes about to counterfeit common stones? Though the more excellent things are, the more difficult it is to make anything that shall be like them in their essential nature and internal virtues; yet the more manifold will the counterfeits be, and the more will art and subtlety be displayed in an exact imitation of the outward appearance. Thus there is the greatest danger of being cheated in buying of medicines that are most excellent and sovereign,

* Mr. Stoddard, in his *Guide to Christ*, speaks of it as a common thing for persons, while in a natural condition, and before they have ever truly accepted of Christ, to have Scripture promises come to them, with a great deal of refreshing: which they take as tokens of God's love, and hope that God has accepted them; and so are confident of their good estate.

though it be most difficult to imitate them with anything of the like value and virtue, and their counterfeits are good for nothing when we have them. So it is with Christian virtues and graces; the subtlety of Satan, and men's deceitful hearts, are wont chiefly to be exercised in counterfeiting those that are in highest repute. So there are perhaps no graces that have more counterfeits than love and humility, these being virtues wherein the beauty of a true Christian does especially appear.

But with respect to love; it is plain by the Scripture that persons may have a kind of religious love, and yet have no saving grace. Christ speaks of many professing Christians that have such love, whose love will not continue, and so shall fail of salvation, Matt. xxiv. 12, 13: "And because iniquity shall abound, the love of many shall wax cold. But he that shall endure unto the end, the same shall be saved." Which latter words plainly show that those spoken of before, whose love shall not endure to the end, but wax cold, should not be saved.

Persons may seem to have love to God and Christ, yea, to have very strong and violent affections of this nature, and yet have no grace. For this was evidently the case with many graceless Jews, such as cried Jesus up so high, following him day and night, without meat, drink, or sleep; such as said, "Lord, I will follow thee whithersoever thou goest," and cried, "Hosanna to the Son of David."*

The apostle seems to intimate that there were many in his days who had a counterfeit love to Christ, in Eph. vi. 24: "Grace be with all them that love our Lord Jesus Christ in sincerity." The last word, in the original, signifies *incorruption;* which shows that the apostle was sensible that there were many who had a kind of love to Christ, whose love was not pure and spiritual.

So also Christian love to the people of God may be counterfeited. It is evident by the Scripture, that there may be strong affections of this kind without saving grace; as there were in the Galatians towards the Apostle Paul, when they were ready to

---

* Agreeable to this, Mr. Stoddard observes, in his *Guide to Christ,* that some sinners have pangs of affection, and give an account that they find a spirit of love to God, and of their aiming at the glory of God, having that which has a great resemblance of saving grace; and that sometimes their common affections are stronger than saving. He supposes that sometimes natural men may have such violent pangs of false affection to God, that they may think themselves willing to be damned.

pluck out their eyes and give them to him; although the apostle expresses his fear that their affections were come to nothing, and that he had bestowed upon them labour in vain, Gal. iv. 11, 15.

VII. *Persons having religious affections of many kinds, accompanying one another, is not sufficient to determine whether they have any gracious affections or no.*

Though false religion is wont to be maimed and monstrous, and not to have that entireness and symmetry of parts which is to be seen in true religion: yet there may be a great variety of false affections together, that may resemble gracious affections.

It is evident that there are counterfeits of all kinds of gracious affections; as of love to God, and love to the brethren, as has been just now observed; so of godly sorrow for sin, as in Pharaoh, Saul, and Ahab, and the children of Israel in the wilderness, Exod. ix. 27, 1 Sam. xxiv. 16, 17, and xxvi. 21, 1 Kings xxi. 27, Numb. xiv. 39, 40; and of the fear of God, as in the Samaritans, "who feared the Lord, and served their own gods" at the same time, 2 Kings xvii. 32, 33; and those enemies of God we read of, Psal. lxvi. 3, who, "through the greatness of God's power, submit themselves to him," or, as it is in the Hebrew, "lie unto him," *i.e.*, yield a counterfeit reverence and submission. So of a gracious gratitude, as in the children of Israel, who sang God's praise at the Red Sea, Psal. cvi. 12; and Naaman the Syrian, after the miraculous cure of his leprosy, 2 Kings v. 15, &c.

So of spiritual joy, as in the stony-ground hearers, Matt. xiii. 20, and particularly many of John the Baptist's hearers, John v. 35. So of zeal, as in Jehu, 2 Kings x. 16, and in Paul before his conversion, Gal. i. 14, Phil. iii. 6, and the unbelieving Jews, Acts xxii. 3, Rom. x. 2. So graceless persons may have earnest religious desires, that may be like Balaam's desires, which he expresses under an extraordinary view that he had of the happy state of God's people as distinguished from all the rest of the world, Numb. xxiii. 9, 10. They may also have a strong hope of eternal life, as the Pharisees had.

And as men, while in a state of nature, are capable of a resemblance of all kinds of religious affections, so nothing hinders but that they may have many of them together. And what appears in fact does abundantly evince that it is very often so indeed. It seems commonly to be so that, when false affections are raised high, many false affections attend each other. The multitude that attended Christ into Jerusalem, after that great miracle of raising Lazarus, seem to have been moved with many religious affections at once, and all in a high degree. They seem to have been filled with admiration; there was a show of a high affection of love, and also of a great degree of reverence, in their laying their garments on the ground for Christ to tread upon; and also of great gratitude to Him, for the great and good works He had wrought, praising Him with loud voices for His salvation. They showed earnest desires for the coming of God's kingdom, which they supposed Jesus was now about to set up, and great hopes of it, expecting it would immediately appear; and hence were filled with joy, by which they were so animated in their acclamations as to make the whole city ring with the noise of them; and appeared great in their zeal and forwardness to attend Jesus, and assist Him without further delay, in the time of the great feast of the passover, to set up His kingdom. And it is easy, from nature, and the nature of the affections, to give an account why, when one affection is raised very high, it should excite others; especially if the affection which is raised high be that of counterfeit love, as it was in the multitude who cried "Hosanna." This will naturally draw many other affections after it. For, as was observed before, love is the chief of the affections, and as it were the fountain of them.

Let us suppose a person who has been for some time in great exercise and terror through fear of hell, and his heart weakened with distress and dreadful apprehensions, and upon the brink of despair, who is all at once delivered by being firmly made to believe, through some delusion of Satan, that God has pardoned him, and accepts him as the object of His dear love, and promises him eternal life; as suppose through some vision, or strong idea or imagination, suddenly excited in him, of a person with a beautiful countenance, smiling on him, and with arms open, and with blood dropping down, which the person conceives to be Christ, without any other enlightening of the understanding to give a view of the spiritual divine excellency of Christ and His fulness, and of the way of salvation revealed in the gospel: or perhaps by some voice or words coming as if they were spoken to him, such as these, " Son, be of good cheer, thy sins be forgiven thee," or, " Fear not, it is your Father's good pleasure to give you the kingdom," which he takes to be immediately spoken by God to him, though there was no preceding acceptance of Christ, or closing of the heart with Him: I say, if we should suppose such a case, what various passions would naturally crowd at once, or one after another, into such a person's mind! It is easy to be accounted for, from mere principles of nature, that a person's heart on such an occasion should be raised up to the skies with transports of joy, and be filled with fervent affection to that imaginary God or Redeemer, who he supposes has thus rescued him from the jaws of such dreadful destruction that his soul was so amazed with the fears of, and has received him with such endearment as a peculiar favourite; and that now he should be filled with admiration and gratitude, and his mouth should be opened, and be full of talk about what he has experienced; and that, for a while, he should think and speak of scarce anything else, and should seem to magnify that God who has done so much for him, and call upon others to rejoice with him, and appear with a cheerful countenance, and talk with a loud voice: and however, before his deliverance, he was full of quarrellings against the justice of God, that now it should be easy for him to submit to God, and own his unworthiness, and cry out against himself, and appear to be very humble before God, and lie at His feet as tame as a lamb; and that he should now confess his unworthiness, and cry out, " Why me? Why me?" (Like Saul, who when Samuel told him that God had appointed him to be king, makes answer, " Am not I a Benjamite, of the smallest of the tribes of Israel, and my family the least of all the families of the tribe of Benjamin? Wherefore then speakest thou so to me?" Much in the language of David, the true saint, 2 Sam. vii. 18, " Who am I, and what is my father's house, that thou hast brought me hitherto?") Nor is it to be wondered at that now he should delight to be with them who acknowledge and applaud his happy circumstances, and should love all such as esteem and admire him and what he has experienced, and have violent zeal against all such as would make nothing of such things, and be disposed only to separate, and as it were to proclaim war with all who be not of his party, and should now glory in his sufferings, and be very much for condemning and censuring all who seem to doubt, or make any difficulty of these things; and while the warmth of his affections lasts, should be mighty forward to take pains, and deny himself, to promote the interest of the party who he imagines favour such things, and seem earnestly desirous to increase the number of them, as the Pharisees compassed sea and land to make one *proselyte*.* And so I might go on and mention many other things which will naturally arise in such circumstances. He must have but slightly considered human nature, who thinks such things as these cannot arise in this manner, without any supernatural interposition of divine power.

As from true divine love flow all Christian affections, so from a counterfeit love in like manner naturally flow other false affections. In both cases, love is the fountain, and the other affections are the streams. The various faculties, principles, and affections of the human nature, are as it were many channels from one fountain: if there be sweet water in the fountain, sweet water will from thence flow out into those various channels; but if the water in the fountain be poisonous, then poisonous streams will also flow out into all those channels. So that the channels and streams will be alike, corresponding one with another; but the great difference will lie in the nature of the water. Or man's nature may be compared to a tree with many branches coming from one root: if the sap in the root be good, there will also be good sap distributed throughout the branches, and the fruit that is brought forth will be good and wholesome; but if the sap in the root and stock be poisonous, so it will be in many branches (as in the other case), and the fruit will be deadly. The tree in both cases may be alike; there may be an exact resemblance in shape; but the difference is found only in eating the fruit. It is thus (in some measure at least) oftentimes beween saints and hypocrites. There is sometimes a very great similitude between true and false experiences, in their appearance, and in what is expressed and related by the subjects of them: and the difference between them is much like the difference between the dreams of Pharaoh's chief butler and baker; they seemed to be much alike, insomuch that when Joseph interpreted the chief butler's dream, that he should be delivered from his imprisonment, and restored to the king's favour and his honourable office in the palace, the

---

* "Associating with godly men does not prove that a man has grace: Ahithophel was David's companion. Sorrows for the afflictions of the church, and desires for the conversion of souls, do not prove it. These things may be found in carnal men, and so can be no evidence of grace." —Stoddard's *Nature of Saving Conversion*.

chief baker had raised hopes and expectations, and told his dream also; but he was woefully disappointed; and though his dream was so much like the happy and well-boding dream of his companion, yet it was quite contrary in its issue.

VIII. *Nothing can certainly be determined concerning the nature of the affections by this, that comforts and joys seem to follow awakenings and convictions of conscience, in a certain order.*

Many persons seem to be prejudiced against affections and experiences that come in such a method, as has been much insisted on by many divines; first, such awakenings, fears, and awful apprehensions, followed with such legal humblings, in a sense of total sinfulness and helplessness, and then, such and such light and comfort. They look upon all such schemes, laying down such methods and steps, to be of men's devising; and particularly if high affections of joy follow great distress and terror, it is made by many an argument against those affections. But such prejudices and objections are without reason or Scripture. Surely it cannot be unreasonable to suppose that, before God delivers persons from a state of sin and exposedness to eternal destruction, He should give them some considerable sense of the evil He delivers them from; that they may be delivered sensibly, and understand their own salvation, and know something of what God does for them. As men that are saved are in two exceeding different states, first a state of condemnation, and then a state of justification and blessedness: and as God, in the work of the salvation of mankind, deals with them suitably to their intelligent rational nature, so it seems reasonable, and agreeable to God's wisdom, that men who are saved should be in these two states sensibly; first, that they should, sensibly to themselves, be in a state of condemnation, and so in a state of woeful calamity and dreadful misery, and so afterwards sensibly in a state of deliverance and happiness; and that they should be first sensible of their absolute extreme necessity, and afterwards of Christ's sufficiency and God's mercy through Him.

And that it is God's manner of dealing with men, to "lead them into a wilderness, before he speaks comfortably to them," and so to order it that they shall be brought into distress, and made to see their own helplessness and absolute dependence on

His power and grace, before He appears to work any great deliverance for them, is abundantly manifest by the Scripture. Then is God wont to " repent himself for his people, when their strength is gone, and there is none shut up or left," and when they are brought to see that their false gods cannot help them, and that the rock in whom they trusted is vain, Deut. xxxii. 36, 37. Before God delivered the children of Israel out of Egypt, they were prepared for it, by being made to " see that they were in an evil case," and " to cry unto God, because of their bondage," Exod. ii. 23, and v. 19. And before God wrought that great deliverance for them at the Red Sea, they were brought into great distress, the wilderness had shut them in, they could not turn to the right hand nor the left; the Red Sea was before them, and the great Egyptian host behind, and they were brought to see that they could do nothing to help themselves, and that if God did not help them, they would be immediately swallowed up; and then God appeared, and turned their cries into songs. So, before they were brought to their rest, and to enjoy the milk and honey of Canaan, God " led them through a great and terrible wilderness, that he might humble them and teach them what was in their heart, and so do them good in their latter end," Deut. viii. 2, 16. The woman that had the issue of blood twelve years was not delivered until she had first " spent all her living on physicians, and could not be healed of any," and so was left helpless, having no more money to spend; and then she came to the Great Physician, without any money or price, and was healed by Him, Luke viii. 43, 44. Before Christ would answer the request of the woman of Canaan, He first seemed utterly to deny her, and humbled her, and brought her to own herself worthy to be called a dog; and then He showed her mercy, and received her as a dear child, Matt. xv. 22, &c. The Apostle Paul, before a remarkable deliverance, was "pressed out of measure, above strength, insomuch that he despaired even of life; he had the sentence of death in himself, that he might not trust in himself, but in God that raiseth the dead," 2 Cor. i. 8, 9, 10. There was first a great tempest; the ship was covered with the waves, and just ready to sink, and the disciples were brought to cry to Jesus, " Lord save us, we perish;" and then the winds and seas were rebuked, and there was a great calm, Matt. viii. 24, 25, 26. The leper, before he is cleansed, must have his mouth stopped by a covering on his upper lip, and was to acknowledge his great misery and utter uncleanness by rending his clothes and crying, " Unclean, unclean," Lev. xiii. 45. And backsliding Israel, before God heals them, are brought to " acknowledge that they have sinned, and have not obeyed the voice of the Lord," and to see that " they lie down in their shame, and that confusion covers them," and " that in vain is salvation hoped for from the hills, and from the multitude of mountains," and that God only can save them, Jer. iii. 23, 24, 25. Joseph, who was sold by his brethren, and therein was a type of Christ, brings his brethren into great perplexity and distress, and brings them to reflect on their sin, and to say, " We are verily guilty "; and at last to resign up themselves entirely into his hands for bondmen; and then reveals himself to them, as their brother and their saviour.

And if we consider those extraordinary manifestations which God made of Himself to saints of old, we shall find that He commonly first manifested Himself in a way which was terrible, and then by those things that were comfortable. So it was with Abraham; first, a horror of great darkness fell upon him, and then God revealed Himself to him in sweet promises, Gen. xv. 12-16. So it was with Moses at Mount Sinai; first, God appeared to him in all the terrors of His dreadful majesty, so that Moses said, " I exceedingly fear and quake," and then He made all His goodness to pass before him, and proclaimed His name, " The Lord God, merciful and gracious," &c. So it was with Elijah; first, there is a stormy wind, and earthquake, and devouring fire, and then a still, small, sweet voice, 1 Kings xix. So it was with Daniel; he first saw Christ's countenance as lightning, that terrified him, and caused him to faint away; and then he is strengthened and refreshed with such comfortable words as these, " O Daniel, a man greatly beloved," Dan. x. So it was with the Apostle John, Rev. i. And there is an analogy observable in God's dispensations and deliverances which He works for His people, and the manifestations which He makes of Himself to them, both ordinary and extraordinary.

But there are many things in Scripture which do more directly show that this is God's ordinary manner in working salvation for the souls of men, and in the manifestations God makes of Himself and of His mercy in Christ, in the ordinary works of His grace on the hearts of sinners. The servant that owed his prince ten thousand talents is first held to his debt, and the king pronounces sentence of condemnation upon him, and commands him to be sold, and his wife and children, and payment to be made; and thus he humbles him, and brings him to own the whole of the debt to be just, and then forgives him all. The prodigal son spends all he has, and is brought to see himself in extreme circumstances, and to humble himself, and own his unworthiness, before he is relieved and feasted by his father, Luke xv. Old inveterate wounds must be searched to the bottom, in order to heal: and the Scripture compares sin, the wound of the soul, to this, and speaks of healing this wound without thus searching of it as vain and deceitful, Jer. viii. 11. Christ, in the work of His grace on the hearts of men, is compared to rain on the new mown grass, grass that is cut down with a scythe, Psal. lxxii. 6, representing His refreshing, comforting influences on the wounded spirit. Our first parents, after they had sinned, were first terrified with God's majesty and justice, and had their sin with its aggravations set before them by their Judge, before they were relieved by the promise of the Seed of the woman. Christians are spoken of as those " that have fled for refuge to lay hold on the hope set before them," Heb. vi. 18, which representation implies great fear and sense of danger preceding. To the like purpose, Christ is called " a hiding place from the wind, and a covert from the tempest, and as rivers of water in a dry place, and as the shadow of a great rock in a weary land," Isa. xxxii. 2. And it seems to be the natural import of the word *Gospel,* glad tidings, that it is news of deliverance and salvation, after great fear and distress. There is also reason to suppose that God deals with particular believers as He dealt with His church, which He first made to hear His voice in the law, with terrible thunders and lightnings, and kept her under that schoolmaster to prepare her for Christ; and then comforted her with the joyful sound of the gospel from Mount Zion. So likewise John the Baptist came to prepare the way for Christ, and prepare men's hearts for His reception, by showing them their sins, and by bringing the self-righteous Jews off from their own righteousness, telling them that they were " a generation of vipers," and showing them their danger of " the wrath to come," telling them that " the axe was laid at the root of the trees," &c.

And if it be indeed God's manner (as I think the foregoing

considerations show that it undoubtedly is), before he gives men
the comfort of a deliverance from their sin and misery, to give
them a considerable sense of the greatness and dreadfulness of
those evils, and their extreme wretchedness by reason of them;
surely it is not unreasonable to suppose that persons, at least
oftentimes, while under these views, should have great distresses
and terrible apprehensions of mind; especially if it be considered
what these evils are that they have a view of, which are no other
than great and manifold sins against the infinite majesty of the
great Jehovah, and the suffering of the fierceness of His wrath
to all eternity. And the more so still, when we have many plain
instances in Scripture of persons that have actually been brought
into great distress by such convictions before they have received
saving consolations: as the multitude at Jerusalem, who were
" pricked in their heart, and said unto Peter and the rest of the
apostles, Men and brethren, what shall we do?"; and the Apostle
Paul, who trembled and was astonished before he was comforted;
and the gaoler, when " he called for a light, and sprang in, and
came trembling, and fell down before Paul and Silas, and said,
Sirs, what must I do to be saved?"

From these things it appears to be very unreasonable in professing Christians to make this an objection against the truth and
spiritual nature of the comfortable and joyful affections which
any have, that they follow such awful apprehensions and distresses as have been mentioned.

On the other hand, it is no evidence that comforts and joys
are right, because they succeed great terrors, and amazing fears
of hell.* This seems to be what some persons lay a great weight
upon, esteeming great terrors an evidence of the great work of
the law wrought on the heart, well preparing the way for solid
comfort; not considering that terror and a conviction of conscience are different things. For though convictions of conscience
do often cause terror, yet they do not consist in it; and terrors
do often arise from other causes. Convictions of conscience,
through the influences of God's Spirit, consist in conviction of
sinfulness of heart and practice, and of the dreadfulness of sin

* Mr. Shepard speaks of " men's being cast down as low as hell by
sorrow and lying under chains, quaking in apprehension of terror to come,
and then raised up to heaven in joy, not able to live; and yet not rent
from lust: and such are objects of pity now, and are like to be the objects
of terror at the great day."—*Parable of the Ten Virgins*, p. 201.

as committed against a God of terrible majesty, infinite holiness and hatred of sin, and strict justice in punishing of it.   But there are some persons that have frightful apprehensions of hell, a dreadful pit ready to swallow them up, and flames just ready to lay hold of them, and devils around them ready to seize them; who at the same time seem to have very little proper enlightenings of conscience really convincing them of their sinfulness of heart and life.   Men can be terrified by the devil, if permission is given to him to do this, as well as by the Spirit of God; it is a work natural to him, and he has many ways of doing it, in a manner tending to no good.

He may exceedingly affright persons by impressing on them images and ideas of many external things, of a countenance frowning, a sword drawn, black clouds of vengeance, words of an awful doom pronounced,* hell gaping, devils coming, and the like, not to convince persons of things that are true and revealed in the Word of God, but to lead them to vain and groundless determinations; as that their day is past, that they are reprobated, that God is implacable, that He has come to a resolution immediately to cut them off, &c.

And the terrors which some persons have are very much owing to the particular constitution and temper they are of.   Nothing is more manifest than that some persons are of such a temper and frame that their imaginations are more strongly impressed with everything they are affected with than others; and the impression on the imagination reacts on the affection, and raises that still higher; and so affection and imagination act reciprocally, one on another, till their affection is raised to a vast height, and the person is swallowed up, and loses all possession of himself.†

* " The way of the Spirit's working when it does convince men, is by enlightening natural conscience.   The Spirit does not work by giving a testimony, but by assisting natural conscience to do its work.   Natural conscience is the instrument in the hand of God to accuse, condemn, terrify, and to urge to duty.   The Spirit of God leads men into the consideration of their danger, and makes them to be affected therewith; Prov. xx. 27, ' The spirit of man is the candle of the Lord, searching all the inward parts of the belly.' "   Stoddard's Guide to Christ.

† The famous Mr. Perkins distinguishes between " those sorrows that come through convictions of conscience, and melancholic passions arising only from mere imagination, strongly conceived in the brain; which, he says, usually come on a sudden, like lightning into a house."—Works, Vol. I, p. 385.

And some speak of a great sight they have of their wickedness, who really, when the matter comes to be well examined into and thoroughly weighed, are found to have little or no convictions of conscience. They tell of a dreadful hard heart, and how their heart lies like a stone, when truly they have none of those things in their minds or thoughts wherein the hardness of men's hearts does really consist. They tell of a dreadful load and sink of sin, a heap of black and loathsome filthiness within them; when, if the matter be carefully inquired into, they have not in view anything wherein the corruption of nature does truly consist, nor have they any thought of any particular thing wherein their hearts are sinfully defective, or fall short of what ought to be in them, or any exercises at all of corruption in them. And many think also they have great convictions of their actual sins, who truly have none. They tell how their sins are set in order before them, they see them stand encompassing them round in a row with a dreadful frightful appearance; when really they have not so much as one of the sins they have been guilty of in the course of their lives coming into view, that they are affected with the aggravations of.

And if persons have had great terrors which really have been from the awakening and convincing influences of the Spirit of God, it doth not thence follow that their terrors must needs issue in true comfort. The unmortified corruption of the heart may quench the Spirit of God (after He has been striving) by leading men to presumptuous and self-exalting hopes and joys, as well as otherwise. It is not every woman who is really in travail that brings forth a real child; but it may be a monstrous production, without anything of the form or properties of human nature belonging to it. Pharaoh's chief baker, after he had lain in the dungeon with Joseph, had a vision that raised his hopes, and he was lifted out of the dungeon, as well as the chief butler; but it was to be hanged.

But if comforts and joys do not only come after great terrors and awakenings, but there be an appearance of such preparatory convictions and humiliations, and brought about very distinctly by such steps and in such a method as has frequently been observable in true converts; this is no certain sign that the light and comforts which follow are true and saving. And for these following reasons:

First, As the devil can counterfeit all the saving operations and graces of the Spirit of God, so he can counterfeit those operations that are preparatory to grace. If Satan can counterfeit those effects of God's Spirit which are special, divine, and sanctifying, so that there shall be a very great resemblance in all that can be observed by others; much more easily may he imitate those works of God's Spirit which are common, and which men, while they are yet his own children, are the subjects of. These works are in no wise so much above him as the others. There are no works of God that are so high and divine, and above the powers of nature, and out of reach of the power of all creatures, as those works of His Spirit, whereby He forms the creature in His own image, and makes it to be a partaker of the divine nature. But if the devil can be the author of such resemblances of these as have been spoken of, without doubt he may of those that are of an infinitely inferior kind. And it is abundantly evident in fact, that there are false humiliations and false submissions, as well as false comforts.* How far was Saul brought, though a very wicked man and of a haughty spirit, when he (though a great king) was brought, in conviction of his sin, as it were to fall down, all in tears, weeping aloud, before David his own subject (and one that he had for a long time mortally hated and openly treated as an enemy), and condemn himself before him, crying out, "Thou art more righteous than I: for thou hast rewarded me good, whereas I have rewarded thee evil!" And at another time, "I have sinned, I have played the fool, I have erred exceedingly," 1 Sam. xxiv. 16, 17, and chap. xxvi. 21. And yet Saul seems then to have had very little of the influences of the Spirit of God, it being after God's Spirit had departed from him, and given him up, and an evil spirit from the Lord troubled him. And if this proud monarch, in a pang of affection, was brought to humble himself so low before a subject that he hated, and still continued an enemy to, there doubtless may be appearances of

---

* The venerable Mr. Stoddard observes, " A man may say, that he can justify God however he deals with him, and yet not be brought off from his own righteousness. Some men justify God from a partial conviction of the righteousness of their condemnation; conscience takes notice of their sinfulness, and tells them that they may be righteously damned; as Pharaoh, who justified God, Exod. ix. 27. And they give some kind of consent to it, but many times it does not continue; they have only a pang upon them that usually dies away after a little time."—*Guide to Christ.*

great conviction and humiliation in men before God, while they yet remain enemies to Him, and though they finally continue so. There is oftentimes in men who are terrified through fears of hell, a great appearance of their being brought off from their own righteousness, when they are not brought off from it in all ways, although they are in many ways that are more plain and visible. They have only exchanged some ways of trusting in their own righteousness for others that are more secret and subtle. Oftentimes a great degree of discouragement, as to many things they used to depend upon, is taken for humiliation: and that is called a submission to God which is no absolute submission, but has some secret bargain in it that it is hard to discover.

Secondly, If the operations and effects of the Spirit of God, in the convictions and comforts of true converts, may be sophisticated, then the order of them may be imitated. If Satan can imitate the things themselves, he may easily put them one after another, in such a certain order. If the devil can make A, B, and C, it is as easy for him to put A first, and B next, and C next, as to range them in a contrary order. The nature of divine things is harder for the devil to imitate than their order. He cannot *exactly* imitate divine operations in their nature, though his counterfeits may be very much like them in external appearance; but he can exactly imitate their order. When counterfeits are made, there is no divine power needful in order to the placing one of them first, and another last. And therefore no order or method of operations and experiences is any certain sign of their divinity. That only is to be trusted to, as a certain evidence of grace, which Satan cannot do, and which it is impossible should be brought to pass by any power short of divine.

Thirdly, We have no certain rule to determine how far God's own Spirit may go in those operations and convictions which in themselves are not spiritual and saving, and yet the person that is the subject of them never be converted, but fall short of salvation at last. There is no necessary connection in the nature of things between anything that a natural man may experience while in a state of nature, and the saving grace of God's Spirit. And if there be no connection in the nature of things, then there can be no known and certain connection at all, unless it be by divine revelation. But there is no revealed certain connection between a state of salvation, and anything that a natural man can be the subject of before he believes in Christ. God has revealed no certain connection between salvation and any qualifications in men, but only grace and its fruits And therefore we do not find any legal convictions, or comforts following these legal convictions, in any certain method or order, ever once mentioned in the Scripture as certain signs of grace, or things peculiar to the saints; although we do find gracious operations and effects themselves so mentioned thousands of times. Which should be enough with Christians, who are willing to have the Word of God rather than their own philosophy, and experiences, and conjectures, as their sufficient and sure guide in things of this nature.

Fourthly, Experience does greatly confirm that persons' seeming to have convictions and comforts following one another in such a method and order, as is frequently observable in true converts, is no certain sign of grace.* I appeal to all those ministers in this land who have had much occasion of dealing with souls in the late extraordinary season, whether there have not been many who do not prove well, that have given a fair account of their experiences, and have seemed to be converted according to rule, *i.e.,* with convictions and affections succeeding distinctly and exactly, in that order and method which has been ordinarily insisted on as the order of the operations of the Spirit of God in conversion.

And as a seeming to have this distinctness as to steps and method is no certain sign that a person is converted, so a being without is no evidence that a person is not converted. For though it might be made evident to a demonstration, on Scripture principles, that a sinner cannot be brought heartily to receive Christ as his Saviour who is not convinced of his sin and misery, and of his own emptiness and helplessness and his just desert of eternal condemnation; and that therefore such convictions must be some way implied in what is wrought in his soul; yet nothing proves it to be necessary that all those things which are implied or presupposed in an act of faith in Christ must be plainly and

---

* Mr. Stoddard, who had much experience of things of this nature, long ago observed that converted and unconverted men cannot be certainly distinguished by the account they give of their experience, the same relation of experiences being common to both; and that many persons have given a fair account of a work of conversion, that have carried well in the eye of the world for several years, but have not proved well at last.—*Appeal to the Learned.*

distinctly wrought in the soul, in so many successive and separate
works of the Spirit, that shall be each one plain and manifest, in
all who are truly converted. On the contrary (as Mr. Shepard
observes), sometimes the change made in a saint, at first, is like
a confused chaos; so that the saints know not what to make of it.
The manner of the Spirit's proceeding in them that are born of
the Spirit is very often exceeding mysterious and unsearchable:
we, as it were, hear the sound of it, the effect of it is discernible;
but no man can tell whence it came, or whither it went. And
it is oftentimes as difficult to know the way of the Spirit in the
new birth, as in the first birth; Eccl. xi. 5, "Thou knowest not
what is the way of the Spirit, or how the bones do grow in the
womb of her that is with child; even so thou knowest not the
works of God that worketh all." The ingenerating of a principle
of grace in the soul seems in Scripture to be compared to the conceiving of Christ in the womb, Gal. iv. 19. And therefore the
Church is called Christ's mother, Cant. iii. 11. And so is every
particular believer, Matt. xii. 49, 50. And the conception of
Christ in the womb of the blessed virgin by the power of the
Holy Ghost, seems to be a designed resemblance of the conception of Christ in the soul of a believer by the power of the same
Holy Ghost. And we know not what is the way of the Spirit, nor
how the bones do grow, either in the womb or heart that conceives this holy child. The new creature may use that language
in Psal. cxxxix. 14, 15, "I am fearfully and wonderfully made;
marvellous are thy works, and that my soul knoweth right well.
My substance was not hid from thee, when I was made in secret."
Concerning the generation of Christ, both in His person, and also
in the hearts of His people, it may be said, as in Isa. liii. 8, "Who
can declare his generation?" We know not the works of God,
that worketh all. "It is the glory of God to conceal a thing"
(Prov. xxv. 2), and to have "his path as it were in the mighty
waters, that his footsteps may not be known"; and especially in
the works of His Spirit on the hearts of men, which are the
highest and chief of His works. And therefore it is said, Isa. xl.
13, "Who hath directed the Spirit of the Lord, or being his coun-
sellor hath taught him?" It is to be feared that some have gone
too far towards directing the Spirit of the Lord, and marking out
His footsteps for Him, and limiting Him to certain steps and
methods. Experience plainly shows, that God's Spirit is unsearch-

able and untraceable, in some of the best of Christians, in the method of His operations in their conversion. Nor does the Spirit of God proceed discernibly in the steps of a particular established scheme, one half so often as is imagined. A scheme of what is necessary, and according to a rule already received and established by common opinion, has a vast (though to many a very insensible) influence in forming persons' notions of the steps and method of their own experiences. I know very well what their way is, for I have had much opportunity to observe it. Very much, at first, their experiences appear like a confused chaos, as Mr. Shepard expresses it: but then those passages of their experience are picked out, that have most of the appearance of such particular steps that are insisted on; and these are dwelt upon in the thoughts, and these are told of from time to time in the relation they give: these parts grow brighter and brighter in their view; and others, being neglected, grow more and more obscure: and what they have experienced is insensibly strained to bring all to an exact conformity to the scheme that is established. And it becomes natural for ministers who have to deal with them, and direct them that insist upon distinctness and clearness of method, to do so too. But yet there has been so much to be seen of the operations of the Spirit of God of late, that they who have had much to do with souls, and are not blinded with a seven-fold veil of prejudice, must know that the Spirit is so exceeding various in the manner of His operating that in many cases it is impossible to trace Him, or find out His way.

What we have principally to do with, in our inquiries into our own state or the directions we give to others, is the nature of the effect that God has brought to pass in the soul. As to the steps which the Spirit of God took to bring that effect to pass, we may leave them to Him. We are often in Scripture expressly directed to try ourselves by the nature of the fruits of the Spirit; but nowhere by the Spirit's method of producing them.* Many do

---

* Mr. Shepard, speaking of the soul's closing with Christ, says, " As a child cannot tell how his soul comes into it, nor it may be when; but afterwards it sees and feels that life; so that he were as bad as a beast that should deny an immortal soul; so here."—*Parable of the Ten Virgins,* p. 609.

" If the man do not know the time of his conversion, or first closing with Christ, the minister may not draw any peremptory conclusion from thence that he is not godly."—*Stoddard's Guide to Christ.*

" Do not think there is no compunction, or sense of sin, wrought in the

greatly err in their notions of a clear work of conversion, calling
that a clear work where the successive steps of influence and
method of experience are clear: whereas that indeed is the clearest work, not where the order of *doing* is clearest, but where the
spiritual and divine nature of the work *done,* and effect *wrought,*
is most clear.

IX. *It is no certain sign that the religious affections which
persons have are such as have in them the nature of true religion, or that they have not, that they dispose persons to spend
much time in religion, and to be zealously engaged in the external duties of worship.*

This has, very unreasonably, of late been looked upon as an
argument against the religious affections which some have had,
that they spend so much time in reading, praying, singing, hearing sermons, and the like. It is plain from the Scripture that it
is the tendency of true grace to cause persons to delight in such
religious exercises. True grace had this effect on Anna the pro-
phetess: Luke ii. 37, "She departed not from the temple, but
served God with fastings and prayers night and day." And grace
had this effect upon the primitive Christians in Jerusalem: Acts
ii. 46. 47, "And they continuing daily with one accord in the
temple, and breaking bread from house to house, did eat their
meat with gladness and singleness of heart, praising God." Grace
made Daniel delight in the duty of prayer, and solemnly to
attend it three times a day, as it also did David: Psal. lv. 17,
"Evening, morning, and at noon will I pray." Grace makes the
saints delight in singing praises to God: Psal. cxxxv. 3, "Sing
praises unto his name, for it is pleasant." And cxlvii. 1, "Praise
ye the Lord; for it is good to sing praises unto our God; for it
is pleasant, and praise is comely." It also causes them to delight
to hear the word of God preached: it makes the gospel a joyful
sound to them, Psal. lxxxix. 15, and makes the feet of those who
publish these good tidings to be beautiful: Isa. lii. 7, "How
beautiful upon the mountains are the feet of him that bringeth

---

soul, because you cannot so clearly discern and feel it; nor the time of
the working, and first beginning of it. I have known many that have come
with their complaints, that they *were never humbled, they never felt it so;*
yet there it hath been, and many times they have seen it by the other
spectacles, and blessed God for it."—*Shepard's Sound Believer,* p. 139.

good tidings!" &c. It makes them love God's public worship: Psal. xxvi. 8, "Lord, I have loved the habitation of thy house, and the place where thine honour dwelleth." And Psal. xxvii. 4, "One thing have I desired of the Lord, that will I seek after, that I may dwell in the house of the Lord all the days of my life, to behold the beauty of the Lord, and to inquire in his temple." Psal. lxxxiv. 1, 2, &c., "How amiable are thy tabernacles, O Lord of hosts! My soul longeth, yea, even fainteth for the courts of the Lord.—Yea, the sparrow hath found an house, and the swallow a nest for herself, where she may lay her young, even thine altars, O Lord of hosts, my King and my God. Blessed are they that dwell in thy house: they will be still praising thee. Blessed is the man in whose heart are the ways of them, who passing through the valley of Baca—go from strength to strength, every one of them in Zion appeareth before God." Ver. 10, "A day in thy courts is better than a thousand."

This is the nature of true grace. But yet, on the other hand, that persons are disposed to abound and to be zealously engaged in the external exercises of religion, and to spend much time in them, is no sure evidence of grace; because such a disposition is found in many that have no grace. So it was with the Israelites of old, whose services were abominable to God; they attended the "new moons, and Sabbaths, and calling of assemblies, and spread forth their hands, and made many prayers," Isa. i. 12-15. So it was with the Pharisees; they "made long prayers, and fasted twice a week." False religion may cause persons to be loud and earnest in prayer: Isa. lviii. 4, "Ye shall not fast as ye do this day, to cause your voice to be heard on high." That religion which is not spiritual and saving may cause men to delight in religious duties and ordinances: Isa. lviii. 2, "Yet they seek me daily, and delight to know my ways, as a nation that did righteousness, and forsook not the ordinance of their God: they ask of me the ordinances of justice; they take delight in approaching to God." It may cause them to take delight in hearing the word of God preached, as it was with Ezekiel's hearers: Ezek. xxxiii. 31, 32, "And they come unto thee as the people cometh, and they sit before thee as my people, and they hear thy words, but they will not do them: for with their mouth they show much love, but their heart goeth after their covetousness. And lo, thou art unto them as a very lovely song of one that hath a pleasant voice, and can play well on an instrument: for they hear thy words, but they do them not." So it was with Herod; he heard John the Baptist gladly, Mark vi. 20. So it was with others of his hearers; "for a season they rejoiced in his light," John v. 35. So the stony ground hearers heard the word with joy.

Experience shows that persons from false religion may be inclined to be exceeding abundant in the external exercises of religion; yea, to give themselves up to them, and devote almost their whole time to them. Formerly a sort of people were very numerous in the Romish church, called *recluses,* who forsook the world, and utterly abandoned the society of mankind, and shut themselves up close in a narrow cell, with a vow never to stir out of it, nor to see the face of any of mankind any more (unless that they might be visited in case of sickness), to spend all their days in the exercise of devotion and converse with God. There were also in old time great multitudes called Hermits and Anchorites, that left the world to spend all their days in lonesome deserts, to give themselves up to religious contemplations and exercises of devotion; some sorts of them having no dwellings but the caves and vaults of the mountains, and no food but the spontaneous productions of the earth. I once lived for many months next door to a Jew (the houses adjoining one to another), and had much opportunity daily to observe him; who appeared to me the devoutest person that ever I saw in my life; a great part of his time being spent in acts of devotion, at his eastern window, which opened next to mine, seeming to be most earnestly engaged, not only in the daytime, but sometimes whole nights.

X. *Nothing can be certainly known of the nature of religious affections by this, that they much dispose persons with their mouths to praise and glorify God.*

This indeed is implied in what has been just now observed, of abounding and spending much time in the external exercises of religion, and was also hinted before; but because many seem to look upon it as a bright evidence of gracious affection, when persons appear greatly disposed to praise and magnify God, to have their mouths full of His praises and affectionately to be calling on others to praise and extol Him, I thought it deserved a more particular consideration.

No Christian will make it an argument against a person that he seems to have such a disposition. Nor can it reasonably be looked upon as an evidence for a person, if those things that have been already observed and proved be duly considered, viz., that persons without grace may have high affections towards God and Christ, and that their affections, being strong, may fill their mouths, and incline them to speak much and very earnestly about the things they are affected with, and that there may be counterfeits of all kinds of gracious affection. But it will appear more evidently and directly that this is no certain sign of grace, if we consider what instances the Scripture gives us of it in those that were graceless. We often have an account of this in the multitude that were present when Christ preached and wrought miracles; Mark ii. 12, "And immediately he arose, took up his bed, and went forth before them all, insomuch that they were all amazed, and glorified God, saying, "We never saw it on this fashion." So Matt. ix. 8, and Luke v. 26. Also Matt. xv. 31, "Insomuch that the multitude wondered when they saw the dumb to speak, the maimed to be whole, the lame to walk, and the blind to see: and they glorified the God of Israel." So we are told that on occasion of Christ's raising the son of the widow of Nain, Luke vii. 16, "There came a fear on all: and they glorified God, saying, That a great prophet is risen up among us; and, That God hath visited his people." So we read of their glorifying Christ, or speaking exceedingly highly of Him: Luke vi. 15, "And he taught in their synagogues, being glorified of all." And how did they praise Him, with loud voices, crying, "Hosanna to the Son of David; hosanna in the highest; blessed is he that cometh in the name of the Lord," a little before he was crucified! And after Christ's ascension, when the apostles had healed the impotent man, we are told that all men glorified God for that which was done, Acts iv. 21. When the Gentiles in Antioch of Pisidia heard from Paul and Barnabas that God would reject the Jews and take the Gentiles to be His people in their room, they were affected with the goodness of God to the Gentiles, "and glorified the word of the Lord:" but all that did so were not true believers, but only a certain elect number of them; as is intimated in the account we have of it, Acts xiii. 48: "And when the Gentiles heard this, they were glad, and glorified the word of the Lord: and as many as were ordained to eternal life, believed." So of old the children of Israel at the Red Sea, "sang God's praise; but soon forgat his works." And the Jews in Ezekiel's time, "with their mouth showed much love, while their heart went after their covetousness." And it is foretold of false professors, and real enemies of religion, that they should show a forwardness to glorify God: Isa. lxvi. 5, "Hear the word of the Lord, ye that tremble at his word. Your brethren that hated you, that cast you out for my name's sake, said, Let the Lord be glorified."

It is no certain sign that a person is graciously affected, if, in the midst of his hopes and comforts, he is greatly affected with God's unmerited mercy to him, that is so unworthy, and seems greatly to extol and magnify free grace. Those that yet remain with unmortified pride and enmity against God, may, when they imagine that they have received extraordinary kindness from God, deplore their unworthiness, and magnify God's undeserved goodness to them. Yet this may arise from no other conviction of their ill deservings, and from no higher principle, than Saul had, who, while he yet remained with unsubdued pride and enmity against David, was brought, though a king, to acknow-ledge his unworthiness, and cry out, "I have played the fool, I have erred exceedingly," and with great affection and admiration to magnify and extol David's unmerited and unexampled kind-ness to him, 1 Sam. xxiv. 16-19, and xxvi. 21; and from no higher principle than that from whence Nebuchadnezzar was affected with God's dispensations that he saw and was the subject of, and praises, extols and honours the King of heaven; and both he, and Darius, in their high affections, call upon all nations to praise God, Dan. iii. 28, 29, 30, and iv. 1-3, 34-37, and vi. 25-27.

XI. *It is no sign that affections are right, or that they are wrong, that they make persons that have them exceeding con-fident that what they experience is divine, and that they are in a good estate.*

It is an argument with some that persons are deluded if they pretend to be assured of their good estate, and to be carried be-yond all doubting of the favour of God; supposing that there is no such thing to be expected in the church of God as a full and absolute assurance of hope; unless it be in some very extraordin-ary circumstances, as in the case of martyrdom: contrary to the doctrine of Protestants, which has been maintained by their most celebrated writers against the Papists; and contrary to the plainest Scripture evidence. It is manifest that it was a common thing for the saints that we have a history or particular account of in Scripture, to be assured. God, in the plainest and most positive manner, revealed and testified his special favour to Noah, Abraham, Isaac, Jacob, Moses, Daniel, and others. Job often speaks of his sincerity and uprightness with the greatest imaginable confidence and assurance, often calling God to witness to it; and says plainly, "I know that my Redeemer liveth, and that I shall see him for myself, and not another," Job xix. 25, &c. David, throughout the book of Psalms, almost everywhere speaks without any hesitancy, and in the most positive manner, of God as his God: glorying in Him as his Portion and Heritage, his Rock and Confidence, his Shield, Salvation, and High Tower, and the like. Hezekiah appeals to God, as one that knew that he had walked before Him in truth, and with a perfect heart, 2 Kings xx. 3. Jesus Christ, in His dying discourse with His eleven disciples, in the 14th, 15th, and 16th chapters of John (which was as it were Christ's last will and testament to His disciples, and to His whole church), often declares His special and everlasting love to them in the plainest and most positive terms; and promises them a future participation with Him in His glory in the most absolute manner; and tells them at the same time that He does so to the end that their joy might be full: John xv. 11, "These things have I spoken unto you, that my joy might remain in you, and that your joy might be full." See also at the conclusion of His whole discourse, chap. xvi. 33: "These things have I spoken unto you, that in me ye might have peace. In the world ye shall have tribulation: but be of good cheer, I have overcome the world." Christ was not afraid of speaking too plainly and positively to them; He did not desire to hold them in the least suspense. And He concluded that last discourse of His with a prayer in their presence, wherein He speaks positively to His Father of those eleven disciples, as having all of them savingly known Him, and believed in Him and received and kept His word; and that they were not of the world; and that for their sakes He sanctified Himself; and that His will was that they should be with Him in His glory; and tells His Father, that He spake those things in His prayer to the end that His joy might be fulfilled in them, verse 13.

By these things it is evident that it is agreeable to Christ's designs, and the contrived ordering and disposition Christ makes of things in His church, that there should be sufficient and abundant provision made that His saints might have full assurance of their glory.

The Apostle Paul, through all his epistles, speaks in an assured strain, ever speaking positively of his special relation to Christ, his Lord and Master and Redeemer, and his interest in and expectation of the future reward. It would be endless to take notice of all places that might be enumerated; I shall mention but three or four: Gal. ii. 20, " Christ liveth in me; and the life which I now live in the flesh, I live by the faith of the Son of God, who loved me, and gave himself for me;" Phil. i. 21, " For to me to live is Christ, and to die is gain;" 2 Tim. i. 12, " I know whom I have believed, and am persuaded that he is able to keep that which I have committed unto him against that day;" 2 Tim. iv. 7, 8, " I have fought a good fight, I have finished my course, I have kept the faith. Henceforth there is laid up for me a crown of righteousness, which the Lord, the righteous Judge, shall give me at that day."

And the nature of the covenant of grace, and God's declared ends in the appointment and constitution of things in that covenant, do plainly show it to be God's design to make ample provision for the saints having an assured hope of eternal life while living here upon earth. For so are all things ordered and contrived in that covenant, that every thing might be made sure on God's part. " The covenant is ordered in all things and sure:" the promises are most full, and very often repeated, and various ways exhibited; and there are many witnesses and many seals; and God has confirmed His promises with an oath. God's declared design in all this is, that the heirs of the promises might have an undoubting hope and full joy, in an assurance of their future glory. Heb. vi. 17, 18, " Wherein God, willing more abundantly to show unto the heirs of promise the immutability of his counsel, confirmed it by an oath: that by two immutable things, in which it was impossible for God to lie, we might have a strong consolation, who have fled for refuge to lay hold on the hope set before us." But all this would be in vain, for any such purpose as the saints' strong consolation, and hope of their obtaining future glory, if their interest in those sure promises in ordinary cases was not ascertainable. For God's promises and oaths, let them be as sure as they will, cannot give strong hope and comfort to any particular person any further than he can know that those promises are made to him. And in vain is provision made in Jesus Christ that believers might be perfect as pertaining to the conscience, as is signified, Heb. ix. 9, if assurance of freedom from the guilt of sin is not attainable.

It further appears that assurance is attainable in ordinary cases, in that all Christians are directed to give all diligence to make their calling and election sure, and are told how they may do it, 2 Pet. i. 5-10. And it is spoken of as a thing very unbecoming of Christians, and an argument of something very blamable in them, not to know whether Christ be in them or no: 2 Cor. xiii. 5, "Know ye not your own selves, how that Jesus Christ is in you, except ye be reprobates?" And it is implied that it is an argument of a very blamable negligence in Christians, if they practise Christianity after such a manner as to remain uncertain of the reward, in 1 Cor. ix. 26: "I therefore so run, not as uncertainly." And to add no more, it is manifest that Christians should know that their interest in the saving benefits of Christianity is a thing ordinarily attainable, because the apostle tells us by what means Christians (and not only the apostles and martyrs) were wont to know this: 1 Cor. ii. 12, "Now we have received, not the spirit of the world, but the Spirit which is of God; that we might know the things that are freely given to us of God." And 1 John ii. 3, "And hereby we do know that we know him, if we keep his commandments." And verse 5, "Hereby know we that we are in him." Chap. iii. 14, "We know that we have passed from death unto life, because we love the brethren;" ver. 19, "Hereby we know that we are of the truth, and shall assure our hearts before him;" ver. 24, "Hereby we know that he abideth in us, by the Spirit which he hath given us." So chap. iv. 13, and chap. v. 2, and 19.

Therefore it must needs be very unreasonable to determine that persons are hypocrites, and their affections wrong, because they seem to be out of doubt respecting their own salvation, and the affections they are the subjects of seem to banish all fears of hell.

On the other hand, it is no sufficient reason to determine that men are saints, and their affections gracious, because the affections they have are attended with an exceeding confidence that their state is good, and their affections divine.* Nothing can be certainly argued from their confidence, how great and strong soever it seems to be. If we see a man that boldly calls God his Father, and commonly speaks in the most bold, familiar, and appropriating language in prayer, "My Father, my dear Redeemer, my sweet Saviour, my Beloved," and the like; and it is a common thing for him to use the most confident expressions before men about the goodness of his state; such as "I know certainly that God is my Father; I know so surely as there is a God in heaven that he is my God; I know I shall go to heaven as well as if I were there; I know that God is now manifesting himself to my soul and is now smiling upon me;" and seems to have done for ever with any inquiry or examination into his state, as a thing sufficiently known, and out of doubt, and to contemn all that so much as intimate or suggest that there is some reason to doubt or fear whether all is right, such things are no signs at all that it is indeed so as he is confident it is.† Such an overbearing,

* " O professor, look carefully to your foundation: ' Be not high minded, but fear.' You have, it may be, done and suffered many things in and for religion; you have excellent gifts and sweet comforts, a warm zeal for God, and high confidence of your integrity: all this may be right, for aught that I, or (it may be) you know: but yet, it is possible it may be false. You have sometimes judged yourselves, and pronounced yourselves upright; but remember your final sentence is not yet pronounced by your Judge. And what if God weigh you over again, in his more equal balance, and should say, *Mene Tekel,* ' Thou art weighed in the balance, and art found wanting?' What a confounded man wilt thou be under such a sentence! *Quæ resplendent in conspectu hominis, sordent in conspectu Judicis; things that are highly esteemed of men, are an abomination in the sight of God:* He seeth not as man seeth. Thy heart may be false, and thou not know it: yea, it may be false, and thou strongly confident of its integrity."—*Flavel's Touchstone of Sincerity.* Works Vol. V, p. 525.
" Some hypocrites are a great deal more confident than many saints."—*Stoddard's Discourse on the Way to know Sincerity and Hypocrisy.*
† " Doth the work of faith in some believers bear upon its top branches the full ripe fruits of a blessed assurance? Lo, what strong confidence, and high-built persuasions, of an interest in God, have sometimes been found in unsanctified ones! Yea, so strong may this false assurance be, that they dare boldly venture to go to the judgment seat of God, and there defend it. Doth the Spirit of God fill the heart of the assured believer with joy unspeakable, and full of glory, giving him, through faith, a prelibation or foretaste of heaven itself, in those first fruits of it? How near to this comes what the apostle supposes may be found in apostates!"
—*Flavel's Husbandry Spiritualized.* Works Vol. V, p. 96.

high-handed, and violent sort of confidence as this, affecting to declare itself with a most glaring show in the sight of men, although it is to be seen in many, has not the countenance of a true Christian assurance: it savours more of the spirit of the Pharisees, who never doubted but that they were saints, and the most eminent of saints, and were bold to go to God, and come up near to Him, and lift up their eyes, and thank Him for the great distinction He had made between them and other men; and when Christ intimated that they were blind and graceless, despised the suggestion: John ix. 40, "And some of the Pharisees which were with him, heard these words, and said unto him, Are we blind also?" If they had had more of the spirit of the publican, who, in a sense of his exceeding unworthiness, stood afar off, and durst not so much as lift up his eyes to heaven, but smote on his breast, and cried out of himself as a sinner, their confidence would have more resembled that of one who humbly trusts and hopes in Christ, and has no confidence in himself.

If we do but consider what the hearts of natural men are, what principles they are under the dominion of, what blindness and deceit, what self-flattery, self-exaltation, and self-confidence reign there, we need not at all wonder that their high opinion of themselves, and confidence of their happy circumstances, be as high and strong as mountains, and as violent as a tempest, when once conscience is blinded, and convictions killed, with false high affections; when, too, those forementioned principles are let loose, fed and prompted by false joys and comforts, excited by some pleasing imaginations, and impressed by Satan transforming himself into an angel of light.

When once a hypocrite is thus established in a false hope, he has not those things to cause him to call his hope in question that oftentimes are the occasion of the doubting of true saints; as, *first*, he has not that cautious spirit, that great sense of the vast importance of a sure foundation, and that dread of being deceived. The comforts of the true saints increase awakening and caution, and a lively sense how great a thing it is to appear before an infinitely holy, just and omniscient Judge. But false comforts put an end to these things and dreadfully stupefy the mind. *Secondly*, The hypocrite has not the knowledge of his own blindness, and the deceitfulness of his own heart, and that mean opinion of his own understanding that the true saint has.

Those that are deluded with false discoveries and affections are evermore highly conceited of their light and understanding. *Thirdly,* The devil does not assault the hope of the hypocrite as he does the hope of a true saint. The devil is a great enemy to a true Christian hope, not only because it tends greatly to the comfort of him that hath it, but also because it is a thing of a holy, heavenly nature, greatly tending to promote and cherish grace in the heart, and a great incentive to strictness and diligence in the Christian life. But he is no enemy to the hope of a hypocrite, which above all things establishes his interest in him that has it. A hypocrite may retain his hope without opposition as long as he lives, the devil never disturbing it nor attempting to disturb it. But there is perhaps no true Christian but what has his hope assaulted by him. Satan assaulted Christ Himself upon this, whether He were the Son of God or no: and the servant is not above his Master, nor the disciple above his Lord; it is enough for the disciple, that is most privileged in this world, to be as his Master. *Fourthly,* He who has a false hope has not that sight of his own corruptions which the saint has. A true Christian has ten times so much to do with his heart and its corruptions as a hypocrite: and the sins of his heart and practice appear to him in their blackness; they look dreadful; and it often appears a very mysterious thing that any grace can be consistent with such corruption, or should be in such a heart. But a false hope hides corruption, covers it all over, and the hypocrite looks clean and bright in his own eyes.

There are two sorts of hypocrites: one that are deceived with their outward morality and external religion, many of whom are professed Arminians in the doctrine of justification: and the other are those that are deceived with false discoveries and elevations; who often cry down works and men's own righteousness, and talk much of free grace, but at the same time make a righteousness of their discoveries and of their humiliation, and exalt themselves to heaven with them. These two kinds of hypocrites, Mr. Shepard, in his Exposition of the Parable of the Ten Virgins, distinguishes by the names of *legal* and *evangelical* hypocrites, and often speaks of the latter as the worse. And it is evident that the latter are commonly by far the more confident in their hope, and with the more difficulty brought off from it: I have scarcely known an instance of such a one, in my life, that has been undeceived. The chief grounds of the confidence of many of them are the very same kind of impulses and supposed revelations (sometimes with texts of Scripture, and sometimes without) that so many of late have had concerning future events; calling these impulses about their good estate the witness of the Spirit; entirely misunderstanding the nature of the witness of the Spirit, as I shall show hereafter. Those that have had visions and impulses about other things, it has generally been to reveal such things as they are desirous and fond of: and no wonder that persons who give heed to such things have the same sort of visions or impressions about their own eternal salvation, to reveal to them that their sins are forgiven them, that their names are written in the book of life, that they are in high favour with God, &c., and especially when they earnestly seek, expect, and wait for evidence of their election and salvation this way, as the surest and most glorious evidence of it. Neither is it any wonder that, when they have such a supposed revelation of their good estate, it raises in them the highest degree of confidence of it. It is found by abundant experience that those who are led away by impulses and imagined revelations are extremely confident: they suppose that the great Jehovah has declared these and those things to them; and having his immediate testimony, a strong confidence is the highest virtue. Hence they are bold to say, I know this or that—I know certainly—I am as sure as that I have a being, and the like; and they despise all argument and inquiry in the case. And, above all things else, it is easy to be accounted for that impressions and impulses about that which is so pleasing, so suiting their self-love and pride, as their being the dear children of God, distinguished from most in the world in His favour, should make them strongly confident; especially when with their impulses and revelations they have high affections, which they take to be the most eminent exercises of grace. I have known of several persons that have had a fond desire of something of a temporal nature, through a violent passion that has possessed them; and they have been earnestly pursuing the thing they have desired should come to pass, and have met with great difficulty and many discouragements in it, but at last have had an impression, or supposed revelation, that they should obtain what they sought; and they have looked upon it as a sure promise from the Most High, which has made them most ridiculously confident, against all manner of reason to convince them to the contrary, and all events working against them. And there is nothing hinders but that persons who are seeking their salvation may be deceived by the like delusive impressions, and be made confident the same way.

The confidence of many of this sort of hypocrites, that Mr. Shepard calls *evangelical hypocrites,* is like the confidence of some mad men who think they are kings; they will maintain it against all manner of reason and evidence. And in one sense it is much more immovable than a truly gracious assurance. A true assurance is not upheld but by the soul's being kept in a holy frame, and grace maintained in lively exercise. If the actings of grace do much decay in the Christian, and he falls into a lifeless frame, he loses his assurance: but this kind of confidence of hypocrites will not be shaken by sin; they (at least some of them) will maintain their boldness in their hope, in the most corrupt frames and wicked ways; which is a sure evidence of their delusion.*

And here I cannot but observe that there are certain doctrines often preached to the people which need to be delivered with more caution and explanation than they frequently are; for, as they are by many understood, they tend greatly to establish this delusion and false confidence of hypocrites. The doctrines I speak of are those of " Christians living by faith, not by sight "; " their giving glory to God, by trusting Him in the dark "; " living upon Christ, and not upon experiences "; " not making their good frames the foundation of their faith "; which are excellent and important doctrines indeed, rightly understood, but corrupt and destructive as many understand them. The Scripture speaks of living or walking by faith and not by sight, in no other way than

---

* Mr. Shepard speaks of it, as a " presumptuous peace, that is not interrupted and broke by evil works." And says, that " the spirit will sigh, and not sing, in that bosom, whence corrupt dispositions and passions break out." And that " though men in such frames may seem to maintain the consolation of the Spirit, and not suspect their hypocrisy, under pretence of trusting the Lord's mercy; yet they cannot avoid the condemnation of the world." *Parable of the Ten Virgins,* p. 223.

Dr. Ames speaks of it as a thing by which the peace of a wicked man may be distinguished from the peace of a godly man, " that the peace of a wicked man continues, whether he performs the duties of piety and righteousness or no; provided those crimes are avoided that appear horrid to nature itself." *Cases of Conscience.*

these, viz., a being governed by a respect to eternal things, that
are the objects of faith, and are not seen, and not by a respect
to temporal things, which are seen; and believing things revealed,
that we never saw with bodily eyes; and also living by faith in
the promise of future things, without yet seeing or enjoying the
things promised, or knowing the way how they can be fulfilled.
This will be easily evident to any one who looks over the Scriptures, which speak of *faith* in opposition to *sight;* as 2 Cor. iv. 18,
and v. 7, Heb. xi. 1, 8, 13, 17, 27, 29, Rom. viii. 24, John xx. 29.
But this doctrine, as it is understood by many, is, that Christians
ought firmly to believe and trust in Christ, without spiritual sight
or light, and although they are in a dark dead frame, and for the
present have no spiritual experiences or discoveries. And it is
truly the duty of those who are thus in darkness, to come out of
darkness into light and believe. But that they should confidently
believe and trust, while they yet remain without spiritual light
or sight, is an anti-scriptural and absurd doctrine. The Scripture is ignorant of any such faith in Christ of the operation of
God, that is not founded in a spiritual sight of Christ. That believing on Christ, which accompanies a title to everlasting life, is
a " seeing the Son, and believing on him," John vi. 40. True faith
in Christ is never exercised any further than persons " behold
as in a glass the glory of the Lord, and have the knowledge of
the glory of God in the face of Jesus Christ," 2 Cor. iii. 18, and
iv. 6. They into whose minds " the light of the glorious gospel
of Christ, who is the image of God, does not shine, believe not,"
2 Cor. iv. 4. That faith which is without spiritual light is not
the faith of the children of the light and of the day, but the presumption of the children of darkness. And therefore to press
and urge them to believe, without any spiritual light or sight,
tends greatly to help forward the delusions of the prince of darkness. Men not only cannot exercise faith without some spiritual
light, but they can exercise faith only just in such proportion as
they have spiritual light. Men will trust in God no further than
they know Him; and they cannot be in the exercise of faith in
Him one ace further than they have a sight of His fulness and
faithfulness in exercise. Nor can they have the exercise of trust
in God any further than they are in a gracious frame. They that
are in a dead carnal frame doubtless ought to trust in God, because that would be the same thing as coming out of their bad

frame and turning to God; but to exhort men confidently to trust in God, and so hold up their hope and peace, though they are not in a gracious frame, and continue still to be so, is the same thing in effect as to exhort them confidently to trust in God, but not with a gracious trust: and what is that but a wicked presumption? It is just as impossible for men to have a strong or lively trust in God when they have no lively exercises of grace, or sensible Christian experiences, as it is for them to be in the lively exercises of grace without the exercises of grace.

It is true that it is the duty of God's people to trust in Him when in darkness, and though they remain still in darkness, in that sense that they ought to trust in God when the aspects of His providence are dark, and look as though God had forsaken them, and did not hear their prayers; and many clouds gather, and many enemies surround them with a formidable aspect, threatening to swallow them up; and all events of providence seem to be against them, all circumstances seem to render the promises of God difficult to be fulfilled. Then God must be trusted out of sight, *i.e.*, when we cannot see which way it is possible for Him to fulfil His word; everything but God's mere word makes it look unlikely, so that, if persons believe, they must hope against hope. Thus the ancient Patriarchs, and Job, and the Psalmist, and Jeremiah, Daniel, Shadrach, Meshach, and Abednego, and the Apostle Paul, gave glory to God by trusting in God in darkness. And we have many instances of such a glorious victorious faith in the eleventh of Hebrews. But how different a thing is this from trusting in God, without spiritual sight, and being at the same time in a dead and carnal frame!

There is also such a thing as spiritual light being let into the soul in one way when it is not in another; and so there is such a thing as the saints trusting in God, and also knowing their good estate, when they are destitute of some kinds of experience. As for instance, they may have clear views of God's sufficiency and faithfulness, and so confidently trust in Him, and know that they are His children; and at the same time not have those clear and sweet ideas of His love as at other times: for it was thus with Christ Himself in His last passion. And they may have views of much of God's sovereignty, holiness, and all-sufficiency, enabling them quietly to submit to Him, and exercise a sweet and most encouraging hope in God's fulness, when they are not satisfied of their own good estate. But how different things are these from confidently trusting in God, without spiritual light or experience!

Those that thus insist on persons living by faith, when they have no experience, and are in very bad frames, are also very absurd in their notions of faith. What they mean by faith is, believing that they are in a good estate. Hence they count it a dreadful sin for them to doubt of their state, whatever frames they are in, and whatever wicked things they do, because it is the great and heinous sin of unbelief; and he is the best man, and puts most honour upon God, that maintains his hope of his good estate the most confidently and immovably, when he has the least light or experience; that is to say, when he is in the worst and most wicked frame and way; because, forsooth, that is a sign that he is strong in faith, giving glory to God, and against hope believes in hope. But what Bible do they learn this notion of faith out of, that it is a man's confidently believing that he is in a good estate?* If this be faith, the Pharisees had faith in an eminent degree, some of whom, Christ teaches, committed the unpardonable sin against the Holy Ghost. The Scripture represents faith as that by which men are brought into a good estate; and therefore it cannot be the same thing as believing that they are already in a good estate. To suppose that faith consists in persons believing that they are in a good estate, is in affect the same thing as to suppose that faith consists in a person's believing that he has faith, or in believing that he believes.

Indeed, persons' doubting of their good estate may in several respects arise from unbelief. It may be from unbelief, or because they have so little faith that they have so little evidence of their good estate: if they had more experience of the actings

---

* "Men do not know that they are godly by believing that they are godly. We know many things by faith, Heb. xi. 3. ' By faith we understand that the worlds were made by the word of God.' Faith is the evidence of things not seen, Heb. xi. 1. Thus men know the Trinity of persons of the Godhead; that Jesus Christ is the Son of God; that he that believes in Him will have eternal life; the resurrection of the dead. And if God should tell a saint that he hath grace, he might know it by believing the word of God. But it is not this way that godly men do know that they have grace. It is not revealed in the Word, and the Spirit of God doth not testify it to particular persons." *Stoddard's Nature of Saving Conversion.*

of faith, and so more experience of the exercise of grace, they would have clearer evidence that their state was good; and so their doubts would be removed. And then their doubting of their state may be from unbelief thus, when, though there be many things that are good evidences of a work of grace in them, yet they doubt very much whether they are really in a state of favour with God, because it is they, those that are so unworthy, and have done so much to provoke God to anger against them. Their doubts in such a case arise from unbelief, as they arise from want of a sufficient sense of, and reliance on, the infinite riches of God's grace, and the sufficiency of Christ for the chief of sinners. They may also be from unbelief, when they doubt of their state, because of the mystery of God's dealings with them; they are not able to reconcile such dispensations with God's favour to them; or when they doubt whether they have any interest in the promises, because the promises from the aspect of providence appear so unlikely to be fulfilled; the difficulties that are in the way are so many and great. Such doubting arises from want of dependence upon God's almighty power, and His knowledge and wisdom, as infinitely above theirs. But yet, in such persons, their unbelief, and their doubting of their state, are not the same thing, though one arises from the other.

Persons may be greatly to blame for doubting of their state on such grounds as these last mentioned; and they may be to blame that they have no more grace, and no more of the present exercises and experiences of it, to be an evidence to them of the goodness of their state: men are doubtless to blame for being in a dead, carnal frame; but when they are in such a frame, and have no sensible experience of the exercises of grace, but on the contrary, are much under the prevalence of their lusts and an unchristian spirit, they are not to blame for doubting of their state. It is as impossible, in the nature of things, that a holy and Christian hope should be kept alive in its clearness and strength in such circumstances, as it is to keep the light in the room when the candle is put out; or to maintain the bright sunshine in the air when the sun is gone down. Distant experiences, when darkened by present prevailing lust and corruption, will never keep alive a gracious confidence and assurance, but one that sickens and decays upon it, as necessarily as a little child by repeated blows on the head with a hammer. Nor is it at all to be lamented that persons doubt of their state in such circumstances: on the contrary, it is desirable and every way best that they should. It is agreeable to that wise and merciful constitution of things, which God hath established, that it should be so. For so hath God contrived and constituted things, in His dispensations towards His own people, that when their love decays, and the exercises of it fail or become weak, fear should arise; for then they need it to restrain them from sin, and to excite them to care for the good of their souls, and so to stir them up to watchfulness and diligence in religion. But God hath so ordered, that when love rises and is in vigorous exercise, then fear should vanish and be driven away; for then they need it not, having a higher and more excellent principle in exercise, to restrain them from sin and stir them up to their duty. There are no other principles which human nature is under the influence of, that will ever make men conscientious, but one of these two, *fear* or *love;* and therefore, if one of these should not prevail as the other decays, God's people, when fallen into dead and carnal frames, when love is asleep, would be lamentably exposed indeed: and therefore God has wisely ordained, that these two opposite principles of love and fear should rise and fall, like the two opposite scales of a balance; when one rises the other sinks. Light and darkness necessarily and unavoidably succeed each other; if light prevails, so much does darkness cease, and no more; and if light decays, so much does darkness prevail. So it is in the heart of a child of God: if divine love decays and falls asleep, and lust prevails, the light and joy of hope go out, and dark fear and doubting arises; and if, on the contrary, divine love prevails and comes into lively exercise, this brings in the brightness of hope, and drives away black lust and fear with it. Love is the spirit of adoption, or the childlike principle; if that slumbers, men fall under fear, which is the spirit of bondage or the servile principle; and so on the contrary. And if it be so, that love, or the spirit of adoption, be carried to a great height, it quite drives away all fear and gives full assurance; agreeable to that of the apostle, 1 John iv. 18, " There is no fear in love, but perfect love casts out fear." These two opposite principles of lust and holy love bring hope and fear into the hearts of God's children in proportion as they prevail; that is, when left to their own natural influence, without something adventitious or accidental intervening; as the distemper of melancholy, doctrinal ignorance, prejudices of education, wrong instruction, false principles, peculiar temptations, &c.

Fear is cast out by the Spirit of God no other way than by the prevailing of love; nor is fear ever maintained but when love is asleep. At such a time, in vain is all the saint's self-examinations, and poring on past experience, in order to establish his peace and get assurance. For it is contrary to the nature of things, as God hath constituted them, that he should have assurance at such a time.

They therefore do directly thwart God's wise and gracious constitution of things, who exhort others to be confident in their hope when in dead frames; under a notion of " living by faith, and not by sight, and trusting God in the dark, and living upon Christ, and not upon experiences;" and warn them not to doubt of their good estate, lest they should be guilty of the dreadful sin of unbelief. And it has a direct tendency to establish the most presumptuous hypocrites, and to prevent their ever calling their state in question, how much soever wickedness rages and reigns in their hearts, and prevails in their lives, under a notion of honouring God, by hoping against hope, and confidently trusting in God, when things look very dark. And, doubtless, vast has been the mischief that has been done this way.

Persons cannot be said to forsake Christ, and live on their experiences of the exercises of grace, merely because they take them and use them as evidences of grace; for there are no other evidences that they can or ought to take. But then may persons be said to live upon their experiences, when they make a righteousness of them, and instead of keeping their eye on God's glory and Christ's excellency, they turn their eyes on to themselves, to entertain their minds by viewing their own attainments and high experiences, and the great things they have met with, and are bright and beautiful in their own eyes. They are rich and increased with goods in their own apprehensions, and think that God has as admiring an esteem of them, on the same account, as they have of themselves : this is living on experiences, and not on Christ, and is more abominable in the sight of God than the gross immoralities of those who make no pretences to religion. But this is a far different thing from a mere improving experiences as evidences of an interest in a glorious Redeemer.

But to return from this digression, I would mention one thing more under the general head that I am upon.

XII. *Nothing can be certainly concluded concerning the nature of religious affections from this, that the outward manifestations of them, and the relation persons give of them, are very affecting and pleasing to the truly godly, and such as greatly gain their charity and win their hearts.*

The true saints have not such a spirit of discerning that they can certainly determine who are godly and who are not. For though they know experimentally what true religion is in the internal exercises of it, yet these are what they can neither feel nor see in the heart of another.* There is nothing in others that comes within their view, but outward manifestations and appearances; but the Scripture plainly intimates that this way of judging what is in men by outward appearances is at best uncertain, and liable to deceit: 1 Sam. xvi. 7, " The Lord seeth not as man seeth; for man looketh on the outward appearance, but the Lord looketh on the heart." Isa. xi. 3, " He shall not judge after the sight of his eyes, neither reprove after the hearing of his ears."†
They commonly are but poor judges and dangerous counsellors in soul cases, who are quick and peremptory in determining persons' states, vaunting themselves in their extraordinary faculty of discerning and distinguishing in these great affairs, as though all was open and clear to them. They betray one of these three things: either that they have had but little experience; or are

* " Men may have the knowledge of their own conversion: the knowledge that other men have of it is uncertain, because no man can look into the heart of another and see the workings of grace there." *Stoddard's Nature of Saving Conversion.*
† Mr. Stoddard observes that " all visible signs are common to converted and unconverted men; and a relation of experiences among the rest." *Appeal to the Learned.*
" O how hard it is for the eye of man to discern betwixt chaff and wheat! And how many upright hearts are now censured, whom God will clear! How many false hearts are now approved whom God will condemn! Men ordinarily have no convictive proofs, but only probable symtoms; which at most beget but a conjectural knowledge of another's state. And they that shall peremptorily judge either way may possibly wrong the generation of the upright, or on the other, absolve and justify the wicked. And truly, considering what has been said, it is no wonder that dangerous mistakes are so frequently made in this matter." *Flavel's Husbandry Spiritualized.* Works Vol. V, p. 97.

persons of a weak judgment; or that they have a great degree of pride and self-confidence, and so of ignorance of themselves. Wise and experienced men will proceed with great caution in such an affair.

When there are many probable appearances of piety in others, it is the duty of the saints to receive them cordially into their charity, and to love them and rejoice in them, as their brethren in Christ Jesus. But yet the best of men may be deceived when the appearances seem to them exceeding fair and bright, even so as entirely to gain their charity and conquer their hearts. It has been a common thing in the church of God for such bright professors, that are received as eminent saints among the saints, to fall away and come to nothing.* And this we need not wonder at, if we consider the things that have been already observed; what things it has been shown may appear in men who are altogether graceless. Nothing hinders but all these things may meet together in men, and yet they be without a spark of grace in their hearts. They may have religious affections of many kinds together; they may have a sort of affection towards God, that bears a great resemblance of dear love to Him; and so a kind of love to the brethren, and great appearances of admiration of God's perfections and works, and sorrow for sin, and reverence, submission, self-abasement, gratitude, joy, religious longings, and zeal for religion and the good of souls. And these affections may come after great awakenings and convictions of conscience; and there may be great appearances of a work of humiliation. Counterfeit love and joy, and other affections, may seem to follow one

* " Be not offended if you see great cedars fall, stars fall from heaven, great professors die and decay: do not think they be all such: do not think that the elect shall fall. Truly, some are such that when they fall, one would think a man truly sanctified might fall away, as the Arminians think: 1 John ii. 19, *They were not of us.* I speak this, because the Lord is shaking; and I look for great apostasies: for God is trying all His friends, through all the Christian world. In Germany what profession was there! Who would have thought it? The Lord, who delights to manifest that openly which was hid secretly, sends a sword and they fall." *Shepard's Parable of the Ten Virgins,* p. 190.
" The saints may approve thee and God condemn thee. Rev. iii. 1, ' Thou hast a name that thou livest, and art dead.' Men may say, There is a true Nathanael; and God may say, There is a self-cozening Pharisee. Reader, thou hast heard of Judas and Demas, of Ananias and Sapphira, of Hymeneus and Philetus, once renowned and famous professors, and thou hast heard how they proved at last." *Flavel's Touchstone of Sincerity.* Works Vol. V, p. 526.

another, just in the same order that is commonly observable in the holy affections of true converts. And these religious affections may be carried to a great height, and may cause abundance of tears, yea, may overcome the nature of those who are the subjects of them, and may make them affectionate, and fervent, and fluent in speaking of the things of God, and dispose them to be abundant in it; and may be attended with many sweet texts of Scripture and precious promises, brought with great impression on their minds; and may dispose them with their mouths to praise and glorify God in a very ardent manner, and fervently to call upon others to praise Him, exclaiming against their unworthiness, and extolling free grace. They may, moreover, dispose them to abound in the external duties of religion, such as prayer, hearing the word preached, singing, and religious conference; and these things may be attended with a great resemblance of a Christian assurance in its greatest height, when the saints mount on eagles' wings above all darkness and doubting. I think it has been made plain that there may be all these things, and yet there be nothing more than the common influences of the Spirit of God, joined with the delusions of Satan and a wicked and deceitful heart. To which I may add, that all these things may be attended with a sweet natural temper, and a good doctrinal knowledge of religion, and a long acquaintance with the saints' way of talking, and of expressing their affections and experiences, and a natural ability and subtlety in accommodating their expressions and manner of speaking to the dispositions and notions of the hearers, with a taking decency of expression and behaviour formed by a good education. How great therefore may the resemblance be, as to all outward expressions and appearances, between a hypocrite and a true saint! Doubtless it is the glorious prerogative of the omniscient God, as the great Searcher of hearts, to be able well to separate between sheep and goats. And what an indecent self-exaltation and arrogance it is, in poor fallible dark mortals, to pretend that they can determine and know who are really sincere and upright before God and who are not!

Many seem to lay great weight on that, and to suppose it to be what may determine them with respect to others' real piety, when they not only tell a plausible story, but when, in giving an account of their experiences, they make such a representation, and speak after such a manner, that the hearers feel their talk; that is to say, when their talk seems to harmonize with their own experience, and their hearts are touched and affected and delighted by what they hear them say, and are drawn out by it in dear love to them. But there is not that certainty in such things, and that full dependence to be had upon them, which many imagine. A true saint greatly delights in holiness; it is a most beautiful thing in his eyes; and God's work, in savingly renewing and making holy and happy, a poor, and before-perishing soul, appears to him a most glorious work: no wonder, therefore, that his heart is touched and greatly affected, when he hears another give a probable account of this work wrought on his own heart, and when he sees in him probable appearances of holiness; whether those pleasing appearances have anything real to answer them or no. And if he uses the same words, which are commonly made use of to express the affections of true saints, and tells of many things following one another in an order agreeable to the method of the experience of him that hears him, and also speaks freely and boldly and with an air of assurance; no wonder the other thinks his experiences harmonize with his own. And if, besides all this, in giving his relation he speaks with much affection; and, above all, if in speaking he seems to show much affection to him to whom he speaks, such an affection as the Galatians did to the Apostle Paul—these things will naturally have a powerful influence to affect and draw his hearer's heart, and open wide the doors of his charity towards him. David speaks as one who had felt Ahithophel's talk, and had once a sweet savour and relish of it. And therefore exceeding great was his surprise and disappointment when he fell; it was almost too much for him: Psal. lv. 12, 13, 14, "It was not an enemy—then I could have borne it—but it was thou, a man mine equal, my guide, and mine acquaintance: we took sweet counsel together, and walked unto the house of God in company."

It is with professors of religion, especially such as become so in a time of outpouring of the Spirit of God, as it is with blossoms in the spring;* there are vast numbers of them upon the

* A time of outpouring of the Spirit of God, reviving religion and producing the pleasant appearances of it in new converts, is in Scripture compared to this very thing, viz., the spring season, when the benign influences of the heavens cause the blossoms to put forth. Cant. ii. 11, 12.

trees, which all look fair and promising; but yet many of them never come to anything. And many of those that in a little time wither up, and drop off and rot under the trees, yet for a while look as beautiful and gay as others; and not only so, but smell sweet, and send forth a pleasant odour; so that we cannot, by any of our senses, certainly distinguish those blossoms which have in them that secret virtue which will afterwards appear in the fruit, and that inward solidity and strength which shall enable them to bear, and cause them to be perfected by the hot summer sun that will dry up the others. It is the mature fruit which comes afterwards, and not the beautiful colours and smell of the blossoms, that we must judge by. So new converts (professedly so), in their talk about things of religion, may appear fair and be very savoury, and the saints may think they talk feelingly. They may relish their talk, and imagine they perceive a divine savour in it, and yet all may come to nothing.

It is strange how hardly men are brought to be contented with the rules and directions Christ has given them, but they must needs go by other rules of their own inventing that seem to them wiser and better. I know of no directions or counsels which Christ ever delivered more plainly than the rules He has given us, to guide us in our judging of others' sincerity, viz., that we should judge of the tree chiefly by the fruit, yet this, it seems, will not do, but other ways are found out which are imagined to be more distinguishing and certain. And woeful have been the mischievous consequences of this arrogant setting up of men's wisdom above the wisdom of Christ. I believe many saints have gone much out of the way of Christ's word in this respect: and some of them have been chastised with whips, and (I had almost said) scorpions, to bring them back again. But many things which have lately appeared, and do now appear, may convince us that ordinarily those who have gone farthest this way, that have been most highly conceited of their faculty of discerning, and have appeared most forward peremptorily and suddenly to determine the state of men's souls, have been hypocrites who have known nothing of true religion.

In the parable of the wheat and tares it is said, Matt. xiii. 26, " When the blade was sprung up, and brought forth fruit, then appeared the tares also." As though the tares were not discerned, nor distinguishable from the wheat, until then, as Mr. Flavel observes.* He mentions it as an observation of Jerome's, that "wheat and tares are so much alike, until the blade of the wheat comes to bring forth the ear, that it is next to impossible to distinguish them." And then Mr. Flavel adds, "How difficult soever it be to discern the difference between wheat and tares, yet doubtless the eye of sense can much easier discriminate them, than the most quick and piercing eye of man can discern the difference between special and common grace. For all saving graces in the saints have their counterfeits in hypocrites; there are similar works in those, which a spiritual and very judicious eye may easily mistake for the saving and genuine effects of a sanctifying spirit."

As it is the ear or the fruit which distinguishes the wheat from the tares, so this is the true Shibboleth that He, who stands as judge at the passages of Jordan, makes use of to distinguish those that shall pass over Jordan into the true Canaan from those that should be slain at the passages. For the Hebrew word Shibboleth signifies an ear of corn. And perhaps the more full pronunciation of Jephthah's friends, Shibboleth, may represent a full ear with fruit in it, typifying the fruits of the friends of Christ, the antitype of Jephthah; and Sibboleth, the more lean pronunciation of the Ephraimites, his enemies, may represent their empty ears, typifying the show of religion in hypocrites without substance and fruit. (Judges xii. 6.) This is agreeable to the doctrine we are abundantly taught in Scripture, viz., that He who is set to judge those that pass through death, whether they have a right to enter into the heavenly Canaan or no, or whether they should be slain, will judge every man according to his works.

We seem to be taught the same things by the rules given for the priest's discerning the leprosy. In many cases it was impossible for the priest to determine whether a man had the leprosy, or whether he were clean, by the most narrow inspection of the appearances that were upon him, until he had waited to see what the appearances would come to, and had shut up the person who showed himself to him one seven days after another; and when he judged, he was to determine by the hair which grew out of the spot that was showed him, which was as it were the fruit that it brought forth.

* *Husbandry Spiritualized*, Works Vol. V, p. 95.

And here, before I finish what I have to say under this head, I would say something to a strange notion some have of late been led away with, of certainly knowing the good estate that others are in, as though it were immediately revealed to them from heaven, by their love flowing out to them in an extraordinary manner. They argue thus, that their love being very sensible and great, it may be certainly known by them who feel it to be a true Christian love: and if it be a true Christian love, the Spirit of God must be the author of it: and inasmuch as the Spirit of God who knows certainly whether others are the children of God or no, and is a Spirit of truth, is pleased by an uncommon influence upon them to cause their love to flow out in an extraordinary manner towards such a person as a child of God; it must needs be, that this infallible Spirit, who deceives none, knows that that person is a child of God. But such persons might be convinced of the falseness of their reasoning, if they would consider whether or no it be not their duty, and what God requires of them, to love those as the children of God who they think are the children of God, and whom they have no reason to think otherwise of, from all that they can see in them, though God, who searches the hearts, knows them not to be His children.

If it be their duty, then it is good, and the want of it sin; and therefore surely the Spirit of God may be the author of it: the Spirit of God, without being a spirit of falsehood, may in such a case assist a person to do his duty, and keep him from sin. But then they argue from the uncommon degree and special manner in which their love flows out to the person, which they think the Spirit of God never would cause if He did not know the object to be a child of God. But then I would ask them, whether or no it is not their duty to love all such as they are bound to think are the children of God, from all that they can see in them, to a very great degree, though God, from other things which He sees that are out of sight to them, knows them not to be so. It is men's duty to love all whom they are bound in charity to look upon as the children of God, with a vastly dearer affection than they commonly do. As we ought to love Christ to the utmost capacity of our nature, so it is our duty to love those who, we think, are so near and dear to Him as His members, with an exceeding dear affection, as Christ has loved us; and therefore it is sin in us not to love them so. We ought to pray to God that

He would by His Spirit keep us from sin, and enable us to do our duty: and may not His Spirit answer our prayers, and enable us to do our duty, in a particular instance, without lying? If He cannot, then the Spirit of God is bound not to help His people to do their duty in some instances, because He cannot do it without being a spirit of falsehood. But surely God is so far a sovereign that He may enable us to do our duty when He pleases, and on what occasion He pleases. When persons think others are His children, God may have other ends in causing their exceedingly endeared love to flow out to them, besides revealing to them whether their opinion of them be right or no: He may have that merciful end in it, to enable them to do their duty, and to keep them from that dreadful infinite evil, sin. And will they say God shall not show them that mercy in such a case? If I am at a distance from home, and hear that in my absence my house is burnt, but my family have, in some extraordinary manner, all escaped the flames; and every thing in the circumstances of the story, as I hear it, makes it appear very credible, it would be sin in me, in such a case, not to feel a very great degree of gratitude to God, though the story indeed be not true. And is not God so sovereign that He may, if He pleases, show me that mercy on that occasion, and enable me to do my duty in a much further degree than I used to do it, and yet not incur the charge of deceitfulness in confirming a falsehood?

It is exceeding manifest that error or mistake may be the occasion of a gracious exercise, and consequently a gracious influence of the Spirit of God, by this: "He that eateth, to the Lord he eateth, and giveth God thanks; and he that eateth not, to the Lord he eateth not, and giveth God thanks!" (Rom. xiv. 6). The apostle is speaking of those, who through erroneous and needless scruples, avoided eating legally unclean meats. By this it is very evident that there may be true exercises of grace, a true respect to the Lord, and particularly a true thankfulness, which may be occasioned by an erroneous judgment and practice. And consequently, an error may be the occasion of those truly holy exercises that are from the infallible Spirit of God. And if so, it is certainly too much for us to determine to how great a degree the Spirit of God may give this holy exercise on such an occasion.

This notion of certainly discerning another's state by love flowing out, is not only not founded on reason or Scripture, but it is anti-scriptural, against the rules of Scripture; which say not a word of any such way of judging the state of others as this, but direct us to judge chiefly by the fruits that are seen in them. And it is against the doctrines of Scripture, which do plainly teach us that the state of others' souls towards God cannot be known by us, as in Rev. ii. 17: "To him that overcometh will I give to eat of the hidden manna, and I will give him a white stone, and in the stone a new name written, which no man knoweth saving he that receiveth it." And Rom. ii. 29, "He is a Jew, which is one inwardly; and circumcision is that of the heart, in the spirit, and not in the letter, whose praise is not of men, but of God." By this last expression, "whose praise is not of men, but of God," the apostle has respect to the insufficiency of men to judge concerning him, whether he be inwardly a Jew or no (as they could easily see by outward marks whether men were outwardly Jews), and would signify, that it belongs to God alone to give a determining voice in this matter. This is confirmed by the same apostle's use of the phrase, in 1 Cor. iv. 5: "Therefore judge nothing before the time, until the Lord come, who both will bring to light the hidden things of darkness, and will make manifest the counsels of the heart: and then shall every man have praise of God." The apostle, in the two foregoing verses, says, "But with me it is a very small thing that I should be judged of you, or of man's judgment: yea, I judge not mine own self. For I know nothing by myself, yet am I not hereby justified; but he that judgeth me is the Lord." And again, it is further confirmed, because the apostle, in this second chapter to the Romans, directs his speech especially to those who had a high conceit of their own holiness, made their boast of God, and were confident of their own discerning, and that they knew God's will, and approved the things which were excellent, or tried the things that differ (as it is in the margin), ver. 19: "And were confident that they were guides of the blind, and a light to them which were in darkness, instructors of the foolish, teachers of babes"; and so took upon them to judge others. See ver. 1, and 17-20.

And how arrogant must the notion be that they have, who imagine they can certainly know others' godliness, when that great Apostle Peter pretends not to say any more concerning Silvanus, than that he was a faithful brother, as he supposed! 1 Pet. v. 12 : though this Silvanus appears to have been a very eminent minister of Christ, an evangelist, a famous light in God's church at that day, and an intimate companion of the apostles. See 2 Cor. i. 19, 1 Thess. i. 1, and 2 Thess. i. 1.

Part III

SHOWING WHAT ARE DISTINGUISHING SIGNS OF TRULY GRACIOUS AND HOLY AFFECTIONS

I COME now to the second thing appertaining to the trial of religious affections which was proposed, viz., To take notice of some things wherein those affections that are spiritual and gracious do differ from those that are not so.

But before I proceed directly to the distinguishing characters, I would previously mention some things which I desire may be observed concerning the marks I shall lay down.

1. That I am far from undertaking to give such signs of gracious affections as shall be sufficient to enable any certainly to distinguish true affection from false in others, or to determine positively which of their neighbours are true professors and which are hypocrites. In so doing, I should be guilty of that arrogance which I have been condemning. Though it be plain that Christ has given rules to all Christians to enable them to judge of professors of religion whom they are concerned with, so far as is necessary for their own safety, and to prevent their being led into a snare by false teachers and false pretenders to religion; and though it be also beyond doubt that the Scriptures do abound with rules which may be very serviceable to ministers, in counselling and conducting souls committed to their care in things appertaining to their spiritual and eternal state; yet it is also evident, that it was never God's design to give us any rules by which we may certainly know who of our fellow professors are His, and to make a full and clear separation between sheep and goats. On the contrary, it was God's design to reserve this to Himself as His prerogative. And therefore no such distinguishing signs as shall enable Christians or ministers to do this are ever to be expected to the world's end: for no more is ever to be expected from any signs that are to be found in the word of God or gathered from it, than Christ designed them for.

2. No such signs are to be expected, that shall be sufficient to enable those saints certainly to discern their own good estate who are very low in grace, or are such as have much departed from God and are fallen into a dead, carnal, and unchristian frame. It is not agreeable to God's design (as has been already observed), that such should know their good estate: nor is it desirable that they should, but, on the contrary, every way best that they should not; and we have reason to bless God, that He made no provision that such should certainly know the state that they are in, any other way than by first coming out of the ill frame and way they are in. Indeed, it is not properly through the defect of the signs given in the Word of God that every saint living, whether strong or weak, and those who are in a bad frame, as well as others, cannot certainly know their good estate by them. For the rules in themselves are certain and infallible, and every saint has, or has had, those things in himself which are sure evidences of grace; for every, even the least, act of grace is so. But the difficulty comes through his defect to whom the signs are given. There is a twofold defect in that saint who is very low in grace or in an ill frame, which makes it impossible for him to know certainly that he has true grace, by the best signs and rules which can be given him. First, there is a defect in the object or the qualification to be viewed and examined. I do not mean an essential defect, because I suppose the person to be a real saint, but a defect in degree. Grace, being very small, cannot be clearly and certainly discerned and distinguished.

Things that are very small we cannot clearly discern as to their form, or distinguish them one from another; though, as they are in themselves, their form may be very different. There is doubtless a great difference between the body of man and the bodies of other animals, in the first conception in the womb: but yet if we should view the different embryos, it might not be possible for us to discern the difference by reason of the imperfect state of the object; but as it comes to greater perfection, the difference becomes very plain. The difference between creatures of very contrary qualities is not so plainly to be seen while they are very young, even after they are actually brought forth, as in their more perfect state. The difference between doves and ravens, or doves and vultures, when they first come out of the egg, is not so evident; but as they grow to their perfection, it is exceeding great and manifest. Another defect attending the grace of those I am speaking of is its being mingled with so much corruption, which clouds and hides it and makes it impossible for it certainly to be known. Though different things that are before us may have in themselves many marks thoroughly distinguishing them one from another, yet if we see them only in a thick smoke, it may nevertheless be impossible to distinguish them. A fixed star is easily distinguishable from a comet in a clear sky; but if we view them through a cloud, it may be impossible to see the difference. When true Christians are in an ill frame, guilt lies on the conscience; which will bring fear, and so prevent the peace and joy of an assured hope.

Secondly. There is in such a case a defect in the eye. As the feebleness of grace and prevalence of corruption obscure the object, so they enfeeble the sight; they darken the sight as to all spiritual objects, of which grace is one. Sin is like some distempers of the eyes that make things to appear of different colours from those which properly belong to them; and like many other distempers that put the mouth out of taste so as to disenable it from distinguishing good and wholesome food from bad, but everything tastes bitter.

Men in a corrupt and carnal frame have their spiritual senses in but poor plight for judging and distinguishing spiritual things.

For these reasons, no signs that can be given will actually satisfy persons in such a case: let the signs that are given be never so good and infallible, and clearly laid down, they will not serve them. It is like giving a man rules how to distinguish visible objects in the dark; the things themselves may be very different, and their difference may be very well and distinctly described to him; yet all is insufficient to enable him to distinguish them, because he is in the dark. And therefore many persons in such a case spend time in a fruitless labour, in poring on past experiences, and examining themselves by signs they hear laid down from the pulpit or that they read in books, when there is other work for them to do, that is much more expected of them, which, while they neglect, all their self-examinations are like to be in vain, if they should spend never so much time in them. The accursed thing is to be destroyed from their camp, and Achan to be slain; and until this be done they will be in trouble.

It is not God's design that men should obtain assurance in any other way than by mortifying corruption, and increasing in grace, and obtaining the lively exercises of it. And although self-examination be a duty of great use and importance, and by no means to be neglected, yet it is not the principal means by which the saints do get satisfaction of their good estate. Assurance is not to be obtained so much by *self-examination* as by *action.* The Apostle Paul sought assurance chiefly this way, even by "forgetting the things that were behind, and reaching forth unto those things that were before, pressing towards the mark for the prize of the high calling of God in Christ Jesus; if by any means he might attain unto the resurrection of the dead." And it was by this means chiefly that he obtained assurance: 1 Cor. ix. 26, "I therefore so run, not as uncertainly." He obtained assurance of winning the prize, more by running than by considering. The swiftness of his pace did more towards his assurance of a conquest than the strictness of his examination. Giving all diligence to grow in grace, by adding to faith, virtue, &c., is the direction that the Apostle Peter gives us for "making our calling and election sure, and having an entrance ministered to us abundantly into Christ's everlasting kingdom;" signifying to us, that without this, our eyes will be dim, and we shall be as men in the dark, that cannot plainly see things past or to come, either the forgiveness of our sins past, or our heavenly inheritance that is future and far off, 2 Pet. i. 5-11.*

Therefore, though good rules to distinguish true grace from counterfeit may in many respects tend to convince hypocrites, and be of great use to the saints, and among other benefits may be very useful to them to remove many needless scruples and establish their hope, yet I am far from pretending to lay down any such rules as shall be sufficient of themselves, without other means, to enable all true saints to see their good estate, or as supposing they should be the principal means of their satisfaction.

---

* "The way to know your godliness is to renew the visible exercises of grace.—The more the visible exercises of grace are renewed, the more certain you will be. The more frequently these actings are renewed, the more abiding and confirmed your assurance will be.

"The more men's grace is multiplied, the more their peace is multiplied; 2 Pet. i. 2, 'Grace and peace be multiplied unto you, through the knowledge of God and of Jesus our Lord.'" *Stoddard's Way to know Sincerity and Hypocrisy.*

3. Nor is there much encouragement, in the experience of present or past times, to lay down rules or marks to distinguish between true and false affections, in hopes of convincing any considerable number of that sort of hypocrites who have been deceived with great false discoveries and affections, and are once settled in a false confidence and high conceit of their own supposed great experiences and privileges. Such hypocrites are so conceited of their own wisdom, and so blinded and hardened with a very great self-righteousness (but very subtle and secret, under the disguise of great humility), and so invincible a fondness of their pleasing conceit of their great exaltation, that it usually signifies nothing at all to lay before them the most convincing evidences of their hypocrisy. Their state is indeed deplorable, and next to those who have committed the unpardonable sin. Some of this sort of persons seem to be most out of the reach of means of conviction and repentance. But yet the laying down of good rules may be a means of preventing such hypocrites, and of convincing many of other kinds of hypocrites; and God is able to convince even this kind, and His grace is not to be limited, nor means to be neglected. And besides, such rules may be of use to the true saints, to detect false affections which they may have mingled with true; and be a means of their religion's becoming more pure, and like gold tried in the fire.

Having premised these things, I now proceed directly to take notice of those things in which true religious affections are distinguished from false.

I. *Affections that are truly spiritual and gracious do arise from those influences and operations on the heart which are spiritual, supernatural and divine.*

I will explain what I mean by these terms, whence will appear their use to distinguish between those affections which are spiritual, and those which are not so.

We find that true saints, or those persons who are sanctified by the Spirit of God, are in the New Testament called spiritual persons. And their being spiritual is spoken of as their peculiar character, and that wherein they are distinguished from those who are not sanctified. This is evident, because those who are spiritual are set in opposition to natural men and carnal men. Thus the spiritual man and the natural man are set in opposition one to another, 1 Cor. ii. 14, 15: "The natural man receiveth not the things of the Spirit of God; for they are foolishness unto him; neither can he know them, because they are spiritually discerned. But he that is spiritual judgeth all things." The Scripture explains itself to mean an ungodly man, or one that has no grace, by a natural man: thus the Apostle Jude, speaking of certain ungodly men that had crept in unawares among the saints (ver. 4, of his epistle), says, v. 19, "These are sensual, having not the Spirit." This the apostle gives as a reason why they behaved themselves in such a wicked manner as he had described. Here the word translated *sensual*, in the original is ψυχικοι (Psychikoi), which is the very same as in those verses in 1 Cor. chap. ii. is translated *natural*. In the like manner, in the continuation of the same discourse, in the next verse but one, spiritual men are opposed to carnal men; which the connection plainly shows means the same as spiritual men and natural men in the foregoing verses; "And I, brethren, could not speak unto you, as unto spiritual, but as unto carnal;" *i.e.*, as in a great measure unsanctified. That by carnal the apostle means corrupt and unsanctified, is abundantly evident by Rom. vii. 25-viii. 13, Gal. v. 16-26, Col. ii. 18. Therefore, if by natural and carnal in these texts be intended unsanctified, then doubtless by spiritual, which is opposed thereto. is meant sanctified and gracious.

And as the saints are called spiritual in Scripture, so we also find that there are certain properties, qualities, and principles, that have the same epithet given them. So we read of a "spiritual mind," Rom. viii. 6, of "spiritual understanding," Col. i. 9, and of "spiritual blessings," Eph. i. 3.

Now it may be observed that the epithet *spiritual*, in these and other parallel texts of the New Testament, is not used to signify any relation of persons or things to the spirit or soul of man, as the spiritual part of man in opposition to the body which is the material part. Qualities are not said to be spiritual, because they have their seat in the soul and not in the body: for there are some properties that the Scripture calls *carnal* or *fleshly*, which have their seat as much in the soul as those properties that are called *spiritual*. Thus it is with pride and self-righteousness, and a man's trusting to his own wisdom, which the apostle calls *fleshly*, Col. ii. 18. Nor are things called spiritual because they are conversant about those things that are immaterial and not corporeal. For so was the wisdom of the wise men and princes of this world conversant about spirits and immaterial beings; whom yet the apostle speaks of as natural men, totally ignorant of those things that are spiritual, 1 Cor. chap. ii. But it is with relation to the Holy Ghost, or Spirit of God, that persons or things are termed spiritual in the New Testament. *Spirit*, as the word is used to signify the third person in the Trinity, is the substantive, of which is formed the adjective *spiritual*, in the Holy Scriptures. Thus Christians are called spiritual persons because they are born of the Spirit, and because of the indwelling and holy influences of the Spirit of God in them. And things are called spiritual as related to the Spirit of God; 1 Cor. ii. 13, 14, "Which things also we speak, not in the words which man's wisdom teacheth, but which the Holy Ghost teacheth; comparing spiritual things with spiritual. But the natural man receiveth not the things of the Spirit of God." Here the apostle himself expressly signifies that by spiritual things he means the things of the Spirit of God, and things which the Holy Ghost teacheth. The same is yet more abundantly apparent by viewing the whole context. Again, Rom. viii. 6, "To be carnally minded is death; to be spiritually minded is life and peace." The apostle explains what he means by being carnally and spiritually minded in what follows in the 9th verse, and shows that by being spiritually minded he means a having the indwelling and holy influences of the Spirit of God in the heart: "But ye are not in the flesh, but in the Spirit, if so be that the Spirit of God dwell in you. Now if any man have not the Spirit of Christ, he is none of his." The same is evident by all the context. But time would fail to produce all the evidence there is of this in the New Testament.

And it must be here observed that, although it is with relation to the Spirit of God and His influences that persons and things are called spiritual, yet not all those persons who are subject to any kind of influence of the Spirit of God are ordinarily called spiritual in the New Testament. They who have only the common influences of God's Spirit are not so called, in the places above, but only those who have the special, gracious, and saving influences of God's Spirit; as is evident, because it has been already proved that by spiritual men is meant godly men, in opposition to natural, carnal, and unsanctified men. And it is most plain that the apostle by spiritually minded (Rom. viii. 6) means graciously minded. And though the extraordinary gifts of the Spirit, which natural men might have, are sometimes called spiritual because they are from the Spirit; yet natural men, whatever gifts of the Spirit they had, were not, in the usual language of the New Testament, called spiritual persons. For it was not by men's having the gifts of the Spirit, but by their having the virtues of the Spirit, that they were called spiritual; as is apparent by Gal. vi. 1: "Brethren, if a man be overtaken in a fault, ye which are spiritual restore such an one in the spirit of meekness." Meekness is one of those virtues which the apostle had just spoken of in the verses next preceding, showing what are the fruits of the Spirit. Those qualifications are said to be spiritual, in the language of the New Testament, which are truly gracious and holy and peculiar to the saints.

Thus, when we read of spiritual wisdom and understanding (as in Col. i. 9, "We desire that ye may be filled with the knowledge of his will, in all wisdom and spiritual understanding"), hereby is intended that wisdom which is gracious, and from the sanctifying influences of the Spirit of God. For, doubtless, by spiritual wisdom is meant that which is opposite to what the Scripture calls natural wisdom; as the spiritual man is opposed to the natural man. And therefore spiritual wisdom is doubtless the same with that wisdom which is from above, that the Apostle James speaks of, Jam. iii. 17: "The wisdom that is from above, is first pure, then peaceable, gentle," &c., for this the apostle opposes to natural wisdom, ver. 15: "This wisdom descendeth not from above, but is earthly, sensual"—the last word in the original is the same that is translated *natural*, in 1 Cor. ii. 14.

So that, although natural men may be the subjects of many influences of the Spirit of God, as is evident by many Scriptures, as Numb. xxiv. 2, 1 Sam. x. 10, and xi. 6, and xvi. 14, 1 Cor. xiii. 1, 2, 3, Heb. vi. 4, 5, 6, and many others, yet they are not, in the sense of the Scripture, spiritual persons; neither are any of those common gifts, qualities, or affections, that are from the influence of the Spirit of God upon them, called spiritual things. The great difference lies in these two things.

1. The Spirit of God is given to the true saints to dwell in them as His proper lasting abode; and to influence their hearts, as a principle of new nature, or as a divine supernatural spring of life and action. The Scriptures represent the Holy Spirit not

only as moving and occasionally influencing the saints, but as dwelling in them as His temple, His proper abode, and everlasting dwelling place, 1 Cor. iii. 16, 2 Cor. vi. 16, John xiv. 16, 17. And He is represented as being there so united to the faculties of the soul that He becomes there a principle or spring of a new nature and life.

So the saints are said to live by Christ living in them, Gal. ii. 20. Christ by His Spirit not only *is* in them, but *lives* in them; they live by His life. His Spirit is united to them as a principle of life in them. They not only drink living water, but this "living water becomes a well or fountain of water" in the soul, "springing up into spiritual and everlasting life," John iv. 14, and thus becomes a principle of life in them. This living water the evangelist himself explains to intend the Spirit of God, chap. vii. 38, 39. The light of the Sun of righteousness does not only shine upon them, but is so communicated to them that they shine also, and become little images of that Sun which shines upon them; the sap of the true vine is not only conveyed into them, as the sap of a tree may be conveyed into a vessel, but is conveyed as sap is from a tree into one of its living branches, where it becomes a principle of life. The Spirit of God being thus communicated and united to the saints, they are from thence properly denominated from Him, and are called *spiritual*.

On the other hand, though the Spirit of God may many ways influence natural men, yet because He is not thus communicated to them as an indwelling principle, they do not derive any denomination or character from Him: for, there being no union, He is not their own. The light may shine upon a body that is very dark or black; and though that body be the subject of the light, yet, because the light becomes no principle of light in it so as to cause the body to shine, hence that body does not properly receive its denomination from it, so as to be called a lightsome body. So the Spirit of God acting upon the soul only, without communicating Himself to be an active principle in it, cannot denominate it spiritual. A body that continues black may be said not to have light, though the light shines upon it: so natural men are said "not to have the Spirit," Jude 19, "sensual or natural" (as the word is elsewhere rendered), "having not the Spirit."

2. Another reason why the saints and their virtues are called spiritual (which is the principal thing) is, that the Spirit of God,

dwelling as a vital principle in their souls, there produces those effects where He exerts and communicates Himself in His own proper nature. Holiness is the nature of the Spirit of God, therefore He is called in Scripture the Holy Ghost. Holiness, which is as it were the beauty and sweetness of the divine nature, is as much the proper nature of the Holy Spirit as heat is the nature of fire, or as sweetness was the nature of that holy anointing oil which was the principal type of the Holy Ghost in the Mosaic dispensation; yea, I may rather say, that holiness is as much the proper nature of the Holy Ghost as sweetness was the nature of the sweet odour of that ointment. The Spirit of God so dwells in the hearts of the saints that He there, as a seed or spring of life, exerts and communicates Himself, in this His sweet and divine nature, making the soul a partaker of God's beauty and Christ's joy, so that the saint has truly fellowship with the Father, and with His Son Jesus Christ, in thus having the communion or participation of the Holy Ghost. The grace which is in the hearts of the saints is of the same nature with the divine holiness, as much as it is possible for that holiness to be which is infinitely less in degree; as the brightness that is in a diamond which the sun shines upon is of the same nature with the brightness of the sun, but only that it is as nothing to it in degree. Therefore Christ says, John iii. 6, "That which is born of the Spirit is spirit;" i.e., the grace that is begotten in the hearts of the saints is something of the same nature with that Spirit, and so is properly called a spiritual nature; after the same manner as that which is born of the flesh is flesh, or that which is born of corrupt nature is corrupt nature.

But the Spirit of God never influences the minds of natural men after this manner. Though He may influence them many ways, yet He never, in any of His influences, communicates Himself to them in His own proper nature. Indeed He never acts disagreeably to His nature, either on the minds of saints or sinners: but the Spirit of God may act upon men agreeably to His own nature, and not exert His proper nature in the acts and exercises of their minds: the Spirit of God may act so, that His actions may be agreeable to His nature, and yet may not at all communicate Himself in His proper nature, in the effect of that action. Thus, for instance, the Spirit of God moved upon the face of the waters, and there was nothing disagreeable to His nature in that action; but yet He did not at all communicate Himself in that action; there was nothing of the proper nature of the Holy Spirit in that motion of the waters. And so He may act upon the minds of men many ways, and not communicate Himself any more than when He acts on inanimate things.

Thus not only the manner of the relation of the Spirit, who is the Operator, to the subject of his operations is different—as the Spirit operates in the saints, as dwelling in them, as an abiding principle of action, whereas He doth not so operate upon sinners —but the influence and operation itself is different, and the effect wrought exceeding different. So that not only the persons are called *spiritual,* as having the Spirit of God dwelling in them, but those qualifications, affections, and experiences, that are wrought in them by the Spirit are also *spiritual,* and therein differ vastly in their nature and kind from all that a natural man is or can be the subject of while he remains in a natural state; and also from all that men or devils can be the authors of. It is a spiritual work in this high sense, and therefore above all other works is peculiar to the Spirit of God. There is no work so high and excellent, for there is no work wherein God doth so much communicate Himself, and wherein the mere creature hath, in so high a sense, a participation of God; so that it is expressed in Scripture by the saints " being made partakers of the divine nature," 2 Pet. i. 4, and " having God dwelling in them, and they in God," 1 John iv. 12, 15, 16; " and having Christ in them," John xvii. 21, Rom. viii. 10; " being the temples of the living God," 2 Cor. vi. 16; " living by Christ's life," Gal. ii. 20; " being made partakers of God's holiness," Heb. xii. 10; " having Christ's love dwelling in them," John xvii. 26; " having his joy fulfilled in them," John xvii. 13; " seeing light in God's light, and being made to drink of the river of God's pleasures," Psal. xxxvi. 8, 9; " having fellowship with God, or communicating and partaking with him (as the word signifies)," 1 John i. 3. Not that the saints are made partakers of the essence of God, and so are *godded* with God, and *christed* with Christ, according to the abominable and blasphemous language and notions of some heretics; but, to use the Scripture phrase, they are made partakers of God's fulness, Eph. iii. 17, 18, 19, John i. 16, that is, of God's spiritual beauty and happiness, according to the measure and capacity of a creature; for so the word *fulness* signifies in Scripture language.

Grace in the hearts of the saints being therefore the most glorious work of God, wherein He communicates of the goodness of His nature, it is doubtless His peculiar work, and in an eminent manner above the power of all creatures. And the influences of the Spirit of God in this, being thus peculiar to God, and being those wherein God does, in so high a manner, communicate Himself, and make the creature partaker of the divine nature (the Spirit of God communicating Himself in His own proper nature) —this is what I mean by those influences that are divine, when I say that " truly gracious affections do arise from those influences that are spiritual and divine."

The true saints only have that which is spiritual; others have nothing which is divine, in the sense that has been spoken of. They not only have not these communications of the Spirit of God in so high a degree as the saints, but have nothing of that nature or kind. For the Apostle James tells us that natural men have not the Spirit; and Christ teaches the necessity of a new birth, or of being born of the Spirit, from this, that he that is born of the flesh has only flesh, and no spirit, John iii. 6. They have not the Spirit of God dwelling in them in any degree; for the apostle teaches that all who have the Spirit of God dwelling in them are His, Rom. viii. 9-11. And a having the Spirit of God is spoken of as a certain sign that persons shall have the eternal inheritance; for it is spoken of as the earnest of it, 2 Cor. i. 22, and v. 5, Eph. i. 14; and a having anything of the Spirit is mentioned as a sure sign of being in Christ, 1 John iv. 13; " Hereby know we that we dwell in him, because he hath given us of his Spirit." Ungodly men not only have not so much of the divine nature as the saints, but they are not partakers of it; which implies that they have nothing of it; for a being partaker of the divine nature is spoken of as the peculiar privilege of the true saints, 2 Pet. i. 4. Ungodly men are not " partakers of God's holiness," Heb. xii. 10. A natural man has no experience of any of those things that are spiritual: the apostle teaches us that he is so far from it that he knows nothing about them, he is a perfect stranger to them, the talk about such things is all foolishness and nonsense to him, he knows not what it means; 1 Cor. ii. 14, " The natural man receiveth not the things of the Spirit of God, for they are foolishness to him: neither can he know them, because they are spiritually discerned." And to the like purpose Christ

teaches us that the world is wholly unacquainted with the Spirit
of God, John xiv. 17 : " Even the Spirit of truth, whom the world
cannot receive, because it seeth him not, neither knoweth him."
And it is further evident that natural men have nothing in them
of the same nature with the true grace of the saints, because the
apostle teaches us that those of them who go farthest in religion
have no charity or true Christian love, 1 Cor. chap. xiii. So Christ
elsewhere reproves the Pharisees, those high pretenders to religion, that they " had not the love of God in them," John v. 42.
Hence natural men have no communion or fellowship with
Christ, or participation with Him (as these words signify), for
this is spoken of as the peculiar privilege of the saints, 1 John
i. 3-7, and 1 Cor. i. 9. And the Scripture speaks of the actual
existence of a gracious principle in the soul, though in its first
beginning, as a seed there planted, as inconsistent with a man's
being a sinner, 1 John iii. 9. And natural men are represented
in Scripture as having no spiritual light, no spiritual life, and no
spiritual being; and therefore conversion is often compared to
opening the eyes of the blind, raising the dead, and a work of
creation (wherein creatures are made entirely new), and becoming new-born children.

From these things it is evident that those gracious influences
which the saints are subjects of, and the effects of God's Spirit
which they experience, are entirely above nature, altogether of a
different kind from anything that men find within themselves
by nature, or only in the exercise of natural principles; and are
things which no improvement of those qualifications or principles
that are natural, no advancing or exalting them to higher degrees, and no kind of composition of them, will ever bring men
to; because they not only differ from what is natural, and from
every thing that natural men experience, in degree and circumstances, but also in kind; and are of a nature vastly more excellent. And this is what I mean by supernatural, when I say that
gracious affections are from those influences that are supernatural.

From hence it follows, that in those gracious exercises and
affections which are wrought in the minds of the saints, through
the saving influences of the Spirit of God, there is a new inward
perception or sensation of their minds, entirely different in its
nature and kind from anything that ever their minds were the

subjects of before they were sanctified. For doubtless, if God by
His mighty power produces something that is new, not only in
degree and circumstances but in its whole nature, and which
could not be produced by any exalting, varying, or compounding
of what was there before, or by adding anything of the like kind
—I say, if God produces something thus new in a mind, that is a
perceiving, thinking, conscious thing, then doubtless something
entirely new is felt, or perceived, or thought; or, which is the
same thing, there is some new sensation or perception of the
mind, which is entirely of a new sort, and which could not be
produced by any exalting, varying, or compounding of the kind
of perceptions or sensations which the mind had before; or there
is what some metaphysicians call a new simple idea. If grace be,
in the sense above described, an entirely new kind of principle,
then the exercises of it are also entirely a new kind of exercises.
And if there be in the soul a new sort of exercises which it is
conscious of, which the soul knew nothing of before, and which
no improvement, composition, or management of what it was
before conscious or sensible of could produce, or anything like it;
then it follows that the mind has an entirely new kind of perception or sensation; and here is, as it were, a new spiritual sense
that the mind has, or a principle of a new kind of perception or
spiritual sensation, which is in its whole nature different from
any former kinds of sensation of the mind, as tasting is diverse
from any of the other senses; and something is perceived by a
true saint, in the exercise of this new sense of mind in spiritual
and divine things, as entirely diverse from anything that is perceived in them by natural men, as the sweet taste of honey is
diverse from the ideas men get of honey by only looking on and
feeling it. So that the spiritual perceptions which a sanctified
and spiritual person has are not only diverse from all that natural
men have after the manner that the ideas or perceptions of the
same sense may differ from one another, but rather as the ideas
and sensations of different senses do differ. Hence the work of
the Spirit of God in regeneration is often in Scripture compared
to the giving a new sense, giving eyes to see and ears to hear,
unstopping the ears of the deaf, and opening the eyes of them
that were born blind, and turning from darkness unto light. And
because this spiritual sense is immensely the most noble and excellent, and that without which all other principles of percep-

tion and all our faculties are useless and vain; therefore the giving this new sense, with the blessed fruits and effects of it in the soul, is compared to a raising the dead, and to a new creation.

This new spiritual sense and the new dispositions that attend it are no new faculties, but are new principles of nature. I use the word principles for want of a word of a more determinate signification. By a principle of nature in this place, I mean that foundation which is laid in nature, either old or new, for any particular manner or kind of exercise of the faculties of the soul; or a natural habit or foundation for action, giving a personal ability and disposition to exert the faculties in exercises of such a certain kind; so that to exert the faculties in that kind of exercises may be said to be his nature. So this new spiritual sense is not a new faculty of understanding, but it is a new foundation laid in the nature of the soul for a new kind of exercises of the same faculty of understanding. So that new holy disposition of heart that attends this new sense is not a new faculty of will, but a foundation laid in the nature of the soul, for a new kind of exercises of the same faculty of will.

The Spirit of God, in all His operations upon the minds of natural men, only moves, impresses, assists, improves, or some way acts upon natural principles; but gives no new spiritual principle. Thus when the Spirit of God gives a natural man visions, as He did Balaam, He only impresses a natural principle, viz., the sense of seeing, immediately exciting ideas of that sense; but He gives no new sense; neither is there anything supernatural, spiritual, or divine in it. So if the Spirit of God impresses on a man's imagination, either in a dream, or when he is awake, any outward ideas of any of the senses, either voices or shapes and colours, it is only exciting ideas of the same kind that he has by natural principles and senses. So if God reveals to any natural man any secret fact, as, for instance, something that he shall hereafter see or hear, this is not infusing or exercising any new spiritual principle, or giving the ideas of any new spiritual sense; it is only impressing, in an extraordinary manner, the ideas that will hereafter be received by sight and hearing —So in the more ordinary influences of the Spirit of God on the hearts of sinners, He only assists natural principles to do the same work to a greater degree which they do of themselves by nature. Thus the Spirit of God by His common influences may assist men's natural ingenuity,

as He assisted Bezaleel and Aholiab in the curious works of the
tabernacle: so He may assist men's natural abilities in political
affairs, and improve their courage and other natural qualifications, as He is said to have put His spirit on the seventy elders,
and on Saul, so as to give him another heart. Likewise God may
greatly assist natural men's reason, in their reasoning about secular things, or about the doctrines of religion, and may greatly
advance the clearness of their apprehensions and notions of
things of religion in many respects, without giving any spiritual
sense. So in those awakenings and convictions that natural men
may have, God only assists conscience, which is a natural principle, to do that work in a further degree which it naturally does.
Conscience naturally gives men an apprehension of right and
wrong, and suggests the relation there is between them and a
retribution: the Spirit of God assists men's consciences to do this
in a greater degree, and helps conscience against the stupifying
influence of worldly objects and their lusts. Many other ways
might be mentioned wherein the Spirit acts upon, assists, and
moves natural principles; but after all it is no more than nature
moved, acted and improved; here is nothing supernatural and
divine. But the Spirit of God in His spiritual influences on the
hearts of His saints, operates by infusing or exercising new,
divine, and supernatural principles; principles which are indeed
a new and spiritual nature, and principles vastly more noble and
excellent than all that is in natural men.

From what has been said it follows that all spiritual and gracious affections are attended with and do arise from some apprehension, idea, or sensation of mind, which is in its whole nature
different, yea, exceeding different, from all that is or can be in
the mind of a natural man. The natural man discerns nothing
of it (agreeable to 1 Cor. ii. 14), and conceives of it no more than
a man without the sense of tasting can conceive of the sweet taste
of honey, or a man without the sense of hearing can conceive of
the melody of a tune, or a man born blind can have a notion of
the beauty of the rainbow.

But here two things must be observed, in order to the right
understanding of this.

1. On the one hand it must be observed, that not everything
which in any respect appertains to spiritual affections is new and
entirely different from what natural men can conceive of and ex-

perience; some things are common to gracious affections with other affections; many circumstances, appendages, and effects are common. Thus a saint's love to God has a great many things appertaining to it which are common with a man's natural love to a near relation; love to God makes a man have desires of the honour of God, and a desire to please Him; so does a natural man's love to his friend make him desire his honour, and desire to please him; love to God causes a man to delight in the thoughts of God, and to delight in the presence of God, and to desire conformity to God, and the enjoyment of God; and so it it is with a man's love to his friend; and many other things might be mentioned which are common to both. But yet that idea which the saint has of the loveliness of God, and that kind of delight he has in that view which is as it were the marrow and quintessence of his love, is peculiar and entirely diverse from anything that a natural man has or can have any notion of. And even in those things that seem to be common, there is something peculiar. Both spiritual and natural love cause desires after the object beloved; but they are not the same sort of desires: there is a sensation of soul in the spiritual desires of one that loves God which is entirely different from all natural desires. Both spiritual love and natural love are attended with delight in the object beloved; but the sensations of delight are not the same, but entirely and exceedingly diverse. Natural men may have conceptions of many things about spiritual affections; but there is something in them which is as it were the nucleus, or kernel of them, that they have no more conception of than one born blind has of colours.

It may be clearly illustrated thus: we will suppose two men; one is born without the sense of tasting, the other has it. The latter loves honey, and is greatly delighted in it because he knows the sweet taste of it; the other loves certain sounds and colours. The love of each has many things that appertain to it which are common; it causes both to desire and delight in the object beloved, and causes grief when it is absent, &c., but yet that idea or sensation which he who knows the taste of honey has of its excellency and sweetness, as the foundation of his love, is entirely different from anything the other has or can have; and that delight which he has in honey is wholly diverse from anything that the other can conceive of, though they both delight in their beloved objects. So both these persons may in some respects love the same object: the one may love a delicious kind of fruit, which is beautiful to the eye and of a delicious taste, not only because he has seen its pleasant colours but knows its sweet taste; the other, perfectly ignorant of this, loves it only for its beautiful colours: there are many things seen, in some respect, to be common to both; both love, both desire, and both delight; but the love and desire and delight of the one, is altogether diverse from that of the other. The difference between the love of a natural man and that of a spiritual man is like to this; but only it must be observed, that in one respect it is vastly greater, viz., that the kinds of excellency which are perceived in spiritual objects by these different kinds of persons, are in themselves vastly more diverse than the different kinds of excellency perceived in delicious fruit by a tasting and a tasteless man; and in another respect it may not be so great, for the spiritual man may have a spiritual sense or taste but in small beginnings, and to a very imperfect degree.

2. On the other hand, it must be observed that a natural man may have religious apprehensions and affections, which may be in many respects very new and surprising to him; and yet what he experiences be nothing like the exercises of a principle of new nature, or the sensations of a new spiritual sense. His affections may be very new, by extraordinarily moving natural principles in a very new degree, and with a great many new circumstances, and a new co-operation of natural affections, and a new composition of ideas. This may be from some extraordinary powerful influence of Satan, and some great delusion; yet there is nothing but nature extraordinarily acted. As if a poor man that had always dwelt in a cottage and had never looked beyond the obscure village where he was born, should in a jest be taken to a magnificent city and prince's court, and there arrayed in princely robes, and set on the throne, with the crown royal on his head, peers and nobles bowing before him, and should be made to believe that he was now a glorious monarch. The ideas he would have, and the affections he would experience, would in many respects be very new, and such as he had no imagination of before; but all this is no more than extraordinarily raising and exciting natural principles, and newly exalting, varying, and compounding such sort of ideas as he has by nature; here is nothing like giving him a new sense.

Upon the whole, I think it is clearly manifest that all truly gracious affections do arise from special and peculiar influences of the Spirit, working that sensible effect or sensation in the souls of the saints, which is entirely different from all that is possible a natural man should experience, not only different in degree and circumstances, but different in its whole nature; so that a natural man not only cannot experience that which is individually the same, but cannot experience anything but what is exceeding diverse, and immensely below it, in its kind; and that which the power of men or devils is not sufficient to produce the like of, or anything of the same nature.

I have insisted largely on this matter, because it is of great importance and use evidently to discover and demonstrate the delusions of Satan in many kinds of false religious affections, which multitudes are deluded by, and probably have been in all ages of the Christian church; and to settle and determine many articles of doctrine concerning the operations of the Spirit of God and the nature of true grace.

Now, therefore, to apply these things to the purpose of this discourse.

Hence it appears, that impressions which some have received in their imagination, or the imaginary ideas which they have of God or Christ, or heaven, or anything appertaining to religion, have nothing in them that is spiritual or of the nature of true grace. Though such things may attend what is spiritual and be mixed with it, yet in themselves they have nothing that is spiritual, nor are they any part of gracious experience.

Here, for the sake of the ignorant, I will explain what is intended by impressions on the imagination, and imaginary ideas. The imagination is that power of the mind whereby it can have a conception or idea of things of an external or outward nature (that is, of such sort of things as are the objects of the outward senses) when those things are not present and are not perceived by the senses. It is called imagination from the word *image;* because thereby a person can have an image of some external thing in his mind, when that thing is not present in reality, nor anything like it. All such things as we perceive by our five external senses, seeing, hearing, smelling, tasting, and feeling, are external things: and when a person has an idea or image of any of these sorts of things in his mind, when they are not there, and when he does not really see, hear, smell, taste, nor feel them; that is to have an imagination of them, and these ideas are imaginary ideas: and when such kinds of ideas are strongly impressed upon the mind, and the image of them in the mind is very lively, almost as if one saw them, or heard them, &c., that is called an impression on the imagination. Thus colours and shapes, and a form of countenance, are outward things, objects of the outward sense of seeing; therefore, when any person has in his mind a lively idea of any shape, or colour, or form of countenance, that is to have an imagination of those things. If he has an idea of such sort of light or darkness as he perceives by the sense of seeing, that is to have an idea of outward light, and so is an imagination. If he has an idea of any marks made on paper, suppose letters and words written in a book, that is to have an external and imaginary idea of such kind of things as we sometimes perceive by our bodily eyes. And when we have the ideas of sounds or voices or words spoken, this is only to have ideas of outward things, viz., of such kind of things as are perceived by the external sense of hearing, and so that also is imagination: and when these ideas are impressed with liveliness almost as if they were really heard with the ears, this is to have an impression on the imagination. And so I might go on, and give instances appertaining to the other three senses of smelling, tasting, and feeling.

Many who have had such things have very ignorantly supposed them to be of the nature of spiritual discoveries. They have had lively ideas of some external shape, and beautiful form of countenance; and this they call spiritually seeing Christ. Some have had impressed upon them ideas of a great outward light; and this they call a spiritual discovery of God's or Christ's glory. Some have had ideas of Christ's hanging on the cross, and His blood running from His wounds; and this they call a spiritual sight of Christ crucified, and the way of salvation by His blood. Some have seen Him with his arms open ready to embrace them; and this they call a discovery of the sufficiency of Christ's grace and love. Some have had lively ideas of heaven, and of Christ on His throne there, and shining ranks of saints and angels; and this they call seeing heaven opened to them. Some from time to time have had a lively idea of a person of a beautiful countenance smiling upon them; and this they call a spiritual discovery of the love of Christ to their souls, and tasting the love of Christ. And they look upon it a sufficient evidence that these things are spiritual discoveries, and that they see them spiritually, because they say they do not see these things with their bodily eyes but in their hearts; for they can see them when their eyes are shut. And in like manner, the imaginations of some have been impressed with ideas of the sense of hearing; they have had ideas of words, as if they were spoken to them, sometimes the words of Scripture, and sometimes other words: they have had ideas of Christ's speaking comfortable words to them. These things they have called having the inward call of Christ, hearing the voice of Christ spiritually in their hearts, having the witness of the Spirit, and the inward testimony of the love of Christ, &c.

The common and less considerate and understanding sort of people are the more easily led into apprehensions that these things are spiritual things, because, spiritual things being invisible and not things that can be pointed forth with the finger, we are forced to use figurative expressions in speaking of them, and to borrow names from external and sensible objects to signify them by. Thus we call a clear apprehension of things spiritual by the name of *light*; and a having an apprehension of things, by the name of *seeing* such things. The conviction of the judgment, and the persuasion of the will, by the word of Christ in the gospel, we signify by spiritually hearing the call of Christ; and the Scripture itself abounds with such like figurative expressions. Persons hearing these often used, and having pressed upon them the necessity of having their eyes opened, and having a discovery of spiritual things, and seeing Christ in His glory, and having the inward call, and the like, they ignorantly look and wait for some such external discoveries and imaginary views as have been spoken of. And when they have them they are confident that now their eyes are opened, now Christ has discovered Himself to them, and they are His children; and hence they are exceedingly affected and elevated with their deliverance and happiness, and many kinds of affections are at once set in a violent motion in them.

But it is exceedingly apparent that such ideas have nothing in them which is spiritual and divine, in the sense wherein it has been demonstrated that all gracious experiences are spiritual and divine. These external ideas are in no wise entirely, and in their whole nature, diverse from all that men have by nature; so far from this, they are ideas of the same sort which we have by the external senses, among the inferior powers of human nature; they are merely ideas of external objects, of the outward, sensitive kind; the same sort of sensations of mind (differing not in degree, but only in circumstances) that we have by those natural principles which are common to us with the beasts, viz., the five external senses. This is a low, miserable notion of spiritual sense, to suppose that it is only a conceiving or imagining that sort of ideas which we have by our animal senses, which senses the beasts have in as great perfection as we; it is, as it were, a turning of Christ, or the divine nature in the soul, into a mere animal. There is nothing wanting in the soul, as it is by nature, to render it capable of being the subject of all these external ideas, without any new principles. A natural man is capable of having an idea, and a lively idea, of shapes, and colours, and sounds, when they are absent, even as capable as a regenerate man is: so there is nothing supernatural in them. And it is known by abundant experience, that it is not the advancing or perfecting of human nature, which makes persons more capable of having such lively and strong imaginary ideas, but on the contrary, the weakness of body and mind, and distempers of body, make persons abundantly more susceptive of such impressions.*

As to a truly spiritual sensation, not only is the manner of its coming into the mind extraordinary, but the sensation itself is totally diverse from all that men have, or can have, in a state of nature, as has been shown. But as to these external ideas, though the way of their coming into the mind is sometimes unusual, yet the ideas in themselves are not the better for that; they are still of no different sort from what men have by their senses; they are of no higher kind, nor a whit better. For instance, the external idea a man has now of Christ hanging on the cross, and shedding His blood, is no better in itself than the external idea that

* " Conceits and whimsies abound most in men of weak reason; children, and such as are cracked in their understanding, have most of them; strength of reason banishes them, as the sun does mists and vapours. But now the more rational any gracious person is, by so much more is he fixed and settled, and satisfied in the grounds of religion; yea, there is the highest and purest reason in religion; and when this change is wrought upon men, it is carried on in a rational way. Isa. i. 18." *Flavel's Preparation for Sufferings.* Works, Vol. VI, p. 32.

the Jews His enemies had, who stood round His cross, and saw this with their bodily eyes. The imaginary idea which men have now of an external brightness and glory of God is no better than the idea the wicked congregation in the wilderness had of the external glory of the Lord at Mount Sinai, when they saw it with their bodily eyes; or any better than that idea which millions of cursed reprobates will have of the external glory of Christ at the Day of Judgment, who shall see and have a very lively idea of ten thousand times greater external glory of Christ than ever yet was conceived in any man's imagination.* Yea, the image of Christ, which men conceive in their imaginations, is not in its own nature of any superior kind to the idea the Papists conceive of Christ, by the beautiful and affecting images of Him which they see in their churches (though the way of their receiving the idea may not be so bad); nor are the affections they have, if built primarily on such imaginations, any better than the affections raised in ignorant people by the sight of those images, which oftentimes are very great; especially when these images, through the craft of the priests, are made to move and speak and weep and the like.† Merely the way of persons receiving these imaginary ideas does not alter the nature of the ideas themselves

* " If any man should see, and behold Christ really and immediately, this is not the saving knowledge of Him. I know the saints do know Christ as if immediately present; they are not strangers by their distance: if others have seen Him more immediately I will not dispute it. But if they have seen the Lord Jesus as immediately as if here on earth, yet Capernaum saw Him so; nay, some of them were disciples for a time, and followed Him, John vi. And yet the Lord was hid from their eyes. Nay, all the world shall see Him in His glory, which shall amaze them; and yet this is far short of having the saving knowledge of Him, which the Lord doth communicate to the elect. So that though you see the Lord so really, as that you become familiar with Him, yet, Luke xiii. 26: ' Lord, have we not eat and drank,' &c.—and so perish." *Shepard's Parable of the Ten Virgins*, p. 311.

† " Satan is transformed into an angel of light: and hence we have heard that some have heard voices; some have seen the very blood of Christ dropping on them, and His wounds in His side: some have seen a great light shining in the chamber; some have been wonderfully affected with their dreams; some in great distress have had inward witness, ' Thy sins are forgiven '; and hence such liberty and joy that they are ready to leap up and down the chamber. O adulterous generation! this is natural and usual with men, they would fain see Jesus, and have Him present to give them peace; and hence Papists have His images. Woe to them that have no other manifested Christ, but such an one." *Shepard's Parable of the Ten Virgins*, p. 312.

that are received; let them be received in what way they will, they are still but external ideas, or ideas of outward appearances, and so are not spiritual. Yea, if men should actually receive such external ideas by the immediate power of the Most High God upon their minds, they would not be spiritual, they would be no more than a common work of the Spirit of God; as is evident in fact in the instance of Balaam, who had impressed on his mind by God Himself a clear and lively outward representation or idea of Jesus Christ, as " the Star rising out of Jacob, when he heard the words of God, and knew the knowledge of the Most High, and saw the vision of the Almighty, falling into a trance," Numb. xxiv. 16, 17, but yet had no manner of spiritual discovery of Christ; that Day Star never spiritually rose in his heart, he being but a natural man.

And as these external ideas have nothing divine or spiritual in their nature, and nothing but what natural men, without any new principles, are capable of; so there is nothing in their nature which requires that peculiar, inimitable and unparalleled exercise of the glorious power of God, in order to their production, which it has been shown there is in the production of true grace. There appears to be nothing in their nature above the power of the devil. It is certainly not above the power of Satan to suggest thoughts to men; because otherwise he could not tempt them to sin. And if he can suggest any thoughts or ideas at all, doubtless imaginary ones, or ideas of things external, are not above his power;* for the external ideas men have are the lowest sort of ideas. These ideas may be raised only by impressions made on the body, by moving the animal spirits, and impressing the brain. Abundant experience does certainly show that alterations in the body will excite imaginary or external ideas in the mind; as often in the case of a high fever, melancholy, &c. These external ideas are as much below the more intellectual exercises of the soul as the body is a less noble part of man than the soul.

And there is not only nothing in the nature of external ideas or imaginations of outward appearances, from whence we can infer that they are above the power of the devil; but it is certain

* " Consider how difficult, yea and impossible it is to determine that such a voice, vision, or revelation is of God, and that Satan cannot feign or counterfeit it: seeing He hath left no certain marks by which we may distinguish one spirit from another." Flavel's Causes and Cures of Mental Terrors. Works, Vol. III, p. 284.

also that the devil can excite, and often hath excited, such ideas. They were external ideas which he excited in the dreams and visions of the false prophets of old, who were under the influence of lying spirits, that we often read of in Scripture, as Deut. xiii. 1, 1 Kings xxii. 22, Ezek. xiii. 7. And they were external ideas that he often excited in the minds of the heathen priests, magicians and sorcerers, in their visions and ecstasies, and they were external ideas that he excited in the mind of the Man Christ Jesus, when he showed Him all the kingdoms of the world, with the glory of them, when those kingdoms were not really in sight.

And if Satan, or any created being, has power to impress the mind with outward representations, then no particular sort of outward representations can be any evidence of a divine power. Almighty power is no more requisite to represent the shape of man to the imagination than the shape of anything else: there is no higher kind of power necessary to form in the brain one bodily shape or colour than another. It needs a no more glorious power to represent the form of the body of a man than the form of a chip or block; though it be of a very beautiful human body, with a sweet smile in his countenance, or arms open, or blood running from the hands, feet and side. That sort of power which can represent blackness or darkness to the imagination can also represent white and shining brightness: the power and skill which can well and exactly paint a straw or a stick of wood on a piece of paper or canvas; the same in kind, only perhaps further improved, will be sufficient to paint the body of a man with great beauty and in royal majesty, or a magnificent city, paved with gold, full of brightness, and a glorious throne. So it is no more than the same sort of power that is requisite to paint one as the other of these on the brain. The same sort of power that can put ink upon paper can put on leaf-gold. So that it is evident to a demonstration, if we suppose it to be in the devil's power to make any sort of external representation at all on the fancy (as without doubt it is, and never any one questioned it who believed there was a devil, that had any agency with mankind): I say, if so, it is demonstrably evident, that a created power may extend to all kinds of external appearances and ideas in the mind. From hence it again clearly appears that no such things have anything in them that is spiritual, supernatural, and divine, in the sense in which it has been proved that all truly gracious experiences have. And though external ideas, through man's make and frame, do ordinarily in some degree attend spiritual experiences, yet these ideas are not part of their spiritual experience, any more than the motion of the blood, and beating of the pulse, that attend experiences, are a part of spiritual experience. And though undoubtedly, through men's infirmity in the present state, and especially through the weak constitution of some persons, gracious affections which are very strong do excite lively ideas in the imagination; yet it is also undoubted, that when persons' affections are founded on imaginations, which is often the case, those affections are merely natural and common, because they are built on a foundation that is not spiritual, and so are entirely different from gracious affections, which, as has been proved, do evermore arise from those operations that are spiritual and divine.

These imaginations do oftentimes raise the carnal affections of men to an exceeding great height:* and no wonder, when the

* There is a remarkable passage of Mr. John Smith (1618-52), in his discourse on the shortness of a Pharisaic righteousness, describing that sort of religion which is built on such a foundation as I am here speaking of. I cannot forbear transcribing the whole of it. Speaking of a sort of Christians whose life is nothing but a strong energy of fancy, he says: " Lest their religion might too grossly discover itself to be nothing else but a piece of art, there may be sometimes such extraordinary motions stirred up within them, which may prevent all their own thoughts, that they may seem to be a true operation of the divine life; when yet all this is nothing else but the energy of their own self-love, touched with some fleshly apprehensions of divine things, and excited by them. There are such things in our Christian religion, which, when a carnal, unhallowed mind takes the chair and gets the expounding of them, may seem very delicious to the fleshly appetites of men; some doctrines and notions of free grace and justification, the magnificent title of God and heirs of heaven, ever flowing streams of joy and pleasure that blessed souls shall swim in to all eternity, a glorious paradise in the world to come always springing up with well-scented and fragrant beauties, a new Jerusalem paved with gold and be-spangled with stars, comprehending in its vast circuit such numberless varieties that a busy curiosity may spend itself about to all eternity. I doubt not but that sometimes the most fleshly and earthly men, that fly in their ambition to the pomp of this world, may be so ravished with the conceits of such things as these, that they may seem to be made partakers of the powers of the world to come. I doubt not but that they might be much exalted with them, as the souls of crazed or distracted persons seem to be sometimes, when their fancies play with those quick and nimble spirits which a distempered frame of body, and unnatural heat in their heads, beget within them. Thus may these blazing comets rise up above the moon, and climb higher than the sun; which yet, because they have no solid consistence of their own, and are of a base and

subjects of them have an ignorant, but undoubting persuasion that they are divine manifestations, which the great Jehovah immediately makes to their souls, therein giving them testimonies in an extraordinary manner of His high and peculiar favour.

Again, it is evident from what has been observed and proved of the manner in which gracious operations and effects in the heart are spiritual, supernatural and divine, that the immediate suggesting of the words of Scripture to the mind has nothing in it which is spiritual.

I have had occasion to say something of this already; and what has been said may be sufficient to evince it; but if the reader

---

earthly alloy, will soon vanish and fall down again, being only borne up by an external force. They may seem to themselves to have attained higher than those noble Christians that are gently moved by the natural force of true goodness: they seem to be *pleniores Deo* (*i.e.*, more full of God) than those that are really informed and actuated by the divine Spirit and do move on steadily and constantly in the way towards heaven. As the seed that was sown in stony ground grew up, and lengthened out its blade faster, than that which was sown in the good and fruitful soil. And as the motions of our sense, and fancy, and passions, while our souls are in this mortal condition, sunk down deeply into the body, are many times more vigorous, and make stronger impressions upon us than those of the higher powers of the soul, which are more subtle, and remote from these mixed animal perceptions: that devotion which is there seated, may seem to have more energy and life in it, than that which gently, and with a more delicate kind of touch spreads itself upon the understanding, and from thence mildly disperses itself through our wills and affections. But however the former may be more boisterous for a time, yet this is of a more consistent and thriving nature. For that proceeding indeed from nothing but a sensual and fleshly apprehension of God and true happiness, is but of a flitting and fading nature; and as the sensible powers and faculties grow more languid, or the sun of divine light shines more brightly upon us, these earthly devotions, like our culinary fires, will abate their heat and fervour. But a true celestial warmth will never be extinguished, because it is of an immortal nature; and being once seated vitally in the souls of men, it will regulate and order all the motions of it in a due manner, as the natural heat, radiated in the hearts of living creatures, hath the dominion and economy of the whole body under it. True religion is no piece of artifice; It is no boiling up of our imaginative powers, nor the glowing heats of passion; though these are too often mistaken for it, when in our jugglings in religion we cast a mist before our own eyes: but it is a new nature, informing the souls of men; it is a Godlike frame of spirit, discovering itself most of all in serene and clear minds, in deep humility, meekness, self-denial, universal love to God and all true goodness, without partiality, and without hypocrisy, whereby we are taught to know God, and knowing Him to love Him, and conform ourselves as much as may be to all that perfection which shines in Him. (*Select Discourses*, 1660).

bears in mind what has been said concerning the nature of spiritual influences and effects, it will be more abundantly manifest
that this is no spiritual effect. For I suppose there is no person
of common understanding who will say or imagine that the bringing of any words (let them be what words they will) to the mind
is an effect of that nature which it is impossible the mind of a
natural man, while he remains in a state of nature, should be the
subject of, or anything like it; or that it requires any new divine
sense in the soul; or that the bringing sounds or letters to the
mind is an effect of so high, holy, and excellent a nature, that
it is impossible any created power should be the cause of it.

As the suggesting of words of Scripture to the mind is only the
exciting in the mind ideas of certain sounds or letters, so it is
only one way of exciting ideas in the imagination; for sounds
and letters are external things, that are the objects of the external
senses of seeing and hearing. Ideas of certain marks upon paper,
such as any of the twenty-four letters, in what ever order, or any
sounds of the voice, are as much external ideas as of any other
shapes or sounds whatsoever; and therefore, by what has been
already said concerning these external ideas, it is evident they
are nothing spiritual; and if at any time the Spirit of God suggests these letters or sounds to the mind, this is a common and
not any special or gracious influence of that Spirit. And therefore it follows from what has been already proved, that those
affections which have this effect for their foundation are no spiritual or gracious affections.

But let it be observed what it is that I say, viz., when this effect—
even the immediate and extraordinary manner of words of Scripture's coming to the mind—is that which excites the affections,
and is properly the foundation of them, then these affections are
not spiritual. It may be so that persons may have gracious affections going with Scriptures which come to their minds, and the
Spirit of God may make use of those Scriptures to excite them;
when it is some spiritual sense, taste or relish they have of the
divine and excellent things contained in those Scriptures that is
the thing which excites their affections, and not the extraordinary
and sudden manner of words being brought to their minds. They
are affected with the instruction they receive from the words, and
the view of the glorious things of God or Christ, and things appertaining to them, that they contain and teach; and not because

the words came suddenly, as though some person had spoken
them to them, thence concluding that God did as it were immediately speak to them. Persons oftentimes are exceedingly affected
on this foundation; the words of some great and high promises
of Scripture came suddenly to their minds, and they look upon
the words as directed immediately by God to them, as though
the words that moment proceeded out of the mouth of God as
spoken to them: so that they take it as a voice from God, immediately revealing to them their happy circumstances, and promising such and such great things to them: and this it is that affects
and elevates them. There is no new spiritual understanding of
the divine things contained in the Scripture, or new spiritual
sense of the glorious things taught in that part of the Bible going
before their affection, and being the foundation of it. All the
new understanding they have, or think they have, to be the
foundation of their affection, is this, that the words are spoken
to them, because they come so suddenly and extraordinarily.
And so this affection is built wholly on the sand, because it is
built on a conclusion for which they have no foundation. For,
as has been shown, the sudden coming of the words to their
minds is no evidence that the bringing them to their minds in
that manner was from God. And if it was true that God brought
the words to their minds, and they certainly knew it, that would
not be spiritual knowledge; it may exist without any spiritual
sense: Balaam might know that the words which God suggested
to him were indeed suggested to him by God, and yet have no
spiritual knowledge. So that these affections which are built on
the notion that texts of Scripture are sent immediately from God,
are built on no spiritual foundation, and are vain and delusive.
Persons who have their affections thus raised, if they should be
asked whether they have any new sense of the excellency of
things contained in those Scriptures, would probably say, *Yes,*
without hesitation: but it is true no otherwise than thus, that
when they have taken up that notion, that the words are spoken
immediately to them, that makes them seem sweet to them, and
they own the things which these Scriptures say to them for excellent things and wonderful things. As for instance, supposing these
were the words which were suddenly brought to their minds,
*Fear not, it is your Father's good pleasure to give you the king-
dom.* Having confidently taken up a notion that the words were

immediately spoken from heaven to them, as an immediate revelation that God was their Father and had given the kingdom to
them, they are greatly affected by it, and the words seem sweet
to them. "Oh," they say, "they are excellent things that are
contained in those words!" But the reason why the promise
seems excellent to them is only because they think it is made to
them immediately; all the sense they have of any glory in them is
only from self-love, and from their own imagined interest in the
words. Not that they had any view or sense of the holy and glorious nature of the kingdom of heaven and the spiritual glory of
that God who gives it, and of His excellent grace to sinful men, in
offering and giving them this kingdom of His own good pleasure,
preceding their imagined interest in these things, and their being
affected by them. On the contrary, they first imagine they are
interested in these things, and then are highly affected with that
consideration, and then can own these things to be excellent. So
that the sudden and extraordinary way of the Scripture's coming
to their mind is plainly the first foundation of the whole; which
is a clear evidence of the wretched delusion they are under.

The first comfort of many persons, and what they call their
conversion, is after this manner: after awakening and terrors,
some comfortable sweet promise comes suddenly and wonderfully
to their minds; and the manner of its coming makes them conclude it comes from God to them; and this is the very thing that
is all the foundation of their faith, and hope, and comfort: from
hence they take their first encouragement to trust in God and in
Christ, because they think that God, by some Scripture so
brought, has now already revealed to them that He loves them,
and has already promised them eternal life. But this is very absurd, for every one with common knowledge of the principles of
religion knows that it is God's manner to reveal His love to men,
and their interest in the promises, after they have believed, and
not before, because they must first believe before they have any
interest in the promises to be revealed. The Spirit of God is a
Spirit of truth and not of lies: He does not bring Scriptures to
men's minds, to reveal to them that they have an interest in God's
favour and promises when they have none, having not yet believed: which would be the case, if God's bringing texts of Scripture to men's minds, to reveal to them that their sins were forgiven, or that it was God's pleasure to give them the kingdom,

or anything of that nature, went before, and was the foundation of their first faith. No promise of the covenant of grace belongs to any man, until he has first believed in Christ; for it is by faith alone that we become interested in Christ and the promises of the new covenant made in Him : and therefore whatever spirit applies the promises of that covenant to a person who has not first believed, as being already his, must be a lying spirit, and that faith which is first built on such an application of promises is built upon a lie. God's manner is not to bring comfortable texts of Scripture to give men assurance of his love and of future happiness, before they have had a faith of dependence.* And if the Scripture which comes to a person's mind be not so properly a promise as an invitation; yet if he makes the sudden or

* Mr. Stoddard, in his *Guide to Christ,* says, that " sometimes, men, after they have been in trouble a while, have some promises come to them with a great deal of refreshing; and they hope God has accepted them " : and says that, " In this case, the minister may tell them that God never gives a faith of assurance before he gives a faith of dependence; for he never manifests His love until men are in a state of favour and reconciliation, which is by faith of dependence. When men have comfortable Scriptures come to them they are apt to take them as tokens of God's love : but men must be brought into Christ, by accepting the offer of the gospel, before they are fit for such manifestations. God's method is, first to make the soul accept of the offers of grace, and then to manifest his good estate unto him." And speaking of those " that seem to be brought to lie at God's foot, and give an account of their closing with Christ, and that God has revealed Christ to them, and drawn their hearts to Him, and they do accept of Christ," he says : " In this case, it is best to examine whether by that light that was given him, he saw Christ and salvation offered to him, or whether he saw that God loved him, or pardoned him : for the offer of grace, and our acceptance, goes before pardon, and therefore must more before the knowledge of it."
Mr. Shepard, in his *Parable of the Ten Virgins,* p. 391, says that " Grace and the love of Christ (the fairest colours under the sun) may be pretended; but if you shall receive, under this appearance, that God witnesseth His love, first by an absolute promise, take heed there; for under this appearance you may as well bring in immediate revelations, and from thence come to forsake the Scriptures."
He also says (p. 141) " Is Christ yours? Yes, I see it. How? By any word or promise? No—Then this is delusion." He adds, " The testimony of the Spirit does not make a man more a Christian, but only evidenceth it; as it is the nature of a witness not to make a thing to be true, but to clear and evidence it." Speaking of them that say they have the witness of the Spirit that makes a difference between them and hypocrites, he says, " the witness of the Spirit makes not the first difference : for first a man is a believer and in Christ, and justified, called and sanctified, before the Spirit does witness it; else the Spirit should witness to an untruth and lie." (P. 224.)

unusual manner of the invitation's coming to his mind the ground on which he believes that he is invited, it is not true faith; because it is built on that which is not the true ground of faith. True faith is built on no precarious foundation: but a determination that the words of such a particular text were, by the immediate power of God, suggested to the mind, at such a time, as though then spoken and directed by God to him because the words came after such a manner, is wholly an uncertain and precarious determination, as has been now shown, and therefore is a false and sandy foundation for faith; and accordingly that faith which is built upon it is false. The only certain foundation which any person has to believe that he is invited to partake of the blessings of the gospel, is, that the Word of God declares that persons so qualified as he is, are invited, and that God, who declares it, is true, and cannot lie. If a sinner be once convinced of the veracity of God, and that the Scriptures are His word, he will need no more to convince and satisfy him that he is invited; for the Scriptures are full of invitations to sinners, to the chief of sinners, to come and partake of the benefits of the gospel; he will not want any new speaking of God to him; what he hath spoken already will be enough with him.

As the first comfort of many persons, and their affections at the time of their supposed conversion, are built on such grounds as these which have been mentioned, so are their joys and hopes and other affections from time to time afterwards. Particular words of Scripture, usually sweet declarations and promises, are suggested to them, which by reason of the manner of their coming they think are immediately sent from God to them. This they look upon as their warrant to take them. They actually make it the main ground of their appropriating them to themselves, and of the comfort they take in them, and the confidence they receive from them. Thus they imagine a kind of conversation is carried on between God and them; and that God from time to time, as it were, immediately speaks to them, satisfies their doubts, testifies his love to them, promises them supports and supplies and His blessing in such and such cases, and reveals to them clearly their interest in eternal blessings. And thus they are often elevated, and have a course of a sudden and tumultuous kind of joys, mingled with a strong confidence and high opinion of themselves; when indeed the main ground of these joys and this confidence is not anything contained in or taught by these Scriptures, as they lie in the Bible, but the manner of their coming to them; which is a certain evidence of their delusion. There is no particular promise in the Word of God that is the saint's, or is any otherwise made to him, or spoken to him, than all the promises of the covenant of grace are his, and are made to him and spoken to him;* though it be true that some of these promises may be more peculiarly adapted to his case than others, and God by His Spirit may enable him better to understand some than others, and to have a greater sense of the preciousness, and glory, and suitableness of the blessings contained in them.

But here some may be ready to say, What! is there no such thing as any particular spiritual application of the promises of Scripture by the Spirit of God? I answer, there is doubtless such a thing as a spiritual and saving application of the invitations and promises of Scripture to the souls of men; but it is also certain that the nature of it is wholly misunderstood by many persons, to the great ensnaring of their own souls, and the giving Satan a vast advantage against them, and against the interest of religion, and the church of God. The spiritual application of a Scripture promise does not consist in its being immediately suggested to the thoughts by some extrinsic agent, and being borne into the mind with this strong apprehension that it is particularly spoken and directed to them at that time; there is nothing of the evidence of the hand of God in this effect, as events have proved in many notorious instances. It is a mean notion of a spiritual application of Scripture; there is nothing in the nature of it at all beyond the power of the devil, if he be not restrained by God; for there is nothing in the nature of the effect that is spiritual or that implies any vital communication of God. A

---

* Mr. Shepard, in his *Sound Believer,* p. 217, says, "Embrace in thy bosom, not only some few promises, but all." And then he asks the question, "When may a Christian take a promise without presumption, as spoken to him?" He answers, "The rule is very sweet, but certain; when he takes all the Scripture, and embraces it as spoken unto him, he may then take any particular promise boldly. My meaning is, when a Christian takes hold, and wrestles with God for the accomplishment of all the promises of the New Testament, when he sets all the commands before him, as a compass and guide to walk after, when he applies all the threatenings to drive him nearer unto Christ, the end of them, then he does well. This no hypocrite can do; this the saints shall do; and by this they may know when the Lord speaks in particular unto them."

truly spiritual application of the Word of God is of a vastly higher nature; as much above the devil's power, as it is for him to apply the Word of God to a dead corpse, so as to raise it to life; or to a stone, to turn it into an angel. A spiritual application of the Word of God consists in applying it to the heart, in spiritually enlightening, sanctifying influences. A spiritual application of an invitation or offer of the gospel consists in giving the soul a spiritual sense or relish of the holy and divine blessings offered, and the sweet and wonderful grace of the Offerer, in making so gracious an offer, and of His holy excellency and faithfulness to fulfil what He offers, and His glorious sufficiency for it; so leading and drawing forth the heart to embrace the offer, and thus giving the man evidence of his title to the thing offered. And so a spiritual application of the promises of Scripture, for the comfort of the saints, consists in enlightening their minds to see the holy excellency and sweetness of the blessings promised, and also the holy excellency of the Promiser, and His faithfulness and sufficiency; thus drawing forth their hearts to embrace the Promiser, and the thing promised; and by this means giving the sensible actings of grace, enabling them to see their grace and their title to the promise. An application not consisting in this divine sense and enlightening of the mind, but consisting only in the word's being borne into the thoughts, as if immediately then spoken, so making persons believe on no other foundation that the promise is theirs, is a blind application, and belongs to the spirit of darkness and not of light.

When persons have their affections raised after this manner, those affections are really not raised by the Word of God; the Scripture is not the foundation of them. It is not anything contained in those Scriptures which come to their minds that raises their affections but the strange manner of the word's being suggested to their minds, and a proposition from thence taken up by them, which indeed is not contained in the Scripture, nor any other, as that his sins are forgiven him, or that it is the Father's good pleasure to give him in particular the kingdom, or the like. There are propositions to be found in the Bible, declaring that persons of such and such qualifications are forgiven and beloved of God: but there are no propositions to be found in the Bible, declaring that such and such particular persons, independent of any previous knowledge of any qualifications, are forgiven and beloved of God: and therefore, when any person is comforted, and affected by any such proposition, it is by another word, a word newly coined, and not any word of God contained in the Bible.* And thus many persons are vainly affected and deluded.

Again, it plainly appears from what has been demonstrated that no revelation of secret facts by immediate suggestion is anything spiritual and divine, in that sense wherein gracious effects and operations are so.

By secret facts I mean things that have been done, or are come to pass, or shall hereafter come to pass, which are secret in that sense that they do not appear to the senses, nor are known by any argumentation, nor any other way, but only by immediate suggestion of the ideas to the mind. Thus for instance, if it should be revealed to me that next year this land would be invaded by a fleet from France, or that such and such persons would then be converted, or that I myself should then be converted; not by enabling me to argue out these events from anything which now appears in providence, but immediately suggesting and bearing in upon my mind, in an extraordinary manner, the apprehension or ideas of these facts, with a strong suggestion or impression on my mind, that I had no hand in myself, that these things would come to pass: or if it should be revealed to me that this day there is a battle fought between the armies of such and such powers in Europe, or that such a prince in Europe was this day converted, or is now in a converted state, having been converted formerly, or that one of my neighbours is converted, or that I myself am converted; not by having any other evidence of any of these facts, from whence I argue them, but an immediate extraordinary suggestion or excitation of these ideas, and a strong impression of them upon my mind: this is a revelation of secret facts by immediate suggestion, as much as if the facts were future; for the facts being past, present, or future, alters not the case, as long as they are secret and hidden from my senses and reason, and not spoken of in Scripture, nor known by me any other way than by immediate suggestion. If I have it revealed to me that a revolution is come to pass this day

* " If God should tell a saint that he has grace, he might know it by believing the Word of God: but it is not in this way that godly men do know that they have grace: it is not revealed in the Word, and the Spirit of God doth not testify it to particular persons." *Stoddard's Nature of Saving Conversion.*

in the Ottoman Empire, it is the very same sort of revelation as if it were revealed to me that such a revolution would come to pass there this day come twelvemonth; because, though one is present and the other future, yet both are equally hidden from me any other way than by immediate revelation. When Samuel told Saul that the asses which he went to seek were found, and that his father had left caring for the asses and sorrowed for him, this was by the same kind of revelation as that by which he told Saul that in the plain of Tabor there should meet him three men going up to God to Bethel (1 Sam. x. 2, 3), though one of these things was future and the other was not. When Elisha told the king of Israel the words that the king of Syria spake in his bed-chamber, it was by the same kind of revelation as that by which he foretold many things to come.

It is evident that this revelation of secret facts by immediate suggestions has nothing of the nature of a spiritual and divine operation, in the sense forementioned. There is nothing at all in the nature of the perceptions or ideas themselves, which are excited in the mind, that is divinely excellent, and so far above all the ideas of natural men; though the manner of exciting the ideas be extraordinary. In those things which are spiritual, as has been shown, not only the manner of producing the effect but the effect wrought is divine, and so vastly above all that can be in an unsanctified mind. Now simply the having an idea of facts, setting aside the manner of producing those ideas, is nothing beyond what the minds of wicked men are susceptible of, without any goodness in them; and they all either have or will have the knowledge of the truth of the greatest and most important facts that have been, are, or shall be.

And as to the extraordinary manner of producing the ideas or perception of facts, even by immediate suggestion, there is nothing in it but what the minds of natural men, while they are yet natural men, are capable of, as is manifest in Balaam and others spoken of in the Scripture. And therefore it appears that there is nothing appertaining to this immediate suggestion of secret facts that is spiritual, in the sense in which it has been proved that gracious operations are so. If there be nothing in the ideas themselves which is holy and divine, and so nothing but what may be in a mind not sanctified, then God can put them into the mind by immediate power without sanctifying it. As there is nothing in the idea of a rainbow that is of a holy and divine nature and nothing hinders but that an unsanctified mind may receive that idea, so God, if He pleases, and when He pleases, immediately and in an extraordinary manner may excite that idea in an unsanctified mind. So also, as there is nothing in the idea or knowledge that such and such particular persons are forgiven and accepted of God, and entitled to heaven, but what unsanctified minds may have and will have concerning many at the day of judgment, so God can, if He pleases, extraordinarily and immediately suggest this to, and impress it upon, an unsanctified mind now: there is no principle wanting in an unsanctified mind to make it capable of such a suggestion or impression, nor is there anything in it necessarily to exclude or prevent such a suggestion.

And if these suggestions of secret facts be attended with texts of Scripture, immediately and extraordinarily brought to mind, about other facts that seem in some respects similar, that does not make the operation to be of a spiritual and divine nature. For that suggestion of words of Scripture is no more divine than the suggestion of the facts themselves, as has been just now demonstrated: and two effects together, which are neither of them spiritual, cannot make up one complex effect that is spiritual.

Hence it follows, from what has been already shown, and often repeated, that those affections which are properly founded on such immediate suggestions, or supposed suggestions, of secret facts, are not gracious affections. Not but that it is possible that such suggestions may be the occasion or accidental cause of gracious affections; for so may a mistake and delusion; but they are never properly the foundation of gracious affections: for gracious affections, as has been shown, are all the effects of an influence and operation which is spiritual, supernatural, and divine. But there are many affections, and high affections, which some have, that have such suggestions or revelations for their very foundation: they look upon these as spiritual discoveries, which is a gross delusion, and this delusion is truly the spring whence their affections flow.

Here it may be proper to observe, that it is exceedingly manifest from what has been said, that what many persons call the witness of the Spirit that they are the children of God, has nothing in it spiritual and divine; and consequently that the affections built upon it are vain and delusive. That which many call the witness of the Spirit is no other than an immediate suggestion and impression of the fact, otherwise secret, that they are converted, or made the children of God, so that their sins are pardoned and God has given them a title to heaven. This kind of knowledge, viz., knowing that a certain person is converted, and delivered from hell, and entitled to heaven, is no divine sort of knowledge in itself. This sort of fact is not that which requires any higher or more divine kind of suggestion, in order to impress it on the mind, than any other fact which Balaam had impressed on his mind. It requires no higher sort of idea or sensation, for a man to have the apprehension of his own conversion impressed upon him, than to have the apprehension of his neighbour's conversion, in like manner impressed : but God, if He pleased, might impress the knowledge of this fact, that He had forgiven his neighbour's sins and given him a title to heaven, as well as any other fact, without any communication of His holiness: the excellency and importance of the fact, does not at all hinder a natural man's mind being susceptible of an immediate suggestion and impression of it. Balaam had as excellent and important and glorious facts as this, immediately impressed on his mind, without any gracious influence; as particularly, the coming of Christ, and His setting up His glorious kingdom, and the blessedness of the spiritual Israel in His peculiar favour, and their happiness living and dying. Yea, Abimelech, king of the Philistines, had God's special favour to a particular person, even Abraham, revealed to him, Gen. xx. 6, 7. So it seems that He revealed to Laban His special favour to Jacob; see Gen. xxxi. 24, and Psal. cv. 15. And if a truly good man should have an immediate revelation or suggestion from God, after the like manner, concerning His favour to his neighbour, or himself, it would be no higher kind of influence; it would be no more than a common sort of influence of God's Spirit; as the gift of prophecy, and all revelation by immediate suggestion is; see 1 Cor. xiii. 2. And though it be true that it is not possible that a natural man should have that individual suggestion from the Spirit of God that he is converted, because it is not true, yet that does not arise from the nature of the influence, or because that kind of influence which suggests such excellent facts is too high for him to be the subject of. The influence which immediately suggests this fact, when it is true, is of no different kind from that which immediately suggests other true facts: and so the kind and nature of the influence is not above what is common to natural men.

But this is a mean ignoble notion of the witness of the Spirit of God given to His dear children, to suppose that there is nothing in the kind and nature of that influence of the Spirit of God, in imparting this high and glorious benefit, but what is common to natural men, altogether unsanctified and the children of hell; and that therefore the benefit or gift itself has nothing of the holy nature of the Spirit of God in it, nothing of a vital communication of that Spirit. This notion greatly debases that high and most exalted kind of influence and operation of the Spirit, which there is in the true witness of the Spirit.* That which is called the witness of the Spirit, Rom. viii., is elsewhere in the New Testament called the seal of the Spirit, 2 Cor. i. 22, Eph. i. 13, and iv. 30, alluding to the seal of princes, annexed to the instrument by which they advanced any of their subjects to some high honour and dignity or peculiar privilege in the kingdom, as a token of their special favour. Which is an evidence that the influence of the Spirit of the Prince of princes, in sealing His favourites, is far from being of a common kind; and that there is no effect of God's Spirit whatsoever which is in its nature more divine; nothing more holy, peculiar, inimitable, and distinguishing of divinity. Nothing is more royal than the royal seal; noth-

---

* The late venerable Stoddard, in his younger time, falling in with the opinion of some others, received this notion of the witness of the Spirit, by way of immediate suggestion; but in the latter part of his life, when he had more thoroughly weighed things, and had more experience, he entirely rejected it; as appears by his treatise of the *Nature of Saving Conversion*: "The Spirit of God doth not testify to particular persons, that they are godly. Some think that the Spirit of God doth testify to some, and they ground it on Rom. viii. 16, 'The Spirit itself beareth witness with our spirit, that we are the children of God.' They think the Spirit reveals it by giving an inward testimony to it; and some godly men think they have had experience of it: but they may easily mistake. When the Spirit of God doth eminently stir up the spirit of faith, and sheds abroad the love of God in the heart, it is easy to mistake it for a testimony. And that is not the meaning of Paul's words. The Spirit reveals things to us by opening our eyes to see what is revealed in the Word; but the Spirit doth not reveal new truths, not revealed in the Word. The Spirit discovers the grace of God in Christ, and thereby draws forth special actings of faith and love, which are evidential; but it doth not work in way of testimony. If God do but help us to receive the revelations in the Word, we shall have comfort enough without new revelations."

ing more sacred, that belongs to a prince, and more peculiarly denoting what belongs to him; it being the very end and design of it to be the most peculiar stamp and confirmation of the royal authority. It is the great note of distinction, whereby that which proceeds from the king, or belongs to him, may be known from every thing else. And therefore undoubtedly the seal of the great King of heaven and earth enstamped on the heart is something high and holy in its own nature, some excellent communication from the infinite fountain of divine beauty and glory; and not merely a making known a secret fact by revelation or suggestion; which is a sort of influence of the Spirit of God that the children of the devil have often been the subjects of. The seal of the Spirit is an effect of the Spirit of God on the heart, which natural men, while such, are so far from a capacity of being the subjects of, that they can have no manner of notion or idea of it. Rev. ii. 17: "To him that overcometh will I give to eat of the hidden manna, and I will give him a white stone, and in the stone a new name written, which no man knoweth saving he that receiveth it." There is all reason to suppose that what is here spoken of is the same mark, evidence, or blessed token of special favour, which is elsewhere called the seal of the Spirit.

What has misled many in their notion of that influence of the Spirit of God we are speaking of, is the word *witness,* its being called the witness of the Spirit. Hence they have taken it, not to be any effect or work of the Spirit upon the heart, giving evidence from whence men may argue that they are the children of God, but an inward immediate suggestion, as though God inwardly spoke to the man, and testified to him, and told him that he was His child, by a kind of a secret voice or impression: not observing the manner in which the word witness or testimony is often used in the New Testament, where such terms often signify, not only a mere declaring and asserting a thing to be true, but holding forth evidence from whence a thing may be argued and proved to be true. Thus Heb. ii. 4, God is said to " bear witness, with signs and wonders, and divers miracles, and gifts of the Holy Ghost." Now these miracles here spoken of are called God's witness, not because they are of the nature of assertions, but evidences and proofs. So Acts xiv. 3: "Long time therefore abode they speaking boldly in the Lord, which gave testimony unto the word of his grace, and granted signs and wonders to be done by their hands." And John v. 36: "But I have greater witness than that of John: for the works which the Father hath given me to finish, the same works that I do, bear witness of me, that the Father hath sent me." Again, chap. x. 25: "The works that I do in my Father's name, they bear witness of me." So the water and the blood are said to bear witness, 1 John v. 8, not that they spoke or asserted anything, but they were proofs and evidences. So God's works of providence, in rain and fruitful seasons, are spoken of as witnesses of God's being and goodness, *i.e.*, they are evidences of these things. And when the Scripture speaks of the seal of the Spirit, it is an expression which properly denotes, not an immediate voice or suggestion, but some work of effect of the Spirit that is left as a divine mark upon the soul, to be an evidence by which God's children might be known. The seals of princes were the distinguishing marks of princes: and thus God's seal is spoken of as God's mark, Rev. vii. 3: "Hurt not the earth, neither the sea, nor the trees, till we have sealed the servants of our God in their foreheads;" together with Ezek. ix. 4, "Set a mark upon the foreheads of the men that sigh and that cry, for all the abominations that be done in the midst thereof." When God sets his seal on a man's heart by His Spirit, there is some holy stamp, some image impressed and left upon the heart by the Spirit, as by the seal upon the wax. And this holy stamp, or impressed image, exhibiting clear evidence to the conscience that the subject of it is a child of God, is the very thing which in Scripture is called the seal of the Spirit, and the witness or evidence of the Spirit. And this image enstamped by the Spirit on God's children's hearts is His own image. That is the evidence by which they are known to be God's children, that they have the image of their Father stamped upon their hearts by the Spirit of adoption. Seals anciently had engraven on them two things, viz., the image and the name of the person whose seal it was. Therefore when Christ says to his spouse, Cant. viii. 6, "Set me as a seal upon thine heart, as a seal upon thine arm," it is as much as to say, let My name and image remain impressed there. The seals of princes were wont to bear their image; so that what they set their seal and royal mark upon had their image left on it. It was the manner of princes of old to have their image engraven on their jewels and precious stones. The image of Augustus, engraven on a precious stone, was used as the seal of the Roman emperors, in Christ's and the apostles' times. And the saints are the jewels of Jesus Christ, the great Potentate, who has the possession of the empire of the universe; and these jewels have his image enstamped upon them by His royal signet, which is the Holy Spirit. And this is undoubtedly what the Scripture means by the seal of the Spirit; especially when it is stamped in so fair and clear a manner as to be plain to the eye of conscience, which is what the Scripture calls our spirit. This is truly an effect that is spiritual, supernatural, and divine. This is in itself of a holy nature, being a communication of the divine nature and beauty. That kind of influence of the Spirit which gives and leaves this stamp upon the heart is such that no natural man can be the subject of anything of the like nature with it. This is the highest sort of witness of the Spirit which it is possible the soul should be the subject of: if there were any such thing as a witness of the Spirit by immediate suggestion or revelation, this would be vastly more noble and excellent, and as much above it as the heaven is above the earth. This the devil cannot imitate.

Another thing which is a full proof that the seal of the Spirit is no revelation of any fact by immediate suggestion, but is grace itself in the soul, is that the seal of the Spirit is called in the Scripture, the *earnest of the Spirit*. It is very plain that the seal of the Spirit is the same thing with the earnest of the Spirit, by 2 Cor. i. 22 : " Who hath also sealed us, and given the earnest of the Spirit in our hearts;" and Eph. i. 13, 14, "In whom, after that ye believed, ye were sealed with that Holy Spirit of promise, which is the earnest of our inheritance, until the redemption of the purchased possession, unto the praise of his glory." Now the earnest is part of the money agreed for, given in hand, as a token of the whole to be paid in due time; a part of the promised inheritance granted now, in token of full possession of the whole hereafter. But surely that kind of communication of the Spirit of God, which is of the nature of eternal glory, is the highest and most excellent kind of communication, something that is in its own nature spiritual, holy and divine, and far from anything that is common: and therefore high above anything of the nature of inspiration, or revelation of hidden facts by suggestion of the Spirit of God, which many natural men have had. What is the earnest and beginning of glory but grace itself, especially in the more lively and clear exercises of it? It is not prophecy, nor tongues, nor knowledge, but that more excellent divine thing, "charity that never faileth," which is a prelibation and beginning of the light, sweetness, and blessedness of heaven, that world of love or charity. Grace is the seed of glory, the dawning of glory in the heart, and therefore grace is the earnest of the future inheritance. What is it that is the beginning or earnest of eternal life in the soul, but spiritual life; and what is that but grace? The inheritance that Christ has purchased for the elect is the Spirit of God; not in any extraordinary gifts, but in His vital indwelling in the heart, exerting and communicating Himself there in His own proper, holy, or divine nature; and this is the sum total of the inheritance that Christ purchased for the elect. For so are things constituted in the affairs of our redemption, that the Father provides the Saviour or purchaser, and the purchase is made of him; and the Son is the purchaser and the price; and the Holy Spirit is the great blessing or inheritance purchased, as is intimated, Gal. iii. 13, 14; and hence the Spirit is often spoken of as the sum of the blessings promised in the gospel, Luke xxiv. 49, Acts i. 4, and chap. ii. 38, 39, Gal. iii. 14, Eph. i. 13. This inheritance was the grand legacy which Christ left His disciples and church, in His last will and testament, John chap. xiv., xv., xvi. This is the sum of the blessings of eternal life, which shall be given in heaven. (Compare John vii. 37, 38, 39, and John iv. 14, with Rev. xxi. 6, and xxii. 1, 17.) It is through the vital communications and indwellings of the Spirit that the saints have all their light, life, holiness, beauty, and joy in heaven; and it is through the vital communications and indwelling of the same Spirit that the saints have all light, life, holiness, beauty and comfort on earth; but only communicated in less measure. And this vital indwelling of the Spirit in the saints, in this less measure and small beginning, is, "the earnest of the Spirit, the earnest of the future inheritance, and the firstfruits of the Spirit," as the apostle calls it, Rom. viii. 22, where, by "the firstfruits of the Spirit," the apostle undoubtedly means the same vital, gracious principle that he speaks of in all the preceding part of the chapter, which he calls Spirit, and sets in opposition to flesh or corruption. Therefore this earnest of the Spirit, and firstfruits of the Spirit, which has been shown to be the same with the seal of the Spirit, is the vital, gracious, sanctifying communication and

influence of the Spirit, and not any immediate suggestion or revelation of facts by the Spirit.*

And indeed the apostle, when (Rom. viii. 16) he speaks of the
Spirit's bearing witness with our spirit that we are the children of
God, does sufficiently explain himself, if his words are but attended
to. What is here expressed is connected with the two preceding
verses, as resulting from what the apostle had said there, as every
reader may see. The three verses together are thus: " For as many
as are led by the Spirit of God, they are the sons of God: for ye
have not received the spirit of bondage again to fear; but ye have
received the spirit of adoption, whereby we cry, Abba, Father: the
Spirit itself beareth witness with our spirits that we are the children of God." Here, what the apostle says, if we take it together,
plainly shows that what he has respect to, when he speaks of the
Spirit's giving us witness or evidence that we are God's children,
is His dwelling in us, and leading us, as a spirit of adoption, or
spirit of a child, disposing us to behave towards God as to a
father. This is the witness or evidence which the apostle speaks
of that we are children, that we have the spirit of children, or
spirit of adoption. And what is that but the spirit of love? There
are two kinds of spirits the apostle speaks of, the spirit of a slave,
or the spirit of bondage, that is fear; and the spirit of a child, or
spirit of adoption, and that is love. The apostle says we have not
received the spirit of bondage, or of slaves, which is a spirit of
fear; but we have received the more ingenuous noble spirit of
children, a spirit of love, which naturally disposes us to go to God
as children to a father, and behave towards God as children. And
this is the evidence or witness which the Spirit of God gives us
that we are His children. This is the plain sense of the apostle;
and so undoubtedly he here is speaking of the very same way of
casting out doubting and fear and the spirit of bondage, which the
Apostle John speaks of, 1 John iv. 18, viz., by the prevailing of
love, that is the spirit of a child. The spirit of bondage works

---

* " After a man is in Christ, not to judge by the work is not to judge
by the Spirit. For the apostle makes the earnest of the Spirit to be the
seal.—Now earnest is part of the money bargained for; the beginning of
heaven, of the light and life of it. He that sees not that the Lord is his
by that, sees no God his at all. Oh, therefore, do not look for a Spirit,
without a word to reveal, nor a word to reveal, without seeing and feeling
of some work first. I thank the Lord, I do but pity those that think otherwise. If a sheep of Christ, Oh, wander not." *Shepard's Parable of the
Ten Virgins*, p. 142.

by fear for the slave fears the rod : but love cries, Abba, Father; it disposes us to go to God, and behave ourselves towards God as children; and it gives us clear evidence of our union to God as His children, and so casts out fear. So that it appears that the witness of the Spirit the apostle speaks of, is far from being any whisper, or immediate suggestion or revelation; but that gracious holy effect of the Spirit of God in the hearts of the saints, the disposition and temper of children, appearing in sweet childlike love to God, which casts out fear or a spirit of a slave.

And the same thing is evident from all the context : it is plain the apostle speaks of the Spirit, over and over again, as dwelling in the hearts of the saints as a gracious principle, set in opposition to the flesh or corruption : and so he does in the words that immediately introduce this passage we are upon, ver. 13, " For if ye live after the flesh, ye shall die : but if ye through the Spirit do mortify the deeds of the body, ye shall live."

Indeed it is past doubt with me, that the apostle has a more special respect to the spirit of grace, or the spirit of love, or spirit of a child, in its more lively actings; for it is perfect love, or strong love only, which so witnesses or evidences that we are children as to cast out fear, and wholly deliver from the spirit of bondage. The strong and lively exercises of a spirit of childlike, evangelical, humble love to God, give clear evidence of the soul's relation to God as His child; which does very greatly and directly satisfy the soul. And though it be far from being true that the soul in this case judges only by an immediate witness, without any sign or evidence, for it judges and is assured by the greatest sign and clearest evidence, yet in this case the saint stands in no need of multiplied signs, or any long reasoning upon them. And though the sight of his relative union with God, and his being in His favour, is not without a medium, because he sees it by that medium, viz., his love, yet his sight of the union of his heart to God is immediate. Love, the bond of union, is seen intuitively : the saint sees and feels plainly the union between his soul and God; it is so strong and lively that he cannot doubt of it. And hence he is assured that he is a child. How can he doubt whether he stands in a childlike relation to God when he plainly sees a childlike union between God and his soul, and hence does boldly, and as it were naturally and necessarily, cry, Abba, Father?

And whereas the apostle says, " the Spirit bears witness with our spirits "; by our spirit here, is meant our conscience, which is called the spirit of man, Prov. xx. 27, "The spirit of man is the candle of the Lord, searching all the inward parts of the belly." We elsewhere read of the witness of this spirit of ours: 2 Cor. i. 12, " For our rejoicing is this, the testimony of our conscience." And 1 John iii. 19, 20, 21 : " And hereby we know that we are of the truth, and shall assure our hearts before him. For if our heart condemn us, God is greater than our heart, and knoweth all things. Beloved, if our heart condemn us not, then have we confidence towards God." When the Apostle Paul speaks of the Spirit of God bearing witness with our spirit, he is not to be understood of two spirits that are two separate, collateral, independent witnesses; but it is by one that we receive the witness of the other : the Spirit of God gives the evidence by infusing and shedding abroad the love of God, the spirit of a child, in the heart, and our spirit or conscience receives and declares this evidence for our rejoicing.

Many have been the mischiefs that have arisen from that false and delusive notion of the witness of the Spirit, that it is a kind of inward voice, suggestion, or declaration from God to man that he is beloved of Him, and pardoned, elected, or the like, sometimes with and sometimes without a text of Scripture; and many have been the false and vain (though very high) affections that have arisen from hence. And it is to be feared that multitudes of souls have been eternally undone by it. I have therefore insisted the longer on this head. But I proceed now to a second characteristic of gracious affections.

II. *The primary ground of gracious affections is the transcendently excellent and amiable nature of divine things as they are in themselves; and not any conceived relation they bear to self, or self-interest.*

I say that the supremely excellent nature of divine things is the first, or primary and original, objective foundation of the spiritual affections of true saints; for I do not suppose that all relation which divine things bear to themselves, and their own particular interest, is wholly excluded from all influence in their gracious affections. For this may have, and indeed has, a secondary and consequential influence in those affections that are truly holy and spiritual, as I shall show how by and by.

It was before observed that the affection of love is, as it were, the fountain of all affection; and particularly that Christian love is the fountain of all gracious affections. Now the divine excellency and glory of God and Jesus Christ, the Word of God, the works of God, and the ways of God, &c., is the primary reason why a true saint loves these things; and not any supposed interest that he has in them, or any conceived benefit that he has received from them, or shall receive from them.

Some say that all love arises from self-love; and that it is impossible in the nature of things for any man to have any love to God, or any other being, but that love to himself must be the foundation of it. But I humbly suppose it is for want of consideration that they say so. They argue, that whoever loves God, and so desires His glory or the enjoyment of Him, desires these things as his own happiness. The glory of God, and the beholding and enjoying His perfections are considered as things agreeable to him, tending to make him happy. He places his happiness in them, and desires them as things, which (if they were obtained) would be delightful to him, or would fill him with delight and joy, and so make him happy. And so, they say, it is from self-love, or a desire of his own happiness, that he desires God should be glorified, and desires to behold and enjoy His glorious perfections. But then they ought to consider a little further, and inquire how the man came to place his happiness in God's being glorified, and in contemplating and enjoying God's perfections. There is no doubt but that after God's glory, and the beholding His perfections, are become so agreeable to him that he places his highest happiness in these things, then he will desire them as he desires his own happiness. But how came these things to be so agreeable to him that he esteems it his highest happiness to glorify God? Is not this the fruit of love? A man must first love God, or have his heart united to Him, before he will esteem God's good his own, and before he will desire the glorifying and enjoying of God as his happiness. It is not strong arguing, that because a man has his heart united to God in love, and, as a fruit of this, desires God's glory and enjoyment as his own happiness, that therefore a desire after this happiness of his own must needs be the cause and foundation of his love. It would be just as

true to argue that, because a father begat a son, therefore his son
certainly begat him. If, after a man loves God, and has his heart
so united to Him as to look upon God as his chief good and on
God's good as his own, it will be a consequence and fruit of this
that even self-love, or love to his own happiness, will cause him to
desire the glorifying and enjoying of God; it will not thence follow
that this very exercise of self-love went before his love to God,
and that his love to God was a consequence and fruit of that.
Something else, entirely distinct from self-love, might be the
cause of this, viz., a change made in the views of his mind, and
relish of his heart, whereby he apprehends a beauty, glory, and
supreme good, in God's nature as it is in itself. This may be the
thing that first draws his heart to Him, and causes his heart to
be united to Him, prior to all considerations of his own interest
or happiness, although after this, and as a fruit of this, he necessarily seeks his interest and happiness in God.

There is a kind of love or affection that a man may have towards persons or things, which does properly arise from self-love.
A preconceived relation to himself, or some respect already manifested by another to him, or some benefit already received or depended on, is truly the first foundation of his love, and what his
affection does wholly arise from; and is what precedes any relish
of or delight in the nature and qualities inherent in the being
beloved, as beautiful and amiable. When the first thing that
draws a man's benevolence to another is the beholding of those
qualifications and properties in him, which appear to him lovely
in themselves, and the subject of them, on this account worthy
of esteem and good will, love arises in a very different manner
than when it first arises from some gift bestowed by another or
depended on from him, as a judge loves and favours a man that
has bribed him; or from the relation he supposes another has to
him, as a man who loves another because he looks upon him as
his child. When love to another arises thus, it does truly and
properly arise from self-love.

That kind of affection to God or Jesus Christ which does thus
properly arise from self-love, cannot be a truly gracious and spiritual love, as appears from what has been said already: for self-
love is a principle entirely natural, and as much in the hearts
of devils as angels; and therefore surely nothing that is the mere
result of it can be supernatural and divine, in the manner before

described.* Christ plainly speaks of this kind of love, as what is nothing beyond the love of wicked men: Luke vi. 32, "If ye love them that love you, what thank have ye? For sinners also love those that love them." And the devil himself knew that that kind of respect to God which was so mercenary as to be only for benefits received or depended on (which is all one), is worthless in the sight of God; otherwise he never would have made use of such a slander before God against Job, as in Job i. 9, 10: "Doth Job fear God for nought? Hast not thou made a hedge about him, and about his house," &c. Nor would God ever have implicitly allowed the objection to have been good, in case the accusation had been true, by allowing that that matter should be tried, and that Job should be so dealt with, that it might appear in the event, whether Job's respect to God was thus mercenary or no, and by putting the proof of the sincerity and goodness of his respect upon that issue.

It is unreasonable to think otherwise, than that the first foundation of a true love to God is that whereby He is in Himself lovely, or worthy to be loved, or the supreme loveliness of His nature. This is certainly what makes him chiefly amiable. What chiefly makes a man or any creature lovely is his excellency; and so what chiefly renders God lovely, and must undoubtedly be the chief ground of true love, is His excellency. God's nature or divinity is infinitely excellent; yea it is infinite beauty, brightness, and glory itself. But how can that be true love of His excellent and lovely nature which is not built on the foundation of its true loveliness? How can that be true love of beauty and brightness which is not for beauty and brightness' sake? How can that be a true prizing of that which is in itself infinitely worthy and precious which is not for the sake of its worthiness and preciousness? This infinite excellency of the divine nature, as it is in itself, is the true ground of all that is good in God in any respect; but how can a man truly and rightly love God without loving Him for that excellency in Him which is the foundation of all that is in any manner of respect good or desirable in Him? If men's affection to God is founded first on His profitableness to them, their affection begins at the wrong end; they regard God

* " There is a natural love to Christ, as to One that doth thee good, and for thine own ends; and spiritual for Himself, whereby the Lord only is exalted." *Shepard's Parable of the Ten Virgins,* p. 49.

only for the utmost limit of the stream of divine good, where it touches them and reaches their interest, and have no respect to that infinite glory of God's nature which is the original good, and the true fountain of all good, the first fountain of all love-liness of every kind, and so the first foundation of all true love.

A natural principle of self-love may be the foundation of great affections towards God and Christ, without seeing anything of the beauty and glory of the divine nature. There is a certain gratitude that is a mere natural thing. Gratitude is one of the natural affections of the soul of man, as well as anger; and there is a gratitude that arises from self-love, very much in the same manner that anger does. Anger in men is an affection excited against another, or in opposition to another, for something in him that crosses self-love: gratitude is an affection one has to-wards another, for loving him or gratifying him, or for some-thing in him that suits self-love. And there may be a kind of gratitude without any true or proper love: as there may be anger without any proper hatred, as in parents towards their children whom they may be angry with, and yet at the same time have a strong habitual love to them. This gratitude is the principle which is an exercise in wicked men as Christ declares concern-ing them in the 6th of Luke, where He says, " Sinners love those that love them "; and as He declares concerning even the pub-licans, who were some of the most carnal and profligate sort of men, Matt. v. 46. This is the very principle that is wrought upon by bribery, in unjust judges; and it is a principle that even the brute beasts do exercise; a dog will love his master that is kind to him. And we see in innumerable instances, that mere nature is sufficient to excite gratitude in men, or to affect their hearts with thankfulness to others for kindnesses received; and sometimes towards them against whom at the same time they have an habit-ual enmity. Thus Saul was once and again greatly affected, and even dissolved with gratitude towards David, for sparing his life, and yet remained an habitual enemy to him. And as men, from mere nature, may be thus affected towards men, so they may to-wards God. Nothing hinders but that the same self-love may work after the same manner towards God as towards men. And we have manifest instances of it in Scripture; as in the children of Israel who sang God's praises at the Red Sea, but soon forgat God's works; and in Naaman the Syrian, who was greatly affected with the miraculous cure of his leprosy, so as to have his heart engaged thenceforward to worship the God that had healed him, and Him only, excepting when it would expose him to be ruined in his temporal interest. So was Nebuchadnezzar greatly affected with God's goodness to him, in restoring him to his reason and kingdom, after his dwelling with the beasts.

Gratitude being thus a natural principle, it renders ingratitude so much the more vile and heinous; because it shows a dreadful prevalence of wickedness, when it even overbears and suppresses the better principles of human nature: as it is mentioned as an evidence of the high degree of the wickedness of many of the heathen, that they were without natural affection, Rom. i. 31. But that the want of gratitude or natural affection is evidence of a high degree of vice, is no argument that all gratitude and natural affection has the nature of virtue or saving grace.

Self-love, through the exercise of mere natural gratitude, may be the foundation of a sort of love to God in many ways. A kind of love may arise from a false notion of God, that men have been educated in or have some way imbibed, as though He were only goodness and mercy, and not revenging justice; or as though the exercises of His goodness were necessary and not free and sovereign; or as though His goodness were dependent on what is in them, and as it were constrained by them. Men on such grounds as these may love a God of their own forming in their imaginations, when they are far from loving such a God as reigns in heaven.

Again, self-love may be the foundation of an affection in men towards God, through a great insensibility of their state with regard to God, and for want of conviction of conscience to make them sensible how dreadfully they have provoked God to anger. They have no sense of the heinousness of sin as against God, and of the infinite and terrible opposition of the holy nature of God against it. And so, having formed in their minds such a God as suits them, and thinking God to be such an one as themselves, who favours and agrees with them, they may like Him very well and feel a sort of love to Him, when they are far from loving the true God. And men's affections may be much moved towards God from self-love, by some remarkable outward benefits received from God; as it was with Naaman, Nebuchadnezzar, and the children of Israel at the Red Sea.

Again, a very high affection towards God may, and often does, arise in men from an opinion of the favour and love of God to them, as the first foundation of their love to Him. After awakenings and distress through fears of hell, they may suddenly get a notion, through some impression on their imagination, or immediate suggestion with or without texts of Scripture, or by some other means, that God loves them, and has forgiven their sins, and made them His children; and this is the first thing that causes their affections to flow towards God and Jesus Christ; and then after this, and upon this foundation, many things in God may appear lovely to them, and Christ may seem excellent. And if such persons are asked whether God appears lovely and amiable in Himself, they would perhaps readily answer, Yes; when indeed, if the matter be strictly examined, this good opinion of God was purchased and paid for in the distinguishing and infinite benefits they imagined they received from God: and they allow God to be lovely in Himself no otherwise than that He has forgiven them, and accepted them, and loves them above most in the world, and has engaged to improve all His infinite power and wisdom in preferring, dignifying, and exalting them, and will do for them just as they would have Him. When once they are firm in this apprehension, it is easy to own God and Christ to be lovely and glorious, and to admire and extol Them. It is easy for them to own Christ to be a lovely person, and the best in the world, when they are first firm in it, that He, though Lord of the universe, is captivated with love to them, and has His heart swallowed up in them, and prizes them far beyond most of their neighbours, and loved them from eternity, and died for them, and will make them reign in eternal glory with Him in heaven. When this is the case with carnal men, their very lusts will make Him seem lovely: pride itself will prejudice them in favour of that which they call Christ: selfish proud man naturally calls that lovely that greatly contributes to his interest, and gratifies his ambition.

And as this sort of persons begin, so they go on. Their affections are raised from time to time, primarily on this foundation of self-love and a conceit of God's love to them. Many have a false notion of communion with God, as though it were carried on by impulses, and whispers, and external representations, immediately made to their imagination. These things they often have; which they take to be manifestations of God's great love to them, and evidences of their high exaltation above others of mankind; and so their affections are often renewedly set a-going.

But the exercises of true and holy love in the saints arise in another way. They do not first see that God loves them, and then see that He is lovely, but they first see that God is lovely, and that Christ is excellent and glorious, and their hearts are first captivated with this view, and the exercises of their love are wont from time to time to begin here, and to arise primarily from these views; and then, consequentially, they see God's love, and great favour to them.* The saint's affections begin with God; and self-love has a hand in these affections consequentially and secondarily only. On the contrary, false affections begin with self, and an acknowledgment of an excellency in God, and an affectedness with it, is only consequential and dependent. In the love of the true saint God is the lowest foundation; the love of the excellency of His nature is the foundation of all the affections which come afterwards, wherein self-love is concerned as a handmaid: but the hypocrite lays himself at the bottom of all, as the first foundation, and lays on God as the superstructure; and even his acknowledgment of God's glory itself depends on his regard to his private interest.

Self-love may not only influence men, so as to cause them to be affected with God's kindness to them separately; but also with God's kindness to them as parts of a community. As a natural principle of self-love, without any other principle, may be sufficient to make a man concerned for the interest of the nation to which he belongs: as for instance, in the present war, self-love may make natural men rejoice at the successes of our nation, and sorry for their disadvantages, they being concerned as members of the body. So the same natural principle may extend further, and even to the world of mankind, and might be affected with the benefits the inhabitants of the earth have, beyond those of the inhabitants of other planets, if we knew that such there were, and how it was with them. So this principle may cause men to be affected with the benefits that mankind have received be-

* " There is a seeing of Christ after a man believes, which is Christ in His love, &c. But I speak of that first sight of Him that precedes the second act of faith; and it is an intuitive or real sight of Him as He is in His glory." *Shepard's Parable of the Ten Virgins*, p. 123.

yond the fallen angels. And hence men, from this principle, may be much affected with the wonderful goodness of God to mankind, His great goodness in giving His Son to die for fallen man, and the marvellous love of Christ in suffering such great things for us, and with the great glory they hear God has provided in heaven for us; looking on themselves as persons concerned and interested, as being some of this species of creatures so highly favoured. The same principle of natural gratitude may influence men here, as in the case of personal benefits.

But these things that I have said do by no means imply, that all gratitude to God is a mere natural thing, and that there is no such thing as a spiritual gratitude, which is a holy and divine affection: they imply no more than that there is a gratitude which is merely natural, and that when persons have affections towards God only or primarily for benefits received, their affection is only the exercise of a natural gratitude. There is doubtless such a thing as a gracious gratitude, which does greatly differ from all that gratitude which natural men experience. It differs in the following respects:

1. True gratitude or thankfulness to God for His kindness to us arises from a foundation laid before, of love to God for what He is in Himself; whereas a natural gratitude has no such antecedent foundation. The gracious stirrings of grateful affection to God, for kindness received, always are from a stock of love already in the heart, established in the first place on the grounds of God's own excellency; and hence the affections are disposed to flow out on occasions of God's kindness. The saint having seen the glory of God, and his heart being overcome by it and captivated with love to Him on that account, his heart hereby becomes tender and easily affected with kindnesses received. If a man has no love to another, yet gratitude may be moved by some extraordinary kindness, as in Saul towards David: but this is not the same kind of thing as a man's gratitude to a dear friend, for whom his heart was before possessed with a high esteem and love, and by this means became tender towards him. Self-love is not excluded from a gracious gratitude; the saints love God for His kindness to them: Psal. cxvi. 1, " I love the Lord, because he hath heard the voice of my supplications." But something else is included; and another love prepares the way and lays the foundation for these grateful affections.

2. In a gracious gratitude men are affected with the attribute of God's goodness and free grace, not only as they are concerned in it, or as it affects their interest, but as a part of the glory and beauty of God's nature. That wonderful and unparalleled grace of God which is manifested in the work of redemption, and shines forth in the face of Jesus Christ, is infinitely glorious in itself, and appears so to the angels; it is a great part of the moral perfection and beauty of God's nature. This would be glorious, whether it were exercised towards us or no; and the saint who exercises a gracious thankfulness for it, sees it to be so, and delights in it as such: though his concern in it serves the more to engage his mind and raise the attention and affection. Self-love here assists as a handmaid, being subservient to higher principles, to lead forth the mind to the view and contemplation, and engage and fix the attention, and heighten the joy and love. God's kindness to them is a glass that God sets before them, wherein to behold the beauty of the attribute of God's goodness. The exercises and displays of this attribute, by this means, are brought near to them, and set right before them. So that in a holy thankfulness to God, the concern our interest has in God's goodness is not the first foundation of our being affected with it; that was laid in the heart before, in that stock of love which was to God for His excellency in Himself, that makes the heart tender and susceptive of such impressions from His goodness to us. Nor is our own interest, or the benefits we have received, the only, or the chief objective ground of the present exercises of the affection, but God's goodness as part of the beauty of His nature; although the manifestations of that lovely attribute, set immediately before our eyes in the exercises of it for us, be the special occasion of the mind's attention to that beauty at that time, and serves to fix the attention and heighten the affection.

Some may perhaps be ready to object, against the whole that has been said, that text, 1 John iv. 19: "We love him, because he first loved us," as though this implied that God's love to the true saints were the first foundation of their love to Him.

In answer to this, I would observe that the apostle's drift in these words is to magnify the love of God to us from hence, that He loved us while we had no love to Him; as will be manifest to any one who compares this verse and the two following with the 9th, 10th, and 11th verses. And that God loved us when we had no love to

Him, the apostle proves by this argument, that God's love to the elect is the ground of their love to Him. And that it is in three ways: 1. The saints' love to God is the fruit of God's love to them, as it is the gift of that love. God gave them a spirit of love to Him, because He loved them from eternity. And in this respect God's love to His elect is the first foundation of their love to Him, as it is the foundation of their regeneration, and the whole of their redemption. 2. The exercises and discoveries that God has made of His wonderful love to sinful men by Jesus Christ, in the work of redemption, is one of the chief manifestations which God has made of the glory of His moral perfection to both angels and men; and so is one main objective ground of the love of both to God, in a good consistence with what was said before. 3. God's love to a particular elect person, discovered by his conversion, is a great manifestation of God's moral perfection and glory to him, and a proper occasion of the excitation of the love of holy gratitude, agreeable to what was before said. And that the saints do in these respects love God, because He first loved them, fully answers the design of the apostle's argument in that place. So that no good argument can be drawn from hence against a spiritual and gracious love in the saints, arising primarily from the excellency of divine things as they are in themselves, and not from any conceived relation they bear to their interest.

And as it is with the love of the saints, so it is with their joy and spiritual delight and pleasure: the first foundation of it is not any consideration or conception of their interest in divine things; but it primarily consists in the sweet entertainment their minds have in the view or contemplation of the divine and holy beauty of these things, as they are in themselves. And this is indeed the main difference between the joy of the hypocrite and the joy of the true saint. The former rejoices in himself; self is the first foundation of his joy: the latter rejoices in God. The hypocrite has his mind pleased and delighted, in the first place, with his own privilege, and the happiness which he supposes he has attained to or shall attain to. True saints have their minds, in the first place, inexpressibly pleased and delighted with the sweet ideas of the glorious and amiable nature of the things of God. And this is the spring of all their delights and the cream of all their pleasures: it is the joy of their joy. This sweet and ravishing entertainment they have in the view of the beautiful and delightful nature of divine things, is the foundation of the joy that they have afterwards in the consideration of their being theirs. But the dependence of the affections of hypocrites is in a contrary order: they first rejoice and are elevated with it, that they are made so much of by God; and then on that ground He seems, in a sort, lovely to them.

The first foundation of the delight a true saint has in Christ is His own perfection; and the first foundation of the delight he has in Christ, is His own beauty; He appears in Himself the chief among ten thousand and altogether lovely. The way of salvation by Christ is a delightful way to him, for the sweet and admirable manifestations of the divine perfections in it: the holy doctrines of the gospel, by which God is exalted and man abased, holiness honoured and promoted, sin greatly disgraced and discouraged, and free and sovereign love manifested, are glorious doctrines in his eyes, and sweet to his taste, prior to any conception of his interest in these things. Indeed, the saints rejoice in their interest in God, and that Christ is theirs, and so they have great reason, but this is not the first spring of their joy. They first rejoice in God as glorious and excellent in Himself, and then secondarily rejoice in the fact that so glorious a God is theirs. They first have their hearts filled with sweetness from the view of Christ's excellency, and the excellency of His grace and the beauty of the way of salvation by Him, and then they have a secondary joy in that so excellent a Saviour and such excellent grace are theirs.* But that which is the true saint's superstructure is the hypocrite's foundation. When they hear of the wonderful things of the gospel, of God's great love in sending His Son, of Christ's dying love to sinners, and of the great things Christ has purchased and promised to the saints, and hear these things eloquently set forth, they may hear with a great deal of pleasure, and be lifted up with what they hear; but if their joy

* Dr. Owen in his *Discourse on the Holy Spirit*, speaking of a common work of the Spirit, says: " The effects of this work on the mind, which is the first subject affected with it, proceeds not so far as to give delight, complacency and satisfaction, in the lovely spiritual nature and excellencies of the things revealed unto it. The true nature of saving illumination consists in this, that it gives the mind such a direct intuitive insight and prospect into spiritual things, as that in their own spiritual nature they suit, please, and satisfy it; so that it is transformed into them, cast into the mould of them, and rests in them."

be examined, it will be found to have no other foundation than this, that they look upon these things as theirs, all this exalts them, they love to hear of the great love of Christ, so vastly distinguishing some from others; for self-love, and even pride itself, makes them affect great distinction from others. No wonder, in this confident opinion of their own good estate, that they feel well under such doctrine, and are pleased in the highest degree in hearing how much God and Christ make of them. So that their joy is really a joy in themselves and not in God.

The joy of hypocrites is in themselves; hence it comes to pass that in their rejoicings and elevations they are wont to keep their eye upon themselves. Having received what they call spiritual discoveries or experiences, their minds are taken up about them, admiring their own experiences. What they are principally taken and elevated with is not the glory of God, or beauty of Christ, but the beauty of their experiences. They keep thinking with themselves, What a good experience is this! What a great discovery is this! What wonderful things have I met with! And so they put their experiences in the place of Christ and His beauty and fulness. Instead of rejoicing in Christ Jesus, they rejoice in their admirable experiences; instead of feeding and feasting their souls in the view of what is without them, viz., the innate, sweet refreshing amiableness of the things exhibited in the gospel, their eyes are off from these things, or at least they view them only as it were sideways. But the object that fixes their contemplation is their experience; and they are feeding their souls, and feasting a selfish principle, with a view of their discoveries. They take more comfort in their discoveries than in Christ discovered, which is the true notion of living upon experiences and frames, and not in using experiences as the signs on which they rely for evidence of their good estate, which some call living on experiences; though it be very observable, that some of them who do so are most notorious for living upon experiences, according to the true notion of it.

The affections of hypocrites are very often after this manner; they are first much affected with some impression on their imagination, or some impulse which they take to be an immediate suggestion or testimony from God of His love and their happiness, and high privileges in some respect, either with or without a text of Scripture; they are mightily taken with this as a great discovery, and hence arise high affections. And when their affections are raised, then they view those high affections, and call them great and wonderful experiences; and they have a notion that God is greatly pleased with those affections; and this affects them more; and so they are affected with their affections. And thus their affections rise higher and higher, until they sometimes are perfectly swallowed up: also self-conceit and a fierce zeal rise withal; and all is built like a castle in the air, on no other foundation but imagination, self-love, and pride.

And as the thoughts of this sort of persons are, so is their talk, for out of the abundance of their heart their mouth speaketh. As in their high affections they keep their eye upon the beauty of their experiences, and greatness of their attainments, so they are great talkers about themselves. The true saint, when under great spiritual affections, from the fulness of his heart, is ready to be speaking much of God and His glorious perfections and works, and of the beauty and amiableness of Christ, and the glorious things of the gospel: but hypocrites, in their high affections, talk more of the discovery, than they do of the thing discovered; they are full of talk about the great things they have met with, the wonderful discoveries they have had, how sure they are of the love of God to them, how safe their condition is, and how they know they shall go to heaven, &c.

A true saint, when in the enjoyment of true discoveries of the sweet glory of God and Christ, has his mind too much captivated and engaged by what he views without himself, to stand at that time to view himself, and his own attainments. It would be a diversion and loss which he could not bear, to take his eye off from the ravishing object of his contemplation, to survey his own experience, and to spend time in thinking with himself, What a high attainment this is, and what a good story I now have to tell others! Nor does the pleasure and sweetness of his mind at that time chiefly arise from the consideration of the safety of his state, or anything he has in view of his own qualifications, experiences, or circumstances; but from the divine and supreme beauty of what is the object of his direct view without himself, which sweetly entertains, and strongly holds his mind.

As the love and joy of hypocrites are all from the source of self-love, so it is with their other affections, their sorrow for sin, their humiliation and submission, their religious desires and zeal. Everything is, as it were, paid for beforehand, in God's highly gratifying their self-love and their lusts, by making so much of them and exalting them so highly, as things are in their imagination. It is easy for nature, corrupt as it is, to love this imaginary God that suits them so well, and to extol Him, and submit to Him, and to be fierce and zealous for Him. The high affections of many are all built on the supposition of their being eminent saints. If that opinion which they have of themselves were taken away, if they thought they were some of the lower form of saints (though they should yet suppose themselves to be real saints), their high affections would fall to the ground. If they only saw a little of the sinfulness and vileness of their own hearts, and their deformity in the midst of their best duties and their best affections, it would knock their affections on the head. Because their affections are built upon self, therefore self-knowledge would destroy them. But as to truly gracious affections, they are built elsewhere; they have their foundation out of self in God and Jesus Christ; and therefore a discovery of themselves, of their own deformity, and the meanness of the experiences, though it will purify their affections, yet it will not destroy them, but in some respects sweeten and heighten them.

III. *Those affections that are truly holy, are primarily founded on the loveliness of the moral excellency of divine things.*

Or (to express it otherwise) a love to divine things for the beauty and sweetness of their moral excellency, is the first beginning and spring of all holy affections.

Here, for the sake of the more illiterate reader, I will explain what I mean by the moral excellency of divine things.

And it may be observed, that the word *moral* is not to be understood here according to the common acceptation of the word, when men speak of morality, and a moral behaviour, meaning an outward conformity to the duties of the moral law, and especially the duties of the second table; or intending no more at farthest than such seeming virtues as proceed from natural principles, in opposition to those virtues that are more inward, spiritual, and divine; as the honesty, justice, generosity, good nature, and public spirit of many of the heathen are called moral virtues, in distinction from the holy faith, love, humility, and heavenly-mindedness of true Christians. I say, the word *moral* is not to be understood thus in this place.

But in order to a right understanding of what is meant, it must be observed that divines commonly make a distinction between moral good and evil and natural good and evil. By moral evil they mean the evil of sin, or that evil which is against duty and contrary to what is right and ought to be. By natural evil they do not mean that evil which is properly opposed to duty; but that which is contrary to mere nature, without any respect to a rule of duty. So the evil of suffering is called natural evil, such as pain and torment, disgrace, and the like: these things are contrary to mere nature, contrary to the nature of both bad and good, hateful to wicked men and devils as well as good men and angels. Likewise, natural defects are called natural evils, as if a child be monstrous, or a natural fool; these are natural evils, but are not moral evils, because they have not properly the nature of the evil of sin. On the other hand, as by moral evil divines mean the evil of sin, or that which is contrary to what is right, so by moral good they mean that which is contrary to sin, or that good in beings who have will and choice, whereby as voluntary agents they are and act as it becomes them to be and to act, or so as is most fit and suitable and lovely. By natural good they mean that good that is entirely of a different kind from holiness or virtue, viz., that which perfects or suits nature, considering nature abstractly from any holy or unholy qualifications, and without any relation to any rule or measure of right and wrong.

Thus pleasure is a natural good; so is honour, so is strength, so is speculative knowledge, human learning, and policy. Thus there is a distinction to be made between the natural good that men are possessed of, and their moral good; and also between the natural and moral good of the angels in heaven. The great capacity of angelic understandings, their great strength, and the honourable circumstances they are in as the great ministers of God's kingdom, whence they are called thrones, dominions, principalities, and powers, is the natural good which they are possessed of; but their perfect and glorious holiness and goodness, their pure and flaming love to God and to the saints and to one another, is their moral good. Likewise, divines make a distinction between the natural and moral perfections of God: by the moral perfections of God, they mean those attributes which God exercises as a moral agent, or whereby the heart and will of God are good, right, and infinitely becoming and lovely; such as His righteousness, truth, faithfulness, and goodness; or, in one word, His holiness. By God's natural attributes or perfections, they mean those attributes wherein, according to our way of conceiving of God, consists, not the holiness or moral goodness of God, but his greatness: such as His power, His knowledge, whereby He knows all things, and His being eternal, from everlasting to everlasting, His omnipresence, and His awful and terrible majesty.

The moral excellency of an intelligent voluntary being is more immediately seated in the heart or will. That intelligent being whose will is truly right and lovely is morally good or excellent.

This moral excellency of an intelligent being, when it is true and real, and not only external or merely seeming and counterfeit, is holiness. Therefore holiness comprehends all the true moral excellency of intelligent beings: there is no other true virtue but real holiness. Holiness comprehends all the true virtue of a good man, his love to God, his gracious love to men, his justice, his charity and bowels of mercies, his gracious meekness and gentleness; all other true Christian virtues that he has, belong to his holiness. So the holiness of God in the more extensive sense of the word, and the sense in which the word is commonly, if not universally, used concerning God in Scripture, is the same with the moral excellency of the divine nature, or His purity and beauty as a moral agent, comprehending all His moral perfections, His righteousness, faithfulness, and goodness. As in holy men, their charity, Christian kindness, and mercy, belong to their holiness; so the kindness and mercy of God belong to His holiness. Holiness in man is but the image of God's holiness; there are not more virtues belonging to the image than are in the Original: derived holiness has not more in it than is in that underived holiness which is its fountain; there is no more than grace for grace, or grace in the image answerable to grace in the Original.

As there are two kinds of attributes in God, according to our way of conceiving of Him, His moral attributes, which are summed up in His holiness, and His natural attributes of strength, knowledge, &c., that constitute the greatness of God; so there is a twofold image of God in man—His moral or spiritual image which is His holiness, that is the image of God's moral excellency (which image was lost by the fall), and God's natural image, consisting in man's reason and understanding, his natural ability, and dominion over the creatures, which is the image of God's natural attribute.

From what has been said, it may easily be understood what I intend, when I say that a love to divine things for the beauty of their moral excellency is the beginning and spring of all holy affections. It has been already shown, under the former head, that the first objective ground of all holy affections is the supreme excellency of divine things as they are in themselves, or in their own nature. I now proceed further, and say more particularly that that kind of excellency of the nature of divine things, which is the first objective ground of all holy affections, is their moral excellency or their holiness. Holy persons, in the exercise of holy affections, do love divine things primarily for their holiness. They love God, in the first place, for the beauty of His holiness or moral perfection, as being supremely amiable in itself. Not that the saints, in the exercise of gracious affections, do love God only for His holiness; all His attributes are amiable and glorious in their eyes; they delight in every divine perfection; the contemplation of the infinite greatness, power, and knowledge, and terrible majesty of God, is pleasant to them. But their love to God for His holiness is what is most fundamental and essential in their love. Here it is that true love to God begins; all other holy love to divine things flows from hence. This is the most essential and distinguishing thing that belongs to a holy love to God, with regard to the foundation of it. A love to God for the beauty of His moral attributes leads to and necessarily causes a delight in God for all His attributes. His moral attributes cannot be without His natural attributes: for infinite holiness supposes infinite wisdom, and an infinite capacity and greatness; and all the attributes of God do as it were imply one another.

The true beauty and loveliness of all intelligent beings does primarily and most essentially consist in their moral excellency or holiness. Herein consists the loveliness of the angels, without which, with all their natural perfections, their strength, and their knowledge, they would have no more loveliness than devils. It is a moral excellency alone, that is in itself, and on its own account, the excellency of intelligent beings. It is this that gives beauty to, or rather is the beauty of, their natural perfections and qualifications. Moral excellency is the excellency of natural excellencies. Natural qualifications are either excellent or otherwise, according as they are joined with moral excellency or not. Strength and knowledge do not render any beings lovely without holiness, but more hateful; though they render them more lovely when joined with holiness. Thus the elect angels are the more glorious for their strength and knowledge, because these natural perfections of theirs are sanctified by their moral perfection. But though the devils are very strong and of great natural understanding, they be not the more lovely: they are more terrible indeed, not more amiable; but on the contrary, the more hateful. The holiness of an intelligent creature is the beauty of all his natural perfections. And so it is in God, according to our way of conceiving of the divine Being: holiness is in a peculiar manner the beauty of the divine nature. Hence we often read of the beauty of holiness, Psal. xxix. 2, xcvi. 9, and cx. 3. This renders all His other attributes glorious and lovely. It is the glory of God's wisdom that it is a holy wisdom, and not a wicked subtlety and craftiness. This makes His majesty lovely, and not merely dreadful and horrible, that it is a holy majesty. It is the glory of God's immutability that it is a holy immutability, and not an inflexible obstinacy in wickedness.

And therefore it must needs be that a sight of God's loveliness must begin here. A true love to God must begin with a delight in His holiness, and not with a delight in any other attribute; for no other attribute is truly lovely without this, and no otherwise than as (according to our way of conceiving of God) it derives its loveliness from this; and therefore it is impossible that other attributes should appear lovely, in their true loveliness, until this is seen; and it is impossible that any perfection of the divine nature should be loved with true love until this is loved. If the true loveliness of all God's perfections arises from the love of His holiness, then the true love of all His perfections arises from the love of His holiness. They that do not see the glory of God's holiness cannot see anything of the true glory of His mercy and grace: they see nothing of the glory of those attributes as excellencies of God's nature, as it is in itself; though they may be affected with them and love them, as they concern their interest: for these attributes are no part of the excellency of God's nature,

as that is excellent in itself, any otherwise than as they are included in His holiness, more largely taken; or as they are a part
of His moral perfection.

As the beauty of the divine nature does primarily consist in
God's holiness, so does the beauty of all divine things. Herein
consists the beauty of the saints, that they are saints or holy ones;
it is the moral image of God in them which is their beauty; and
that is their holiness. Herein consists the beauty and brightness
of the angels of heaven, that they are holy angels and so not
devils. Dan. iv. 13, 17, 23, Matt. xxv. 31, Mark viii. 38, Acts x. 22,
Rev. xiv. 10. Herein consists the beauty of the Christian religion
above all other religions, that it is so holy a religion. Herein
consists the excellency of the word of God, that it is so holy:
Psal. cxix. 140, "Thy word is very pure: therefore thy servant
loveth it." Ver. 128, "I esteem all thy precepts concerning all
things to be right; and I hate every false way." Ver. 138, "Thy
testimonies that thou hast commanded are righteous and very
faithful." And 172, "My tongue shall speak of thy word; for
all thy commandments are righteousness." And Psal. xix. 7-10,
"The law of the Lord is perfect, converting the soul; the testimony of the Lord is sure, making wise the simple. The statutes
of the Lord are right, rejoicing the heart: the commandment of
the Lord is pure, enlightening the eyes. The fear of the Lord
is clean, enduring for ever: the judgments of the Lord are true
and righteous altogether. More to be desired are they than gold,
yea, than much fine gold; sweeter also than honey, and the honey-
comb." Herein does primarily consist the amiableness and beauty
of the Lord Jesus, whereby He is the chief among ten thousand
and altogether lovely, even in that He is the holy one of God,
Acts iii. 14, and God's holy child, Acts iv. 27, and He that is holy,
and He that is true, Rev. iii. 7. All the spiritual beauty of His
human nature—His meekness, lowliness, patience, heavenliness,
love to God, love to men, condescension to the mean and vile, and
compassion to the miserable—all is summed up in His holiness.
And the beauty of His divine nature, of which the beauty of His
human nature is the image and reflection, also primarily consists
in His holiness. Herein primarily consists the glory of the gospel,
that it is a holy gospel, and so bright an emanation of the holy
beauty of God and Jesus Christ. Herein consists the spiritual
beauty of its doctrines, that they are holy doctrines or doctrines

according to godliness. And herein consists the spiritual beauty
of the way of salvation by Jesus Christ, that it is so holy a way.
And herein chiefly consists the glory of heaven, that it is the
holy city, the holy Jerusalem, the habitation of God's holiness
and so of His glory, Isa. lxiii. 15. All the beauties of the new
Jerusalem, as it is described in the last two chapters of Revelation, are but various representations of this. See chap. xxi. 2, 10,
11, 18, 21, 27, chap. xxii. 1, 3.

It is primarily on account of this kind of excellency that the
saints love all these things. Thus they love the word of God because it is very pure. It is on this account they love the saints;
and on this account chiefly it is that heaven is lovely to them,
and those holy tabernacles of God amiable in their eyes: it is on
this account that they love God; and on this account primarily
it is that they love Christ, and that their hearts delight in the
doctrines of the gospel, and sweetly acquiesce in the way of salvation therein revealed.*

Under the head of the first distinguishing characteristic of
gracious affection, I observed, that there is given to those that
are regenerated a new supernatural sense, that is as it were a certain divine spiritual taste. It is in its whole nature diverse from
any former kinds of sensation of the mind, as tasting is diverse
from any of the other five senses, and something is perceived by
a true saint in the exercise of this new sense of mind, in spiritual
and divine things, as entirely different from anything that is perceived in them by natural men, as the sweet taste of honey is
diverse from the ideas men get of honey by looking on it or feeling it. Now the beauty of holiness is that which is perceived
by this spiritual sense, so diverse from all that natural men can
perceive. This kind of beauty is the quality that is the immediate

* " To the right closing with Christ's person, this is also required, to
taste the bitterness of sin as the greatest evil: else a man will never close
with Christ, for His holiness in Him, and from Him, as the greatest good.
For we told you, that that is the right closing with Christ for Himself,
when it is for his holiness. Ask a whorish heart what beauty he sees in
the person of Christ; he will, after he has looked over His kingdom, His
righteousness, and all His works, see a beauty in them because they do
serve his turn, to comfort him only. Ask a virgin; he will see his happiness in all; but that which makes the Lord amiable is His holiness, which
is in him to make him holy too. As in marriage, it is the personal beauty
draws the heart. And hence I have thought it reason, that he that loves
the brethren for a little grace, will love Christ much more." *Shepard's
Parable of the Ten Virgins,* p. 139.

object of this spiritual sense; this is the sweetness that is the proper object of this spiritual taste. The Scripture often represents
the beauty and sweetness of holiness as the grand object of a
spiritual taste and spiritual appetite. This was the sweet food of
the holy soul of Jesus Christ, John iv. 32, 34: "I have meat to
eat that ye know not of.—My meat is to do the will of him that
sent me, and to finish his work." I know of no part of the Holy
Scriptures where the nature and evidences of true and sincere
godliness are so much of set purpose and so fully and largely insisted on and delineated, as the 119th Psalm. The Psalmist declares his design in the first verses of the Psalm, and he keeps his
eye on this design all along, and pursues it to the end: but in this
Psalm the excellency of holiness is represented as the immediate
object of a spiritual taste, relish, appetite, and delight of God's
law. That grand expression and emanation of the holiness of
God's nature, and prescription of holiness to the creature, is all
along represented as the food and entertainment, and as the great
object of the love, the appetite, the complacence and rejoicing of
the gracious nature, which prizes God's commandments above
gold, yea, the finest gold, and to which they are sweeter than the
honey and honey-comb; and that upon account of their holiness,
as I observed before. The same Psalmist declares, that this is the
sweetness that a spiritual taste relishes in God's law: Psal. xix.
7, 8, 9, 10, "The law of the Lord is perfect; the commandment
of the Lord is pure; the fear of the Lord is clean; the statutes of
the Lord are right, rejoicing the heart;—the judgments of the
Lord are true, and righteous altogether; more to be desired are
they than gold, yea, than much fine gold; sweeter also than
honey, and the honey-comb."

A holy love has a holy object. The holiness of love consists
especially in this, that it is the love of that which is holy, for its
holiness; so that it is the holiness of the object which is the
quality whereon it fixes and terminates. A holy nature must
needs love that in holy things chiefly which is most agreeable to
itself. But surely that in divine things which above all others
is agreeable to a holy nature, is holiness, because holiness must
be above all other things agreeable to holiness; for nothing can
be more agreeable to any nature than itself; holy nature must be
above all things agreeable to holy nature: and so the holy nature
of God and Christ, and the Word of God, and other divine things,

must be above all other things agreeable to the holy nature that is in the saints.

And again, a holy nature doubtless loves holy things, especially on the account of that for which sinful nature has enmity against them; but that for which sinful nature is chiefly at enmity against holy things, is their holiness. It is for this that the carnal mind is at enmity against God, and against the law of God, and the people of God. Now it is just arguing from contraries; from contrary causes to contrary effects; from opposite natures to opposite tendencies. We know that holiness is of a directly contrary nature to wickedness; as therefore it is the nature of wickedness chiefly to oppose and hate holiness, so it must be the nature of holiness chiefly to tend to, and delight in holiness.

The holy nature of the saints and angels in heaven (where the true tendency of it best appears) is principally engaged by the holiness of divine things. This is the divine beauty which chiefly engages the attention, admiration, and praise of the bright and burning seraphim: Isa. vi. 3, "One cried unto another, and said, Holy, holy, holy is the Lord of hosts, the whole earth is full of his glory." And Rev. iv. 8, "They rest not day and night, saying, Holy, holy, holy, Lord God Almighty, which was, and is, and is to come." So the glorified saints, chap. xv. 4, "Who shall not fear thee, O Lord, and glorify thy name? For thou only art holy."

And the Scriptures represent the saints on earth as adoring God primarily on this account, and admiring and extolling all God's attributes, either as deriving loveliness from his holiness, or as being a part of it. Thus when they praise God for His power, His holiness is the beauty that engages them: Psal. xcviii. 1, "O sing unto the Lord a new song, for he hath done marvellous things: his right hand, and his holy arm hath gotten him the victory." So when they praise Him for His justice and terrible majesty: Psal. xcix. 2, 3, "The Lord is great in Zion, and he is high above all people. Let them praise thy great and terrible name; for it is holy." Ver. 5, "Exalt ye the Lord our God, and worship at his footstool; for he is holy." Ver. 8, 9, "Thou wast a God that forgavest them, though thou tookest vengeance of their inventions. Exalt ye the Lord our God, and worship at his holy hill: for the Lord our God is holy." So when they praise God for His mercy and faithfulness: Psal. xcvii. 11, 12, "Light is sown for the righteous, and gladness for the upright in heart. Rejoice in the Lord, ye righteous; and give thanks at the remembrance of his holiness." 1 Sam. ii. 2, "There is none holy as the Lord: for there is none beside thee; neither is there any rock like our God."

By this therefore all may try their affections, and particularly their love and joy. Various kinds of creatures show the difference of their natures very much in the different things they relish as their proper good, one delighting in that which another abhors. Such a difference is there between true saints and natural men: natural men have no sense of the goodness and excellency of holy things, at least for their holiness; they have no taste for that kind of good; and so may be said not to know that divine good, or not to see it; it is wholly hid from them. But the saints, by the mighty power of God, have it discovered to them; they have that supernatural, most noble and divine sense given them, by which they perceive it; and it is this that captivates their hearts, and delights them above all things. It is the most amiable and sweet thing to the heart of a true saint that is to be found in heaven or earth, that which above all others attracts and engages his soul, and that wherein above all things he places his happiness, and which he looks to for solace and entertainment to his mind in this world, and full satisfaction and blessedness in another. By this, you may examine your love to God, and to Jesus Christ, and to the Word of God, and your joy in them, and also your love to the people of God, and your desires after heaven; whether they be from a supreme delight in this sort of beauty, without being primarily moved by your imagined interest in them, or expectations from them. There are many high affections, great seeming love and rapturous joys, which have nothing of this holy relish belonging to them.

Particularly, by what has been said you may try your discoveries of the glory of God's grace and love, and your affections arising from them. The grace of God may appear lovely two ways; either as *bonum utile*, a profitable good to me, that which greatly serves my interest, and so suits my self-love; or as *bonum formosum*, a beautiful good in itself, and part of the moral and spiritual excellency of the divine nature. In this latter respect it is that the true saints have their hearts affected, and love captivated, by the free grace of God.

From the things that have been said, it appears that, if persons have a great sense of the natural perfections of God, and are greatly affected with them, or have any other sight or sense of God than that which consists in, or implies a sense of the beauty of His moral perfections, it is no certain sign of grace; as particularly men's having a great sense of the awful greatness and terrible majesty of God; for this is only God's natural perfection, and what men may see, and yet be entirely blind to the beauty of His moral perfection, and have nothing of that spiritual taste which relishes this divine sweetness.

It has been shown already, in what was said upon the first distinguishing mark of gracious affections, that that which is spiritual is entirely different in its nature from all that it is possible any graceless person should be the subject of while he continues graceless. But it is possible for those who are wholly without grace to have a clear sight and very great and affecting sense of God's greatness, His mighty power, and awful majesty; for this is what the devils have, though they have lost the spiritual knowledge of God, consisting in a sense of the amiableness of His moral perfections. They are perfectly destitute of any sense or relish of that kind of beauty, yet they have a very great knowledge of the natural glory of God (if I may so speak), or His awful greatness and majesty; this they behold, and are affected with the apprehensions of, and therefore tremble before Him. This glory of God all shall behold at the day of judgment; God will make all rational beings to behold it to a great degree indeed, angels and devils, saints and sinners: Christ will manifest His infinite greatness and awful majesty to every one in a most open, clear, and convincing manner, and in a light that none can resist, " when he shall come in the glory of his Father, and every eye shall see him." Then they shall cry to the mountains to fall upon them, to hide them from the face of Him that sits upon the throne. God will make all His enemies to behold this, and to live in a most clear and affecting view of it, in hell to all eternity. God hath often declared His immutable purpose to make all His enemies to know Him in this respect, in so often annexing these words to the threatenings He denounces against them: " And they shall know that I am the Lord "; Yea, He hath sworn that all men shall see His glory in this respect: Numb. xiv. 21, " As truly as I live, all the earth shall be filled with the glory of the Lord." And this kind of manifestation of God is very often spoken of in Scripture, as made, or to be made, in the sight of God's enemies in this world, Exod. ix. 16, xiv. 18, and xv. 16, Psal. lxvi. 3, and xlvi, 10, and other places innumerable. This was a manifestation which God made of Himself in the sight of that wicked congregation at Mount Sinai, deeply affecting them with it, so that all the people in the camp trembled. Wicked men and devils will see and have a great sense of everything that appertains to the glory of God, except the beauty of his moral perfection. They will see His infinite greatness and majesty, His infinite power, and will be fully convinced of His omniscience, and His eternity and immutability. They will see and know everything appertaining to his moral attributes themselves, except their beauty and amiableness; they will see and know that He is perfectly just and righteous and true, and that He is a holy God, of purer eyes than to behold evil, who cannot look on iniquity. They will see the wonderful manifestations of His infinite goodness and free grace to the saints; and there is nothing will be hid from their eyes, but only the beauty of these moral attributes, and that beauty of the other attributes which arises from it. And so natural men in this world are capable of having a very affecting sense of everything that appertains to God, but this only. Nebuchadnezzar had a great and very affecting sense of the infinite greatness and awful majesty of God, of His supreme and absolute dominion, His mighty and irresistible power, and His sovereignty. He saw that he and all the inhabitants of the earth were nothing before Him, and also had a great conviction in his conscience of His justice, and an affecting sense of His great goodness, Dan. iv. 1, 2, 3, 34, 35, 37. And the sense that Darius had of God's perfections seems to be very much like his, Dan. vi. 25, &c. But saints and angels behold that glory of God which consists in the beauty of His holiness; and it is this sight only that will melt and humble the hearts of men, wean them from the world, draw them to God, and effectually change them. A sight of the awful greatness of God may overpower men's strength, and be more than they can endure; but if the moral beauty of God be hid, the enmity of the heart will remain in its full strength. No love will be enkindled; the will, instead of being effectually gained, will remain inflexible. But the first glimpse of the moral and spiritual glory of God shining into the heart produces all these effects as it were with omnipotent power, which nothing can withstand.

The sense that natural men may have of the awful greatness of God may affect them various ways; it may not only terrify them, but it may elevate them, and raise their joy and praise, according to their circumstances. This will be the natural effect of it, under the real or supposed receipt of some extraordinary mercy from God, by the influence of mere principles of nature. It has been shown already that the receipt of kindness may, by the influence of natural principles, affect the heart with gratitude and praise to God; but if a person, at the same time that he receives remarkable kindness from God, has a sense of His infinite greatness, and that he is but nothing in comparison of Him, surely this will naturally raise his gratitude and praise the higher, for kindness to one so much inferior. A sense of God's greatness had this effect upon Nebuchadnezzar, under the receipt of that extraordinary favour of his restoration, after he had been driven from men and had his dwelling with the beasts. A sense of God's exceeding greatness raises his gratitude very high, so that he does, in the most lofty terms, extol and magnify God, and calls upon all the world to do it with him. If a natural man, at the same time that he is greatly affected with God's infinite greatness and majesty, entertains a strong conceit that this great God has made him His child and special favourite, and promised him eternal glory in His highest love, will not this have a tendency, according to the course of nature, to raise his joy and praise to a great height.

Therefore, it is beyond doubt that too much weight has been laid, by many persons of late, on discoveries of God's greatness, awful majesty, and natural perfection, operating after this manner, without any real view of the holy majesty of God. And experience does abundantly confirm what reason and Scripture declare as to this matter; there having been very many persons, who have seemed to be overpowered with the greatness and majesty of God, and consequently elevated in the manner that has been spoken of, who have been very far from having appearances of a Christian spirit and temper in any manner of proportion, or fruits in practice in any wise agreeable; but their discoveries have worked in a way contrary to the operation of truly spiritual discoveries.

Not that a sense of God's greatness and natural attributes is not exceeding useful and necessary. For, as I observed before, this is implied in a manifestation of the beauty of God's holiness. Though that be something beyond it, it supposes it, as the greater supposes the less. And though natural men may have a sense of the natural perfections of God, yet undoubtedly this is more frequent and common with the saints than with natural men. Grace tends to enable men to see these things in a better manner than natural men do; and not only enables them to see God's natural attributes, but that beauty of those attributes, which (according to our way of conceiving of God) is derived from His holiness.

IV. *Gracious affections arise from the mind being enlightened, rightly and spiritually to understand or apprehend divine things.*

Holy affections are not heat without light; but evermore arise from the information of the understanding, some spiritual instruction that the mind receives, some light or actual knowledge. The child of God is graciously affected because he sees and understands something more of divine things than he did before, more of God or Christ, and of the glorious things exhibited in the gospel; he has some clearer and better view than he had before, when he was not affected. Either he receives some understanding of divine things that is new to him, or has his former knowledge renewed after the view was decayed: 1 John iv. 7, " Every one that loveth, knoweth God." Phil. i. 9, " I pray that your love may abound more and more in knowledge and in all judgment." Rom. x. 2, " They have a zeal of God, but not according to knowledge." Col. iii. 10, " The new man, which is renewed in knowledge." Psalm xliii. 3, 4, " O send out thy light and thy truth; let them lead me; let them bring me unto thy holy hill." John vi. 45, " It is written in the prophets, And they shall be all taught of God. Every man therefore that hath heard, and hath learned of the Father, cometh unto me." Knowledge is the key that first opens the hard heart, and enlarges the affections, and so opens the way for men into the kingdom of heaven; Luke xi. 52, " Ye have taken away the key of knowledge."

Now there are many affections which do not arise from any light in the understanding. And when it is thus, it is a sure evidence that these affections are not spiritual, let them be ever so

high.* Indeed, they have some new apprehensions which they
had not before. Such is the nature of man that it is impossible
his mind should be affected, unless it be by something that he
apprehends, or that his mind conceives. But in many persons
those apprehensions or conceptions that they have, wherewith
they are affected, have nothing of the nature of knowledge or
instruction in them. As for instance, when a person is affected
with a lively idea, suddenly excited in his mind, of some shape
or very beautiful pleasant form of countenance, or some shining
light, or other glorious outward appearance: here is something
apprehended or conceived by the mind; but there is nothing of
the nature of instruction in it, persons become never the wiser
by such things, or more knowing about God, or a Mediator between God and man, or the way of salvation by Christ, or anything contained in any of the doctrines of the gospel. By these
external ideas persons have no further acquaintance with God
as to any of the attributes or perfections of His nature; nor have
they any further understanding of His word, or of His ways or
works. Truly spiritual and gracious affections are not raised after
this manner; these arise from the enlightening of the understanding to understand the things that are taught of God and Christ,
in a new manner. There is a new understanding of the excellent nature of God and His wonderful perfections, some new view
of Christ in His spiritual excellencies and fulness. Things that
appertain to the way of salvation by Christ are opened to him
in a new manner, and he now understands those divine and spiritual doctrines which once were foolishness to him. Such enlightenings of the understanding as these are things entirely different in their nature from strong ideas of shapes and colours,
and outward brightness and glory, or sounds and voices. That
all gracious affections do arise from some instruction or enlightening of the understanding, is therefore a further proof that affections which arise from such impression on the imagination, are
not gracious affections.

Hence, also, it appears that affections arising from texts of

* " Many that have had mighty strong affections at first conversion,
afterwards become dry, and wither, and consume, and pine, and die away:
and now their hypocrisy is manifest; if not to all the world by open profaneness, yet to the discerning eye of living Christians, by a formal,
barren, unsavoury, unfruitful heart and course; because they never had
light to conviction enough as yet."

Scripture coming to the mind are vain, when no instruction received in the understanding from those texts, or anything taught
in those texts, is the ground of the affection, but the manner of
their coming to the mind.   When Christ makes the Scripture
a means of the heart's burning with gracious affection, it is by
opening the Scriptures to their understandings; Luke xxiv. 32,
"Did not our heart burn within us, while he talked with us by
the way, and while he opened to us the Scriptures?"   It appears
also that the affection which is occasioned by the coming of a
text of Scripture must be vain, when the affection is founded on
something that is supposed to be taught by it, which really is
not contained in it, nor in any other Scripture; because such supposed instruction is not real instruction, but a mistake and misapprehension of the mind.   As for instance, when persons suppose that they are expressly taught by some Scripture coming
to their minds, that they in particular are beloved of God,
or that their sins are forgiven, that God is their Father, and the
like.   This is a mistake or misapprehension; for the Scripture
nowhere reveals the individual persons who are beloved, expressly; but only by consequence, by revealing the qualifications
of persons that are beloved of God: and therefore this matter
is not to be learned from Scripture any other way than by consequence, and from these qualifications; for things are not to be
learned from the Scripture any other way than they are taught
in the Scripture.

Affections really arise from ignorance, rather than instruction,
in these instances which have been mentioned; as likewise in
some others that might be mentioned.   As some, when they find
themselves free of speech in prayer, call it God's being with them.
This affects them more, and so their affections are set a-going and
increased; when they look not into the cause of this freedom of
speech, which may arise many other ways besides God's spiritual
presence.   So some are much affected with some apt thoughts that
come into their minds about the Scripture, and call it the Spirit
of God teaching them.   So they ascribe many of the workings
of their own minds, which they have a high opinion of, and are
pleased and taken with, to the special immediate influences of
God's Spirit; and so are mightily affected with their privilege.
And there are some instances of persons in whom it seems manifest that the first ground of their affection is some bodily sensa-

tion. The animal spirits, by some cause (and probably sometimes by the devil) are suddenly and unaccountably put into a very agreeable motion, causing persons to feel pleasantly in their bodies; the animal spirits are put into such a motion as is wont to be connected with the exhilaration of the mind; and the soul, by the laws of the union of soul and body, hence feels pleasure. The motion of the animal spirits does not first arise from any affection or apprehension of the mind whatsoever; but the very first thing that is felt is an exhilaration of the animal spirits, and a pleasant external sensation, it may be, in their breasts. Hence, through ignorance, the person being surprised, begins to think, surely this is the Holy Ghost coming into him. And then the mind begins to be affected and raised. There is first great joy, and then many other affections, in a very tumultuous manner, putting all nature, both body and mind, into a mighty ruffle. For though, as I observed before, it is the soul only that is the seat of the affections, yet this hinders not but that bodily sensations may, in this manner, be an occasion of affections in the mind.

And though men's religious affections truly arise from some instruction or light in the understanding, yet the affection is not gracious unless the light which is the ground of it be spiritual. Affections may be excited by that understanding of things which they obtain merely by human teaching, with the common improvement of the faculties of the mind. Men may be much affected by knowledge of things of religion that they obtain this way; as some philosophers have been mightily affected, and almost carried beyond themselves, by the discoveries they have made in mathematics and natural philosophy. So men may be much affected from common illuminations of the Spirit of God, in which God assists men's faculties to a greater degree of that kind of understanding of religious matters, which they have in some degree by only the ordinary exercise and improvement of their own faculties. Such illuminations may much affect the mind, as in many whom we read of in Scripture that were once enlightened. But these affections are not spiritual.

There is such a thing, if the Scriptures are of any use to teach us anything, as a spiritual, supernatural understanding of divine things that is peculiar to the saints, and which those who are not saints have nothing of. It is this kind of understanding, apprehending or discerning of divine things, that natural men have nothing of, as the apostle speaks, 1 Cor. ii. 14: "But the natural man receiveth not the things of the Spirit of God, for they are foolishness unto him; neither can he know them, because they are spiritually discerned." It is certainly a kind of seeing or discerning spiritual things peculiar to the saints, which is spoken of in 1 John iii. 6: "Whosoever sinneth, hath not seen him, neither known him." 3 John 11, "He that doeth evil hath not seen God." And John vi. 40, "This is the will of him that sent me, that every one that seeth the Son, and believeth on him, may have everlasting life." Chap. xiv. 19, "The world seeth me no more; but ye see me." Chap. xvii. 3, "This is eternal life, that they might know thee, the only true God, and Jesus Christ whom thou hast sent." Matt. xi. 27, "No man knoweth the Son, but the Father; neither knoweth any man the Father, save the Son, and he to whomsoever the Son will reveal him." John xii. 45, "He that seeth me seeth him that sent me." Psal. ix. 10, "They that know thy name, will put their trust in thee." Phil. iii. 8, "I count all things but loss, for the excellency of the knowledge of Christ Jesus my Lord:"—ver. 10, "That I may know him." And innumerable other places there are, all over the Bible, which show the same. And that there is such a thing as an understanding of divine things, which in its nature and kind is wholly different from all knowledge that natural men have, is evident from this, that there is an understanding of divine things which the Scripture calls spiritual understanding, Col. i. 9: "We do not cease to pray for you, and to desire that you may be filled with the knowledge of his will, in all wisdom and spiritual understanding." It has been already shown, that that which is spiritual, in the ordinary use of that word in the New Testament, is entirely different in nature and kind from all which natural men are, or can be the subjects of.

From hence it may be surely inferred wherein spiritual understanding consists. For if there be in the saints a kind of apprehension or perception, which is in its nature perfectly diverse from all that natural men have, or that it is possible they should have until they have a new nature; it must consist in their having a certain kind of ideas or sensations of mind which are simply diverse from all that is or can be in the minds of natural men. And that is the same thing as to say that it consists in the sensations of a new spiritual sense which the souls of natural men have not; as is evident by what has been repeatedly observed. But I have already shown what that new spiritual sense is which the saints have given them in regeneration, and what is the object of it. I have shown that the immediate object of it is the supreme beauty and excellency of the nature of divine things, as they are in themselves. And this is agreeable to the Scripture. The apostle very plainly teaches that the great thing discovered by spiritual light, and understood by spiritual knowledge, is the glory of divine things, 2 Cor. iv. 3, 4: "But if our gospel be hid, it is hid to them that are lost; in whom the god of this world hath blinded the minds of them that believe not, lest the light of the glorious gospel of Christ, who is the image of God, should shine unto them;" together with ver. 6: "For God, who commanded the light to shine out of darkness, hath shined in our hearts, to give the light of the knowledge of the glory of God in the face of Jesus Christ." And chap. iii. 18, preceding: "But we all with open face, beholding as in a glass the glory of the Lord, are changed into the same image, from glory to glory, even as by the Spirit of the Lord." And it must needs be so, for, as has been before observed, the Scripture often teaches that all true religion summarily consists in the love of divine things. And therefore that kind of understanding or knowledge which is the proper foundation of true religion must be the knowledge of the loveliness of divine things. For doubtless, that knowledge which is the proper foundation of love is the knowledge of loveliness. What that beauty of divine things is, which is the proper and immediate object of a spiritual sense of mind, was showed under the last head insisted on, viz., that it is the beauty of their moral perfection. Therefore it is in the view or sense of this, that spiritual understanding does more immediately and primarily consist. And indeed it is plain it can be nothing else; for (as has been shown) there is nothing pertaining to divine things, besides the beauty of their moral excellency and those properties and qualities of divine things which this beauty is the foundation of, but what natural men and devils can see and know, and will know fully and clearly to all eternity.

From what has been said, therefore, we come necessarily to this conclusion, concerning that wherein spiritual understanding consists, viz., that it consists in "a cordial sense of the supreme beauty and sweetness of the holiness or moral perfection of divine things, together with all that discerning and knowledge of things of religion, that depends upon and flows from such a sense."

Spiritual understanding consists primarily in a cordial sense, or a sense of heart, of that spiritual beauty. I say, a sense of heart; for it is not speculation merely that is concerned in this kind of understanding; nor can there be a clear distinction made between the two faculties of understanding and will as acting distinctly and separately in this matter. When the mind is sensible of the sweet beauty and amiableness of a thing, that implies a sensibleness of sweetness and delight in the presence of the idea of it: and this sensibleness of the amiableness or delightfulness of beauty carries in the very nature of it the sense of the heart.

There is a distinction to be made between a mere notional understanding, wherein the mind only beholds things in the exercise of a speculative faculty, and the sense of the heart, wherein the mind does not only speculate and behold but relishes and feels. That sort of knowledge, by which a man has a sensible perception of amiableness and loathsomeness, or of sweetness and nauseousness, is not just the same sort of knowledge with that by which he knows what a triangle is and what a square is. The one is mere speculative knowledge, the other sensible knowledge in which more than the mere intellect is concerned; the heart is the proper subject of it, or the soul as a being that not only beholds, but has inclination, and is pleased or displeased. And yet there is the nature of instruction in it; as he that has perceived the sweet taste of honey, knows much more about it, than he who has only looked upon, and felt it.

The apostle seems to make a distinction between mere speculative knowledge of the things of religion and spiritual knowledge. The former he terms the form of knowledge and of the truth, Rom. ii. 20, "Which hast the form of knowledge and of the truth in the law." The latter is often represented by relishing, smelling, or tasting: 2 Cor. ii. 14, "Now thanks be to God, which always causeth us to triumph in Christ, and maketh manifest the savour of his knowledge by us in every place." Matt. xvi. 23. "Thou savourest not the things that be of God, but those that be of men." 1 Pet. ii. 2, 3, "As new born babes, desire the sincere milk of the word, that ye may grow thereby; if so be ye have tasted that the Lord is gracious." Cant. i. 3, "Because of the savour of thy good ointments, thy name is as ointment poured forth, therefore do the virgins love thee;" compared with 1 John ii. 20, " But ye have an unction from the Holy One, and ye know all things."

Spiritual understanding primarily consists in this sense or taste of the moral beauty of divine things; so that no knowledge can be called spiritual, any further than it arises from this and has this in it. But, secondarily, it includes all that discerning and knowledge of things of religion, which depends upon and flows from such a sense.

When the true beauty and amiableness of the holiness, or true moral good, that is in divine things is discovered to the soul, it, as it were, opens a new world to its view. This shows the glory of all the perfections of God and of every thing appertaining to the divine Being. For, as was observed before, the beauty of all arises from God's moral perfection. This shows the glory of all God's works, both of creation and providence. For it is the special glory of them, that God's holiness, righteousness, faithfulness, and goodness, are so manifested in them; and without these moral perfections there would be no glory in that power and skill with which they are wrought. The glorifying of God's moral perfections is the special end of all the works of God's hands. By this sense of the moral beauty of divine things is understood the sufficiency of Christ as a Mediator; for it is only by the discovery of the beauty of the moral perfection of Christ that the believer is let into the knowledge of the excellency of His Person, so as to know anything more of it than the devils do; and it is only by the knowledge of the excellency of Christ's Person that any know His sufficiency as a Mediator; for the latter depends upon, and arises from, the former. It is by seeing the excellency of Christ's Person that the saints are made sensible of the preciousness of His blood, and its sufficiency to atone for sin; for therein consists the preciousness of Christ's blood, that it is the blood of so excellent and amiable a Person. And on this depends the meritoriousness of His obedience, and the sufficiency and prevalence of His intercession. By this sight of the moral beauty of divine things is seen the beauty of the way of salvation by Christ; for that consists in the beauty of the moral perfections of God, which wonderfully shines forth in every step of this method of salvation from beginning to end. By this is seen the fitness and suitableness of this way: for this wholly consists in its tendency to deliver us from sin and hell, and to bring us to the happiness which consists in the possession and enjoyment of moral good in a way sweetly agreeing with God's moral perfections. And in the way being contrived so as to attain these ends, consists the excellent wisdom of that way. By this is seen the excellency of the Word of God. Take away all the moral beauty and sweetness in the Word, and the Bible is left wholly a dead letter, a dry, lifeless, tasteless thing. By this is seen the true foundation of our duty, the worthiness of God to be so esteemed, honoured, loved, submitted to, and served, as He requires of us, and the amiableness of the duties themselves that are required of us. And by this is seen the true evil of sin; for he who sees the beauty of holiness must necessarily see the hatefulness of sin, its contrary. By this men understand the true glory of heaven, which consists in the beauty and happiness that is in holiness. By this is seen the amiableness and happiness of both saints and angels. He that sees the beauty of holiness, or true moral good, sees the greatest and most important thing in the world, which is the fulness of all things, without which all the world is empty, no better than nothing, yea, worse than nothing. Unless this is seen, nothing is seen that is worth the seeing; for there is no other true excellency or beauty. Unless this be understood, nothing is understood that is worthy of the exercise of the noble faculty of understanding. This is the beauty of the Godhead, and the divinity of Divinity (if I may so speak), the good of the infinite Fountain of good; without which, God Himself (if that were possible) would be an infinite evil; without which we ourselves had better never have been; and without which there had better have been no being. He therefore in effect knows nothing that knows not this; his knowledge is but the shadow of knowledge, or the form of knowledge, as the apostle calls it. Well therefore may the Scriptures represent those who are destitute of that spiritual sense by which is perceived the beauty of holiness, as totally blind, deaf, and senseless, yea, dead. And well may regeneration, in which this divine sense is given to the soul by its Creator, be represented as opening the blind eyes, and raising the dead, and bringing a person into a new world. For if what has been said be considered, it will be manifest, that when a person has this sense and knowledge given him, he will view nothing as he did before; though before he knew all things " after the flesh, yet henceforth he will know them so no more; and he is become a new creature; old things are passed away, behold all things are become new," agreeable to 2 Cor. v. 16, 17.

And besides the things that have been already mentioned, there arises from this sense of spiritual beauty all true experimental knowledge of religion, which is of itself as it were a new world of knowledge. He that sees not the beauty of holiness knows not what one of the graces of God's Spirit is, he is destitute of any idea or conception of all gracious exercises of the soul, and all holy comforts and delights, and all effects of the saving influences of the Spirit of God on the heart; and so is ignorant of the greatest works of God, the most important and glorious effects of His power upon the creature: and also is wholly ignorant of the saints as saints. He knows not what they are, and in effect is ignorant of the whole spiritual world.

Things being thus, it plainly appears that God's implanting of that spiritual supernatural sense which has been spoken of, makes a great change in a man. And were it not for the very imperfect degree in which this sense is commonly given at first, or the small degree of this glorious light that first dawns upon the soul, the change made by this spiritual opening of the eyes in conversion would be much greater and more remarkable every way, than if a man, who had been born blind, and with only the other four senses should continue so a long time, and then at once should have the sense of seeing imparted to him, in the midst of the clear light of the sun, discovering a world of visible objects. For though sight be more noble than any of the other external senses, yet this spiritual sense is infinitely more noble than that, or any other principle of discerning that a man naturally has, and the object of this sense infinitely greater and more important.

This sort of understanding is that knowledge of divine things from whence all truly gracious affections proceed; by which therefore all affections are to be tried. Those affections that arise wholly from any other kind of knowledge, or result from any other kind of apprehensions of mind, are vain.

From what has been said may be learned wherein the most essential difference lies between that light or understanding which is given by the common influences of the Spirit of God on the hearts of natural men, and that saving instruction which is given to the saints. The latter primarily and most essentially lies in beholding the holy beauty that is in divine things, which is the only true moral good, and which the soul of fallen man is by nature totally blind to. The former consists only in a further understanding, through the assistance of natural principles, of those things which men may know, in some measure, by the alone ordinary exercise of their faculties. And this knowledge consists only in the knowledge of those things pertaining to religion which are natural. Thus for instance, in those awakenings of the conscience that natural men are often subject to, the Spirit of God gives no knowledge of the true moral beauty which is in divine things; but only assists the mind to a clearer idea of the guilt of sin, or its relation to punishment, and its connection with the evil of suffering (without any sight of its true moral evil, or odiousness as sin), and a clearer idea of the natural perfections of God, wherein consists, not His holy beauty and glory, but His awful and terrible greatness. It is a clear sight of this that will fully awaken the consciences of wicked men at the day of judgment, without any spiritual light. And it is a lesser degree of the same that awakens the consciences of natural men, without spiritual light, in this world. The same discoveries are in some measure given in the conscience of an awakened sinner in this world, which will be given more fully in the consciences of sinners at the day of judgment. The same kind of sight or apprehension of God, in a lesser degree, makes awakened sinners in this world sensible of the dreadful guilt of sin against so great and terrible a God, and sensible of its amazing punishment, and fills them with fearful apprehensions of divine wrath. This will thoroughly convince all wicked men of the infinitely dreadful nature and guilt of sin, and astonish them with apprehensions of wrath, when Christ shall come in the glory of His power and majesty, and every eye shall see Him, and all the kindreds of the earth shall wail because of Him. And in those common illuminations which are sometimes given to natural men, exciting in them some kind of religious desire, love, and joy, the mind is only assisted to a clearer apprehension of the natural good that is in divine things. Thus sometimes, under common illuminations, men are raised with the ideas of the natural good that is in heaven: as its outward glory, its ease, its honour and advancement, all persons there being the objects of the high favour of God. So there are many things exhibited in the gospel concerning God and Christ and the way of salvation that have a natural good in them, which suits the natural principle of self-love. Thus in the great goodness of God to sinners, and the wonderful dying love of Christ, there is a natural good which all men love as they love themselves; as well as a spiritual and holy beauty which is seen only by the regenerate. Therefore there are many things appertaining to the word of God's grace delivered in the gospel, which may cause natural men, when they hear it, anon with joy to receive it. All that love which natural men have to God and Christ, and to Christian virtues and good men, is not from any sight of the amiableness of the holiness, or true moral excellency of these things, but only for the sake of the natural good there is in them. All natural men's hatred of sin is as much from principles of nature, as men's hatred of a tiger for his rapaciousness, or their aversion to a serpent for his poison and hurtfulness. And all their love of Christian virtue is from no higher principle than their love of a man's good nature, which appears amiable to natural men; but no otherwise than silver and gold appear amiable in the eyes of a merchant, or than the blackness of the soil is beautiful in the eyes of the farmer.

From what has been said of the nature of spiritual understanding, it appears that spiritual understanding does not consist in any new doctrinal knowledge, or in having suggested to the mind any new proposition not before read or heard of; for it is plain that this suggesting of new propositions is a thing entirely diverse from giving the mind a new state or relish of beauty and sweetness.* It is also evident that spiritual knowledge does not consist in any new doctrinal explanation of any part of the Scripture; for still, this is but doctrinal knowledge or the knowledge of propositions; the doctrinal explaining of any part of Scripture is only

---

* Calvin, in his Institutes, Book I, Chap. ix. § 1, says, " The office of the Spirit promised us, is not to make new and unheard-of revelations, or to coin some new kind of doctrine, by which we may be led away from the received doctrine of the gospel; but to seal and confirm to us that very doctrine which is by the gospel." And in the same place he speaks of some that in those days maintained the contrary notion, pretending to be immediately led by the Spirit, as persons that were governed by a most haughty self-conceit: and not so properly to be looked upon as only labouring under a mistake, but as driven by a sort of raving madness.

giving us to understand what are the propositions contained or taught in that part of Scripture.

Hence it appears that the spiritual understanding of the Scripture, does not consist in opening to the mind the mystical meaning of the Scripture, in its parables, types, and allegories; for this is only a doctrinal explication of the Scripture. He that explains what is meant by the stony ground, and the seeds springing up suddenly and quickly withering away, only explains what propositions or doctrines are taught in it. So he that explains what is typified by Jacob's ladder, and the angels of God ascending and descending on it, or what was typified by Joshua's leading Israel through Jordan, only shows what propositions are hid in these passages. And many men can explain these types, who have no spiritual knowledge. It is possible that a man might know how to interpret all the types, parables, enigmas, and allegories in the Bible, and not have one beam of spiritual light in his mind; because he may not have the least degree of that spiritual sense of the holy beauty of divine things which has been spoken of, and may see nothing of this kind of glory in anything contained in any of these mysteries, or any other part of the Scripture. It is plain, by what the apostle says, that a man might understand all such mysteries, and have no saving grace, 1 Cor. xiii. 2: "And though I have the gift of prophecy, and understand all mysteries, and all knowledge, and have not charity, it profiteth me nothing." They therefore are very foolish who are exalted in an opinion of their own spiritual attainments, from notions that come into their minds, of the mystical meaning of these and those passages of Scripture, as though it was a spiritual understanding of these passages, immediately given them by the Spirit of God. Their affections may be highly raised, but what has been said shows the vanity of such affections.

From what has been said, it is also evident that it is not spiritual knowledge for persons to be informed of their duty, by having it immediately suggested to their minds that such and such outward actions or deeds are the will of God. If we suppose that it is truly God's manner thus to signify His will to His people by immediate inward suggestions, such suggestions have nothing of the nature of spiritual light. Such kind of knowledge would only be one kind of doctrinal knowledge. A proposition concerning the will of God is as properly a doctrine of religion as a pro-

position concerning the nature of God or a work of God; and
a having either of these kinds of propositions, or any other proposition, declared to a man, either by speech or inward suggestion, differs vastly from a having the holy beauty of divine things
manifested to the soul, wherein spiritual knowledge does most
essentially consist. Thus there was no spiritual light in Balaam;
though he had the will of God immediately suggested to him by
the Spirit of God from time to time, concerning the way that he
should go, and what he should do and say.

It is manifest, therefore, that a being led and directed in this
manner is not that holy and spiritual leading of the Spirit of
God, which is peculiar to the saints, and a distinguishing mark
of the sons of God, spoken of in Rom. viii. 14: "For as many as
are led by the Spirit of God, they are the sons of God." Gal.
v. 18, "But if ye be led by the Spirit, ye are not under the law."

And if persons have the will of God concerning their actions
suggested to them by some text of Scripture, suddenly and extraordinarily brought to their minds, which text, as the words lay
in the Bible before they came to their minds, related to the action
and behaviour of some other person, but they suppose, as God
sent the words to them, He intended something further by them,
and meant some particular action of theirs; I say, if persons
should have the will of God thus suggested to them with texts
of Scripture, it alters not the case. That the suggestion is accompanied with an apt text of Scripture does not give it the nature
of spiritual instruction. As for instance, if a person in New England, on some occasion, were at a loss to know whether it was
his duty to go into some popish or heathenish land, where he was
like to be exposed to many difficulties and dangers, and should
pray to God that He would show him the way of his duty; and
after earnest prayer, should have those words which God spake
to Jacob suddenly and extraordinarily brought to his mind, as
if they were spoken to him; "Fear not to go down into Egypt;
for I will go with thee; and I will also surely bring thee up again."
(Gen. xlvi. 3-4.) In which words, though as they lay in the Bible
before they came to his mind, they related only to Jacob, and his
behaviour, yet he supposes that God has a further meaning, as
they were brought and applied to him; that thus they are to be
understood in a new sense, that by Egypt is to be understood the
particular country he has in his mind, and that the action in-

tended is his going thither, and that the meaning of the promise is that God would bring him back into New England again. There is nothing of the nature of a spiritual or gracious leading of the Spirit in this, for there is nothing of the nature of spiritual understanding in it. Thus to understand texts of Scripture is not to have a spiritual understanding of them. Spiritually to understand the Scripture is rightly to understand what is in the Scripture, and what was in it before it was understood: it is to understand rightly what used to be contained in the meaning of it, and not the making of a new meaning. When the mind is enlightened spiritually and rightly to understand the Scripture, it is enabled to see that in the Scripture which before was not seen by reason of blindness. But if it was by reason of blindness, that is an evidence that the same meaning was in it before, otherwise it would have been no blindness not to see it; it is no blindness not to see a meaning which is not there. Spiritually enlightening the eyes to understand the Scripture, is to open the eyes: Psal. cxix. 18, "Open thou mine eyes, that I may behold wondrous things out of thy law;" which argues that the reason why the same was not seen in the Scripture before, was that the eyes were shut; which would not be the case if the meaning that is now understood was not there before, but is now newly added to the Scripture, by the manner of the Scripture's coming to the mind. This making a new manner to the Scripture is the same thing as making a new Scripture; it is an adding to the word, which is threatened with so dreadful a curse. Spiritually to understand the Scripture is to have the eyes of the mind opened, to behold the wonderful spiritual excellency of the glorious things contained in the true meaning of it, and that always were contained in it, ever since it was written; to behold the amiable and bright manifestations of the divine perfections, and of the excellency and sufficiency of Christ, and the excellency and suitableness of the way of salvation by Christ, and the spiritual glory of the precepts and promises of the Scripture, &c., which things are, and always were, in the Bible, and would have been seen before if it had not been for blindness, without having any new sense added, by the words being sent by God to a particular person, and spoken anew to him, with a new meaning.

As to a gracious leading of the Spirit, it consists in two things: partly in instructing a person in his duty by the Spirit, and partly in powerfully inducing him to comply with that instruction. But so far as the gracious leading of the Spirit lies in instruction, it consists in a person's being guided by a spiritual and distinguishing taste of that which has in it true moral beauty. I have shown that spiritual knowledge primarily consists in a taste or relish of the amiableness and beauty of that which is truly good and holy. This holy relish is a thing that discerns and distinguishes between good and evil, between holy and unholy, without being at the trouble of a train of reasoning. As he who has a true relish of external beauty knows what is beautiful by looking upon it; he stands in no need of a train of reasoning about the proportion of the features, in order to determine whether that which he sees be a beautiful countenance or no; he needs nothing, but only the glance of his eye. He who has a correct musical ear knows whether the sound he hears be true harmony; he does not need first to be at the trouble of the reasonings of a mathematician about the proportion of the notes. He that has a healthy palate knows what is good food as soon as he tastes it, without the reasoning of a physician about it. There is a holy beauty and sweetness in words and actions, as well as a natural beauty in countenances and sounds, and sweetness in food: Job xii. 11, "Doth not the ear try words, and the mouth taste his meat?" When a holy and amiable action is suggested to the thoughts of a holy soul, that soul, if in the lively exercise of its spiritual taste, at once sees a beauty in it, and so inclines to it and closes with it. On the contrary, if an unworthy unholy action be suggested to it, its sanctified eye sees no beauty in it and is not pleased with it; its sanctified taste relishes no sweetness in it, but on the contrary, it is nauseous to it. Yea, its holy taste and appetite leads it to think of that which is truly lovely, and naturally suggests it; as a healthy taste and appetite naturally suggests the idea of its proper object. Thus a holy person is led by the Spirit, as he is instructed and led by his holy taste and disposition of heart; whereby, in the lively exercise of grace, he easily distinguishes good and evil, and knows at once what is a suitable amiable behaviour towards God and towards man, in this case and the other, and judges what is right, as it were spontaneously and of himself, without a particular deduction, by any other arguments than the beauty that is seen, and goodness that is tasted. Thus Christ blames the Pharisees, that they did not, even of their own selves, judge what was right, without needing miracles to prove it, Luke xii. 57. The apostle seems plainly to have respect to this way of judging of spiritual beauty, in Rom. xii. 2: "Be ye transformed by the renewing of your mind, that ye may prove what is that good, and acceptable, and perfect will of God."

There is such a thing as good taste of natural beauty (which learned men often speak of) that is exercised about temporal things, in judging of them; as about the justness of a speech, the goodness of style, the beauty of a poem, the gracefulness of deportment. A late great philosopher of our nation writes thus upon it: "To have a taste, is to give things their real value, to be touched with the good, to be shocked with the ill; not to be dazzled with false lustres, but in spite of all colours, and every thing that might deceive or amuse, to judge soundly. Taste and judgment, then, should be the same thing; and yet it is easy to discern a difference. The judgment forms its opinions from reflection: the reason on this occasion fetches a kind of circuit, to arrive at its end; it supposes principles, it draws consequences, and it judges; but not without a thorough knowledge of the case; so that after it has pronounced, it is ready to render a reason of its decrees. Good taste observes none of these formalities; ere it has time to consult, it has taken its side; as soon as ever the object is presented, the impression is made, the sentiment formed. As the ear is wounded with a harsh sound, as the smell is soothed with an agreeable odour, before ever the reason have meddled with those objects to judge of them, so the taste opens itself at once, and prevents all reflection. They may come afterwards to confirm it, and discover the secret reasons of its conduct; but it was not in its power to wait for them. Frequently it happens not to know them at all, and what pains soever it uses, cannot discover what it was determined it to think as it did. This conduct is very different from what the judgment observes in its decisions: unless we choose to say that good taste is, as it were, a first motion, or a kind of instinct of right reason, which hurries on with rapidity, and conducts more securely, than all the reasonings she could make; it is a first glance of the eye, which discovers to us the nature and relations of things in a moment."

Now as there is such a kind of taste of the mind as this, which philosophers speak of, whereby persons are guided in their judgment of the natural beauty, gracefulness, propriety, nobleness, and sublimity of speeches and action, whereby they judge as it were by the glance of the eye, or by inward sensation, and the first impression of the object; so there is likewise such a thing as a divine taste, given and maintained by the Spirit of God, in the hearts of the saints, whereby they are in like manner led and guided in discerning and distinguishing the true spiritual and holy beauty of actions; and that more easily, readily, and accurately, as they have more or less of the Spirit of God dwelling in them. And thus " the sons of God are led by the Spirit of God " in their behaviour in the world.

A holy disposition and spiritual taste, where grace is strong and lively, will enable the soul to determine what actions are right and becoming Christians, not only more speedily but far more éxactly than the greatest abilities without it. This may be illustrated by the manner in which some habits of mind and dispositions of heart, of a nature inferior to true grace, will teach and guide a man in his actions. For instance, if a man be a very good-natured man, his good nature will teach him better how to act benevolently amongst mankind, and will direct him on every occasion to those speeches and actions which are agreeable to rules of goodness, than the strongest reason will a man of a morose temper. So if a man's heart be under the influence of an entire friendship and most endeared affection to another, though he be a man of an indifferent capacity, yet this habit of his mind will direct him, far more readily and exactly, to a speech and deportment which shall in all respects be sweet and kind, and agreeable to a benevolent disposition of heart, than the greatest capacity without it. He has, as it were, a spirit within him that guides him. The habit of his mind is attended with a taste by which he immediately relishes that air and mien which is benevolent, and disrelishes the contrary. It causes him to distinguish between one and the other in a moment, more precisely than the most accurate reasonings can find out in many hours. The nature and inward tendency of a stone or other heavy body that is let fall from aloft, shows the way to the centre of the earth more exactly in an instant than the ablest mathematician, without it, could determine by his most accurate observations, in a whole day. Thus it is that a spiritual disposition and taste teaches and guides a man in his behaviour in the world. So an

eminently humble, or meek, or charitable disposition, will direct
a person of mean capacity to such a behaviour, as is agreeable
to Christian rules of humility, meekness and charity, far more
readily and precisely than the most diligent study and elaborate
reasonings of a man of the strongest faculties, who has not a
Christian spirit within him. So also will a spirit of love to God, and
holy fear and reverence towards God, and filial confidence in God,
and a heavenly disposition, teach and guide a man in his behaviour.

It is an exceedingly difficult thing for a wicked man, destitute
of Christian principles in his heart to guide him, to know how
to demean himself like a Christian, with the life and beauty and
heavenly sweetness of a truly holy, humble, Christ-like behaviour.
He knows not how to put on these garments, neither do they fit
him: Eccl. x. 2, 3, " A wise man's heart is at his right hand; but
a fool's heart at his left. Yea also, when he that is a fool walketh
by the way, his wisdom faileth him, and he saith to everyone
that he is a fool;" with ver. 15, " The labour of the foolish wear-
ieth every one of them, because he knoweth not how to go to
the city." Prov. x. 32, " The lips of the righteous know what is
acceptable." Chap. xv. 2, " The tongue of the wise useth knowledge aright; but the mouth of fools poureth out foolishness."
And chap. xvi. 23, " The heart of the wise teacheth his mouth,
and addeth learning to his lips."

The saints, in thus judging of actions by a spiritual taste, have
not a particular recourse to the express rules of God's word, with
respect to every word and action that is before them, the good or
evil of which they thus judge: but yet their taste itself, in general,
is subject to the rule of God's word, and must be tried by that, and
a right reasoning upon it. As a man of a healthy palate judges
of particular morsels by his taste; but yet his palate itself must
be judged of, whether it be healthy or no, by certain rules and
reasons. But a spiritual taste of soul mightily helps the soul in
its reasonings on the Word of God, and in judging of the true
meaning of its rules: for it removes the prejudices of a depraved
appetite, and naturally leads the thoughts in the right channel.
It casts a light on the Word of God, and causes the true meaning
most naturally to come to mind, through the harmony there is
between the disposition and relish of a sanctified soul and the true
meaning of the rules of God's Word. Yea, this harmony tends
to bring the texts themselves to mind on proper occasions; as the

particular state of the stomach and palate tends to bring such particular meats and drinks to mind as are agreeable to that state. Thus the children of God are led by the Spirit of God, in judging of actions themselves, and in their meditations upon, and judging of, and applying the rules of God's holy Word: and so God "teaches them his statutes, and causes them to understand the way of his precepts "; which the Psalmist so often prays for.

But this leading of the Spirit is a thing exceedingly diverse from that which some call so; which consists not in teaching them God's statutes and precepts, that He has already given, but in giving them new precepts by immediate inward speech or suggestion; and has in it no tasting the true excellency of things, or judging or discerning the nature of things at all. They do not determine what is the will of God by any taste or relish, or any manner of judging of the nature of things, but by an immediate dictate concerning the thing to be done; there is no such thing as any judgment or wisdom in the case. Whereas in that leading of the Spirit which is peculiar to God's children, is imparted that true wisdom and holy discretion so often spoken of in the Word of God; which is high above the other way, as the stars are higher than a glow worm. Balaam and Saul (who sometimes were led by the Spirit in that other way) never had it and no natural man can have, without a change of nature.

What has been said of the nature of spiritual understanding, as consisting most essentially in a divine supernatural sense and relish of the heart, not only shows that there is nothing of it in this falsely supposed leading of the Spirit, but also shows the difference between spiritual understanding and all kinds and forms of enthusiasm—all imaginary sights of God and Christ and heaven, all supposed witnessing of the Spirit, and testimonies of the love of God by immediate inward suggestion, and all impressions of future events, and immediate revelations of any secret facts whatsoever; all enthusiastical impressions and applications of words of Scripture, as though they were words now immediately spoken by God to a particular person, in a new meaning and carrying something more in them than the words contain as they lie in the Bible; and all interpretations of the mystical meaning of the Scripture by supposed immediate revelation. None of these things consist in a divine sense and relish of the heart of the holy beauty and excellency of divine things; nor have they anything to do with such a sense; but all consist in impressions in the head; all are impressions on the imagination, and consist in the exciting of external ideas in the mind, either of outward shapes and colours, or words spoken, or letters written, or ideas of things external and sensible, belonging to actions done or events accomplished or to be accomplished. An enthusiastical supposed manifestation of the love of God is made by the exciting an idea of a smiling countenance, or some other pleasant outward appearance, or by the idea of pleasant words spoken, or written, or excited in the imagination, or by some pleasant bodily sensation. When persons have an imaginary revelation of some secret fact, it is by exciting external ideas; either of some words, implying a declaration of that fact, or some visible or sensible circumstances of such a fact. So the supposed leading of the Spirit to do the will of God, is either by exciting the idea of words (which are outward things) in their minds, either the words of Scripture or other words, which they look upon as an immediate command of God; or else by exciting and impressing strongly the ideas of the outward actions themselves. So when an interpretation of a Scripture type or allegory is immediately, in an extraordinary way, strongly suggested, it is by suggesting words, as though one secretly whispered and told the meaning, or by exciting other ideas in the imagination.

Experiences and discoveries such as these, commonly raise the affections of such as are deluded by them to a great height, and make a mighty uproar in both soul and body. And a very great part of the false religion that has been in the world, from one age to another, consists in such discoveries as these, and in the affections that flow from them. In such things consisted the experiences of the ancient Pythagoreans among the heathen, and many others among them, who had strange ecstasies and raptures, and pretended to a divine afflatus and immediate revelations from heaven. In such things as these seem to have consisted the experiences of the Essenes, an ancient sect among the Jews at and after the time of the apostles. In such things as these consisted the experiences of many of the ancient Gnostics, the Montanists, and many other sects of ancient heretics in the primitive ages of the Christian church. In such things as these consisted the pretended immediate converse with God and Christ and saints and angels of heaven, of the monks, anchorites, and recluses, that formerly abounded in the Church of Rome. In such things consisted the pretended high experiences and great spirituality of many sects of enthusiasts, that swarmed in the world after the Reformation; such as the Anabaptists, Antinomians, and Familists, the followers of Nicholas Storch, Thomas Münzer, John Becold, Henry Pfeiffer, David George, Casper Swenckfield, Henry Nicholas, Johannes Agricola Eislebius; and the many wild enthusiasts that were in England in the days of Oliver Cromwell; and the followers of Mrs. Anne Hutchinson in New England; as appears by the particular and large accounts given of all these sects by that eminently holy man, Mr. Samuel Rutherford, in his " Display of the Spiritual Antichrist." And in such things as these consisted the experiences of the late French prophets and their followers. In these things also seems to lie the religion of the many kinds of enthusiasts of the present day. It is chiefly by such sort of religion as this that Satan transforms himself into an angel of light: and it is that which he has ever most successfully made use of to confound hopeful and happy revivals of religion, from the beginning of the Christian church to this day. When the Spirit of God is poured out to begin a glorious work, then the old serpent, as fast as possible and by all means, introduces this bastard religion, and mingles it with the true; which has from time to time soon brought all things into confusion. The pernicious consequence of it is not easily imagined or conceived of, until we see and are amazed with the awful effects of it, and the dismal desolation it has made. If the revival of true religion be very great in its beginning, yet if this bastard comes in, there is danger of its doing as Gideon's bastard Abimelech did, who never left until he had slain all his threescore and ten true-born sons, excepting one that was forced to flee. Great and strict therefore should be the watch and guard that ministers maintain against such things, especially at a time of great awakening: for men, especially the common people, are easily bewitched with such things, they having such a glaring and glistering show of high religion. The devil hides his own shape, and appears as an angel of light, that men may not be afraid of him but adore him.

The imagination or fancy seems to be that wherein are formed all those delusions of Satan, which those are carried away with who are under the influence of false religion and counterfeit graces and affections. Here is the devil's grand lurking place, the very nest of foul and delusive spirits. It is very much to be doubted whether the devil can come at the soul of man at all to affect it, or to excite any thought or motion, or produce any effect whatsoever in it, any other way than by the fancy, which is that power of the soul, by which it receives ideas of outward and sensible things. As to the laws and means which the Creator has established for the intercourse and communication of unbodied spirits, we know nothing about them; we do not know by what medium they manifest their thoughts to each other, or excite thoughts in each other. But as to spirits that are united to bodies, those bodies are their medium of communication. They have no other medium of acting on other creatures, or being acted on by them, than the body. Therefore it is not to be supposed that Satan can excite any thought, or produce any effect in the soul of man, any otherwise than by some motion of the animal spirits, or by causing some motion or alteration in something which appertains to the body. There is this reason to think that the devil cannot produce thoughts in the soul immediately, or any other way than by the medium of the body, that he cannot immediately see or know the thoughts of the soul: it is abundantly declared in the Scripture to be peculiar to the omniscient God to do that. But it is not likely that the devil can immediately produce an effect which is out of the reach of his immediate view. It seems unreasonable to suppose that his immediate agency should be out of his own sight, or that it should be impossible for him to see what he himself immediately does. Is it not unreasonable to suppose that any spirit or intelligent agent should, by the act of his will, produce effects according to his understanding, or agreeable to his own thoughts, and that immediately, and yet the effects produced be beyond the reach of his understanding, or where he can have no immediate perception of them? But if this be so, that the devil cannot produce thoughts in the soul immediately, or any other way than by the animal spirits or by the body, then it follows that he never brings to pass anything in the soul, but by the imagination or fancy, or by exciting external ideas. For we know that alterations in the body do immediately excite no other sort of ideas in the mind, but external ones, or those of the outward senses. As to reflection, abstraction, reasoning, and those thoughts and inward motions which are the fruits of these acts of the mind, they are not the nearest effects of impressions on the body. So that it must be only by the imagination that Satan has access to the soul, to tempt and delude it, or suggest anything to it.* And this seems to be the reason why persons that are under the disease of melancholy are commonly so visibly and remarkably subject to the suggestions and temptations of Satan; that being a disease which peculiarly affects the animal spirits, and is attended with weakness of that part of the body which is the foundation of the animal spirits, even the brain, which is, as it were, the seat of the fancy. It is by impressions made on the brain that any ideas are excited in the mind, by the motion of the animal spirits, or any changes made in the body. The brain being thus weakened and diseased, it is less under the command of the higher faculties of the soul, and yields the more easily to extrinsic impressions, and is overpowered by the disordered motions of the animal spirits; and so the devil has greater advantage to affect the mind by working on the imagination. And thus Satan, when he casts in those

* " The imagination is that room of the soul wherein the devil doth often appear. Indeed (to speak exactly) the devil hath no efficient power over the rational part of a man; he cannot change the will, he cannot alter the heart of a man. So that the utmost he can do, in tempting a man to sin, is by suasion and suggestion only. But how doth the devil do this? Even by working upon the imagination. He observeth the temper and bodily constitution of a man; and thereupon suggests to his fancy, and injects his fiery darts thereinto, by which the mind will come to be wrought upon. The devil then, though he hath no imperious efficacy over thy will, yet he can thus stir and move thy imagination, and thou being naturally destitute of grace, canst not withstand these suggestions: hence it is that any sin in thy imagination, though but in the outward works of the soul, yet doth quickly lay hold on all. And indeed, by this means, do arise those horrible delusions, that are in many erroneous ways of religion; all is because their imaginations are corrupted. Yea, how often are these diabolical delusions of the imagination taken for the gracious operation of God's Spirit! It is from hence that many have pretended to enthusiasms: they leave the Scriptures, and wholly attend to what they perceive and feel within them." *Anthony Burgess, On Original Sin* (1659).

The great François Turretine, speaking on that question, What is the power of angels? says, " As to bodies, there is no doubt but that they can do a great deal upon all sorts of elementary and sublunary bodies, to move them locally, and variously to agitate them. It is also certain, that they can act upon the external and internal senses to excite them or to bind them. But as to the rational soul itself, they can do nothing immediately upon that; for to God alone, who knows and searches the hearts, and who has them in His hands, does it also appertain to bow and move them whithersoever He will. But angels can act upon the rational soul, only mediately, by imaginations." (*Institutio theologicae elencticae:* 1680-83.)

horrid suggestions into the minds of many melancholy persons
in which they have no hand themselves, he does it by exciting
imaginary ideas, either of some dreadful words or sentences or
other horrid outward ideas. And when he tempts other persons
who are not melancholy, he does it by presenting to the imagination in a lively and alluring manner the objects of their lusts,
or by exciting ideas of words and so by them exciting thoughts;
or by promoting an imagination of outward actions, events, or
circumstances. Innumerable are the ways by which the mind
may be led on to all kind of evil thoughts, by the exciting of external ideas in the imagination.

If persons keep no guard at these avenues of Satan, by which
he has access to the soul to tempt and delude it, they will be
likely to have enough of him. And especially if, instead of guard-
ing against him, they lay themselves open to him, and seek and
invite him, because he appears as an angel of light, and counterfeits the illuminations and graces of the Spirit of God by inward
whispers, and immediate suggestions of facts and events, pleasant voices, beautiful images, and other impressions on the imagination. There are many who are deluded by such things, and
are lifted up with them, and seek after them, that have a continued course of them and can have them almost when they will;
and especially when their pride and vainglory have most occasion
for them, to make a show of them before company. It is with
them something as it is with those who are professors of the art
of telling where lost things are to be found, by impressions made
on their imaginations; they laying themselves open to the devil,
he is always on hand to give them the desired impression.

Before I finish what I would say on this head of imaginations,
counterfeiting spiritual light, and affections arising from them, I
would renewedly (to prevent misunderstanding of what has been
said) desire it may be observed that I am far from determining
that no affections are spiritual which are attended with imaginary ideas. Such is the nature of man that he can scarcely think
of anything intensely, without some kind of outward ideas. They
arise and interpose themselves unavoidably in the course of a
man's thoughts; though oftentimes they are very confused, and
are not what the mind regards. When the mind is much engaged and the thoughts intense, oftentimes the imagination is
more strong, and the outward idea more lively, especially in per-

sons of some constitutions of body. But there is a great difference between these two things, viz., lively imaginations arising
from strong affections, and strong affections arising from lively
imaginations. The former may be, and doubtless often is, an
accompaniment of truly gracious affections. The affections do
not arise from the imagination, nor have any dependence upon
it; but on the contrary, the imagination is only the accidental
effect or consequent of the affection, through the infirmity of
human nature. But when the latter is the case, as it often is, and
the affection arises from the imagination, and is built upon it
as its foundation, instead of a spiritual illumination or discovery,
then is the affection, however elevated, worthless and vain. And
this is the drift of what has been now said, of impressions on the
imagination. Having observed this, I proceed to another mark
of gracious affections.

V. *Truly gracious affections are attended with a reasonable
and spiritual conviction of the reality and certainty of divine
things.*

This seems to be implied in the text that was laid as the foundation of this discourse: "Whom having not seen, ye love; in
whom, though now ye see him not, yet believing, ye rejoice with
joy unspeakable, and full of glory."

All those who are truly gracious persons have a solid, full,
thorough and effectual conviction of the truth of the great things
of the gospel; I mean, that they no longer halt between two opinions. The great doctrines of the gospel cease to be any longer
doubtful things or matters of opinion, which, though probable,
are yet disputable; but with them, they are points settled and
determined, as undoubted and indisputable; so that they are not
afraid to venture their all upon their truth. Their conviction is
an effectual conviction; so that the great, spiritual, mysterious,
and invisible things of the gospel have the influence of real and
certain things upon them; they have the weight and power of
real things in their hearts; and accordingly rule in their affections, and govern them through the course of their lives. With
respect to Christ's being the Son of God and Saviour of the
world, and the great things He has revealed concerning Himself
and his Father, and another world, they have not only a pre-
dominating opinion that these things are true, and so yield their

assent, as they do in many other matters of doubtful speculation; but they see that it is really so; their eyes are opened so that they see that really Jesus is the Christ, the Son of the living God. And as to the things which Christ has revealed of God's eternal purposes and designs concerning fallen man, and the glorious and everlasting things prepared for the saints in another world, they see that they are so indeed; and therefore these things are of great weight with them, and have a mighty power upon their hearts and influence over their practice, in some measure answerable to their infinite importance.

That all true Christians have such a kind of conviction of the truth of the things of the gospel is abundantly manifest from the Holy Scriptures. I will mention a few places of many : Matt. xvi. 15, 16, 17, "But whom say ye that I am? Simon Peter answered and said, Thou art the Christ, the Son of the living God. And Jesus answered and said unto him, Blessed art thou, Simon Bar-jona; my Father which is in heaven hath revealed it unto thee." John vi. 68, 69, " Thou hast the words of eternal life. And we believe and are sure that thou art that Christ, the Son of the living God." John xvii. 6, 7, 8, "I have manifested thy name unto the men which thou gavest me out of the world. Now they have known that all things whatsoever thou hast given me, are of thee. For I have given unto them the words which thou gavest me; and they have received them, and have known surely that I came out from thee, and they have believed that thou didst send me." Acts viii. 37, "If thou believest with all thy heart, thou mayest." 2 Cor. iv. 11-14, "We which live, are alway delivered unto death for Jesus' sake.—Death worketh in us. —We having the same spirit of faith, according as it is written, I believed, and therefore have I spoken; we also believe, and therefore speak; knowing that he which raised up the Lord Jesus, shall raise up us also by Jesus, and shall present us with you." Ver. 16, " For which cause we faint not." And ver. 18, " While we look not at the things which are seen," &c. And chap. v. 1, " For we know, that if our earthly house of this tabernacle were dissolved, we have a building of God." And ver. 6, 7, 8, " Therefore we are always confident, knowing that whilst we are at home in the body, we are absent from the Lord : (for we walk by faith, not by sight). We are confident, I say, and willing rather to be absent from the body, and present with the Lord." 2 Tim i. 12, " For the which cause, I also suffer these things; nevertheless I am not ashamed; for I know whom I have believed, and am persuaded that he is able to keep that which I have committed unto him against that day." Heb. iii. 6, "Whose house are we, if we hold fast the confidence and the rejoicing of the hope firm unto the end." Heb. xi. 1, "Now faith is the substance of things hoped for, the evidence of things not seen"; together with that whole chapter. 1 John iv. 13-16, "Hereby know we that we dwell in him, and he in us, because he hath given us of his Spirit. And we have seen, and do testify, that the Father sent the Son to be the Saviour of the world. Whosoever shall confess that Jesus is the Son of God, God dwelleth in him, and he in God. And we have known and believed the love that God hath to us." Chap. v. 4, 5, "For whatsoever is born of God overcometh the world; and this is the victory that overcometh the world, even our faith. Who is he that overcometh the world, but he that believeth that Jesus is the Son of God?"

Thus are truly gracious affections attended with a conviction and persuasion of the truth of the things of the gospel, and a sight of their evidence and reality, as these and other Scriptures demonstrate.

There are many religious affections which are not attended with such a conviction of the judgment. There are many apprehensions and ideas which some have, that they call divine discoveries, which are affecting, but not convincing. Though for a little while they may seem to be more persuaded of the truth of the things of religion than they used to be, and may yield a forward assent, like many of Christ's hearers, who believed for a while; yet they have no thorough and effectual conviction. There is no great abiding change in them in this respect, that, whereas formerly they did not realize the great things of the gospel, now these things, with regard to reality and certainty, appear new to them, and they behold them quite in another view than they used to do. There are many persons who have been exceedingly raised with religious affections, and think they have been converted, but they do not seem to be any more convinced of the truth of the gospel than they used to be; or at least, there is no remarkable alteration. They are not men who live under the influence and power of a realizing conviction of the infinite and eternal things which the gospel reveals; if they were, it would be impossible for them to live as they do. Their affections, because they are not attended with a thorough conviction of the mind, are not at all to be depended on; however great a show and noise they make, it is like the blaze of tow or crackling of thorns, or like the forward flourishing blade on stony ground, that has no root nor deepness of earth to maintain its life.

Some persons, under high affections and a confident persuasion of their good estate, have that which they very ignorantly call a seeing of the truth of the Word of God, but which is very far from it. They have some texts of Scripture coming to their minds in a sudden and extraordinary manner, immediately declaring unto them (as they suppose) that their sins are forgiven, or that God loves them and will save them; and, it may be, have a chain of Scriptures coming one after another to the same purpose; and they are convinced that it is truth. They are confident that it is certainly so, that their sins are forgiven, and God does love them. They say they know it is so; and when the words of Scripture are suggested to them, and as they suppose immediately spoken to them by God, they are ready to cry out, "Truth, truth! It is certainly so! The Word of God is true!" And this they call a seeing the truth of the Word of God. Whereas the whole of their faith amounts to no more than only a strong confidence of their own good estate, and so a confidence that these words are true which they suppose tell them they are in a good estate: when indeed (as was shown before) there is no Scripture which declares that any person is in a good estate directly, or any other way than by consequence. So that this, instead of being a real sight of the truth of the Word of God, is a sight of nothing but a phantom, and is wholly a delusion. Truly to see the truth of the Word of God, is to see the truth of the gospel; which is the glorious doctrine the Word of God contains concerning God and Jesus Christ, and the way of salvation by Him, and the world of glory that He is entered into and purchased for all them who believe; and not a revelation that such and such particular persons are true Christians and shall go to heaven. Therefore those affections which arise from no other persuasion of the truth of the Word of God than this, arise from delusion and not true conviction, and consequently are themselves delusive and vain.

But if the religious affections that persons have do indeed arise from a strong persuasion of the truth of the Christian religion, their affections are not the better unless their persuasion be a reasonable persuasion or conviction. By a reasonable conviction, I mean a conviction founded on real evidence, or upon that which is a good reason or just ground of conviction. Men may have a strong persuasion that the Christian religion is true, when their persuasion is not at all built on evidence, but altogether on education and the opinion of others; as many Mahometans are strongly persuaded of the truth of the Mahometan religion, because their fathers and neighbours and nation believe it. That belief of the truth of the Christian religion which is built on the very same grounds with a Mahometan's belief of the Mahometan religion, is the same sort of belief. And though the thing believed happens to be better, yet that does not make the belief itself to be of a better sort; for though the thing believed happens to be true, yet the belief of it is not owing to this truth, but to education. And as the conviction is no better than the Mahometan's conviction, so the affections that flow from it are no better in themselves than the religious affections of Mahometans.

But if the belief of Christian doctrines be not merely from education, but indeed from reasons and arguments which are offered, it will not from thence necessarily follow that their affections are truly gracious: for in order to that, it is requisite not only that the belief which their affections arise from, should be a reasonable, but also a spiritual belief or conviction. I suppose none will doubt but that some natural men do yield a kind of assent of their judgment to the truth of the Christian religion, from the rational proofs or arguments that are offered to evince it. Judas, without doubt, thought Jesus to be the Messiah, from the things which he saw and heard; but yet all along was a devil. So in John ii. 23-25, we read of many that believed in Christ's name when they saw the miracles that He did; whom yet Christ knew had not that within them, which was to be depended on. So Simon the sorcerer believed, when he beheld the miracles and signs which were done; but yet remained in the gall of bitterness, and bond of iniquity, Acts viii. 13, 23. And if there is such a belief or assent of the judgment in some natural men, none can doubt but that religious affections may arise from that assent or belief; as we read of some who believed for a while, that were greatly affected, and anon with joy received the Word.

It is evident that there is such a thing as a spiritual belief or conviction of the truth of the things of the gospel, or a belief that is peculiar to those who are spiritual, or who are regenerated, and have the Spirit of God in His holy communications, and dwelling in them as a vital principle. So that the conviction they have does not only differ from that which natural men have in its concomitants, in that it is accompanied with good works; but the belief itself is diverse. The assent and conviction of the judgment is of a kind peculiar to those who are spiritual, and that which natural men are wholly destitute of. This is evident by the Scripture, if anything at all is so: John xvii. 8, "They have believed that thou didst send me." Tit. i. 1, "According to the faith of God's elect, and the acknowledging of the truth which is after godliness." John xvi. 27, "The Father himself loveth you, because ye have loved me, and have believed that I came out from God." 1 John iv. 15, "Whosoever shall confess that Jesus is the Son of God, God dwelleth in him, and he in God." Chap. v. 1, "Whosoever believeth that Jesus is the Christ, is born of God." Ver. 10, "He that believeth on the Son of God hath the witness in himself."

What a spiritual conviction of the judgment is, we are naturally led to determine from what has been said already, under the former head of a spiritual understanding. The conviction of the judgment arises from the illumination of the understanding; the passing of a right judgment on things depends on having a right apprehension or idea of things. And therefore it follows, that a spiritual conviction of the truth of the great things of the gospel is such a conviction as arises from having a spiritual view or apprehension of those things in the mind. And this is also evident from the Scripture, which often represents that a saving belief of the reality and divinity of the things proposed and exhibited to us in the gospel, is from the Spirit of God's enlightening the mind and causing it to have right apprehensions of the nature of those things, and so as it were unveiling things, or revealing them, and enabling the mind to view them and see them as they are. Luke x. 21, 22, "I thank thee, O Father, Lord of heaven and earth, that thou hast hid these things from the wise and prudent, and hast revealed them unto babes: even so, Father, for so it seemed good in thy sight. All things are delivered unto me of my Father: and no man knoweth who the Son is, but the Father; and who the Father is, but the Son, and he to whom the

Son will reveal him." John vi. 40, " And this is the will of him that sent me, that every one which seeth the Son, and believeth on him, may have everlasting life," where it is plain that true faith arises from a spiritual sight of Christ. And John xvii. 6, 7, 8, " I have manifested thy name unto the men which thou gavest me out of the world. Now they have known that all things whatsoever thou hast given me are of thee. For I have given unto them the words which thou gavest me; and they have received them, and have known surely that I came out from thee, and they have believed that thou didst send me." Christ's manifesting God's name to the disciples, or giving them a true apprehension and view of divine things, was that whereby they knew that Christ's doctrine was of God, and that Christ Himself was of Him, and was sent by Him. Matt. xvi. 16, 17, " Simon Peter said, Thou art the Christ, the Son of the living God. And Jesus answered and said unto him, Blessed art thou, Simon Bar-jona: for flesh and blood hath not revealed it unto thee, but my Father which is in heaven." 1 John v. 10, " He that believeth on the Son of God, hath the witness in himself." Gal. i. 14, 15, 16, " Being more exceedingly zealous of the traditions of my fathers. But when it pleased God, who separated me from my mother's womb, and called me by his grace, to reveal his Son in me, that I might preach him among the heathen; immediately I conferred not with flesh and blood."

If it be so that that is a spiritual conviction of the divinity and reality of the things exhibited in the gospel, which arises from a spiritual understanding of them, I have shown already what that is, viz., a sense and taste of the divine, supreme, and holy excellency and beauty of those things. So that then is the mind spiritually convinced of the divinity and truth of the great things of the gospel, when that conviction arises, either directly or remotely, from such a sense or view of their divine excellency and glory as is there exhibited. This clearly follows from things that have been already said: and for this the Scripture is very plain and express, 2 Cor. iv. 3-6: "But if our gospel be hid, it is hid to them that are lost; in whom the god of this world hath blinded the minds of them that believe not, lest the light of the glorious gospel of Christ, who is the image of God, should shine unto them. For we preach not ourselves, but Christ Jesus the Lord; and ourselves your servants for Jesus' sake. For God, who commanded the light to shine out of darkness, hath shined in our hearts, to give the light of the knowledge of the glory of God in the face of Jesus Christ "; together with the last verse of the fore-going chapter, which introduces this, " But we all, with open face beholding as in a glass the glory of the Lord, are changed into the same image, from glory to glory, even as by the Spirit of the Lord." Nothing can be more evident, than that a saving belief of the gospel is here spoken of by the apostle as arising from the mind's being enlightened to behold the divine glory of the things it exhibits.

This view or sense of the divine glory and unparalleled beauty of the things exhibited to us in the gospel, has a tendency to convince the mind of their divinity two ways; first, directly, and secondly, more indirectly and remotely. 1. A view of this divine glory directly convinces the mind of the divinity of these things, as this glory is in itself a direct, clear, and all-conquering evidence of it; especially when clearly discovered, or when this supernatural sense is given in a good degree.

He that has his judgment thus directly convinced and assured of the divinity of the things of the gospel by a clear view of their divine glory, has a reasonable conviction; his belief and assurance is altogether agreeable to reason; because the divine glory and beauty of divine things is in itself a real evidence of their divinity, and the most direct and strong evidence. He that truly sees the divine, transcendent, supreme glory of those things which are divine, does, as it were, know their divinity intuitively. He not only argues that they are divine, but he sees that they are divine. He sees that in them wherein divinity chiefly consists, for in this glory, which is so vastly and inexpressibly distinguished from the glory of artificial things and all other glory, does mainly consist the true notion of divinity. God is God, distinguished from all other beings and exalted above them, chiefly by His divine beauty, which is infinitely diverse from all other beauty. They therefore that see the stamp of this glory in divine things, they see divinity in them, they see God in them, and so see them to be divine; because they see that in them wherein the truest idea of divinity does consist. Thus a soul may have a kind of intuitive knowledge of the divinity of the things exhibited in the gospel; not that he judges the doctrines of the gospel to be from God, without any argument or deduction at all; but it is without any long chain of arguments; the argument is but one, and the evidence direct; the mind ascends to the truth of the gospel by but one step, and that is its divine glory.

It would be very strange, if any professing Christian should deny it to be possible that there should be an excellency in divine things, which is so transcendent and exceedingly different from what is in other things, that, if it were seen, it would evidently distinguish them. We cannot rationally doubt but that things that are divine, and that appertain to the Supreme Being, are vastly different from things that are human: that there is a God-like, high, and glorious excellency in them, that does so distinguish them from the things which are of men that the difference is ineffable; and therefore such as, if seen, will have a most convincing, satisfying influence upon any one that they are what they are, viz., divine. Doubtless there is that glory and excellency in the divine Being, by which he is so infinitely distinguished from all other beings, that if it were seen, He might be known by it. It would therefore be very unreasonable to deny that it is possible for God to give manifestations of this distinguishing excellency in things by which He is pleased to make Himself known; and that this distinguishing excellency may be clearly seen in them. There are natural excellencies, that are very evidently distinguishing of the subjects or authors, to any one who beholds them. How vastly is the speech of an understanding man different from that of a little child! And how greatly distinguished is the speech of some men of great genius, as Homer, Cicero, Milton, Locke, Addison, and others, from that of many other understanding men! There are no limits to be set to the degrees of manifestation of mental excellency that there may be in speech. But the appearances of the natural perfections of God, in the manifestations he makes of Himself, may doubtless be unspeakably more evidently distinguishing than the appearances of those excellencies of worms of the dust, in which they differ one from another. He that is well acquainted with mankind and their works, by viewing the sun may know it is no human work. And it is reasonable to suppose, that when Christ comes at the end of the world, in the glory of His Father, it will be with such ineffable appearances of divinity as will leave no doubt to the inhabitants of the world, even the most obstinate infidels, that He who appears is a divine person. But, above all, do the manifestations of the moral and spiritual glory of the divine Being (which is the proper beauty of the divinity) bring their own evidence, and tend to assure the heart. Thus the disciples were assured that Jesus was the Son of God, " for they beheld his glory, the glory as of the only begotten of the Father, full of grace and truth," John i. 14. When Christ appeared in the glory of His transfiguration to His disciples, with that outward glory to their bodily eyes which was a sweet and admirable symbol and semblance of His spiritual glory, together with His spiritual glory itself manifested to their minds; the manifestation of glory was such as did perfectly and with good reason assure them of His divinity; as appears by what the Apostle Peter says concerning it, 2 Pet. i. 16, 17, 18, " For we have not followed cunningly devised fables, when we made known unto you the power and coming of our Lord Jesus Christ, but were eyewitnesses of his majesty. For he received from God the Father honour and glory, when there came such a voice to him from the excellent glory, This is my beloved Son, in whom I well pleased. And this voice which came from heaven we heard, when we were with him in the holy mount." The apostle calls that mount the holy mount, because the manifestations of Christ which were made to their minds, and which their minds were especially impressed and ravished with, were the glory of His holiness, or the beauty of His moral excellency; or, as another of these disciples who saw it, expresses it, " his glory, as full of grace and truth."

Now this distinguishing glory of the divine Being has its brightest appearance and manifestation in the things proposed and exhibited to us in the gospel, in the doctrines there taught, the word there spoken, and the divine counsels and acts and works there revealed. These things have the clearest, most admirable, and distinguishing representations and exhibitions of the glory of God's moral perfections, that ever were made to the world. And if there be such a distinguishing, evidential manifestation of divine glory in the gospel, it is reasonable to suppose that there may be such a thing as seeing it. What should hinder but that it may be seen? It is no argument that it cannot be seen, that some do not see it, though they may be discerning men in temporal matters. If there be such ineffable, distinguishing, evidential excellencies in the gospel, it is reasonable to suppose that they are such as are not to be discerned but by the special influence and enlightenings of the Spirit of God. There is need of uncommon force of mind to discern the distinguishing excellencies of the works of authors of great genius. Those things in Milton, which, to mean judges appear tasteless and imperfections, are his inimitable excellencies in the eyes of those, who are of greater discerning and better taste. And if there be a book which God is the author of, it is most reasonable to suppose that the distinguishing glories of His Word are of such a kind, as that the sin and corruption of men's hearts, which above all things alienate men from the Deity, and make the heart dull and stupid to any sense or taste of those things wherein the moral glory of the divine perfections consists: I say it is but reasonable to suppose that this would blind men from discerning the beauties of such a book; and that therefore they will not see them, but as God is pleased to enlighten them, and restore a holy taste to discern and relish divine beauties.

This sense of the spiritual excellency and beauty of divine things also tends directly to convince the mind of the truth of the gospel. Very many of the most important things declared in the gospel are hid from the eyes of natural men, the truth of which in effect consists in this excellency, or so immediately depends upon it, and results from it, that in this excellency being seen, the truth of those things is seen. As soon as ever the eyes are opened to behold the holy beauty and amiableness that is in divine things, a multitude of most important doctrines of the gospel that depend upon it (which all appear strange and dark to natural men) are at once seen to be true. As for instance, hereby appears the truth of what the Word of God declares concerning the exceeding evil of sin; for the same eye that discerns the transcendent beauty of holiness, necessarily therein sees the exceeding odiousness of sin: the same taste which relishes the sweetness of true moral good, tastes the bitterness of moral evil. And by this means a man sees his own sinfulness and loathsomeness, for he has now a sense to discern objects of this nature, and so sees the truth of what the Word of God declares concerning the exceeding sinfulness of mankind, which before he did not see. He now sees the dreadful pollution of his heart, and the desperate depravity of his nature, in a new manner; for his soul has now a sense given it to feel the pain of such a disease; and this shows him the truth of what the Scripture reveals concerning the corruption of man's nature, his original sin, and the ruinous, undone condition man is in; also his need of a Saviour, and of the mighty power of God to renew his heart and change his nature. Men, by seeing the true excellency of holiness, do see the glory of all those things which both reason and Scripture show to be in the divine Being; for it has been shown that the glory of them depends on this: and hereby they see the truth of all that the Scripture declares concerning God's glorious excellency and majesty, His being the Fountain of all good, the only happiness of the creature, &c. And this again shows the mind the truth of what the Scripture teaches concerning the evil of sin against so glorious a God; and also the truth of what it teaches concerning sin's just desert of that dreadful punishment which it reveals; and also concerning the impossibility of our offering any satisfaction or sufficient atonement for that which is so infinitely evil and heinous. And this again shows the truth of what the Scripture reveals concerning the necessity of a Saviour, to offer an atonement of infinite value for sin. And this sense of spiritual beauty that has been spoken of, enables the soul to see the glory of those things which the gospel reveals concerning the person of Christ; and so enables it to see the exceeding beauty and dignity of His person, appearing in what the gospel exhibits of His word, works, acts, and life. This apprehension of the superlative dignity of His person shows the truth of what the gospel declares concerning the value of His blood and righteousness, and so the infinite excellency of that offering He has made to God for us, and its sufficiency to atone for our sins and recommend us to God. And thus the Spirit of God reveals the way of salvation by Christ; thus the soul sees the fitness and suitableness of this way of salvation, the admirable wisdom of the contrivance, and the perfect answerableness of the provision that the gospel exhibits (as made for us) to our necessities. A sense of true divine beauty being given to the soul, the soul discerns the beauty of every part of the gospel scheme. This also shows the soul the truth of what the Word of God declares concerning man's chief happiness, as consisting in holy exercises and enjoyments. This shows the truth of what the gospel declares concerning the unspeakable glory of the heavenly state. What the prophecies of the Old Testament and the writings of the apostles declare concerning the glory of the Messiah's kingdom, is now all plain; and also what the Scripture teaches concerning the reasons and grounds of our duty. The truth of all these things revealed in the Scripture and many more that might be mentioned, appears to the soul, only by the imparting of that spiritual taste of divine beauty which has been spoken of, they being hidden things to the soul before.

And besides all this, the truth of all those things which the Scripture says about experimental religion is hereby known; for they are now experienced. And this convinces the soul that One who knew the heart of man better than we know our own hearts, and perfectly knew the nature of virtue and holiness, was the author of the Scriptures. And the opening to view, with such clearness, of such a world of wonderful and glorious truth in the gospel, that before was unknown, being quite above the view of a natural eye, but which now appears so clear and bright, has a powerful and invincible influence on the soul, to persuade it of the divinity of the gospel.

Unless men may come to a reasonable solid persuasion and conviction of the truth of the gospel, by the internal evidences of it and by a sight of its glory, it is impossible that those who are illiterate, and unacquainted with history should have any thorough and effectual conviction of it at all. They may without this see a great deal of probability of it; it may be reasonable for them to give much credit to what learned men and historians tell them; and they may tell them so much that it may look very probable and rational to them that the Christian religion is true, so that they would be very unreasonable not to entertain this opinion. But to have a conviction so clear and evident and assuring as to be sufficient to induce them with boldness to sell all, confidently and fearlessly to run the venture of the loss of all things and of enduring the most exquisite and long-continued torments, and to trample the world under foot and count all things but dung for Christ: the evidence they can have from history cannot be sufficient. It is impossible that men, who have not something of a general view of the historical world, or of the events of history from age to age, should come at the force of arguments for the truth of Christianity drawn from history, to that degree as effectually to induce them to venture their all upon it. After all that learned men have said to them, there will remain innumerable doubts on their minds. They will be ready, when pinched with some great trial of their faith, to say, " How

do I know this or that? How do I know when these histories
were written? Learned men tell me these histories were so and
so attested in their day; but how do I know that there were such
attestations then? They tell me there is equal reason to believe
these facts, as any whatsoever that are related at such a distance;
but how do I know that other facts which are related of those
ages, are true? Thus endless doubts and scruples will remain.

But the gospel was not given only for learned men. There are
at least nineteen in twenty, if not ninety-nine in a hundred, of
those for whom the Scriptures were written, that are not capable
of any certain or effectual conviction of the divine authority of
the Scriptures by such arguments as learned men make use of.
If men who have been brought up in heathenism must wait for
a clear and certain conviction of the truth of Christianity until
they have learning and acquaintance with the histories of politer
nations, enough to see clearly the force of such kind of arguments, it will make the evidence of the gospel to them immensely
cumbersome, and will render the propagation of the gospel
among them infinitely difficult. Miserable is the condition of the
Houssatunnuck Indians and others, who have lately manifested
a desire to be instructed in Christianity, if they can come at no
evidence of its truth sufficient to induce them to sell all for Christ,
in any other way but this.

It is unreasonable to suppose that God has provided for His
people no more than probable evidence of the truth of the gospel.
He has with great care abundantly provided and given them the
most convicting, assuring, satisfying and manifold evidence of
His faithfulness in the covenant of grace; and as David says,
" made a covenant, ordered in all things and sure." Therefore it
is rational to suppose that, at the same time, He would not fail
of ordering the matter so that there should not be wanting as
great and clear evidence that this is His covenant, and that these
promises are His promises; or, which is the same thing, that the
Christian religion is true and that the gospel is His word. Otherwise in vain are those great assurances He has given of His faithfulness in His covenant, by confirming it with His oath and so
variously establishing it by seals and pledges. For the evidence
that it is His covenant is properly the foundation on which all
the force and effect of those other assurances do stand. We may
therefore undoubtedly suppose and conclude that there is some

sort of evidence which God has given, that this covenant and these promises are His, beyond all mere probability; that there are some grounds of assurance of it held forth, which, if we are not blind to them, tend to give a higher persuasion than any arguing from history, human tradition, &c., which the illiterate and unacquainted with history are capable of; yea, that which is good ground of the highest and most perfect assurance, that mankind have in any case whatsoever; agreeable to those high expressions which the apostle uses, Heb. x. 22, " Let us draw near in full assurance of faith." And Col. ii. 2, " That their hearts might be comforted, being knit together in love, and unto all riches of the full assurance of understanding, to the acknowledgment of the mystery of God, and of the Father, and of Christ." It is reasonable to suppose that God would give the greatest evidence of those things which are greatest, and the truth of which is of greatest importance to us : and that we therefore, if we are wise and act rationally, shall have the greatest desire of having full, undoubting and perfect assurance of. But it is certain that such an assurance is not to be attained by the greater part of them who live under the gospel, by arguments fetched from ancient traditions, histories, and monuments.

And if we come to fact and experience, there is not the least reason to suppose that one in a hundred of those who have been sincere Christians, and have had a heart to sell all for Christ, have come by their conviction of the truth of the gospel this way. If we read over the histories of the many thousands that died martyrs for Christ since the beginning of the Reformation, who have cheerfully undergone extreme tortures in a confidence of the truth of the gospel, and consider their circumstances and advantages, how few of them were there that we can reasonably suppose ever came by their assured persuasion this way; or, indeed, for whom it was possible reasonably to receive so full and strong an assurance from such arguments! Many of them were weak women and children, and the greater part of them illiterate persons, many of whom had been brought up in popish ignorance and darkness, and were but newly come out of it, and lived and died in times wherein those arguments for the truth of Christianity from antiquity and history had been but very imperfectly handled. And indeed, it is but very lately that these arguments have been set in a clear and convincing light, even by learned men themselves : and since it has been done, there never were fewer thorough believers among those who have been educated in the true religion. Infidelity never prevailed so much in any age as in this, wherein these arguments are handled to the greatest advantage.

The true martyrs of Jesus Christ are not those who have only been strong in opinion that the gospel of Christ is true, but those that have seen the truth of it; as the very name of martyrs or witnesses (by which they are called in Scripture) implies. Those are very improperly called witnesses of the truth of anything, who only declare they are very much of opinion that such a thing is true. Those only are proper witnesses who can and do testify that they have seen the truth of the thing they assert : John iii. 11, "We speak that we do know, and testify that we have seen." John i. 34, "And I saw and bare record that this is the Son of God." 1 John iv. 14, "And we have seen and do testify, that the Father sent the Son to be the Saviour of the world." Acts xxii. 14, 15, "The God of our fathers hath chosen thee, that thou shouldest know his will, and see that Just One, and shouldest hear the voice of his mouth; for thou shalt be his witness unto all men, of what thou hast seen and heard." The true martyrs of Jesus Christ are called His witnesses; and all the saints, who by their holy practice under great trials, declare that faith which is the substance of things hoped for, and the evidence of things not seen, are called witnesses, Heb. xi. 1, and xii. 1. By their profession and practice they declare their assurance of the truth and divinity of the gospel. Having had the eyes of their minds enlightened to see divinity in the gospel, they behold that unparalleled, ineffably excellent, and truly divine glory shining in it, which is altogether distinguishing, evidential, and convincing : so that they may truly be said to have seen God in it, and so can speak in the style of witnesses. They not only say that they think the gospel is divine, but that it is divine, giving it in as their testimony because they have seen it to be so. Doubtless Peter, James and John, after they had seen that excellent glory of Christ in the mount, would have been ready, when they came down, to speak in the language of witnesses, and to say positively that Jesus is the Son of God. As Peter says, they were eyewitnesses, 2 Pet. i. 16. All nations will be ready positively to say this, when they shall behold His glory at the day of judgment; though what will be universally seen will be only His natural glory, and not His moral and spiritual glory which is much more distinguishing.

But yet it must be noted that, among those who have a spiritual sight of the divine glory of the gospel, there is a great variety of degrees of strength of faith, as there is a vast variety of the degrees of clearness of views of this glory. But there is no true and saving faith, or spiritual conviction of the judgment of the truth of the gospel, that has nothing in it of this manfestation of its internal evidence in some degree. The gospel of the blessed God does not go abroad a-begging for its evidence, so much as some think; it has its highest and most proper evidence in itself. Some make great use of external arguments, and these are not to be neglected but highly prized and valued; for they may be greatly serviceable to awaken unbelievers, and bring them to serious consideration, and to confirm the faith of true saints; yea, they may be in some respect subservient to the begetting of a saving faith in men. Yet what was said before remains true, that there is no spiritual conviction of the judgment but what arises from an apprehension of the spiritual beauty and glory of divine things: for, as has been observed, this apprehension or view has a tendency to convince the mind of the truth of the gospel two ways, either directly or indirectly. Having therefore already observed how it does this directly, I proceed now,

2. To observe how a view of this divine glory does convince the mind of the truth of Christianity more indirectly.

First, It does so, as the prejudices of the heart against the truth of divine things are hereby removed, so that the mind thereby lies open to the force of the reasons which are offered. The mind of man is naturally full of enmity against the doctrines of the gospel; which is a disadvantage to those arguments that prove their truth, and causes them to lose their force upon the mind. But when a person has discovered to him the divine excellency of Christian doctrines, this destroys that enmity, and removes the prejudices, and sanctifies the reason, and causes it to be open and free. Hence is a vast difference, as to the force that arguments have to convince the mind. Hence was the very different effect which Christ's miracles had to convince the disciples, from what they had to convince the scribes and Pharisees: not that the disciples had a stronger reason, or had their reason more improved; but their reason was sanctified, and those blinding prejudices which the scribes and Pharisees were under were removed by the sense they had of the excellency of Christ and his doctrine.

Secondly, It not only removes the hindrances of reason, but positively helps reason. It makes even the speculative notions more lively. It assists and engages the attention of the mind to that kind of objects which causes it to have a clearer view of them, and more clearly to see their mutual relations. The ideas themselves, which otherwise are dim and obscure, by this means have a light cast upon them, and are impressed with greater strength, so that the mind can better judge of them; as he that beholds the objects on the face of the earth, when the light of the sun is cast upon them, is under greater advantage to discern them in their true forms and mutual relations, and to see the evidences of divine wisdom and skill in their contrivance, than he that sees them in a dim starlight or twilight.

What has been said may serve in some measure to show the nature of a spiritual conviction of the judgment of the truth and reality of divine things, and so to distinguish truly gracious affections from others; for gracious affections are evermore attended with such a conviction of the judgment.

But before I dismiss this head, it will be needful to observe the ways whereby some are deceived with respect to this matter, and take notice of several things that are sometimes taken for a spiritual and saving belief of the truth of the things of religion, which are indeed very diverse from it.

1. There is a degree of conviction of the truth of the great things of religion that arises from the common enlightenings of the Spirit of God. That more lively and sensible apprehension of the things of religion, with respect to what is natural in them —such as natural men have who are under awakenings and common illuminations—will give some degree of conviction beyond what they had before they were thus enlightened. Hereby they see the manifestations of the natural perfections of God, such as His greatness, power, and awful majesty; which tends to convince the mind, that this is the Word of a great and terrible God. From the tokens there are of God's greatness and majesty in His Word and works, which they have a great sense of from the common influence of the Spirit of God, they may have a much greater conviction that these are indeed the words and works of

a very great invisible Being. And the lively apprehension of the greatness of God, which natural men may have, tends to make them sensible of the great guilt which sin against such a God brings, and the dreadfulness of His wrath. And this tends to cause them more easily and fully to believe the revelation the Scripture makes of another world, and of the extreme misery it threatens there to be inflicted on sinners. And so from that sense of the great natural good there is in the things of religion, which is sometimes given in common illuminations, men may be the more induced to believe the truth of religion. These things persons may have, and yet have no sense of the beauty and amiableness of the moral and holy excellency that is in the things of religion; and therefore no spiritual conviction of their truth. But yet such convictions are sometimes mistaken for saving convictions, and the affections flowing from them for saving affections.

2. The extraordinary impressions which are made on the imaginations of some persons, in the visions and immediate strong impulses and suggestions that they have, as though they saw sights and had words spoken to them, may and often do beget a strong persuasion of the truth of invisible things. Though the general tendency of such things in their final issue is to draw men off from the Word of God, and to cause them to reject the gospel, and to establish unbelief and atheism, yet for the present, they may, and often do beget a confident persuasion of the truth of some things that are revealed in the Scriptures; yet their confidence is founded in delusion, and so nothing worth. As for instance, if a person has by some invisible agent immediately and strongly impressed on his imagination the appearance of a bright light, and glorious form of a Person seated on a throne with great external majesty and beauty, uttering some remarkable words with great force and energy. The person who is the subject of such an operation may be from hence confident that there are invisible agents, spiritual beings, for he knows that he had no hand himself in this extraordinary effect which he has experienced. He may also be confident that this is Christ whom he saw and heard speaking: and this may make him confident that there is a Christ, and that Christ reigns on a throne in heaven, as he saw Him; and he may also be confident that the words which he heard Him speak are true. But in the same manner the lying miracles of the Papists may beget in the minds of

ignorant deluded people a strong persuasion of the truth of many things declared in the New Testament. Thus when the images of Christ in Popish churches are on some extraordinary occasions made by priestcraft to appear to the people as if they wept, and shed fresh blood, and moved, and uttered such and such words, the people may be verily persuaded that it is a miracle wrought by Christ Himself; and from thence may be confident there is a Christ, and that what they are told of His death and sufferings, and resurrection, and ascension, and present government of the world is true; for they may look upon this miracle as a certain evidence of all these things, and a kind of ocular demonstration of them. This may be the influence of these lying wonders for the present; though the general tendency of them is not to convince that Jesus Christ is come in the flesh, but finally to promote atheism. Even the intercourse which Satan has with witches, and their often experiencing his immediate power, has a tendency to convince them of the truth of some of the doctrines of religion; as particularly the reality of an invisible world, or world of spirits, contrary to the doctrine of the Sadducees. The general tendency of Satan's influence is delusion: but yet he may mix some truth with his lies, that his lies may not be so easily discovered.

There are multitudes that are deluded with a counterfeit faith from impressions on their imagination, in the manner which has been now spoken of. They say they know that there is a God, for they have seen Him; they know that Christ is the Son of God, for they have seen Him in His glory; they know that Christ died for sinners, for they have seen Him hanging on the cross, and His blood running from His wounds; they know there is a heaven and a hell, for they have seen the misery of the damned souls in hell and the glory of saints and angels in heaven (meaning some external representations, strongly impressed on their imagination); they know that the Scriptures are the Word of God, and that such and such promises in particular are His Word, for they have heard Him speak them to them; they came to their minds suddenly and immediately from God, without their having any hand in it.

3. Persons may seem to have their belief of the truth of the things of religion greatly increased, when the foundation of it is only a persuasion they have received of their interest in them.

They first, by some means or other, take up a confidence that
if there be a Christ and heaven, they are theirs; and this prejudices them more in favour of the truth of them. When they
hear of the great and glorious things of religion, it is with this
notion, that all these things belong to them. Hence they easily
become confident that they are true; they look upon it to be
greatly for their interest that they should be true. It is very obvious what a strong influence men's interest and inclinations have
on their judgments. While a natural man thinks that, if there
be a heaven and a hell, the latter and not the former belongs to
him; then he will be hardly persuaded that there is a heaven or
hell: but when he comes to be persuaded that hell belongs only
to other folks and not to him, then he can easily allow the reality
of hell, and protests against the senselessness and sottishness of
others in neglecting means of escape from it: and being confident that he is a child of God, and that God has promised
heaven to him, he may seem strong in the faith of its reality,
and may have a great zeal against that infidelity which denies it.

But I proceed to another distinguishing sign of gracious affections.

VI. *Gracious affections are attended with evangelical humiliation.*

Evangelical humiliation is a sense that a Christian has of his
own utter insufficiency, despicableness, and odiousness, with an
answerable frame of heart.

There is a distinction to be made between a legal and evangelical humiliation. The former is what men may be the subjects of, while they are yet in a state of nature, and have no gracious affections; the latter is peculiar to true saints. The former is
from the common influence of the Spirit of God, assisting natural
principles, and especially natural conscience; the latter is from
the special influences of the Spirit of God, implanting and exercising supernatural and divine principles: the former is from the
mind's being assisted to a greater sense of the things of religion
as to their natural properties and qualities, and particularly of
the natural perfections of God, such as His greatness, and terrible
majesty, which were manifested to the congregation of Israel in
giving the law at mount Sinai; the latter is from a sense of the
transcendent beauty of divine things in their moral qualities. In

the former, a sense of the awful greatness and natural perfections of God, and of the strictness of His law, convinces men that they are exceeding sinful and guilty and exposed to the wrath of God, as it will convince wicked men and devils at the day of judgment; but they do not see their own odiousness on account of sin; they do not see the hateful nature of sin; a sense of this is given in evangelical humiliation by a discovery of the beauty of God's holiness and moral perfection. In a legal humiliation, men are made sensible that they are little and nothing before the great and terrible God, and that they are undone, and wholly insufficient to help themselves; as wicked men will be at the day of judgment: but they have not an answerable frame of heart, consisting in a disposition to abase themselves, and exalt God alone. This disposition is given only in evangelical humiliation, by overcoming the heart and changing its inclination, by a discovery of God's holy beauty. In a legal humiliation, the conscience is convinced, as the consciences of all will be most perfectly at the day of judgment; but because there is no spiritual understanding, the will is not bowed nor the inclination altered: this is done only in evangelical humiliation. In legal humiliation, men are brought to despair of helping themselves; in evangelical, they are brought voluntarily to deny and renounce themselves; in the former, they are subdued and forced to the ground; in the latter, they are brought sweetly to yield, and freely and with delight to prostrate themselves at the feet of God.

Legal humiliation has in it no spiritual good, nothing of the nature of true virtue; whereas evangelical humiliation is that wherein the excellent beauty of Christian grace does very much consist. Legal humiliation is useful, as a means in order to evangelical; as a common knowledge of the things of religion is a means requisite in order to spiritual knowledge. Men may be legally humbled and have no humility: as the wicked at the day of judgment will be thoroughly convinced that they have no righteousness but are altogether sinful, exceedingly guilty, and justly exposed to eternal damnation, and be fully sensible of their own helplessness without the least mortification of the pride of their hearts: but the essence of evangelical humiliation consists in such humility as becomes a creature in itself exceeding sinful, under a disposition of grace. It is a man's mean esteem of himself, as in himself nothing, and altogether contemptible and odious; attended with a mortification of a disposition to exalt himself, and a free renunciation of his own glory.

This is a great and most essential thing in true religion. The whole frame of the gospel, and every thing appertaining to the new covenant, and all God's dispensations towards fallen man, are calculated to bring to pass this effect in the hearts of men. They that are destitute of this have no true religion, whatever profession they may make and how high soever their religious affections may be: Hab. ii. 4, "Behold, his soul which is lifted up is not upright in him: but the just shall live by his faith;" *i.e.*, he shall live by his faith on God's righteousness and grace, and not by his own goodness and excellency. God has abundantly manifested in His Word that this is what He has a peculiar respect to in His saints, and that nothing is acceptable to Him without it. Psalm xxxiv. 18, "The Lord is nigh unto them that are of a broken heart, and saveth such as be of a contrite spirit." Psalm li. 17, "The sacrifices of God are a broken spirit: a broken and a contrite heart, O God, thou wilt not despise." Psalm cxxxviii. 6, "Though the Lord be high, yet hath he respect unto the lowly." Prov. iii. 34. "He giveth grace unto the lowly." Isa. lvii. 15, "Thus saith the high and lofty One that inhabiteth eternity, whose name is holy; I dwell in the high and holy place, with him also that is of a contrite and humble spirit, to revive the spirit of the humble, and to revive the heart of the contrite ones." Isa. lxvi. 1, 2, "Thus saith the Lord, the heaven is my throne, and the earth is my footstool: but to this man will I look, even to him that is poor, and of a contrite spirit, and trembleth at my word." Micah vi. 8, "He hath showed thee, O man, what is good; and what doth the Lord require of thee, but to do justly, and to love mercy, and to walk humbly with thy God?" Matt. v. 3, "Blessed are the poor in spirit; for their's is the kingdom of heaven." Matt. xviii. 3, 4, "Verily I say unto you, Except ye be converted, and become as little children, ye shall not enter into the kingdom of heaven. Whosoever therefore shall humble himself as this little child, the same is greatest in the kingdom of heaven." Mark x. 15, "Verily I say unto you, Whosoever shall not receive the kingdom of God as a little child, he shall not enter therein." The centurion spoken of in Luke vii., acknowledged that he was not worthy that Christ should enter under his roof, and that he was not worthy to come to Him. See the manner of the woman's coming to Christ, that was a sinner, Luke vii. 37, &c.,: "And behold, a woman in the city, which was a sinner, when she knew that Jesus sat at meat in the Pharisee's house, brought an alabaster box of ointment, and stood at his feet behind him weeping, and began to wash his feet with tears, and did wipe them with the hairs of her head." She did not think the hair of her head, which is the natural crown and glory of a woman (1 Cor. xi. 15), too good to wipe the feet of Christ withal. Jesus most graciously accepted her, and said to her, "Thy faith hath saved thee, go in peace." The woman of Canaan submitted to Christ, in His saying, "It is not meet to take the children's bread and cast it to dogs," and did as it were own that she was worthy to be called a dog; whereupon Christ said unto her, "O woman, great is thy faith: be it unto thee even as thou wilt," Matt. xv. 26, 27, 28. The prodigal son said, "I will arise and go to my father, and I will say unto him, Father, I have sinned against heaven and before thee, and am no more worthy to be called they son: make me as one of thy hired servants," Luke xv. 18, &c. See also Luke xviii, 9, &c.: "And he spake this parable unto certain which trusted in themselves that they were righteous, and despised others, &c. The publican, standing afar off, would not so much as lift up his eyes to heaven, but smote upon his breast, saying, God be merciful to me a sinner. I tell you, this man went down to his house justified rather than the other: for every one that exalteth himself shall be abased; and he that humbleth himself shall be exalted." Matt. xxviii. 9, "And they came and held him by the feet, and worshipped him." Col. iii. 12, "Put ye on, as the elect of God, humbleness of mind." Ezek. xx. 41, 42, "I will accept you with your sweet savour, when I bring you out from the people, &c. And there shall ye remember your ways, and all your doings, wherein ye have been defiled; and ye shall loathe yourselves in your own sight, for all your evils that ye have committed." Chap. xxxvi. 26, 27, 31, "A new heart also will I give unto you—and I will put my Spirit within you, and cause you to walk in my statutes, &c. Then shall ye remember your own evil ways, and your doings that were not good, and shall loathe yourselves in your own sight, for your iniquities, and for your abominations." Chap. xvi. 63, "That thou mayest remember and be confounded, and never open thy mouth any more because of thy shame, when I am pacified toward thee for all that thou hast done, saith the Lord God." Job xlii. 6, "I abhor myself, and repent in dust and ashes."

As we would therefore make the Holy Scriptures our rule in judging of the nature of true religion, and judging of our own religious qualifications and state, it concerns us greatly to look at this humiliation as one of the most essential things pertaining to true Christianity.* This is the principal part of the great Christian duty of self-denial. That duty consists in two things, viz., *first,* in a man's denying his worldly inclinations, and in forsaking and renouncing all worldly objects and enjoyments; and, *secondly,* in denying his natural self-exaltation, and renouncing his own dignity and glory, and in being emptied of himself; so that he does freely and from his very heart, as it were, renounce himself and annihilate himself. This the Christian does in evangelical humiliation. And this latter is the greatest and most difficult part of self-denial: although they always go together, and one never truly is, where the other is not; yet natural men can come much nearer to the former than the latter. Many anchorites and recluses have abandoned (though without any true mortification) the wealth and pleasures and common enjoyments of the world, who were far from renouncing their own dignity and righteousness. They never denied themselves for Christ, but only sold one lust to feed another; sold a beastly lust to pamper a devilish one; and so were never the better, but their latter end was worse than their beginning. They turned out one black devil to let in seven white ones that were worse than the first, though of a fairer countenance. It is inexpressible, and almost inconceivable, how strong a self-righteous, self-exalting disposition is naturally in man; and what he will not do and suffer to feed and gratify it: and what lengths have been gone in a seeming self-denial in other respects, by Essenes and Pharisees among the Jews, and by Papists, many sects of heretics, and enthusiasts among professing Christians; and by many Mahometans; and by Pythagorean philosophers and others among the heathen; and all

* Calvin, in his *Institutes,* Book II, chap. 2, § 11, says, "I was always exceedingly delighted with that saying of Chrysostom, 'The foundation of our philosophy is humility'; and yet more pleased with that of Augustine: 'As the orator, when asked, What is the first precept in eloquence? answered, Delivery: What is the second? Delivery: What is the third? Delivery: so if you ask me concerning the precepts of the Christian religion, I will answer, first, second, and third, Humility.'"

to do sacrifice to this Moloch of spiritual pride or self-righteousness; and that they may have something wherein to exalt themselves before God and above their fellow creatures.

That humiliation which has been spoken of, is what all the
most glorious hypocrites, who make the most splendid show of
mortification to the world, and high religious affection, do grossly
fail in. Were it not that this is so much insisted on in Scripture
as a most essential thing in true grace, one would be tempted to
think that many of the heathen philosophers were truly gracious, in whom was so bright an appearance of many virtues, and
also great illuminations and inward fervours and elevations of
mind, as though they were truly the subjects of divine illapses
and heavenly communications.* It is true that many hypocrites
make great pretences to humility as well as other graces; and very
often there is nothing whatsoever which they make a higher profession of. They endeavour to make a great show of humility in
speech and behaviour; but they commonly make bungling work
of it, though glorious work in their own eyes. They cannot find
out what a humble speech and behaviour is, or how to speak and
act so that there may indeed be a savour of Christian humility
in what they say and do. That sweet humble air and mien is
beyond their art, being not led by the Spirit, or naturally guided
to a behaviour becoming holy humility, by the vigour of a lowly

* " Albeit the Pythagoreans were thus famous for Judaic mysterious
wisdom, and many moral as well as natural accomplishments, yet were
they not exempted from boasting and pride; which was indeed a vice most
epidemic, and as it were congenial, among all the philosophers; but in a
more particular manner, among the Pythagoreans, who abounded in the
sense and commendation of their own excellencies. Thus indeed does
proud nature delight to walk in the sparks of its own fire. And although
many of these old philosophers, could, by the strength of their own lights
and heats, together with some common elevations of spirit (peradventure
from a more than ordinary, though not special and saving assistance of
the Spirit), abandon many grosser vices; yet they were all deeply im-
mersed in that miserable cursed abyss of spiritual pride; so that all their
natural and moral and philosophic attainments did feed, nourish, strengthen and render most inveterate this hell-bred pest of their hearts. Yea,
those of them that seemed most modest, as the Academics, who professed
they knew nothing, and the Cynics, who greatly decried, both in words
and habits, the pride of others, yet even they abounded in the most notorious and visible pride. So connatural and morally essential to corrupt nature,
is this envenomed root, fountain, and plague of spiritual pride; especially
where there is any natural moral or philosophic excellence to feed the
same. Whence, Augustine rightly judged all these philosophic virtues to
be but splendid sins." (Theophilus Gale: *Court of the Gentiles:* 1672).

spirit within them. And therefore they have no other way, many
of them, but only to be much in declaring that they be humble,
and telling how they were humbled to the dust at such and such
times, and abounding in very bad expressions which they use
about themselves; such as, "I am the least of all saints, I am a
poor vile creature, I am not worthy of the least mercy or that
God should look upon me! Oh, I have a dreadful wicked heart!
My heart is worse than the devil! Oh, this cursed heart of mine,"
&c. Such expressions are very often used, not with a heart that
is broken, not with spiritual mourning, not with the tears of her
that washed Jesus' feet, not as "remembering and being confounded, and never opening their mouth more because of their
shame, when God is pacified," as the expression is, Ezek. xvi. 63,
but with a light air, with smiles in the countenance, or with a
Pharisaical affectation. And we must believe that they are thus
humble, and see themselves so vile, upon the credit of their saying so; for there is nothing appears in them of any savour of
humility in the manner of their deportment and deeds that they
do. There are many that are full of expressions of their own
vileness, who yet expect to be looked upon as eminent and bright
saints by others, as their due; and it is dangerous for any so much
as to hint the contrary, or to carry it towards them any otherwise than as if we looked upon them as some of the chief of
Christians. There are many that are much in exclaiming against
their wicked hearts and their great shortcomings and unprofit-
ableness, and speaking as though they looked on themselves as
the meanest of the saints; who yet, if a minister should seriously
tell them the same things in private, and should signify that he
feared they were very low and weak Christians, and thought they
had reason solemnly to consider of their great barrenness and un-
profitableness and falling so much short of many others, it would
be more than they could digest; they would think themselves
highly injured, and there would be a danger of a rooted prejudice
in them against such a minister.

There are some that are abundant in talking against legal doctrines, legal preaching, and a legal spirit, who do but little understand the thing they talk against. A legal spirit is a more subtle
thing than they imagine; it is too subtle for them. It lurks, and
operates, and prevails in their hearts, and they are most notoriously guilty of it, at the same time when they are inveighing

against it. So far as a man is not emptied of himself, and of his own righteousness and goodness, in whatever form or shape, so far he is of a legal spirit. A spirit of pride of man's own righteousness, morality, holiness, affection, experience, faith, humiliation, or any goodness whatsoever, is a legal spirit. It was no pride in Adam before the fall to be of a legal spirit; because of his circumstances, he might seek acceptance by his own righteousness. But a legal spirit in a fallen, sinful creature can be nothing else but spiritual pride; and reciprocally, a spiritually proud spirit is a legal spirit. There is no man living that is lifted up with a conceit of his own experiences and discoveries, and upon the account of them glisters in his own eyes, but what trusts in his experiences, and makes a righteousness of them; however he may use humble terms, and speak of his experiences as of the great things God has done for him, and it may be calls upon others to glorify God for them; yet he that is proud of his experiences arrogates something to himself, as though his experiences were some dignity of his. And if he looks on them as his own dignity, he necessarily thinks that God looks on them so too; for he necessarily thinks his own opinion of them to be true; and consequently judges that God looks on them as he does; and so unavoidably imagines that God looks on his experiences as a dignity in him, as he looks on them himself; and that he glisters as much in God's eyes, as he does in his own. And thus he trusts in what is inherent in him, to make him shine in God's sight, and recommend him to God: and with this encouragement he goes before God in prayer; and this makes him expect much from God; and this makes him think that Christ loves him, and that He is willing to clothe him with His righteousness; because he supposes that He is taken with his experiences and grace. And this is a high degree of living on his own righteousness; and such persons are in the high road to hell. Poor deluded wretches, who think they look so glistering in God's eyes, when they are a smoke in His nose, and are many of them more odious to Him than the most impure beast in Sodom, that makes no pretence to religion! To do as these do, is to live upon experiences, according to the true notion of it; and not to do as those who only make use of spiritual experiences as evidences of a state of grace, and in that way receive hope and comfort from them.

There is a sort of men, who indeed abundantly cry down

works, and cry up faith in opposition to works, and set up themselves very much as evangelical persons in opposition to those that are of a legal spirit, and make a fair show of advancing Christ and the gospel and the way of free grace, who are indeed some of the greatest enemies to the gospel way of free grace, and the most dangerous opposers of pure humble Christianity.

There is a pretended great humiliation, and being dead to the law and emptied of self, which is one of the biggest and most elated things in the world. Some there are who have made great profession of experience of a thorough work of the law on their hearts, and of being brought fully off from works, whose conversion has savoured most of a self-righteous spirit of any that ever I had opportunity to observe. And some who think themselves quite emptied of themselves, and are confident that they are abased in the dust, are full as they can hold with the glory of their own humility, and lifted up to heaven with a high opinion of their own abasement. Their humility is a swelling, self-conceited, confident, showy, noisy, assuming humility. It seems to be the nature of spiritual pride to make men conceited and ostentatious of their humility. This appears in that first born of pride among the children of men, that would be called " his Holiness," even the " man of sin," that exalts himself above all that is called God or is worshipped; he styles himself " Servant of servants "; and to make a show of humility, washes the feet of a number of poor men at his inauguration.

For persons to be truly emptied of themselves, and to be poor in spirit and broken in heart, is quite another thing, and has other effects than many imagine. It is astonishing how greatly many are deceived about themselves as to this matter, imagining themselves most humble when they are most proud, and their behaviour is really the most haughty. The deceitfulness of the heart of man appears in no one thing so much as this of spiritual pride and self-righteousness. The subtlety of Satan appears in its height, in his managing of persons with respect to this sin. And perhaps one reason may be that here he has most experience; he knows the way of its coming in; he is acquainted with the secret springs of it : it was his own sin. Experience gives vast advantage in leading souls, either in good or evil.

But though spiritual pride be so subtle and secret an iniquity, and commonly appears under a pretext of great humility; yet there are two things by which it may (perhaps universally and surely) be discovered and distinguished.

The first thing is this: he that is under the prevalence of this distemper is apt to think highly of his attainments in religion, as comparing himself with others. It is natural for him to fall into that thought of himself that he is an eminent saint, that he is very high amongst the saints, and has distinguishingly good and great experiences. That is the secret language of his heart: Luke xviii. 11, "God, I thank thee that I am not as other men." And Isa. lxv. 5, "I am holier than thou." Hence such are apt to put themselves forward among God's people, and as it were to take a high seat among them, as if there was no doubt of it but it belonged to them. They, as it were, naturally take the highest room, which Christ condemns, Luke xiv. 7, &c. This they do by being forward to take upon them the place and business of the chief; to guide, teach, direct, and manage. "They are confident that they are guides of the blind, a light of them which are in darkness, instructors of the foolish, teachers of babes," Rom. ii. 19, 20. It is natural for them to take it for granted that it belongs to them to do the part of dictators and masters in matters of religion; and so they implicitly affect to be called of men " Rabbi," which is by interpretation " Master," as the Pharisees did, Matt. xxiii. 6, 7, *i.e.*, they are yet apt to expect that others should regard them, and yield to them, as masters in matters of religion.*

But he whose heart is under the power of Christian humility is of a contrary disposition. If the Scriptures are at all to be relied on, such an one is apt to think his attainments in religion to be comparatively mean, and to esteem himself low among the saints, and one of the least of them. Humility, or true lowliness of mind, disposes persons to think others better than themselves: Phil. ii. 3, "In lowliness of mind, let each esteem other better than themselves." Hence they are apt to think the lowest room belongs to them, and their inward disposition naturally leads them to obey that precept of our Saviour, Luke xiv. 10. It is not natural to them to take it upon them to do the part of teachers; but on

* " There be two things wherein it appears that a man has only common gifts, and no inward principle: 1. These gifts ever puff up, and make a man something in his own eyes, as the Corinthian knowledge did, and many a private man thinks himself fit to be a minister." *Shepard's Parable of the Ten Virgins*, p. 287.

the contrary, they are disposed to think that they are not the persons, that others are fitter for it than they; as it was with Moses and Jeremiah (Exod. iii. 11, Jer. i. 6), though they were such eminent saints, and of great knowledge. It is not natural to them to think that it belongs to them to teach, but to be taught; they are much more eager to hear, and to receive instruction from others, than to dictate to others: James i. 19, " Be ye swift to hear, slow to speak." And when they do speak, it is not natural to them to speak with a bold, masterly air; but humility disposes them rather to speak, trembling. Hos. xiii. 1, " When Ephraim spake trembling, he exalted himself in Israel; but when he offended in Baal, he died." They are not apt to assume authority, and to take upon them to be chief managers and masters; but rather to be subject to other: James iii. 1, 2, " Be not many masters." 1 Pet. v. 5, " All of you be subject one to another, and be clothed with humility." Eph. v. 21, " Submitting yourselves one to another in the fear of God."

There are some persons that naturally think highly of their experiences; and they do often themselves speak of their experiences as very great and extraordinary; they freely speak of the great things they have met with. This may be spoken and meant in a good sense. In one sense, every degree of saving mercy is a great thing. It is indeed a thing great, yea, infinitely great, for God to bestow the least crumb of children's bread on such dogs as we are in ourselves; and the more humble a person is that hopes that God has bestowed such mercy on him, the more apt will he be to call it a great thing that he has met with in this sense. But if, by great things which they have experienced they mean comparatively great spiritual experiences, or great compared with others' experiences, or beyond what is ordinary, which is evidently oftentimes the case; then for a person to say, I have met with great things, is the very same thing as to say, I am an eminent saint, and have more grace than ordinary. For to have great experiences, if the experiences be true and worth the telling of, is the same thing as to have great grace: there is no true experience, but the exercise of grace; and exactly according to the degree of true experience is the degree of grace and holiness. The persons that talk thus about their experiences, when they give an account of them, expect that others should admire them. Indeed they do not call it boasting to talk after this manner about their experiences, nor do they look upon it as any sign of pride; because they say, "they know that it was not they that did it, it was free grace; they are things that God has done for them; they would acknowledge the great mercy God has shown them, and not make light of it." But so it was with the Pharisee that Christ tells us of, Luke xviii. He in words gave God the glory of making him to differ from other men; God, I thank thee, says he, that I am not as other men.* Their verbally ascribing it to the grace of God that they are holier than other saints, does not hinder their forwardness to think so highly of their holiness as a sure evidence of the pride and vanity of their minds. If they were under the influence of a humble spirit, their attainments in religion would not be so apt to shine in their own eyes, nor would they so much admire their own beauty. The Christians that are really the most eminent saints, and therefore have the most excellent experiences and are the greatest in the kingdom of heaven, humble themselves as a little child, Matt. xviii. 4; because they look on themselves as but little children in grace, and their attainments to be but the attainments of babes in Christ, and are astonished at and ashamed of the low degrees of their love and their thankfulness, and their little knowledge of God. Moses, when he had been conversing with God in the mount, and his face shone so bright in the eyes of others as to dazzle their eyes, wist not that his face shone. There are some persons that go by the name of high professors, and some will own themselves to be high professors; but eminently humble saints, that will shine brightest in heaven, are not at all apt to profess high. I do not believe there is an eminent saint in the world that is a high professor. Such will be much more likely to profess themselves to be least of all saints, and to think that every saint's attainments and experiences are higher than his.†

* Calvin, in his *Institutes,* Book III, chap. xii. § 7, speaking of this Pharisee, observes, "In his public confession he acknowledges that the righteousness that he has is the gift of God: but because he trusts that he is righteous, he goes away out of the presence of God unaccepted and odious."

† Luther, as his words are cited by Rutherford in his *Display of the Spiritual Antichrist,* says thus: "So is the life of a Christian, that he that has begun seems to himself to have nothing; but strives and presses forward that he may apprehend: whence Paul says, I count not myself to have apprehended. For indeed nothing is more pernicious to a believer than that presumption that he has already apprehended, and has no

Such is the nature of grace and of true spiritual light that they naturally dispose the saints in the present state to look upon their grace and goodness little, and their deformity great. And they that have the most grace and spiritual light of any in this world have most of this disposition; as will appear most clear and evident to any one that soberly and thoroughly weighs the nature and reason of things, and considers the things following.

That grace and holiness is worthy to be called little, that is little in comparison of what it ought to be. And little it seems to one that is truly gracious: for such an one has his eye upon the rule of his duty. A conformity to that is what he aims at; it is what his soul struggles and reaches after; and it is by that that he estimates and judges of what he does and what he has. To a gracious soul, and especially to one eminently gracious, that holiness appears little, which is little of what it should be; little of what he sees infinite reason for, and obligation to. If his holiness appears to him to be at a vast distance from this, it naturally appears despicable in his eyes, and not worthy to be mentioned as any beauty or amiableness in him. For the like reason as a hungry man naturally accounts that which is set before him but a little food, a small matter, not worth mentioning, that is nothing in comparison of his appetite. Or as the child of a great prince, that is jealous for the honour of his father, and beholds the respect which men show him, naturally looks on that honour and respect very little, and not worthy to be regarded, which is nothing in comparison of that which the dignity of his father requires.

But that is the nature of true grace and spiritual light, that it opens to a person's view the infinite reason there is that he should be holy in a high degree. And the more grace he has, and the

---

further need of seeking. Hence also many fall back, and pine away in spiritual security and slothfulness. So Bernard says, ' To stand still in God's way, is to go back.' Wherefore this remains to him that has begun to be a Christian, to think that he is not yet a Christian, but to seek that he may be a Christian, that he may glory with Paul, ' I am not, but I desire to be ', a Christian not yet finished but only in his beginnings. Therefore he is not a Christian that is a Christian, that is, he that thinks himself a finished Christian and is not sensible how he falls short. We reach after heaven but we are not in heaven. Woe to him that is wholly renewed, that is, that thinks himself to be so. That man, without doubt, has never so much as begun to be renewed, nor did he ever taste what it is to be a Christian."

more this is opened to view, the greater sense he has of the infinite excellency and glory of the divine Being, and of the infinite
dignity of the person of Christ, and the boundless length and
breadth and depth and height of the love of Christ to sinners.
And as grace increases, the field opens more and more to a distant view, until the soul is swallowed up with the vastness of the
object, and the person is astonished to think how much it becomes him to love this God and this glorious Redeemer that
has so loved man, and how little he does love. And so the more
he apprehends, the more the smallness of his grace and love
appears strange and wonderful : and therefore he is more ready
to think that others are beyond him. For, wondering at the littleness of his own grace, he can scarcely believe that so strange a
thing happens to other saints. It is amazing to him that one
that is really a child of God, and that has actually received the
saving benefits of that unspeakable love of Christ, should love
no more : and he is apt to look upon it as a thing peculiar to
himself, a strange and exempt instance; for he sees only the
outside of other Christians, but he sees his own inside.

Here the reader may possibly object that love to God is really
increased in proportion as the knowledge of God is increased;
and therefore how should an increase of knowledge in a saint
make his love appear less, in comparison of what is known? To
which I answer, that although grace and the love of God in the
saints be answerable to the degree of knowledge or sight of God;
yet it is not in proportion to the object seen and known. The
soul of a saint, by having something of God opened to sight, is
convinced of much more than is seen. There is something seen
that is wonderful; and that sight brings with it a strong conviction of something vastly beyond that is not immediately seen.
So that the soul, at the same time, is astonished at its ignorance,
and that it knows so little, as well as that it loves so little. And
as the soul, in a spiritual view, is convinced of infinitely more
in the object, yet beyond sight; so it is convinced of the capacity
of the soul to know vastly more, if the clouds and darkness were
but removed. This causes the soul, in the enjoyment of a spiritual view, to complain greatly of spiritual ignorance and want
of love, and to long and reach after more knowledge and more
love.

Grace and the love of God in the most eminent saints in this world is truly very little in comparison of what it ought to be. The highest love that ever any attain in this life, is poor, cold, exceedingly low, and not worthy to be named in comparison of what our obligations appear to be; and this will appear from the joint consideration of these two things, viz.: 1. The reason God has given us to love Him, in the manifestations he has made of His infinite glory, in His Word, and in His works; and particularly in the gospel of His Son, and what He has done for sinful man by Him. And, 2. The capacity there is in the soul of man, by those intellectual faculties which God has given it, of seeing and understanding the reasons which God has given us to love him. How small indeed is the love of the most eminent saint on earth, in comparison of what these things jointly considered do require! Grace tends to convince men of this, and especially eminent grace; for grace is of the nature of light, and brings truth to view. And therefore he that has much grace apprehends much more than others the great height to which his love ought to ascend; and he sees better than others how little a way he has risen towards that height. And when he estimates his love by the whole height of his duty, it appears astonishingly little and low in his eyes.

And the eminent saint, having such a conviction of the high degree in which he ought to love God is shown not only the littleness of his grace but the greatness of his remaining corruption. In order to judge how much corruption or sin we have remaining in us, we must take our measure from that height to which the rule of our duty extends. The whole of the distance we are at from that height is sin: for failing of duty is sin; otherwise our duty is not our duty, and by how much the more we fall short of our duty, so much the more sin have we. Sin is no other than disagreeableness, in a moral agent, to the law or rule of his duty. And therefore the degree of sin is to be judged of by the rule: so much disagreeableness to the rule, so much sin, whether it be in defect or excess. Therefore if men in their love to God do not come up half way to that height which duty requires, then they have more corruption in their hearts than grace; because there is more goodness wanting than is there. All that is wanting is sin: it is an abominable defect, and appears so to the saints, especially those that are eminent. It appears exceeding abominable to them that Christ should be loved so little, and thanked so little for His dying love. It is in their eyes hateful ingratitude.

And then the increase of grace has a tendency another way, to cause the saints to think their deformity vastly more than their goodness. It not only tends to convince them that their corruption is much greater than their goodness, which is indeed the case; but it also tends to cause the deformity that there is in the least sin, or the least degree of corruption, to appear so great as vastly to outweigh all the beauty there is in their greatest holiness. The least sin against an infinite God has an infinite hatefulness or deformity in it; but the highest degree of holiness in a creature has not an infinite loveliness in it: and therefore the loveliness of it is as nothing in comparison of the deformity of the least sin. That every sin has infinite deformity and hatefulness in it is most demonstrably evident; because what the evil, or iniquity, or hatefulness of sin consists in, is the violating of an obligation, or the being or doing contrary to what we should be or do, or are obliged to. And therefore, by how much the greater the obligation is that is violated, so much the greater is the iniquity and hatefulness of the violation. But certainly our obligation to love and honour any being is in some proportion to his loveliness and honourableness, or to his worthiness to be loved and honoured by us; which is the same thing. We are surely under greater obligation to love a more lovely being, than a less lovely; and if a Being be infinitely lovely or worthy to be loved by us, then our obligations to love Him are infinitely great; and therefore, whatever is contrary to this love, has in it infinite iniquity, deformity, and unworthiness. But on the other hand, with respect to our holiness or love to God, there is not an infinite worthiness in that. The sin of the creature against God is ill deserving and hateful in proportion to the distance there is between God and the creature: the greatness of the object, and the meanness and inferiority of the subject, aggravates it. But it is the reverse with regard to the worthiness of the respect of the creature to God; it is worthless, and not worthy, in proportion to the meanness of the subject. So much the greater the distance between God and the creature, so much the less is the creature's respect worthy of God's notice or regard. A great degree of superiority increases the obligation on the inferior to regard the superior, and so makes the want of regard more hateful. But a great degree of inferiority diminishes the worth of the regard of the inferior; because the more he is inferior, the less he is worthy of notice; the less he is, the less is what he can offer worth; for he can offer no more than himself, in offering his best respect; and therefore as he is little, and little worth, so is his respect little worth. And the more a person has of true grace and spiritual light, the more will it appear thus to him; the more will he appear to himself infinitely deformed by reason of sin, and the less will the goodness that is in his grace, or good experience, appear in proportion to it. For indeed it is nothing to it; it is less than a drop to the ocean; for finite bears no proportion at all to that which is infinite. But the more a person has of spiritual light, the more do things appear to him, in this respect, as they are indeed. Hence it most demonstrably appears that true grace is of that nature, that the more a person has of it, with remaining corruption, the less does his goodness and holiness appear in proportion to his deformity; and not only to his past deformity, but to his present deformity, in the sin that now appears in his heart, and the abominable defects of his highest and best affections and brightest experiences.

The nature of many high religious affections, and great discoveries (as they are called) in many persons that I have been acquainted with, is to hide and cover over the corruption of their hearts, and to make it seem to them as if all their sin was gone, and to leave them without complaints of any hateful evil left in them (though it may be they cry out much of their past unworthiness). This is a sure and certain evidence that their discoveries (as they call them) are darkness and not light. It is darkness that hides men's pollution and deformity; but light let into the heart discovers it, searches it out in its secret corners, and makes it plainly to appear; especially that penetrating, all-searching light of God's holiness and glory. It is true that saving discoveries may for the present hide corruption in one sense; they restrain the positive exercises of it, such as malice, envy, covetousness, lasciviousness, murmuring, &c., but they bring corruption to light in that which is privative, viz., that there is not more love, not more humility, not more thankfulness. These defects appear most hateful in the eyes of those who have the most eminent exercises of grace. They are very

burdensome, and cause the saints to exclaim against their lean-
ness and odious pride and ingratitude. And whatever positive
exercises of corruption at any time arise, and mingle themselves
with eminent actings of grace, grace will exceedingly magnify
the view of them, and render their appearance far more heinous
and horrible.

The more eminent saints are, and the more they have of the
light of heaven in their souls, the more do they appear to themselves as the most eminent saints in this world do to the saints
and angels in heaven. How can we rationally suppose the most
eminent saints on earth appear to them, if beheld any otherwise
than covered over with the righteousness of Christ, and their
deformities swallowed up and hid in the coruscation of the
beams of His abundant glory and love? How can we suppose
our most ardent love and praises appear to them that behold
the beauty and glory of God without a vail? How does our
highest thankfulness for the dying love of Christ appear to them,
who see Christ as He is, who know as they are known, and see
the glory of the person of Him that died, and the wonders of
His dying love, without any cloud of darkness? And how do
they look on the deepest reverence and humility with which
worms of the dust on earth approach that infinite Majesty
which they behold? Do they appear great to them, or so much
as worthy of the name of reverence and humility? The reason
why the highest attainments of the saints on earth appear so
mean to them, is because they dwell in the light of God's glory
and see God as He is. And it is in this respect with the saints
on earth as it is with the saints in heaven, in proportion as they
are more eminent in grace.

I would not be understood to mean that the saints on earth
have in all respects the worst opinion of themselves when they
have most of the exercises of grace. In many respects it is otherwise. With respect to the positive exercises of corruption, they
may appear to themselves freest and best when grace is most in
exercise, and worst when the actings of grace are lowest. And
when they compare themselves with themselves at different
times, they may know, when grace is in lively exercise, that it is
better with them than it was before (though before, in the time
of it, they did not see so much badness as they see now). And
when afterwards they sink again in the frame of their minds, they

may know that they sink, and have a new argument of their great remaining corruption, and a rational conviction of a greater vileness than they saw before; and many have more of a sense of guilt, and a kind of legal sense of their sinfulness by far, than when in the lively exercise of grace. But yet it is true, and demonstrable from the forementioned considerations, that the children of God never have so much of a sensible and spiritual conviction of their deformity, and so great and quick and abasing a sense of their present vileness and odiousness, as when they are highest in the exercise of true and pure grace; and never are they so much disposed to set themselves low among Christians as then. And thus he that is greatest in the kingdom, or most eminent in the church of Christ, is the same that humbles himself as the least infant among them; agreeable to that great saying of Christ, Matt. xviii. 4.

A true saint may know that he has some true grace: and the more grace there is, the more easily is it known, as was observed and proved before. But yet it does not follow that an eminent saint is easily sensible that he is an eminent saint, when compared with others. I will not deny that it is possible that he that has much grace, and is an eminent saint, may know it. But he will not be apt to know it; it will not be a thing obvious to him. That he is better than others, and has higher experiences and attainments, is not a foremost thought; nor is it that which from time to time readily offers itself. It is a thing that is not in his way, but lies far out of sight; he must take pains to convince himself of it; there will be need of a great command of reason, and a high degree of strictness and care in arguing, to convince himself. And if he be rationally convinced by a very strict consideration of his own experiences, compared with the great appearances of low degrees of grace in some other saints, it will hardly seem real to him that he has more grace than they; and he will be apt to lose the conviction that he has by pains obtained. Nor will it seem at all natural to him to act upon that supposition. This may be laid down as an infallible thing, that the person who is apt to think that he, as compared with others, is a very eminent saint, much distinguished in Christian experience, in whom this is a first thought that rises of itself and naturally offers itself—he is certainly mistaken; he is no eminent saint, but under the great prevailings of a proud and self-righteous spirit. And if this be habitual with the man, and is statedly the prevailing temper of his mind, he is no saint at all. So surely as the word of God is true, he has not the least degree of any true Christian experience.

Experiences that appear to be of that tendency, and which from time to time elevate the subject of them with a great conceit of those experiences, are certainly vain and delusive. Those supposed discoveries that naturally blow up the person with an admiration of the eminency of his discoveries, and fill him with conceit that now he has seen, and knows more than most other Christians, have nothing of the nature of true spiritual light in them. All true spiritual knowledge is such that, the more a person has of it, the more is he sensible of his own ignorance; as is evident by 1 Cor. viii. 2: "He that thinketh he knoweth anything, he knoweth nothing yet as he ought to know." Agur, when he had a great discovery of God, and a sense of the wonderful height of His glory and of His marvellous works, acknowledging His greatness and incomprehensibleness, at the same time had the deepest sense of his own brutish ignorance, and looked upon himself as the most ignorant of all the saints. Prov. xxx. 2, 3, 4: "Surely I am more brutish than any man, and have not the understanding of a man. I neither learned wisdom, nor have the knowledge of the holy. Who hath ascended up into heaven, or descended? Who hath gathered the wind in his fists? Who hath bound the waters in a garment? Who hath established all the ends of the earth? What is his name, and what is his son's name, if thou canst tell?"

For a man to be highly conceited of his spiritual and divine knowledge, is for him to be wise in his own eyes, if anything is, and therefore it comes under those prohibitions: Prov. iii. 7, "Be not wise in thine own eyes." Rom. xii. 16, "Be not wise in your own conceits." It brings men under that woe, Isa. v. 21: "Woe unto them that are wise in their own eyes, and prudent in their own sight!" Those that are thus wise in their own eyes are some of the least likely to get good of any in the world. Experience shows the truth of that, Prov. xxvi. 12: "Seest thou a man wise in his own conceit? There is more hope of a fool than of him."

To this some may object, that the Psalmist, when we must suppose that he was in a holy frame, speaks of his knowledge as eminently great and far greater than that of other saints: Psal. cxix. 99, 100, "I have more understanding than all my teachers: for thy testimonies are my meditation. I understand more than the ancients; because I keep thy precepts."

To this I answer two things:

(1.) There is no restraint to be laid upon the Spirit of God, as to what He shall reveal to a prophet, for the benefit of His church, who is speaking or writing under immediate inspiration. The Spirit of God may reveal to such an one, and dictate to him to declare to others, secret things that otherwise would be hard, yea impossible, for him to find out. As He may reveal to him mysteries, that otherwise would be above the reach of his reason; or things in a distant place, that he cannot see; or future events, that it would be impossible for him to know and declare, if they were not extraordinarily revealed to him; so the Spirit of God might reveal to David this distinguishing benefit he had received by conversing much with God's testimonies, and use him as His instrument to record it for the benefit of others, to excite them to the like duty and to use the same means to gain knowledge. Nothing can be gathered concerning the natural tendency of the ordinary gracious influences of the Spirit of God from what David declares of his distinguishing knowledge under the extraordinary influences of God's Spirit, immediately dictating to him the divine mind by inspiration, and using David as His instrument to write what He pleased for the benefit of His church, any more than we can reasonably argue that it is the natural tendency of grace to incline men to curse others and wish the most dreadful misery to them that can be thought of, because David, under inspiration, often curses others and prays that such misery may come upon them.

(2.) It is not certain that the knowledge David here speaks of is spiritual knowledge, wherein holiness fundamentally consists. It may refer to that greater revelation which God made to him of the Messiah and the things of His future kingdom, and the far more clear and extensive knowledge that he had of the mysteries and doctrines of the gospel than others; as a reward for his keeping God's testimonies. In this, it is apparent by the Book of Psalms that David far exceeded all that had gone before him.

Secondly. Another infallible sign of spiritual pride is present when persons think highly of their humility. False experiences are commonly attended with a counterfeit humility. It is the very nature of a counterfeit humility to be highly conceited of itself. False religious affections have generally a tendency, especially when raised to a great height, to make persons think that their humility is great, and accordingly to take much notice of their great attainments in this respect, and admire them. But eminently gracious affections (I scruple not to say it) are evermore of a contrary tendency, and have universally a contrary effect in those that have them. They indeed make them very sensible what reason there is that they should be deeply humbled, and cause them earnestly to thirst and long after it; but they make their present humility, or that which they have already attained to, to appear small, and their remaining pride great and exceedingly abominable.

The reason why a proud person should be apt to think his humility great, and why a very humble person should think his humility small, may be easily seen, if it be considered that it is natural for persons, in judging of the degree of their own humiliation, to take their measure from that which they esteem their proper height, or the dignity wherein they properly stand. That may be great humiliation in one that is no humiliation at all in another; because the degree of honourableness or considerableness wherein each does properly stand, is very different. For some great man to stoop to loose the latchet of the shoes of another great man, his equal, or to wash his feet, would be taken notice of as an act of abasement in him; and he, being sensible of his own dignity, would look upon it so himself. But if a poor slave is seen stooping to unloose the shoes of a great prince, nobody will take any notice of this as any act of humiliation in him, or token of any great degree of humility: not would the slave himself, unless he be horribly proud and ridiculously conceited of himself: and if after he had done it, he should, in his talk and behaviour, show that he thought his abasement great in it, and had his mind much upon it as an evidence of his being very humble; would not everybody cry out upon him, "Who do you think yourself to be, that you should think this that you have done such a deep humiliation?" This would make it plain to a demonstration that this slave was swollen with a high degree of pride and vanity of mind, as much as if he

declared in plain terms, "I think myself to be some great one."
And the matter is no less plain and certain when worthless, vile,
and loathsome worms of the dust put a similar construction on
their acts of abasement before God, and think it a token of great
humility in them that they acknowledge themselves to be so
mean and unworthy, and behave themselves as those that are
so inferior. The very reason why such outward acts and such
inward exercises look like great abasement in such an one, is
because he has a high conceit of himself. Whereas, if he
thought of himself more justly, these things would appear
nothing to him, and his humility in them worthy of no regard.
He would rather be astonished at his pride, that one so infinitely
despicable and vile is brought no lower before God. When he
says in his heart, "This is a great act of humiliation; it is certainly a sign of great humility in me that I should feel thus and
do so," his meaning is, "This is great humility for me, for such
an one as I that am so considerable and worthy." He considers
how low he is now brought, and compares this with the height
of dignity on which he in his heart thinks he properly stands,
and the distance appears very great, and he calls it all mere
humility, and as such admires it. Whereas, in him that is truly
humble and really sees his own vileness and loathsomeness before God, the distance appears the other way. When he is
brought lowest of all, it does not appear to him that he is
brought below his proper station, but that he is not come to it.
He appears to himself yet vastly above it, he longs to get lower,
that he may come to it, but appears at a great distance from it.
And this distance he calls pride. And therefore his pride
appears great to him, and not his humility. For although he is
brought much lower than he used to be, yet it does not appear
to him worthy of the name of humiliation, for him that is so
infinitely mean and detestable to come down to a place, which,
though it be lower than what he used to assume, is yet vastly
higher than what is proper for him. Men would hardly count it
worthy of the name of humility, in a contemptible slave that
formerly affected to be a prince, to have his spirit so far brought
down as to take the place of a nobleman; when this is still so
far above his proper station.

All men in the world, in judging of the degree of their own
and others' humility, consider two things, viz., the real degree of

dignity they stand in, and the degree of abasement with the relation it bears to that real dignity. Thus the complying with the same low place or low act may be an evidence of great humility in one, that evidences but little or no humility in another. But truly humble Christians have so mean an opinion of their own real dignity, that all their self-abasement, when considered with relation to that and compared to that, appears very small to them. It does not seem to them to be any great humility, or any abasement to be made much of, for such poor, vile, abject creatures as they to lie at the foot of God.

The degree of humility is to be judged of by the degree of abasement, and the degree of the cause for abasement: but he that is truly and eminently humble never thinks his humility great. The cause why he should be abased appears so great, and the abasement of the frame of his heart so greatly short of it, that he takes much more notice of his pride than his humility.

Every one that has been conversant with souls under convictions of sin knows that those who are greatly convinced of sin, are not apt to think themselves greatly convinced. And the reason is this: men judge of the degree of their own convictions of sin by two things jointly considered, viz., the degree of sense which they have of guilt and pollution, and the degree of cause they have for such a sense, in the degree of their real sinfulness. It is really no argument of any great conviction of sin, for some men to think themselves to be sinful beyond most others in the world; because they are so indeed, very plainly and notoriously. And therefore a far less conviction of sin may incline such an one to think so than another; he must be very blind indeed not to be sensible of it. But he that is truly under great convictions of sin, naturally thinks that the cause he has to be sensible of guilt and pollution is greater than others have; and therefore he ascribes his sensibleness of this to the greatness of his sin, and not to the greatness of his sensibility. It is natural for one under great convictions to think himself one of the greatest of sinners in reality, and also that it is so very plainly and evidently; for the greater his convictions are, the more plain and evident it seems to be to him. And therefore it necessarily seems to him so plain and so easy to him to see it, that it may be seen without much conviction. That man is under great convictions whose conviction is great in proportion to his sin. But no man that is

truly under great convictions thinks his conviction great in proportion to his sin. For if he does, it is a certain sign that he
inwardly thinks his sins small. And if that be the case, it is
a certain evidence that his conviction is small. And this, by the
way, is the main reason that persons, when under a work of
humiliation, are not sensible of it at the time of it.

And as it is with conviction of sin, just so it is, by parity of
reasoning, with respect to men's conviction or sensibleness of
their own meanness and vileness, their own blindness and impotence, and all that low sense that a Christian has of himself,
in the exercise of evangelical humiliation. So that in a high
degree of this, the saints are never disposed to think their
sensibleness of their own meanness, filthiness, and impotence, to
be great, for it never appears great to them considering the cause.

An eminent saint is not apt to think himself eminent in anything. All his graces and experiences are ready to appear to
him to be comparatively small, but especially his humility.
There is nothing that appertains to Christian experience and
true piety, that is so much out of his sight as his humility. He
is a thousand times more quicksighted to discern his pride than
his humility. That he easily discerns, and is apt to take much
notice of, but he hardly discerns his humility. On the contrary,
the deluded hypocrite that is under the power of spiritual pride
is so blind to nothing as his pride, and so quicksighted to
nothing, as the shows of humility that are in him.

The humble Christian is more apt to find fault with his own
pride than with other men's. He is apt to put the best construction on others' words and behaviour, and to think that
none are so proud as himself. But the proud hypocrite is quick
to discern the mote in his brother's eye, in this respect, while he
sees nothing of the beam in his own. He is very often de-
nouncing others' pride, finding fault with others' apparel and
way of living; and is affected ten times as much with his neighbour's ring or riband as with all the filthiness of his own heart.

From the disposition there is in hypocrites to think highly of
their humility, it comes about that counterfeit humility is forward to put itself forth to view. Those that have it are apt to
be much in speaking of their humiliations, setting them forth in
high terms, and making a great outward show of humility in
affected looks, gestures, manner of speech, meanness of apparel,

or some affected singularity. So it was of old with the false prophets, Zech. xiii. 4; so it was with the hypocritical Jews, Isa. lviii. 5, and so Christ tells us it was with the Pharisees, Matt. vi. 16. But it is contrariwise with true humility; they that have it, are not apt to display their eloquence in setting it forth, or to speak of the degree of their abasement in strong terms.* It does not affect to show itself in any singular outward meanness of apparel, or way of living, agreeable to what is implied in Matt. vi. 17, "But thou, when thou fastest, anoint thine head, and wash thy face." Col. ii. 23. "Which things have indeed a show of wisdom in will worship, and humility, and neglecting of the body." Nor is true humility a noisy thing; it is not loud and boisterous. The Scripture represents it as of a contrary nature. Ahab, when he had a visible humility, a resemblance of true humility, went softly, 1 Kings xxi. 27. A penitent, in the exercise of true humiliation, is represented as still and silent, Lam. iii. 28: "He sitteth alone and keepeth silence, because he hath borne it upon him." And silence is mentioned as what attends humility, Prov. xxx. 32: "If thou hast done foolishly in lifting up thyself, or if thou hast thought evil, lay thine hand upon thy mouth."

Thus I have particularly and largely shown the nature of that true humility that attends holy affections, in its tendency to cause persons to think meanly of their attainments in religion as compared with the attainments of others, and particularly of their attainments in humility: and have shown the contrary tendency of spiritual pride to dispose persons to think their attainments in these respects to be great. I have insisted the longer on this, because I look upon it as a matter of great importance, as it affords a certain distinction between true and counterfeit humility; and also as this disposition of hypocrites to look on themselves as better than others is what God has declared to be very hateful to Him, "a smoke in his nose, and a

---

* It is an observation of Mr. Jeremiah Jones (1693-1724), in his excellent treatise on the Canon of the New Testament, that the evangelist Mark, who was the companion of St. Peter, and is supposed to have written his gospel under the direction of that apostle, when he mentions Peter's repentance after his denying his Master, does not use such strong terms to set it forth as the other evangelists; he only uses these words, "When he thought thereon, he wept," Mark xiv. 72; whereas the other evangelists say thus, "He went out, and wept bitterly," Matt. xxvi. 75, Luke xxii. 62.

fire that burneth all the day," Isa. lxv. 5. It is mentioned as an instance of the pride of the inhabitants of that holy city (as it was called), Jerusalem, that they esteemed themselves far better than the people of Sodom, and so looked upon them as worthy to be overlooked and disregarded by them: Ezek. xvi. 56, "For thy sister Sodom was not mentioned by thy mouth in the day of thy pride."

Let not the reader lightly pass over these things in application to himself. If you once have taken it in that it is a bad sign for a person to be apt to think himself a better saint than others, there will arise a blinding prejudice in your own favour; and there will probably be need of a great strictness of self-examination in order to determine whether it be so with you. If on the proposal of the question, you answer, "No, it seems to me none are so bad as I," do not let the matter pass off so; but examine again whether or no you do not think yourself better than others on this very account, because you imagine you think so meanly of yourself. Have not you a high opinion of this humility? And if you answer again, "No; I have not a high opinion of my humility; it seems to me I am as proud as the devil"; yet examine again whether self-conceit do not rise up under this cover—whether on this very account that you think yourself as proud as the devil, you do not think yourself to be very humble.

From this opposition that there is between the nature of a true and of a counterfeit humility, as to the esteem that the subjects of them have of themselves, arises a manifold contrariety of temper and behaviour.

A truly humble person having such a mean opinion of his righteousness and holiness, is poor in spirit. For a person to be poor in spirit, is to be in his own sense and apprehension poor, as to what is in him, and to be of an answerable disposition. Therefore a truly humble person, especially one eminently humble, naturally behaves himself in many respects as a poor man. "The poor useth entreaties, but the rich answereth roughly." A poor man is not disposed to quick and high resentment when he is among the rich: he is apt to yield to others, for he knows others are above him: he is not stiff and self-willed; he is patient with hard fare; he expects no other than to be despised, and takes it patiently; he does not take it hein-

ously that he is overlooked and but little regarded; he is prepared to be in a low place; he readily honours his superiors; he
takes reproofs quietly; he readily honours others as above him;
he easily yields to be taught, and does not claim much to his
understanding and judgment; he is not over nice or humour-
some, and has his spirit subdued to hard things; he is not assuming, nor apt to take much upon him, but it is natural for him to
be subject to others.   Thus it is with the humble Christian.
Humility is (as the great Mastricht* expresses it) a kind of holy
pusillanimity.

A man that is very poor is a beggar; so is he that is poor in
spirit. There is a great difference between those affections that
are gracious, and those that are false. Under the former, the
person continues still a poor beggar at God's gates, exceeding
empty and needy; but the latter make men appear to themselves
rich, and increased with goods, and not very necessitous; they
have a great stock in their own imaginaton for their subsistence.†

A poor man is modest in his speech and behaviour; so, and
much more, and more certainly and universally, is one that is
poor in spirit; he is humble and modest in his behaviour among
men. It is in vain for any to pretend that they are humble, and
as little children before God, when they are haughty, assuming,
and impudent in their behaviour among men. The apostle in-

* Peter van Mastricht (1630-1706), author of *Theoretico-practica theo-
logia*, published in 1724.
† " This spirit ever keeps a man poor and vile in his own eyes, and
empty.—When the man hath got some knowledge, and can discourse
pretty well, and hath some taste of the heavenly gift, some sweet illapses
of grace, and so his conscience is pretty well quieted: and if he hath got
some answer to his prayers, and hath sweet affections, he grows full: and
having ease to his conscience, casts off sense and daily groaning under
sin.   And hence the spirit of prayer dies: he loses his esteem of God's
ordinances, feels not such need of them; or gets no good, feels no life or
power by them.—This is the woeful condition of some; but yet they know
it not.   But now he that is filled with the Spirit, the Lord empties him;
and the more the longer he lives.   So that though others think he needs
not much grace, yet he accounts himself the poorest." *Shepard's Parable
of the Ten Virgins*, p. 556.
" After all fillings, be ever empty, hungry, and feeling need, and praying for more." Ibid. p. 581.
" Truly, brethren, when I see the curse of God upon many Christians
that are now grown full of their parts, gifts, peace, comforts, abilities,
duties, I stand adoring the riches of the Lord's mercy to a little handful
of poor believers, not only in making them empty, but in keeping them
so all their days." *Shepard's Sound Believer*, p. 217.

forms us that the design of the gospel is to cut off all glorying, not only before God, but also before men, Rom. iv. 1, 2. Some pretend to great humiliation, that are very haughty, audacious, and assuming in their external appearance and behaviour: but they ought to consider those Scriptures, Psal. cxxxi. 1, "Lord, my heart is not haughty, nor mine eyes lofty; neither do I exercise myself in great matters, or in things too high for me." Prov. vi. 16, 17, "These six things doth the Lord hate; yea, seven are an abomination unto him: a proud look, &c."—Chap. xxi. 4, "An high look, and a proud heart are sin." Psal. xxviii. 27, "Thou wilt bring down high looks." And Psal. ci. 5, "Him that hath an high look and a proud heart will not I suffer." 1 Cor. xiii. 4, 5. "Charity vaunteth not itself, doth not behave itself unseemly." There is a certain amiable modesty and fear, arising from humility, that belongs to a Christian behaviour among men, that the Scripture often speaks of, 1 Pet. iii. 15, "Be ready to give an answer to every man that asketh you—with meekness and fear." Romans xiii. 7, "Fear to whom fear." 2 Cor. vii. 15, "Whilst he remembereth the obedience of you all, how with fear and trembling ye received him." Eph. vi. 5, "Servants, be obedient to them that are your masters according to the flesh, with fear and trembling." 1 Pet. ii. 18, "Servants, be subject to your masters with all fear." 1 Pet. iii. 2, "While they behold your chaste conversation coupled with fear." 1 Tim. ii. 9, "That women adorn themselves in modest apparel, with shamefacedness and sobriety." In this respect a Christian is like a little child; a little child is modest before men, and his heart is apt to be possessed with fear and awe among them.

The same spirit will dispose a Christian to honour all men: 1 Pet. ii. 17, "Honour all men." A humble Christian is not only disposed to honour the saints in his behaviour; but others also, in all those ways that do not imply a visible approbation of their sins. Thus Abraham, the great pattern of believers, honoured the children of Heth: Gen. xxiii. 7, "Abraham stood up, and bowed himself to the people of the land." This was a remarkable instance of a humble behaviour towards them that were out of Christ, and that Abraham knew to be accursed, and therefore would by no means suffer his servant to take a wife to his son from among them; and Esau's wives, being of these children of Heth, were a grief of mind to Isaac and Rebekah.

So Paul honoured Festus: Acts xxvi. 25, "I am not mad, most noble Festus." Not only will Christian humility dispose persons to honour those wicked men that are out of the visible church, but also false brethren and persecutors. As Jacob, when he was in an excellent frame, having just been wrestling all night with God, and received the blessing, honoured Esau, his false and persecuting brother: Gen. xxxiii. 3, "Jacob bowed himself to the ground seven times, until he came near to his brother Esau." So he called him lord; and commanded all his family to honour him in like manner.

Thus I have endeavoured to describe the heart and behaviour of one that is governed by a truly gracious humility, as exactly agreeable to the Scriptures as I am able.

Now, it is out of such a heart as this that all truly holy affections do flow. Christian affections are like Mary's precious ointment that she poured on Christ's head, that filled the whole house with a sweet odour. That was poured out of an alabaster box; so gracious affections flow out to Christ out of a pure heart. That was poured out of a broken box; until the box was broken, the ointment could not flow, nor diffuse its odour; so gracious affections flow out of a broken heart. Gracious affections are also like those of Mary Magdalene (Luke vii. at the latter end), who also pours precious ointment on Christ out of an alabaster broken box, anointing therewith the feet of Jesus, when she had washed them with her tears and wiped them with the hair of her head. All gracious affections that are a sweet odour to Christ, and that fill the soul of a Christian with a heavenly sweetness and fragrancy, are broken-hearted affections. A truly Christian love, either to God or men, is a humble broken-hearted love. The desires of the saints, however earnest, are humble desires. Their hope is a humble hope; and their joy, even when it is unspeakable and full of glory, is a humble broken-hearted joy, and leaves the Christian more poor in spirit, and more like a little child, and more disposed to a universal lowliness of behaviour.

VII. *Another thing, wherein gracious affections are distinguished from others, is, that they are attended with a change of nature.*

All gracious affections do arise from a spiritual understanding, in which the soul has the excellency and glory of divine things discovered to it, as was shown before. But all spiritual discoveries are transforming, and not only make an alteration of the present exercise, sensation, and frame of the soul; but such power and efficacy have they, that they make an alteration in the very nature of the soul: 2 Cor. iii. 18, "But we all with open face, beholding as in a glass the glory of the Lord, are changed into the same image, from glory to glory, even as by the Spirit of the Lord." Such power as this is properly divine power, and is peculiar to the Spirit of the Lord: other power may make an alteration in men's present frames and feelings: but it is the power of a Creator only that can change the nature, or give a new nature. And no discoveries or illuminations but those that are divine and supernatural will have this supernatural effect. But this effect all those discoveries have that are truly divine. The soul is deeply affected by these discoveries, and so affected as to be transformed.

Thus it is with those affections that the soul is the subject of in its conversion. The Scripture representations of conversion do strongly imply and signify a change of nature: such as "being born again; becoming new creatures; rising from the dead; being renewed in the spirit of the mind, dying to sin, and living to righteousness; putting off the old man, and putting on the new man; a being ingrafted into a new stock; a having a divine seed implanted in the heart; a being made partakers of the divine nature," &c.

Therefore if there be no great and remarkable abiding change in persons that think they have experienced a work of conversion, vain are all their imaginations and pretences, however they have been affected.* Conversion is a great and universal change of the man, turning him from sin to God. A man may be restrained from sin, before he is converted; but when he is converted, he is not only restrained from sin, his very heart and nature is turned from it unto holiness: so that thenceforward he becomes a holy person, and an enemy to sin. If, therefore, after a person's high affections at his supposed first conversion,

* "I would not judge of the whole soul's coming to Christ, so much by sudden pangs as by inward bent. For the whole soul, in affectionate expressions and actions, may be carried to Christ; but being without this bent and change of affections, it is unsound." *Shepard's Parable of the Ten Virgins*, p. 322.

it comes to that in a little time that there is no very sensible or remarkable alteration in him as to those bad qualities and evil habits which before were visible in him, and he is ordinarily under the prevalence of the same kind of dispositions that he used to be, and the same thing seems to belong to his character; if he appears as selfish and carnal, as stupid and perverse, as unchristian and unsavoury as ever; it is greater evidence against him than the brightest story of experiences that ever was told is for him.   For in Christ Jesus neither circumcision, nor uncircumcision, neither high profession, nor low profession, neither a fair story, nor a broken one, avails anything; but a new creature.

If there be a very great alteration visible in a person for a while, if it be not abiding, but he afterwards returns, in a stated manner, to be much as he used to be; it appears to be no change of nature, for nature is an abiding thing.   A swine that is of a filthy nature may be washed, but the swinish nature remains; and a dove that is of a cleanly nature may be defiled, but its cleanly nature remains.*

Indeed, allowances must be made for the natural temper; conversion does not entirely root out the natural temper; those sins which a man by his natural constitution was most inclined to before his conversion, he may be most apt to fall into still. Yet conversion will make a great alteration even with respect to these sins.   Though grace, while imperfect, does not root out an evil natural temper, yet it is of great power and efficacy with respect to it, to correct it.   The change that is wrought in conversion is a universal change.   Grace changes a man with respect to whatever is sinful in him; the old man is put off and the new man put on; he is sanctified throughout; and the man becomes a new creature, old things are passed away and all things are become new; all sin is mortified, constitutional sins as well as others.   If a man before his conversion was by his natural con-

---

* " It is with the soul as with water; all the cold may be gone, but the native principle of cold remains still.   You may remove the burning of lusts, not the blackness of nature.   Where the power of sin lies, change of conscience from security to terror, change of life from profaneness to civility, and fashions of the world, to escape the pollutions thereof, change of lusts, may quench them for a time: but the nature is never changed in the best hypocrite that ever was." *Shepard's Parable of the Ten Virgins*, p. 307.

stitution especially inclined to lasciviousness, or drunkenness, or maliciousness, converting grace will make a great alteration in him with respect to these evil dispositions; so that, however he may be still most in danger of these sins, yet they shall no longer have dominion over him, nor will they any more be properly his character. Yea, true repentance does in some respects especially turn a man against his own iniquity, that wherein he has been most guilty and has chiefly dishonoured God. He that forsakes other sins but saves his leading sin, the iniquity he is chiefly inclined to, is like Saul when sent against God's enemies the Amalekites with a strict charge to save none of them alive, but utterly to destroy them, small and great; who utterly destroyed inferior people, but saved the king, the chief of them all, alive.

Some foolishly make it an argument in favour of their discoveries and affections, that when they are gone they are left wholly without any life or sense, or anything beyond what they had before. They think it an evidence that what they experienced was wholly of God, and not of themselves, because (say they) when God is departed, all is gone; they can see and feel nothing, and are no better than they used to be.

It is very true that all grace and goodness in the hearts of the saints is entirely from God; and they are universally and immediately dependent on Him for it. But yet these persons are mistaken, as to the manner of God's communicating Himself and His Holy Spirit, in imparting saving grace to the soul. He gives His Spirit to be united to the faculties of the soul, and to dwell there after the manner of a principle of nature; so that the soul, in being endued with grace, is endued with a new nature: but nature is an abiding thing. All the exercises of grace are entirely from Christ: but are not from Him as a living agent moves and stirs what is without life, and which yet remains lifeless. The soul has life communicated to it, so that through Christ's power, it has inherent in itself a vital nature. In the soul where Christ savingly is, there He lives. He not only lives without it, so as violently to actuate it, but He lives in it, so that the soul also is alive. Grace in the soul is as much from Christ, as the light in a glass, held out in the sunbeams, is from the sun. But this represents the manner of the communication of grace to the soul only in part; because the glass remains as it

was, the nature of it not being at all changed; it is as much without any lightsomeness in its nature as ever. But the soul of a
saint receives light from the Sun of Righteousness, in such a
manner that its nature is changed, and it becomes properly a
luminous thing; not only does the sun shine in the saints, but
they also become little suns, partaking of the nature of the
Fountain of their light. In this respect, the manner of their
derivation of light is like that of the lamps in the tabernacle,
rather than that of a reflecting glass; which, though they were
lit up by fire from heaven, yet thereby became themselves burning shining things. The saints not only drink of the water of
life that flows from the original fountain, but this water becomes a fountain of water in them, springing up there and
flowing out of them, John iv. 14, and chap. vii. 38, 39. Grace
is compared to a seed implanted, that not only is in the ground,
but has hold of it, has root there, and grows there, and is an
abiding principle of life and nature there.

As it is with spiritual discoveries and affections given at first
conversion, so it is in all subsequent illuminations and affections
of that kind; they are all transforming. There is a like divine
power and energy in them as in the first discoveries; they still
reach the bottom of the heart, and affect and alter the very
nature of the soul, in proportion to the degree in which they
are given. And a transformation of nature is continued and
carried on by them to the end of life, until it is brought to perfection in glory. Hence the progress of the work of grace in the
hearts of the saints is represented in Scripture as a continued
conversion and renovation of nature. So the apostle exhorts
those that were at Rome, " beloved of God, called to be saints,"
and that were subjects of God's redeeming mercies, " to be transformed by the renewing of their mind:" Rom. xii. 1, 2, " I
beseech you therefore, by the mercies of God, that ye present
your bodies a living sacrifice; and be not conformed to this
world: but be ye transformed by the renewing of your mind ";
compared with chap. i. 7. So the apostle, writing to the " saints
and faithful in Christ Jesus," that were at Ephesus (Eph. i. 1),
those who were once dead in trespasses and sins, but were now
quickened and raised up, and made to sit together in heavenly
places in Christ, and created in Christ Jesus unto good works,
that were once far off, but were now made nigh by the blood of

Christ, and that were no more strangers and foreigners, but fellow citizens with the saints, and of the household of God, and that were built together for a habitation of God through the Spirit; I say, the apostle, writing to these, tells them, "that he ceased not to pray for them, that God would give them the spirit of wisdom and revelation, in the knowledge of Christ; the eyes of their understanding being enlightened, that they might know, or experience, what was the exceeding greatness of God's power towards them that believe, according to the working of his mighty power, which he wrought in Christ, when he raised him from the dead, and set him at his own right hand in the heavenly places." Eph. i. 16, to the end. In this the apostle has respect to the glorious power and work of God in converting and renewing the soul; as is most plain by the sequel. So the apostle exhorts the same persons " to put off the old man, which is corrupt according to the deceitful lusts; and be renewed in the spirit of their minds; and to put on the new man, which after God is created in righteousness and true holiness," Eph. iv. 22, 23, 24.

There is a sort of high affections that some have from time to time, that leave them without any manner of appearance of an abiding effect. They go off suddenly; so that from the very height of their emotion and seeming rapture, they pass at once to be quite dead and void of all sense and activity. It surely is not wont to be thus with high gracious affections;* they leave a sweet savour and a relish of divine things on the heart, and a stronger bent of soul towards God and holiness. As Moses' face not only shone while he was in the mount, extraordinarily conversing with God, but it continued to shine after he came down from the mount. When men have been conversing with Christ in an extraordinary manner, there is a sensible effect of it remaining upon them; there is something remarkable in their disposition and frame, which if we take knowledge of and trace to its cause, we shall find it is because they have been with Jesus, Acts iv. 13.

* " Do you think the Holy Ghost comes on a man as on Balaam, by immediate acting, and then leaves him, and then he has nothing?" *Shepard's Parable of the Ten Virgins,* p. 203.

VIII. *Truly gracious affections differ from those affections that are false and delusive, in that they tend to, and are attended with, the lamb-like, dove-like spirit and temper of Jesus Christ.*

In other words, they naturally beget and promote such a spirit of love, meekness, quietness, forgiveness and mercy, as appeared in Christ.

The evidence of this in the Scripture is very abundant. If we judge of the nature of Christianity and the proper spirit of the gospel by the Word of God, this spirit is what may, by way of eminency, be called the Christian spirit; and may be looked upon as the true and distinguishing disposition of the hearts of Christians as Christians. When some of the disciples of Christ said something, through inconsideration and infirmity, that was not agreeable to such a spirit, Christ told them that they knew not what manner of spirit they were of, Luke ix. 55, implying that this spirit that I am speaking of is the proper spirit of His religion and kingdom. All that are truly godly, and real disciples of Christ, have this spirit in them; and not only so, but they are of this spirit. It is the spirit by which they are so possessed and governed that it is their true and proper character. This is evident by what the wise man says, Prov. xvii. 27 (having respect plainly to such a spirit as this): "A man of understanding is of an excellent spirit "; and by the particular description Christ gives of the qualities and temper of such as are truly blessed, that shall obtain mercy, and are God's children and heirs: Matt. v. 5, 7, 9, "Blessed are the meek: for they shall inherit the earth. Blessed are the merciful: for they shall obtain mercy. Blessed are the peacemakers: for they shall be called the children of God." And that this spirit is the special character of the elect of God is manifested by Col. iii. 12, 13: "Put on therefore, as the elect of God, holy and beloved, bowels of mercies, kindness, humbleness of mind, meekness, long-suffering; forbearing one another, and forgiving one another." The apostle, speaking of that temper and disposition which he speaks of as the most excellent and essential thing in Christianity, and that without which none are true Christians, and the most glorious profession and gifts are nothing (calling this spirit by the name of charity), he describes it thus, 1 Cor. xiii. 4, 5: "Charity suffereth long, and is kind; charity envieth not;

charity vaunteth not itself, is not puffed up, doth not behave itself unseemly, seeketh not her own, is not easily provoked, thinketh no evil." And the same apostle, designedly declaring the distinguishing marks and fruits of true Christian grace, chiefly insists on the things that appertain to such a temper and spirit as I am speaking of, Gal. v. 22, 23: "The fruit of the Spirit is love, joy, peace, long-suffering, gentleness, goodness, faith, meekness, temperance." And so does the Apostle James, in describing true grace, or that wisdom that is from above, with the declared design that others who are of a contrary spirit may not deceive themselves, and lie against the truth in professing to be Christians, when they are not, James iii. 14-17: "If ye have bitter envying and strife in your hearts, glory not; and lie not against the truth. This wisdom descendeth not from above, but is earthly, sensual, devilish. For where envying and strife is, there is confusion and every evil work. But the wisdom that is from above is first pure, then peaceable, gentle, and easy to be entreated, full of mercy and good fruits."

Everything that appertains to holiness of heart does, indeed, belong to the nature of true Christianity and the character of Christians; but a spirit of holiness as appearing in some particular graces may more especially be called the Christian spirit or temper. Some amiable qualities and virtues, more especially agree with the nature of the gospel constitution, and Christian profession; because there is a special agreeableness in them with those divine attributes which God has more remarkably manifested and glorified in the work of redemption by Jesus Christ, the grand subject of the Christian revelation; and also a special agreeableness with those virtues that were so wonderfully exercised by Jesus Christ towards us in that affair, and the blessed example He hath therein set us; and likewise because they are peculiarly agreeable to the special drift and design of the work of redemption, and the benefits we thereby receive, and the relation that it brings us into to God and one another. These virtues are such as humility, meekness, love, forgiveness, and mercy. These things therefore especially belong to the character of Christians, as such.

These things are spoken of as what are especially the character of Jesus Christ Himself, the great Head of the Christian church. They are so spoken of in the prophecies of the Old Testament;

as in that cited in Matt. xxi. 5: "Tell ye the daughter of Sion, Behold, thy King cometh unto thee, meek, and sitting upon an ass, and a colt the foal of an ass." So Christ himself speaks of them, Matt. xi. 29: "Learn of me, for I am meek and lowly in heart." The same appears by the name by which Christ is so often called in Scripture, viz., the Lamb. And as these things are especially the character of Christ, so they are also especially the character of Christians. Christians are Christlike; none deserve the name of Christians, that are not so in their prevailing character. "The new man is renewed, after the image of him that created him." Col. iii. 10. All true Christians behold as in a glass the glory of the Lord, and are changed into the same image, by His Spirit, 2 Cor. iii. 18. The elect are all predestinated to be conformed to the image of the Son of God, that He might be the first born among many brethren, Rom. viii. 29. As we have borne the image of the first man, that is earthy, so we must also bear the image of the heavenly; for as is the earthy, such are they also that are earthy; and as is the heavenly, such are they also that are heavenly, 1 Cor. xv. 47, 48, 49. Christ is full of grace, and Christians all receive of His fulness, and grace for grace; *i.e.*, there is grace in Christians answering to grace in Christ, such an answerableness as there is between the wax and the seal. There is character for character: such kind of graces, such a spirit and temper; the same things that belong to Christ's character belong to theirs. In that disposition, wherein Christ's character does in a special manner consist, does His image in a special manner consist. Christians who shine by reflecting the light of the Sun of Righteousness shine with the same sort of brightness, the same mild, sweet, and pleasant beams. These lamps of the spiritual temple, that are enkindled by fire from heaven, burn with the same sort of flame. The branch is of the same nature with the stock and root, has the same sap, and bears the same sort of fruit. The members have the same kind of life with the head. It would be strange if Christians should not be of the same temper and spirit that Christ is of, when they are His flesh and His bone, yea, are one spirit, 1 Cor. vi. 17; and so live, that it is not they that live but Christ that lives in them. A Christian spirit is Christ's mark that he sets upon the souls of his people; His seal in their foreheads, bearing his image and superscription. Christians are the followers of Christ; and they are so, as they are obedient to that call of Christ, Matt. vi. 28, 29, "Come unto me—and learn of me: for I am meek and lowly in heart." They follow him as the Lamb: Rev. xiv. 4, "These are they which follow the Lamb whithersoever he goeth." True Christians are, as it were, clothed with the meek, quiet and loving temper of Christ; for as many as are in Christ have put on Christ. And in this respect the church is clothed with the sun, not only by being clothed with His imputed righteousness, but also by being adorned with his graces, Rom. xiii. 14. Christ, the great Shepherd, is himself a Lamb, and believers are also lambs; all the flock are lambs: John xxi. 15, "Feed my lambs." Luke x. 3, "I send you forth as lambs among wolves." The redemption of the church by Christ from the power of the devil, was typified of old by David's delivering the lamb out of the mouth of the lion and the bear.

That such manner of virtue as has been spoken of, is the very nature of the Christian spirit, or the spirit that worketh in Christ and in His members, is evident by this, that the dove is the very symbol or emblem chosen of God to represent it. Those things are fittest emblems of other things which best represent that which is most distinguishing in their nature. The Spirit that descended on Christ when he was anointed of the Father, descended on him like a dove. The dove is a noted emblem of meekness, harmlessness, peace and love. But the same Spirit that descended on the Head of the church descends to the members. "God hath sent forth the Spirit of his Son into your hearts," Gal. iv. 6. And "if any man have not the Spirit of Christ, he is none of his," Rom. viii. 9. There is but one Spirit to the whole mystical body, Head and members, 1 Cor. vi. 17, Eph. iv. 4. Christ breathes His own Spirit on His disciples, John xx. 22. As Christ was anointed with the Holy Ghost descending on Him like a dove, so Christians also "have an anointing from the Holy One," 1 John ii. 20, 27. And they are anointed with the same oil; it is the same "precious ointment on the head, that goes down to the skirts of the garments." And on both, it is a spirit of peace and love. Psalm cxxxiii. 1, 2, "Behold, how good and how pleasant it is for brethren to dwell together in unity! It is like the precious ointment upon the head, that ran down upon the beard, even Aaron's beard, that went down to the skirts of his garments." The oil on Aaron's garments had the same sweet and inimitable odour with that on his head; the smell of the same sweet spices, Christian affections, and a Christian behaviour, is but the flowing out of the savour of Christ's sweet ointments.   Because the church has a dove-like temper and disposition, therefore it is said of her that she has doves' eyes. Cant. i. 15: "Behold, thou art fair my love; behold, thou art fair, thou hast doves' eyes."   And chap. iv. 1, "Behold, thou art fair, my love, behold, thou art fair; thou hast doves' eyes within thy locks."   The same is said of Christ, chap. v. 12: "His eyes are as the eyes of doves."   And the church is frequently compared to a dove in Scripture: Cant. ii. 14, "O my dove, that art in the clefts of the rock."   Chap. v. 2, "Open to me, my love, my dove." And chap. vi. 9, "My dove, my undefiled is but one."   Psal. lxviii. 13, "Ye shall be as the wings of a dove covered with silver, and her feathers with yellow gold." And lxxiv. 19, "O deliver not the soul of thy turtle-dove unto the multitude of the wicked."   The dove that Noah sent out of the ark, that could find no rest for the sole of her foot until she returned, was a type of a true saint.

Meekness is so much the character of the saints, that the meek and the godly are used as synonymous terms in Scripture: so in Psalm xxxvii. 10, 11, the wicked and the meek are set in opposition one to another, as wicked and godly: "Yet a little while, and the wicked shall not be; but the meek shall inherit the earth." So Psal. cxlvii. 6, "The Lord lifteth up the meek: he casteth the wicked down to the ground."

It is doubtless very much on this account, that Christ represents all His disciples, all the heirs of heaven, as little children: Matt. xix. 14, "Suffer little children, and forbid them not to come unto me; for of such is the kingdom of heaven." Matt. x. 42, "Whosoever shall give to drink unto one of these little ones a cup of cold water only in the name of a disciple, verily I say unto you, he shall in no wise lose his reward." Matt. xviii. 6, "Whoso shall offend one of these little ones, &c." Ver 10. "Take heed that ye despise not one of these little ones." Ver. 14, "It is not the will of your Father which is in heaven, that one of these little ones should perish." John xiii. 33, "Little children, yet a little while I am with you." Little children are innocent and harmless; they do not do a great deal of mischief in the world; men need not be afraid of them; they are no dangerous sort of persons; their anger does not last long, they do not lay up injuries in high resentment, entertaining deep and rooted malice. So Christians in malice are children, 1 Cor. xiv. 20. Little children are not guileful and deceitful, but plain and simple; they are not versed in the arts of fiction and deceit; and are strangers to artful disguises. They are yielding and flexible, and not wilful and obstinate; do not trust to their own understanding, but rely on the instruction of parents and others of superior understanding. Here is therefore a fit and lively emblem of the followers of the Lamb. Persons being thus like little children is not only a thing highly commendable, and what Christians approve of and aim at, and which some of extraordinary proficiency attain to: but it is their universal character, and absolutely necessary in order to entering into the kingdom of heaven: Matt. xviii. 3, "Verily I say unto you, Except ye be converted and become as little children, ye shall not enter into the kingdom of heaven." Mark x. 15, "Verily I say unto you, Whosoever shall not receive the kingdom of God as a little child, he shall not enter therein."

But here some may be ready to say, Is there no such thing as Christian fortitude, and boldness for Christ, being good soldiers in the Christian warfare, and coming out boldly against the enemies of Christ and His people?

To which I answer, There doubtless is such a thing. The whole Christian life is compared to a warfare, and fitly so. The most eminent Christians are the best soldiers, endued with the greatest degrees of Christian fortitude. It is the duty of God's people to be steadfast and vigorous in their opposition to the designs and ways of such as are endeavouring to overthrow the kingdom of Christ and the interest of religion. But yet many persons seem to be quite mistaken concerning the nature of Christian fortitude. It is an exceeding diverse thing from a brutal fierceness, or the boldness of beasts of prey. True Christian fortitude consists in strength of mind, through grace, exerted in two things; in ruling and suppressing the evil and unruly passions and affections of the mind; and in steadfastly and freely exerting and following good affections and dispositions, without being hindered by sinful fear or the opposition of enemies. But the passions that are restrained and kept under, in the exercise of this Christian strength and fortitude, are those very passions that are vigorously and violently exerted in a false boldness for Christ. And those affections that are vigorously exerted in true fortitude are those Christian holy affections that are directly contrary to them. Though Christian fortitude appears in withstanding and counteracting the enemies that are without us; yet it much more appears in resisting and suppressing the enemies that are within us; because they are our worst and strongest enemies and have greatest advantage against us. The strength of the good soldier of Jesus Christ appears in nothing more than in steadfastly maintaining the holy calm, meekness, sweetness, and benevolence of his mind, amidst all the storms, injuries, strange behaviour, and surprising acts and events of this evil and unreasonable world. The Scripture seems to intimate that true fortitude consists chiefly in this: Prov. xvi. 32, "He that is slow to anger is better than the mighty; and he that ruleth his spirit than he that taketh a city."

The directest and surest way in the world to make a right judgment of what is a holy fortitude in fighting with God's enemies, is to look to the Captain of all God's hosts, and our great Leader and Example, and see wherein his fortitude and valour appeared, in His chief conflict, and in the time of the greatest battle that ever was or ever will be fought with these enemies, when He fought with them all alone, and of the people there was none with Him. He exercised His fortitude in the highest degree that ever He did, and got that glorious victory that will be celebrated in the praises and triumphs of all the hosts of heaven throughout all eternity. Behold Jesus Christ in the time of His last sufferings, when his enemies in earth and hell made their most violent attack upon Him, compassing him round on every side like rending and roaring lions. Doubtless here we shall see the fortitude of a holy warrior and champion in the cause of God in its highest perfection and greatest lustre, and an example fit for the soldiers to follow that fight under this Captain. But how did He show His holy boldness and valour at that time? Not in the exercise of any fiery passions; not in fierce and violent speeches, vehemently declaiming against the intolerable wickedness of opposers, giving them their own in plain terms: but in not opening His mouth when afflicted and oppressed, in going as a lamb to the slaughter, and, as a sheep before his shearers is dumb, not opening his mouth; praying that the Father would forgive His cruel enemies because they knew not what they did; not shedding others' blood, but with all-conquering patience and love shedding his own. Indeed, one of his disciples, that made a forward pretence to boldness for Christ and confidently declared he would sooner die with Christ than deny Him, began to lay about him with a sword: but Christ meekly rebukes him, and heals the wound he gives. Never was the patience, meekness, love, and forgiveness of Christ so gloriously manifest as at that time. Never did He appear so much a Lamb, and never did he show so much of the dove-like spirit as at that time. If therefore we see any of the followers of Christ, in the midst of the most violent, unreasonable, and wicked opposition of God's and his own enemies, maintaining under all this temptation, the humility and quietness and gentleness of a lamb, and the harmlessness and love and sweetness of a dove, we may well judge that here is a good soldier of Jesus Christ.

When persons are fierce and violent, and exert their sharp and bitter passions, it shows weakness instead of strength and fortitude. 1 Cor. iii. 1, 3: "And I, brethren, could not speak unto you as unto spiritual, but as unto carnal, even as unto babes in Christ. For ye are yet carnal: for whereas there is among you envying, and strife, and divisions, are ye not carnal, and walk as men?"

There is a pretended boldness for Christ that arises from no better principle than pride. A man may be forward to expose himself to the dislike of the world, and even to provoke their displeasure, out of pride. For it is the nature of spiritual pride to cause men to seek distinction and singularity; and so oftentimes to set themselves at war with those that they call carnal, that they may be more highly exalted among their party. True boldness for Christ is universal, and overcomes all, and carries men above the displeasure of friends and foes; so that they will forsake all rather than Christ; and will rather offend all parties, and be thought meanly of by all, than offend Christ. And that duty which tries whether a man is willing to be despised by them that are of his own party, and thought the least worthy to be regarded by them, is a much more proper trial of his boldness for Christ than his being forward to expose himself to the reproach of opposers. The apostle declined to

seek glory, not only of heathens and Jews, but of Christians; as
he declares, 1 Thess. ii. 6.*   He is bold for Christ that has Christian fortitude enough to confess his fault openly, when he has
committed one that requires it, and as it were to come down
upon his knees before opposers.   Such things as these are vastly
greater evidence of holy boldness than resolutely and fiercely
confronting opposers.

As some are much mistaken concerning the nature of true
boldness for Christ, so they are concerning Christian zeal. It is
indeed a flame, but a sweet one; or rather it is the heat and
fervour of a sweet flame.   For the flame of which it is the heat
is no other than that of divine love or Christian charity, which
is the sweetest and most benevolent thing that is, or can be, in
the heart of man or angel.   Zeal is the fervour of this flame, as
it ardently and vigorously goes out towards the good that is its
object; and so, consequentially, in opposition to the evil that is
contrary to it and impedes it.   There is indeed opposition, and
vigorous opposition, that is a part of it, or rather is an attendant
of it; but it is against things and not persons.   Bitterness against
the persons of men is no part of it, but is very contrary to it;
insomuch that so much the warmer true zeal is, and the higher
it is raised, so much the further are persons from such bitterness, and so much fuller of love both to the evil and to the good.
It is no other, in its very nature and essence, than the fervour
of Christian love.   And as to what opposition there is in it to
things, it is firstly and chiefly against the evil things in the
person himself, who has this zeal: against the enemies of God
and holiness that are in his own heart (as these are most in view,
and what he has most to do with); and but secondarily against
the sins of others.   And therefore there is nothing in a true
Christian zeal that is contrary to that spirit of meekness, gentleness, and love, that spirit of a little child, a lamb and dove, that
has been spoken of; but it is entirely agreeable to it, and tends to
promote it.

But to say something particularly concerning this Christian
spirit, as exercised in these three things—forgiveness, love, and

* Mr. Shepard, speaking of hypocrites affecting applause, says, " Hence
men forsake their friends, and trample under foot the scorns of the
world : they have credit elsewhere.   To maintain their interest in the love
of godly men, they will suffer much." *Parable of the Ten Virgins*, p. 285.

mercy—I would observe that the Scripture is very clear and express concerning the absolute necessity of each of these, as belonging to the temper and character of every Christian.

It is so as to a forgiving spirit, or a disposition to overlook and forgive injuries. Christ gives it to us both as a negative and positive evidence, and is express in teaching us that, if we are of such a spirit, it is a sign that we are in a state of forgiveness and favour ourselves: and that, if we are not of such a spirit, we are not forgiven of God. He seems to take special care that we should take good notice of it, and always bear it on our minds: Matt. vi. 12, 14, 15, "Forgive us our debts, as we forgive our debtors. For if ye forgive men their trespasses, your heavenly Father will also forgive you. But if ye forgive not men their trespasses, neither will your Father forgive your trespasses." Christ expresses the same again at another time, Mark xi. 25, 26, and again in Matt. xviii. 22-35, in the parable of the servant that owed his lord ten thousand talents, but would not forgive his fellow servant a hundred pence; and therefore was delivered to the tormentors. In the application of the parable Christ says, ver. 35, "So likewise shall my heavenly Father do also unto you, if ye from your hearts forgive not every one his brother their trespasses."

That all true saints are of a loving, benevolent, and beneficent temper, the Scripture is very plain and abundant. Without it, the apostle tells us, though we should speak with the tongues of men and angels, we are as a sounding brass, or a tinkling cymbal; and though we have the gift of prophecy, and understand all mysteries and all knowledge, yet without this spirit we are nothing. There is no one virtue or disposition of the mind that is so often and so expressly insisted on, in the marks that are laid down in the New Testament whereby to know true Christians. It is often given as a sign that is peculiarly distinguishing, by which all may know Christ's disciples, and by which they may know themselves; and is often laid down both as a negative and positive evidence. Christ calls the law of love, by way of eminency, His commandment: John xiii. 34, "A new commandment give I unto you, that ye love one another; as I have loved you, that ye also love one another." And chap. xv. 12, "This is my commandment, that ye love one another, as I have loved you." And ver. 17, "These things I command you, that

ye love one another." And says, chap. xiii. 35, "By this shall all
men know that ye are my disciples, if ye have love one to
another." And chap. xiv. 21 (still with a special reference to this
which he calls His commandment), "He that hath my commandments, and keepeth them, he it is that loveth me." The
beloved disciple who had so much of this sweet temper himself,
abundantly insists on it in his epistles. Not one of the apostles
is so express in laying down signs of grace, for professors to
try themselves by, as he; and in his signs he insists scarcely on
anything else, but a spirit of Christian love, and an agreeable
practice: 1 John ii. 9, 10, "He that saith he is in the light, and
hateth his brother, is in darkness even until now. He that
loveth his brother abideth in the light, and there is none occasion of stumbling in him." Chap. iii. 14, "We know that we
have passed from death unto life, because we love the brethren.
He that loveth not his brother abideth in death." Ver. 18, 19,
"My little children, let us not love in word, neither in tongue;
but in deed and in truth. And hereby we know that we are of
the truth, and shall assure our hearts before him." Ver. 23, 24,
"This is his commandment, that we should love one another.
And he that keepeth his commandments dwelleth in him, and
he in him; and hereby we know that he abideth in us, by the
Spirit which he hath given us." Chap. iv. 7, 8, "Beloved, let us
love one another: for love is of God; and every one that loveth
is born of God, and knoweth God. He that loveth not, knoweth
not God: for God is love." Ver. 12, 13, "No man hath seen
God at any time. If we love one another, God dwelleth in us,
and his love is perfected in us. Hereby know we that we
dwell in him, and he in us, because he hath given us of his
Spirit." Ver. 16, "God is love; and he that dwelleth in love
dwelleth in God, and God in him." Ver. 20, "If a man say, I
love God, and hateth his brother, he is a liar; for he that loveth
not his brother whom he hath seen, how can he love God whom
he hath not seen?"

The Scripture is as plain as possible that none are true saints,
but those whose true character it is that they are of a disposition
to pity and relieve their fellow creatures, who are poor, indigent,
and afflicted: Psal. xxxvii. 21, "The righteous showeth mercy,
and giveth." Ver. 26, "He is ever merciful, and lendeth." Psal.
cxii. 5, "A good man showeth favour, and lendeth." Ver. 9, "He

hath dispersed and given to the poor." Prov. xiv. 31, "He
that honoureth his Maker hath mercy on the poor." Prov. xxi.
26, "The righteous giveth, and spareth not." Jer. xxii. 16, "He
judged the cause of the poor and needy, then it was well with
him: was not this to know me? saith the Lord." Jam. i. 27,
"Pure religion and undefiled before God and the Father, is this,
To visit the fatherless and widows in their affliction," &c.   Hos.
vi. 6, "For I desired mercy, and not sacrifice; and the knowledge
of God more than burnt offerings."   Matt. v. 7, "Blessed are the
merciful; for they shall obtain mercy."   2 Cor. viii. 8, "I speak
not by commandment, but by occasion of the forwardness of
others, and to prove the sincerity of your love."   Jam. ii 13—16,
"For he shall have judgment without mercy, that hath showed
no mercy.   What doth it profit, my brethren, though a man say
he hath faith, and have not works?   Can faith save him?   If a
brother or sister be naked, and destitute of daily food, and one
of you say unto them, Depart in peace, be ye warmed and filled;
notwithstanding ye give them not those things which are needful
to the body; what doth it profit?"   1 John iii. 17, "Whoso hath
this world's good, and seeth his brother have need, and shutteth
up his bowels of compassion from him, how dwelleth the love of
God in him?"   Christ in the description He gives us of the day of
judgment, Matt. xxv. (which is the most particular that we have
in all the Bible), represents that judgment will be passed at that
day, according as men have been found to have been of a merciful spirit and practice or otherwise.   Christ's design in giving
such a description of the process of that day is plainly to possess
all his followers with the apprehension that, unless this is their
spirit and practice, there is no hope of their being accepted and
owned by Him at that day.   Therefore this is an apprehension
that we ought to be possessed with.   We find in Scripture that a
righteous man and a merciful man are synonymous expressions,
Isa: lvii. 1, "The righteous perisheth, and no man layeth it to
heart; and merciful men are taken away, none considering that
the righteous is taken away from the evil to come."

Thus we see how full, clear and abundant, the evidence from
Scripture is, that those who are truly gracious are under the
government of that lamb-like, dove-like Spirit of Jesus Christ,
and that this is essentially and eminently the nature of the
saving grace of the gospel and the proper spirit of true Christi-

anity. We may therefore undoubtedly determine that all truly Christian affections are attended with such a spirit, and that this is the natural tendency of the fear and hope, the sorrow and the joy, the confidence and the zeal of true Christians.

None will understand me, to mean that true Christians have no remains of a contrary spirit, and can never, in any instances, be guilty of a behaviour disagreeable to such a spirit. But this I affirm, and shall affirm until I deny the Bible to be anything worth, that everything in Christians that belongs to true Christianity is of this tendency, and works this way; and that there is no true Christian upon earth, but is so under the prevailing power of such a spirit that he is properly denominated from it, and it is truly and justly his character. Therefore ministers, and others, have no warrant from Christ to encourage persons that are of a contrary character and behaviour to think they are converted, because they tell a fair story of illuminations and discoveries. In so doing, they would set up their own wisdom against Christ's, and judge against that rule by which Christ has declared all men should know his disciples. Some persons place religion so much in certain transient illuminations and impressions (especially if they are in a particular method and order), and so little in the spirit and temper persons are of, that they greatly deform religion, and form notions of Christianity quite different from what it is as delineated in the Scriptures. The Scripture knows of no such true Christians, as are of a sordid, selfish, cross and contentious spirit. Nothing can be invented that is a greater absurdity than a morose, hard, close, high-spirited, spiteful, true Christian. We must learn the way of bringing men to rules, and not rules to men, straining and stretching the rules of God's word to take in ourselves, and some of our neighbours, until we make them wholly of none effect.

It is true that allowances must be made for men's natural temper, with regard to these things, as well as others; but not such allowances as to allow men that once were wolves and serpents, to be now converted without any remarkable change in the spirit of their mind. The change made by true conversion is wont to be most remarkable and sensible, with respect to the past notorious wickedness of the person. Grace has as great a tendency to restrain and mortify such sins as are contrary to the spirit that has been spoken of, as it has to mortify drunkenness or lasciviousness. Yea, the Scripture represents the change wrought by gospel grace as especially appearing in an alteration of the former sort: Isa. xi. 6-9. "The wolf shall dwell with the lamb, and the leopard shall lie down with the kid: and the calf, and the young lion, and the fatling together, and a little child shall lead them. And the cow and the bear shall feed, their young ones shall lie down together: and the lion shall eat straw like the ox. And the sucking child shall play on the hole of the asp, and the weaned child shall put his hand on the cockatrice' den. They shall not hurt nor destroy in all my holy mountain: for the earth shall be full of the knowledge of the Lord, as the waters cover the sea." And to the same purpose is Isa. lxv. 25. Accordingly we find that in the primitive times of the Christian church, converts were remarkably changed in this respect: Tit. iii. 3, &c., "For we ourselves also were sometimes foolish, disobedient, deceived, serving divers lusts and pleasures, living in malice and envy, hateful and hating one another. But after that the kindness and love of God our Saviour toward man appeared—he saved us by the washing of regeneration, and renewing of the Holy Ghost." And Col. iii. 7, 8, "In the which ye also walked sometime, when ye lived in them. But now ye also put off all these: anger, wrath, malice, blasphemy, filthy communication out of your mouth."

IX. *Gracious affections soften the heart and are attended and followed with a Christian tenderness of spirit.*

False affections, however persons may seem to be melted by them while they are new, have a tendency in the end to harden the heart. With the delusion that attends them, they finally tend to stupefy the mind, and shut it up against those affections wherein tenderness of heart consists: and the effect of them at last is that persons become less affected with their present and past sins, and less conscientious with respect to future sins, less moved with the warnings and cautions of God's word or God's chastisements in His providence, more careless of the frame of their hearts and the manner and tendency of their behaviour, less quick-sighted to discern what is sinful, less afraid of the appearance of evil, than they were while they were under legal awakenings and fears of hell. Now they have been the subjects of such and such impressions and affections, and have a high opinion of themselves, and look on their state to be safe; they can be much more easy than before, in living in the neglect of duties that are troublesome and inconvenient; and are much more slow and partial in complying with difficult commands. They are in no measure so alarmed at the appearance of their own defects and transgressions; are emboldened to favour themselves more with respect to the labour and painful care and exactness in their walk, and more easily yield to temptations, and the solicitations of their lusts; and have far less care of their behaviour when they come into the holy presence of God in the time of public or private worship. Formerly it may be, under legal convictions, they took much pains in religion, and denied themselves in many things: but now they think themselves out of danger of hell, they very much put off the burden of the cross, save themselves the trouble of difficult duties, and allow themselves more of the enjoyment of their ease and their lusts.

Such persons as these, instead of embracing Christ as their Saviour from sin, trust in Him as the Saviour of their sins. Instead of flying to Him as their refuge from their spiritual enemies, they make use of Him as the defence of their spiritual enemies from God, and to strengthen them against Him. They make Christ the minister of sin, and great officer and vicegerent of the devil, to strengthen his interest, and make him above all things in the world strong against Jehovah; so that they may sin against Him with good courage, and without any fear, being effectually secured from restraints by His most solemn warnings and most awful threatenings. They trust in Christ to preserve to them the quiet enjoyment of their sins, and to be their shield to defend them from God's displeasure; while they come close to Him, even to His bosom, the place of His children, to fight against Him, with their mortal weapons hid under their skirts.* However, some of these at the same time make a great profession

* " These are hypocrites that believe, but fail in regard of the use of the gospel, and of the Lord Jesus. And these we read of, Jude 3, viz., of some men that did turn grace into wantonness. For therein appears the exceeding evil of man's heart, that not only the law, but also the glorious gospel of the Lord Jesus, works in him all manner of unrighteousness. And it is too common for men at the first work of conversion, Oh then to cry for grace and Christ, and afterwards grow licentious, live and lie in the breach of the law, and take their warrant for their course from the gospel!" *Shepard's Parable of the Ten Virgins*, p. 203.

of love to God, and assurance of His favour, and great joy in tasting the sweetness of His love.

After this manner they trusted in Christ, of whom the Apostle Jude speaks, who crept in among the saints unknown, but were really ungodly men, turning the grace of God into lasciviousness, Jude 4. These are they that trust in their being righteous; and because God has promised that the righteous shall surely live, or certainly be saved, are therefore emboldened to commit iniquity; whom God threatens in Ezek. xxxiii. 13: "When I shall say to the righteous, that he shall surely live; if he trust to his own righteousness, and commit iniquity, all his righteousness shall not be remembered; but for his iniquity that he hath committed, he shall die for it."

Gracious affections are of a quite contrary tendency; they turn a heart of stone more and more into a heart of flesh. A holy love and hope are principles that are vastly more efficacious upon the heart to make it tender, and to fill it with a dread of sin or whatever might displease and offend God, and to engage it to watchfulness and care and strictness, than a slavish fear of hell. Gracious affections, as was observed before, flow out of a contrite heart, or (as the word signifies) a bruised heart, bruised and broken with godly sorrow; which makes the heart tender, as bruised flesh is tender and easily hurt. Godly sorrow has much greater influence to make the heart tender, than mere legal sorrow from selfish principles.

The tenderness of the heart of a true Christian is elegantly signified by our Saviour, in his comparing such a one to a little child. The flesh of a little child is very tender; so is the heart of one that is new born. This is represented in what we are told of the cure of Naaman's leprosy by his washing in Jordan; which was undoubtedly a type of the renewing of the soul, by washing in the laver of regeneration. We are told, 2 Kings v. 14, "That he went down, and dipped himself seven times in Jordan, according to the saying of the man of God; and his flesh came again like unto the flesh of a little child." Not only is the flesh of a little child tender, but his mind is tender. A little child has his heart easily moved, wrought upon and bowed: so is a Christian in spiritual things. A little child is apt to be affected with sympathy, to weep with them that weep, and cannot well bear to see others in distress: so it is with a Christian, John xi. 35,

Rom. xii. 15, 1 Cor. xii. 26. A little child is easily won by kindness: so is a Christian. A little child is easily affected with grief at temporal evils, and has his heart melted, and falls a-weeping: thus tender is the heart of a Christian with regard to the evil of sin. A little child is easily affrighted at the appearance of outward evils, or anything that threatens his hurt: so is a Christian apt to be alarmed at the appearance of moral evil and anything that threatens the hurt of the soul. A little child, when he meets enemies or fierce beasts, is not apt to trust his own strength, but flies to his parents for refuge: so a saint is not self-confident in engaging spiritual enemies, but flies to Christ. A little child is apt to be suspicious of evil in places of danger, afraid in the dark, afraid when left alone, or far from home: so is a saint apt to be sensible of his spiritual dangers, jealous of himself, full of fear when he cannot see his way plain before him, afraid to be left alone, and to be at a distance from God: Prov. xxviii. 14, "Happy is the man that feareth alway: but he that hardeneth his heart shall fall into mischief." A little child is apt to be afraid of superiors, and to dread their anger, and tremble at their frowns and threatenings: so is a true saint with respect to God: Psal. cxix. 120, "My flesh trembleth for fear of thee; and I am afraid of thy judgments." Isa. lxvi. 2, "To this man will I look, even to him that is poor, and trembleth at my word." Ver. 5, "Hear the word of the Lord, ye that tremble at his word." Ezra. ix. 4, "Then were assembled unto me every one that trembled at the words of the God of Israel." Chap. x. 3, "According to the counsel of my lord, and of those that tremble at the commandment of our God." A little child approaches superiors with awe: so do the saints approach God with holy awe and reverence: Job xiii. 11, "Shall not his excellency make you afraid? and his dread fall upon you?" Holy fear is so much the nature of true godliness, that it is called in Scripture by no other name more frequently than the fear of God.

Hence gracious affections do not tend to make men bold, forward, noisy, and boisterous; but rather to speak trembling: Hos: xiii. 1, "When Ephraim spake trembling, he exalted himself in Israel; but when he offended in Baal, he died." It tends to clothe them with a kind of holy fear in all their behaviour towards God and man; agreeably to Psal. ii. 11, 1 Pet. iii. 15, 2 Cor. vii. 15, Eph. vi. 5, 1 Pet. iii. 2, Rom. xi. 20.

But here some may object and say, Is there no such thing as a holy boldness in prayer and the duties of divine worship? I answer, there is doubtless such a thing; and it is chiefly to be found in eminent saints, persons of great degrees of faith and love. But this holy boldness is not in the least opposite to reverence; though it be to disunion and servility. It abolishes or lessens that disposition which arises from moral distance or alienation; and also distance of relation, as that of a slave; but not at all that which becomes the natural distance, whereby we are infinitely inferior. No boldness in poor sinful worms of the dust, that have a right sight of God and themselves, will prompt them to approach to God with less fear and reverence than spotless and glorious angels in heaven, who cover their faces before his throne, Isa. vi. Rebecca (who in her marriage with Isaac, in almost all its circumstances, was manifestly a great type of the church, the spouse of Christ), when she meets Isaac, lights off from her camel, and takes a veil and covers herself; although she was brought to him as his bride, to be with him in the nearest relation and most intimate union that mankind are ever united one to another.* Elijah, that great prophet, who had so much holy familiarity with God, at a time of special nearness to God, even when he conversed with Him in the mount, wrapped his face in his mantle. Which was not because he was terrified with any servile fear, by the terrible wind, and earthquake, and fire; but after these were all over, and God spake to him as a friend, in a still small voice: 1 Kings xix. 12, 13, "And after the fire, a still small voice; and it was so, when Elijah heard it, he wrapped his face in his mantle." And Moses, with whom God spake face to face, as a man speaks with his friend, and who was distinguished from all the prophets in the familiarity with God that he was admitted to: at a time when he was brought nearest of all, when God showed him His glory in that same mount where he afterwards spake to Elijah: "He made haste, and bowed his head toward the earth, and worshipped," Exod. xxxiv. 8. There is in some persons a most unsuitable and insufferable boldness, in their addresses to the great Jehovah, in an affectation of a holy boldness, and ostentation of eminent nearness and fami-

* Dr. William Ames (1576-1633), in his *Cases of Conscience*, Book III. chap. iv., speaks of a holy modesty in the worship of God as one sign of true humility.

liarity; the very thoughts of which would make them shrink into nothing, with horror and confusion, if they saw the distance that is between God and them. They are like the Pharisee, that boldly came up near in a confidence of his own eminency in holiness. Whereas, if they saw their vileness, they would be more like the publican that " stood afar off, and durst not so much as lift up his eyes to heaven; but smote upon his breast, saying, God be merciful to me a sinner." It becomes such sinful creatures as we, to approach a holy God (although with faith, and without terror) with contrition and penitent shame and confusion of face. It is foretold that this should be the disposition of the church, in the time of her highest privileges on earth in her latter day of glory, when God should remarkably comfort her by revealing his covenant mercy to her, Ezek. xvi. 60, to the end: "I will establish unto thee an everlasting covenant. Then thou shalt remember thy ways and be ashamed. And I will establish my covenant with thee, and thou shalt know that I am the Lord; that thou mayest remember, and be confounded, and never open thy mouth any more because of thy shame, when I am pacified toward thee for all that thou hast done, saith the Lord God." The woman that we read of in the 7th chapter of Luke, that was an eminent saint, and had much of that true love which casts out fear, by Christ's own testimony (ver. 47), approached Christ in an amiable and acceptable manner, when she came with humble modesty, reverence and shame, standing at His feet and weeping behind Him, as not being fit to appear before His face, and washed his feet with her tears.

One reason why gracious affections are attended with tenderness of spirit is that true grace tends to promote convictions of conscience. Persons are wont to have convictions of conscience before they have any grace: and if afterwards they are truly converted and have true repentance, and joy, and peace in believing, this has a tendency to put an end to terrors, but has no tendency to put an end to convictions of sin; it rather increases them. Grace does not stupefy a man's conscience, but makes it more able thoroughly to discern the sinfulness of that which is sinful, and to receive a greater conviction of the heinous and dreadful nature of sin. It makes a man more convinced of his own sinfulness and of the wickedness of his heart; and consequently it has a tendency to make him more jealous of his heart. Grace

tends to give the soul a further and better conviction of the same
things concerning sin, that it was convinced of under a legal
work of the Spirit of God; viz., its great contrariety to the will
and law and honour of God, the greatness of God's hatred of it
and displeasure against it, and the dreadful punishment it
exposes to and deserves. And not only so, but it convinces the
soul of something further concerning sin, that it saw nothing
of while only under legal convictions; and that is the infinitely
hateful nature of sin, and its dreadfulness upon that account.
And this makes the heart tender with respect to sin; like David's
heart, that smote him when he had cut off Saul's skirt. The
heart of a true penitent is like a burnt child that dreads the fire.
Whereas, on the contrary, he that has had a counterfeit repentance, and false comforts and joys, is like iron that has been
suddenly heated and quenched; it becomes much harder than
before. A false conversion puts an end to convictions of conscience; and so either takes away, or much diminishes, that con-
scientiousness which was manifested under a work of the law.

All gracious affections have a tendency to promote this Christian tenderness of heart—not only a godly sorrow, but also a
gracious joy: Psal. ii. 11, " Serve the Lord with fear, and rejoice
with trembling." As also a gracious hope: Psal. xxxiii. 18,
" Behold, the eye of the Lord is upon them that fear him; upon
them that hope in his mercy." And Psal. cxlvii. 11, " The Lord
taketh pleasure in them that fear him, in those that hope in
his mercy." Yea, the most confident and assured hope, that is
truly gracious, has this tendency. The higher a holy hope is
raised, the more there is of this Christian tenderness. The
banishing of a servile fear by a holy assurance is attended with
a proportionable increase of a reverential fear. The diminishing
of the fear of the fruits of God's displeasure in future punishment is attended with a proportionable increase of fear of His
displeasure itself; the diminishing of the fear of hell, with an
increase of the fear of sin. The vanishing of jealousies concerning the person's state is attended with a proportionable increase
of jealousy of heart, in a distrust of its strength, wisdom, sta-
bility, faithfulness, &c. The less apt he is to be afraid of natural
evil (having his heart fixed, trusting in God, and so not afraid of
evil tidings), the more apt he is to be alarmed with the appearance of moral evil, or the evil of sin. As he has more holy bold-

ness, so he has less of self-confidence, and more modesty. As he is more sure than others of deliverance from hell, so he has more of a sense of the desert of it. He is less apt than others to be shaken in faith; but more apt than others to be moved with solemn warnings, and with God's frowns, and with the calamities of others. He has the firmest comfort, but the softest heart. Richer than others, he is the poorest of all in spirit: the tallest and strongest saint, but the least and tenderest child among them.

X. *Another thing wherein those affections that are truly gracious and holy differ from those that are false, is beautiful symmetry and proportion.*

Not that the symmetry of the virtues, and gracious affections of the saints, is perfect in this life: it oftentimes is in many things defective, through the imperfection of grace, lack of proper instructions, errors in judgment, some particular unhappiness of natural temper, defects in education, and many other disadvantages that might be mentioned. But yet there is in no wise that monstrous disproportion in gracious affections, and the various parts of true religion in the saints, that is very commonly to be observed in the false religion and counterfeit graces of hypocrites.

In the truly holy affections of the saints is found that proportion which is the natural consequence of the universality of their sanctification. They have the whole image of Christ upon them: they have put off the old man, and have put on the new man entire in all his parts and members. It hath pleased the Father that in Christ all fulness should dwell: there is in Him every grace; He is full of grace and truth: and they that are Christ's " of his fulness receive, and grace for grace " (John i. 14, 16); there is every grace in them which is in Christ; grace for grace; that is, grace answerable to grace. There is no grace in Christ but there is its image in believers to answer it: the image is a true image; and there is something of the same beautiful proportion in the image which is in the original; there is feature for feature, and member for member. There is symmetry and beauty in God's workmanship. The natural body, which God hath made, consists of many members; and all are in a beautiful proportion. So it is in the new man, consisting of various graces and affections. The body of one that was born a perfect child may fail of exact proportion through distemper, weakness, or the injury of some of its members; yet the disproportion is in no measure like that of those who are born monsters.

It is with hypocrites, as it was with Ephraim of old, at a time when God greatly complains of His people's hypocrisy, Hos. vii. 8: "Ephraim is a cake not turned," half roasted and half raw: There is commonly no manner of uniformity in their affections.

There is in many of them a great partiality with regard to the several kinds of religious affections: great affections in some things, and no manner of proportion in others. A holy hope and a holy fear go together in the saints, as has been observed from Psal. xxxiii. 18, and cxlvii. 11. But in some hypocrites is the most confident hope, while they are void of reverence, self-jealousy and caution, and while they to a great degree cast off fear. In the saints, joy and holy fear go together, though the joy be never so great: as it was with the disciples, in that joyful morning of Christ's resurrection, Matt. xxviii. 8: "And they departed quickly from the sepulchre, with fear and great joy."* But many hypocrites rejoice without trembling: their joy is of that sort that it is truly opposite to godly fear.

But, particularly, one great difference between saints and hypocrites is this, that the joy and comfort of the former is attended with godly sorrow and mourning for sin. They have not only sorrow to prepare them for their first comfort, but after they are comforted and their joy established. It is foretold of the church of God that they should mourn and loathe themselves for their sins, after they were returned from the captivity and were settled in the land of Canaan, the land of rest flowing with milk and honey, Ezek. xx. 42, 43: "And ye shall know that I am the Lord, when I shall bring you into the land of Israel, into the country for the which I lifted up mine hand to give it to your fathers. And there shall ye remember your ways, and all your doings, wherein ye have been defiled; and ye shall loathe yourselves in your own sight, for all your evils that ye have committed." As also in Ezek. xvi. 61-63. A true saint is like a

---

* " Renewed care and diligence follows the sealings of the Spirit. Now is the soul at the foot of Christ, as Mary was at the sepulchre, with fear and great joy. He that travels the road with a rich treasure about him is afraid of a thief in every bush." *Flavel's Sacramental Meditations.* Works Vol. VI, p. 407.

little child in this respect. He never had any godly sorrow before he was born again, but since has it often in exercise: as a little child, before it is born and while it remains in darkness, never cries; but as soon as it sees the light, it begins to cry; and thenceforward is often crying. Although Christ hath borne our griefs and carried our sorrows, so that we are freed from the sorrow of punishment, and may now sweetly feed upon the comforts Christ hath purchased for us, yet that hinders not but that our feeding on these comforts should be attended with the sorrow of repentance. Thus of old, the children of Israel were commanded evermore to feed upon the paschal lamb with bitter herbs. True saints are spoken of in Scripture, not only as those that have mourned for sin, but as those that do mourn, whose manner it is still to mourn: Matt. v. 4, " Blessed are they that mourn; for they shall be comforted."

Not only is there often in hypocrites an essential deficiency as to the various kinds of religious affections, but also a strange partiality and disproportion in the same affections with regard to different objects.

Thus, as to the affection of love, some make high pretences and a great show of love to God and Christ, and it may be have been greatly affected with what they have heard or thought concerning Them: but they have not a spirit of love and benevolence towards men, but are disposed to contention, envy, revenge, and evil speaking; and will, it may be, suffer an old grudge to rest in their bosoms towards a neighbour for seven years together, if not twice seven years; living in real ill-will and bitterness of spirit towards him: and, it may be, in their dealings with their neighbours are not very strict and conscientious in observing the rule of " doing to others as they would that they should do to them." On the other hand, there are others who appear as if they had a great deal of benevolence to men, and are very good natured and generous in their way, but have no love to God.

And as to love to men, there are some that have flowing affections to some; but their love is far from being of so extensive and universal a nature as a truly Christian love is. They are full of dear affections to some, and full of bitterness towards others. They are knit to their own party, them that approve of them, love them and admire them; but are fierce against those that oppose and dislike them. Matt. v. 45, 46, " Be like your Father which is in heaven; for he maketh his sun to rise on the evil and on the good. For if ye love them which love you, what reward have ye? Do not even the publicans the same?" Some show a great affection to their neighbours, and pretend to be ravished with the company of the children of God abroad; but at the same time are uncomfortable and churlish towards their wives and other near relations at home, and are very negligent of relative duties. And as to the great love to sinners and opposers of religion, and the great concern for their souls, that there is an appearance of in some, even to extreme distress and agony—singling out a particular person from among a multitude for its object—there being at the same time no general compassion to sinners that are in equally miserable circumstances, but what is in a monstrous disproportion; this seems not to be of the nature of gracious affection. Not that I suppose it to be at all strange that a truly gracious compassion to souls should be exercised much more to some persons than others that are equally miserable, especially on some particular occasions. There may many things happen to fix the mind and affect the heart with respect to a particular person, at a particular time; and without doubt some saints have been in great distress for the souls of particular persons, so as to be as it were in travail for them. But when persons appear, at particular times, in racking agonies for the soul of some single person, far beyond what has been usually heard or read of in eminent saints, but appear to be persons that have a spirit of meek and fervent love, charity, and compassion to mankind in general, in a far less degree than they: I say, such agonies are greatly to be suspected, for reasons already given; viz., that the Spirit of God is wont to give graces and gracious affections in a beautiful symmetry and proportion.

And as there is a monstrous disproportion in the love of some in its exercises towards different persons, so there is in their seeming exercises of love towards the same persons. Some men show a love to others as to their outward man; they are liberal of their worldly substance, and often give to the poor, but have no love to, or concern for, the souls of men. Others pretend a great love to men's souls that are not compassionate and charitable towards their bodies. To make a great show of love, pity, and distress for souls, costs them nothing; but in order to show mercy to men's bodies, they must part with money out of their

pockets. But a true Christian love to our brethren extends both
to their souls and bodies, and herein is like the love and compassion of Jesus Christ. He showed mercy to men's souls, by
labouring for them in preaching the gospel to them; and showed
mercy to their bodies in going about doing good, healing all
manner of sickness and disease among the people. We have a
remarkable instance of Christ's having compassion at once both
to men's souls and bodies, and showing compassion by feeding
both, in Mark vi. 34, &c.: "And Jesus when he came out, saw
much people, and was moved with compassion towards them,
because they were as sheep not having a shepherd; and he began
to teach them many things." Here was his compassion to their
souls. And in the sequel we have an account of His compassion
to their bodies, because they had been a long while having
nothing to eat; He fed five thousand of them with five loaves and
two fishes. And if the compassion of professing Christians
towards others does not work in the same ways, it is a sign that
it is no true Christian compassion.

And furthermore, it is a sign that affections are not of the
right sort, if persons seem to be much affected with the bad
qualities of their fellow Christians, as the coldness and lifeless-
ness of other saints, but are in no proportion affected with their
own defects and corruptions. A true Christian may be affected
with the coldness and unsavouriness of other saints, and may
mourn much over it: but at the same time, he is not apt to be
so much affected with the badness of anybody's heart as his
own; this is most in his view; this he is most quick-sighted to
discern; this he sees most of the aggravations of, and is most
ready to lament. A lesser degree of virtue will bring him to pity
himself and be rather concerned at his own calamities, than
rightly to be affected with others' calamities. And if men have
not attained to the less, we may determine they never attained
to the greater.

And here, by the way, I would observe, that it may be laid
down as a general rule, that if persons pretend that they come to
high attainments in religion, but have never yet arrived to the
lesser attainments, it is a sign of a vain pretence. If persons pretend that they have got beyond mere morality, to live a spiritual
and divine life, but really have not come to be so much as moral
persons: or pretend to be greatly affected with the wickedness of

their hearts, and are not affected with the palpable violations of
God's commands in their practice, which is a lesser attainment:
or if they pretend to be brought to be even willing to be damned
for the glory of God, but have no forwardness to suffer a little in
their estates and names and worldly convenience, for the sake of
their duty: or if they pretend that they are not afraid to venture
their souls upon Christ, and commit their all to God, trusting to
His bare word, and the faithfulness of His promises, for their
eternal welfare, but at the same time have not confidence enough
in God to dare to trust Him with a little of their estates, bestowed
to pious and charitable uses; I say, when it is thus with persons,
their pretences are manifestly vain. He that is in a journey, and
imagines he has got far beyond such a place in his road, and
never yet came to it, must be mistaken; and he is not yet arrived
to the top of the hill that never yet got half way thither. But
this by the way.

The same that has been observed of the affection of love is
also to be observed of other religious affections. Those that are
true extend in some proportion to the various things that are
their due and proper objects; but when they are false they are
commonly strangely disproportionate. So it is with religious
desires and longings: these in the saints, are to those things that
are spiritual and excellent in general, and that in some proportion to their excellency, importance or necessity, or their near
concern in them; but in false longing it is often far otherwise.
They will strangely run, with an impatient vehemence, after
something of less importance, when other things of greater importance are neglected. Thus, for instance, some persons from
time to time are attended with a vehement inclination, and unaccountably violent pressure, to declare to others what they
experience, and to exhort others; when there is at the same time
no inclination, in any measure equal to it, to other things, to
which true Christianity has as great, yea, a greater tendency;
as the pouring out of the soul before God in secret, earnest
prayer and praise to Him, and for more conformity to Him, and
living more to His glory, &c. We read in Scripture of "groan-
ings that cannot be uttered," of "soul-breakings for the longing
it hath," and of "longings, thirstings, and pantings," much more
frequently than we read of the former inclinations.

And so as to hatred and zeal; when these are from right principles, they are against sin in general in some proportion to the degree of sinfulness: Psal. cxix. 128, 104, " I hate every false way." But a false hatred and zeal against sin is against some particular sin only. Thus some seem to be very zealous against profaneness and pride in apparel, who themselves are notorious for covetousness, closeness, and it may be backbiting, envy towards superiors, turbulency of spirit towards rulers, and rooted ill-will to them that have injured them. False zeal is against the sins of others, but he that has true zeal, exercises it chiefly against his own sins; though he shows also a proper zeal against prevailing and dangerous iniquity in others. Some pretend to have a great abhorrence of their own sins of heart, and cry out much against their inward corruption; and yet make light of sins in practice, and seem to commit them without much restraint or remorse, though these imply sin both in heart and life.

As there is a much greater disproportion in the exercises of false affections than of true as to different objects, so there is also as to different times. For although true Christians are not always alike—yea, there is very great difference at different times, and the best have reason to be greatly ashamed of their unsteadiness—yet there is in no wise that instability and inconstancy in the hearts of those who are true virgins, " that follow the Lamb whithersoever he goeth," which is in false-hearted professors. The righteous man is truly said to be one whose heart is fixed, trusting in God, Psal. cxii. 7, and to have his heart established with grace. Heb. xiii. 9, and to hold on his way, Job. xvii. 9: " The righteous shall hold on his way, and he that hath clean hands shall wax stronger and stronger." It is spoken of as a note of the hypocrisy of the Jewish church, that they were as a swift dromedary, traversing her ways.

If therefore persons are religious only by fits and starts; if they now and then seem to be raised up to the clouds in their affections, and then suddenly fall down again, lose all, and become quite careless and carnal, and this is their manner of carrying on religion; if they appear greatly moved and mightily engaged in religion only in extraordinary seasons, in the time of a remarkable outpouring of the Spirit, or other uncommon dispensation of providence, or upon the real or supposed receipt of some extraordinary temporal mercy, or suppose that they are newly converted, or have lately had what they call a great discovery; but quickly return to such a frame, that their hearts are chiefly upon other things, and the prevailing bent of their affections is ordinarily towards the things of this world, they clearly evince their unsoundness. When they are like the children of Israel in the wilderness, who had their affections highly raised by what God had done for them at the Red Sea, and sang His praise, and soon fell a-lusting after the fleshpots of Egypt; but then again, when they came to Mount Sinai, and saw the great manifestations God made of Himself there, seemed to be greatly engaged again, and mightily forward to enter into covenant with God, saying, " All that the Lord hath spoken will we do, and be obedient," but then quickly made them a golden calf—I say, when it is thus with persons, it is a sign of the unsoundness of their affections.* They are like the waters in the time of a shower of rain, which, during the shower and a little after, run like a brook and flow abundantly, but are presently quite dry; and when another shower comes, then they will flow again. Whereas a true saint is like a stream from a living spring, which, though it may be greatly increased by a shower of rain and diminished in time of drought, yet constantly runs (John iv. 14, " The water that I shall give him, shall be in him a well of water, springing up, &c."): or like a tree planted by such a stream, that has a constant supply at the root and is always green, even in time of the greatest drought: Jer. xvii. 7, 8, " Blessed is the man that trusteth in the Lord, and whose hope the Lord is. For he shall be as a tree planted by the waters, and that spreadeth

* Dr. John Owen (in his *Discourse on the Holy Spirit*, Book III. Chap. ii. Sect. 18), speaking of a common work of the Spirit, says, " This work operates greatly on the affections: we have given instances in the fear, sorrow, joy and delight, about spiritual things, that are stirred up and acted thereby: but yet it comes short in two things of a thorough work upon the affections themselves. For first, it doth not fix them. And secondly, it doth not fill them."

" There is (says Dr. John Preston) a certain love, by fits, which God accepts not: when men come and offer to God great promises, like the waves of the sea, as big as mountains: oh, they think they will do much for God! But their minds change; and they become as those high waves, which at last fall level with the other waters."

Mr. John Flavel, speaking of these changeable professors, says, " These professors have more of the moon than of the sun: little light, less heat, and many changes. They deceive many, yea, they deceive themselves, but cannot deceive God. They want that ballast and establishment in themselves, that would have kept them tight and steady." *Touchstone of Sincerity*. Works Vol. V, p. 519.

out her roots by the river, and shall not see when heat cometh, but her leaf shall be green; and shall not be careful in the year of drought, neither shall cease from yielding fruit." Many hypocrites are like comets that appear for a while with a mighty blaze; but are very unsteady and irregular in their motion (and are therefore called wandering stars, Jude 13), and their blaze soon disappears, and they appear but once in a great while. But the true saints are like the fixed stars, which, though they rise and set, and are often clouded, yet are steadfast in their orb, and may truly be said to shine with a constant light. Hypocritical affections are like a violent motion; as that of the air moved with winds (Jude 12), but gracious affections are more a natural motion; like the stream of a river, which, though it has many turns hither and thither, and may meet with obstacles, and runs more freely and swiftly in some places than others; yet in the general, with a steady and constant course, tends the same way until it gets to the ocean.

And as there is a strange unevenness and disproportion in false affections at different times, so there often is in different places. Some are greatly affected when in company, but have nothing that bears any manner of proportion to it in secret, in close meditation, secret prayer, and conversing with God, when alone and separated from all the world.* A true Christian doubtless delights in religious fellowship and Christian conversa-tion, and finds much to affect his heart in it; but he also delights at times to retire from all mankind, to converse with God in solitary places. And this also has its peculiar advantages for

---

* " The Lord is neglected secretly, yet honoured openly; because there is no wind in their chambers to blow their sails; and therefore there they stand still. Hence many men keep their profession when they lose their affection. They have by the one a name to live (and that is enough) though their hearts be dead. And hence so long as you love and com-mend them, so long they love you; but if not, they will forsake you. They were warm only by another's fire, and hence, having no principle of life within, soon grow dead. This is the water that turns a Pharisee's mill." *Shepard's Parable of the Ten Virgins*, p. 285.

"The hypocrite (says Mr. Flavel) is not for the closet, but the syna-gogue, Matt. vi. 5, 6. It is not his meat and drink to retire from the clamour of the world, to enjoy God in secret." *Touchstone of Sincerity*. Works Vol. V, p. 567.

Dr. Ames in his *Cases of Conscience*, Lib. III. Chap. v., speaks of it as a thing by which sincerity may be known, " That persons be obedient in the absence, as well as in the presence of lookers on; in secret, as well as, yea more than, in public:" alleging Phil. ii. 12, and Matt. vi. 6.

fixing his heart and engaging his affections. True religion disposes persons to be much alone in solitary places for holy meditation and prayer. So it wrought in Isaac, Gen. xxiv. 63. And
which is much more, so it wrought in Jesus Christ. How often
do we read of His retiring into mountains and solitary places for
holy converse with His Father! It is difficult to conceal great
affections, but yet gracious affections are of a much more silent
and secret nature than those that are counterfeit. So it is with
the gracious sorrow of the saints for their own sins. Thus the
future gracious mourning of true penitents, at the beginning of
the latter day glory, is represented as being so secret as to be
hidden from the companions of their bosom, Zech. xii. 12, 13,
14: "And the land shall mourn, every family apart, the family
of the house of David apart, and their wives apart: the family
of the house of Nathan apart, and their wives apart: the family
of the house of Levi apart, and their wives apart: the family of
Shimei apart, and their wives apart: all the families that remain,
every family apart, and their wives apart." So it is with their
sorrow for the sins of others. The saints' pains and travailing for
the souls of sinners are chiefly in secret places: Jer. xiii. 17, "If
ye will not hear it, my soul shall weep in secret places for your
pride, and mine eye shall weep sore, and run down with tears,
because the Lord's flock is carried away captive." So it is with
gracious joys: they are hidden manna, in this respect, as well
as others, Rev. ii. 17.

The Psalmist seems to speak of his sweetest comforts, as those
that were to be had in secret: Psal. lxiii. 5, 6, "My soul shall be
satisfied as with marrow and fatness; and my mouth shall praise
thee with joyful lips: when I remember thee upon my bed, and
meditate on thee in the night watches." Christ calls forth His
spouse away from the world into retired places, that He may
give her His sweetest love: Cant. vii. 11, 12, "Come, my beloved
let us go forth into the field; let us lodge in the villages: there
will I give thee my loves." The most eminent divine favours
that the saints obtained, that we read of in Scripture, were in
their retirement. The principal manifestations that God made
of Himself and His covenant mercy to Abraham, were when he
was alone, apart from his numerous family; as any one will
judge that carefully reads his history. Isaac received that special
gift of God to him, Rebekah, who was so great a comfort to him,

and by whom he obtained the promised seed, walking alone, meditating in the field. Jacob was retired for secret prayer when Christ came to him, and he wrestled with Him and obtained the blessing. God revealed himself to Moses in the bush, when he was in a solitary place in the desert, in Mount Horeb (Exod. iii.). And afterwards, when God showed him His glory and he was admitted to the highest degree of communion with God that ever he enjoyed, he was alone in the same mountain, and continued there forty days and forty nights, and then came down with his face shining. God came to those great prophets, Elijah and Elisha, and conversed freely with them, chiefly in their retirement. Elijah conversed alone with God at Mount Sinai, as Moses did. And when Jesus Christ had the greatest prelibation of His future glory, when He was transfigured, it was not when He was with the multitude, or with the twelve disciples, but retired into a solitary place in a mountain with only three select disciples, charging them that they should tell no man until He was risen from the dead. When the angel Gabriel came to the blessed virgin, and when the Holy Ghost came upon her and the power of the Highest overshadowed her, she seems to have been alone, and in this matter hid from the world; her nearest and dearest earthly friend Joseph, that had betrothed her, knew nothing of the matter. She that first partook of the joy of Christ's resurrection was alone with Christ at the sepulchre, John xx. And when the beloved disciple was favoured with those wonderful visions of Christ and His future dispensations towards the church and the world, he was alone in the isle of Patmos. Not but that we have also instances of great privileges that the saints have received when with others; or that there is not much in Christian conversation, and social and public worship, tending greatly to refresh and rejoice the hearts of the saints. But this is all that I aim at by what has been said, to show that it is the nature of true grace, that however it loves Christian society in its place, yet in a peculiar manner it delights in retirement and secret converse with God. So that if persons appear greatly engaged in social religion, and but little in the religion of the closet, and are often highly affected when with others, and but little moved when they have none but God and Christ to converse with, it looks very darkly upon their religion.

XI. *Another great and very distinguishing difference between gracious affections and others is, that the higher gracious affections are raised, the more is a spiritual appetite and longing of soul after spiritual attainments increased. On the contrary, false affections rest satisfied in themselves.**

The more a true saint loves God with a gracious love, the more he desires to love Him, and the more uneasy is he at his want of love to Him; the more he hates sin, the more he desires to hate it, and laments that he has so much remaining love to it; the more he mourns for sin, the more he longs to mourn for sin; the more his heart is broke, the more he desires it should be broke: the more he thirsts and longs after God and holiness, the more he longs to long, and breathe out his very soul in longings after God. The kindling and raising of gracious affections is like kindling a flame; the higher it is raised, the more ardent it is; and the more it burns, the more vehemently does it tend and seek to burn. So that the spiritual appetite after holiness and an increase of holy affections, is much more lively and keen in those that are eminent in holiness, than in others; and more when grace and holy affections are in their most lively exercise than at other times. It is as much the nature of one that is spiritually new-born, to thirst after growth in holiness, as it is the nature of a new-born babe to thirst after the mother's breast: 1 Pet. ii. 2, 3, " As new-born babes, desire the sincere milk of the word, that ye may grow thereby: if so be ye have tasted that the Lord is gracious." The most that the saints have in this world is but a taste, a prelibation of that future glory which is their proper fulness; it is only an earnest of their future inheritance, 2 Cor. i. 22, and v. 5, and Eph. i. 14. The most eminent saints in this state are but children, compared with their future, which is their proper state of maturity and perfection; as the apostle observes, 1 Cor. xiii. 10, 11. The greatest eminence that the saints arrive at in this world has no tendency to satiety, or to abate their desires after more; but, on the contrary, makes them more eager to press forward; as is evident by the apostle's words, Phil. iii. 13, 14, 15: " Forgetting those things which are behind, and reaching forth unto those things which are before, I press

* " There is in true grace an infinite circle: a man by thirsting receives, and receiving thirsts for more."—*Shepard's Parable of the Ten Virgins*, p. 218.

toward the mark. Let us therefore, as many as be perfect, be thus minded."

The reasons of it are, that the more persons have of holy affections, the more they have of that spiritual taste which I have spoken of elsewhere; whereby they perceive the excellency, and relish the divine sweetness, of holiness. And the more grace they have, while in this state of imperfection, the more they see their imperfection and emptiness, and distance from what ought to be: and so the more do they see their need of grace; as I showed at large before, when speaking of the nature of evangelical humiliation. Besides, grace, as long as it is imperfect, is of a growing nature, and in a growing state. We see it to be so with all living things, that while they are in a state of imperfection, and in their growing state, their nature seeks after growth; and so much the more as they are more healthy and prosperous. Therefore the cry of every true grace is like that cry of true faith, Mark ix. 24: "Lord, I believe; help thou my unbelief." And the greater spiritual discoveries and affections the true Christian has, the more does he become an earnest beggar for grace and spiritual food, that he may grow; and the more earnestly does he pursue after it by all proper means and endeavours; for true and gracious longings after holiness are no idle ineffectual desires.

But here some may object and say, How is this consistent with what all allow, that spiritual enjoyments are of a soul-satisfying nature?

I answer, its being so will appear to be not at all inconsistent with what has been said, if it be considered in what manner spiritual enjoyments are said to be of a soul-satisfying nature. Certainly they are not of so cloying a nature, that he who has anything of them, though but in a very imperfect degree, desires no more. But spiritual enjoyments are of a soul-satisfying nature in the following respects. 1. They in their kind and nature are fully adapted to the nature, capacity, and need of the soul of man. So that those who find them desire no other kind of enjoyments; they sit down fully contented with that kind of happiness which they have, desiring no change, nor inclining to wander about any more, saying, "Who will show us any good?" The soul is never cloyed, never weary; but perpetually giving up itself, with all its powers, to this happiness. But not that those who have something of this happiness desire no more of the same. 2. They are satisfying also in this respect, that they answer the expectation of the appetite. When the appetite is high to anything, the expectation is consequently so. Appetite to a particular object implies expectation in its nature. This expectation is not satisfied by worldly enjoyments. The man who pursues these expects to have a great accession of happiness, but is disappointed. But it is not so with spiritual enjoyments; these fully answer and satisfy the expectation. 3. The gratification and pleasure of spiritual enjoyments is permanent. It is not so with worldly enjoyments. They in a sense satisfy particular appetites: but the appetite, in being satisfied, is glutted, and then the pleasure is over: and as soon as that is over, the general appetite of human nature after happiness returns, but is empty, and without anything to satisfy it. So that the glutting of a particular appetite does but take away from, and leave empty, the general thirst of nature. 4. Spiritual good is satisfying, as there is enough in it to satisfy the soul as to degree, if obstacles were but removed, and the enjoying faculty duly applied. There is room enough here for the soul to extend itself; here is an infinite ocean. If men be not satisfied here as to degree of happiness, the cause is with themselves; it is because they do not open their mouths wide enough.

But these things do not argue that a soul has no appetite excited after more of the same, that has tasted a little; or that the appetite will not increase until it comes to fulness of enjoyment; as bodies that are attracted to the earth tend to it more strongly, the nearer they come to the attracting body, and are not at rest out of the centre. Spiritual good is of a satisfying nature; and for that very reason, the soul that tastes and knows its nature, will thirst after it, and a fulness of it, that it may be satisfied. And the more a man experiences and knows this excellent, unparalleled, exquisite, and satisfying sweetness, the more earnestly will he hunger and thirst for more, until he comes to perfection. And therefore this is the nature of spiritual affections, that the greater they be, the greater the appetite and longing is after grace and holiness.

But with those joys and other religious affections that are false and counterfeit, it is otherwise. If before there was a great desire of some sort after grace as these affections rise, that desire ceases or is abated. It may be before, while the man was under legal convictions and much afraid of hell, he earnestly longed that he might obtain spiritual light in his understanding, and faith in Christ, and love to God: but now, when these false affections are risen that deceive him, and make him confident that he is converted and his state good, there are no more earnest longings after light and grace; for his end is answered; he is confident that his sins are forgiven him, and that he shall go to heaven, and so he is satisfied. And especially when false affections are raised very high, they put an end to longings after grace and holiness. The man now is far from appearing to himself a poor empty creature; on the contrary he is rich, and increased with goods, and hardly conceives of anything more excellent than what he has already attained to.

Hence there is an end to many persons' earnestness in seeking, after they have once obtained that which they call their conversion; or at least, after they have had those high affections that make them fully confident of it. Before, while they looked upon themselves as in a state of nature, they were engaged in seeking after God and Christ, and cried earnestly for grace, and strove in the use of means: but now they act as though they thought their work was done; they live upon their first work, or some high experiences that are past; and there is an end to their crying and striving after God and grace. But the holy principles that actuate a true saint have a far more powerful influence to stir him up to earnestness in seeking God and holiness, than servile fear. Hence seeking God is spoken of as one of the distinguishing characters of the saints; and " Seekers after God " is one of the names by which the godly are called in Scripture: Psal. xxiv. 6, "This is the generation of them that seek him, that seek thy face, O Jacob!" Psal. lxix. 6, "Let not those that seek thee be confounded for my sake." Ver. 32, "The humble shall see this and be glad: and your heart shall live that seek God." And lxx. 4, "Let all those that seek thee rejoice and be glad in thee: and let such as love thy salvation say continually, Let God be magnified." The Scriptures everywhere represent the seeking, striving, and labour of a Christian, as being chiefly after his conversion, and his conversion as being but the beginning of his work. And almost all that is said in the New Testament, of men's watching, giving earnest heed to themselves, running the race that is set before them, striving and agonizing, wrestling not with flesh and blood but principalities and powers, fighting, putting on the whole armour of God, and standing, pressing forward, reaching forth, continuing instant in prayer, crying to God day and night; I say, almost all that is said in the New Testament of these things, is spoken of and directed to the saints. Where these things are applied to sinners' seeking conversion once, they are spoken of the saints' prosecution of the great business of their high calling ten times. But many in these days have got into a strange anti-scriptural way, of having all their striving and wrestling over before they are converted; and so having an easy time of it afterwards, to sit down and enjoy their sloth and indolence; as those that now have a supply of their wants, and are become rich and full. But when the Lord " fills the hungry with good things, these rich are like to be sent away empty," Luke i. 53.

But doubtless there are some hypocrites, that have only false affections, who will think they are able to stand this trial; and will readily say that they desire not to rest satisfied with past attainments, but to be pressing forward; they desire more, they long after God and Christ, and desire more holiness, and seek it. But the truth is, their desires are not properly the desires of appetite after holiness for its own sake, or for the moral excellency and holy sweetness that is in it, but only for by-ends. They long after clearer discoveries that they may be better satisfied about the state of their souls; or because in great discoveries self is gratified, in being made so much of by God, and so exalted above others. They long to taste the love of God (as they call it) more than to have more love to God. Or, it may be, they have a kind of forced or fancied longings; because they think they must long for more grace, otherwise it will be a dark sign upon them. But such things as these are far different from the natural, and as it were necessary, appetite and thirsting of the new man after God and holiness. There is an inward burning desire that a saint has after holiness, as natural to the new creature as vital heat is to the body. There is a holy breathing and panting after the Spirit of God to increase holiness, which is as natural to a holy nature as breathing is to a living body. And holiness or sanctification is more directly the object of it than any manifestation of God's love and favour. This is the meat and drink that is the object of the spiritual appetite: John iv. 34, "My meat is to do the will of him that sent me, and to finish his work." Where we read in Scripture of the desires, longings, and thirstings of the saints, righteousness and God's laws are much more frequently mentioned as the object of them than anything else. The saints desire the sincere milk of the Word, not so much to testify God's love to them, as that they may grow thereby in holiness. I have shown before that holiness is that good which is the immediate object of a spiritual taste. But undoubtedly the same sweetness that is the chief object of a spiritual taste, is also the chief object of a spiritual appetite. Grace is the godly man's treasure: Isa. xxxiii. 6. "The fear of the Lord is his treasure." Godliness is the gain that he is covetous and greedy of. 1 Tim. vi. 6. Hypocrites long for discoveries, more for the present comfort of the discovery, and the high manifestation of God's love in it, than for any sanctifying influence of it. But neither a longing after great discoveries or after great tastes of the love of God, nor a longing to be in heaven, nor a longing to die, are in any measure so distinguishing marks of true saints as longing after a more holy heart, and after living a more holy life.

But I am come now to the last distinguishing mark of holy affections that I shall mention.

XII. *Gracious and holy affections have their exercise and fruit in Christian practice.*

I mean, they have that influence and power upon him who is the subject of them, that they cause that a practice, which is universally conformed to, and directed by, Christian rules, should be the practice and business of his life.

This implies three things: 1. That his behaviour or practice in the world, be universally conformed to, and directed by, Christian rules. 2. That he makes a business of such a holy practice above all things; that it be a business which he is chiefly engaged in, and devoted to, and pursues with highest earnestness and diligence: so that he may be said to make this practice of religion eminently his work and business. And, 3. That he persists in it to the end of life: so that it may be said, not only to be his business at certain seasons, the business of Sabbath days, or certain extraordinary times, or the business of a month, or a year, or of seven years, or his business under certain circumstances; but the business of his life; it being that business which he perseveres in through all changes, and under all trials as long as he lives.

The necessity of each of these, in all true Christians, is most clearly and fully taught in the Word of God.

1. It is necessary that men should be universally obedient: 1 John iii. 3, &c., "Every man that hath this hope in him purifieth himself, even as he is pure. And ye know that he was manifested to take away our sins; and in him is no sin. Whosoever abideth in him sinneth not; whosoever sinneth, hath not seen him, neither known him. He that doeth righteousness is righteous even as he is righteous: he that committeth sin is of the devil." Chap. v. 18, "We know that whosoever is born of God sinneth not, but he that is begotten of God keepeth himself, and that wicked one toucheth him not." John xv. 14, "Ye are my friends, if ye do whatsoever I command you."

If one member only be corrupt, and we do not cut it off, it will carry the whole body to hell. Matt. v. 29, 30. Saul was commanded to slay all God's enemies, the Amalekites; and he slew all but Agag, and the saving him alive proved his ruin. Caleb and Joshua entered into God's promised rest, because they wholly followed the Lord, Numb. xiv. 24, and xxxii. 11, 12, Deut. i. 36, Josh. xiv. 6, 8, 9, 14. Naaman's hypocrisy appeared in that, however he seemed to be greatly affected with gratitude to God for healing his leprosy, and engaged to serve him, yet in one thing he desired to be excused. Herod, though he feared John, and observed him, and heard him gladly, and did many things; yet was condemned, in that in one thing he would not hearken to him, even in parting with his beloved Herodias. So that it is necessary that men should part with their dearest iniquities, which are as their right hand and right eyes, sins that most easily beset them, and which they are most exposed to by their natural inclinations, evil customs, or particular circumstances, as well as others. As Joseph would not make known himself to his brethren who had sold him, until Benjamin the beloved child of the family, that was most hardly parted with, was delivered up; no more will Christ reveal His love to us, until we part with our dearest lusts, and until we are brought to comply with the most difficult duties, and those that we have the greatest aversion to.

It is important to observe, that in order to a man's being truly
said to be universally obedient, his obedience must not only consist in negatives, or in universally avoiding wicked practices, consisting in sins of commission, but he must also be universal in
the positives of religion. Sins of omission are as much breaches
of God's commands as sins of commission. Christ, in Matt. xxv.,
represents those on the left hand as being condemned and cursed
to everlasting fire for sins of omission: "I was an hungred, and
ye gave me no meat," &c. A man therefore cannot be said to be
universally obedient, and of a Christian conversation, only because he is no thief, nor oppressor, nor fraudulent person, nor
drunkard, nor tavern-haunter, nor whore-master, nor rioter, nor
night-walker, nor unclean, nor profane in his language, nor
slanderer, nor liar, nor furious, nor malicious, nor reviler. He is
falsely said to be of a conversation that becomes the gospel, who
goes thus far and no farther. But, in order to this, it is necessary that he should also be of a serious, religious, devout, humble,
meek, forgiving, peaceful, respectful, condescending, benevolent,
merciful, charitable and beneficent walk and conversation. Without such things as these, he does not obey the laws of Christ, laws
that He and His apostles did abundantly insist on as of the
greatest importance and necessity.

2. In order to men's being true Christians, it is necessary that
they prosecute the business of religion and the service of God
with great earnestness and diligence, as the work which they
devote themselves to, and make the main business of their lives.
All Christ's peculiar people not only do good works, but are
zealous of good works, Tit. ii. 14. No man can do the service of
two masters at once. They that are God's true servants do give
up themselves to His service, and make it as it were their whole
work, therein employing their whole hearts and the chief of
their strength: Phil. iii. 13, "This one thing I do." Christians,
in their effectual calling, are not called to idleness, but to labour
in God's vineyard, and spend their day in doing a great and
laborious service. All true Christians comply with this call (as
is implied in its being an effectual call), and do the work of
Christians; which is everywhere in the New Testament compared to those exercises wherein men are wont to exert their
strength with the greatest earnestness, as running, wrestling,
fighting. All true Christians are good and faithful soldiers of

Jesus Christ, and "fight the good fight of faith;" for none but those who do so, "ever lay hold on eternal life." Those who "fight as those that beat the air," never win the crown of victory. "They that run in a race, run all, but one wins the prize," and they that are slack and negligent in their course do not "so run as that they may obtain." The kingdom of heaven is not to be taken but by violence. Without earnestness there is no getting along in that narrow way that leads to life; and so no arriving at that state of glorious life and happiness which it leads to. Without earnest labour there is no ascending the steep and high hill of Zion, and so no arriving at the heavenly city on the top of it. Without a constant laboriousness there is no stemming the swift stream in which we swim, so as ever to come to that fountain of water of life that is at the head of it. There is need that we should "watch and pray always, in order to our escaping those dreadful things that are coming on the ungodly, and our being counted worthy to stand before the Son of man." There is need of our "putting on the whole armour of God, and doing all, to stand," in order to our avoiding a total overthrow, and being utterly destroyed by "the fiery darts of the devil." There is need that we should "forget the things that are behind, and be reaching forth to the things that are before, and pressing towards the mark for the prize of the high calling of God in Christ Jesus," in order to our obtaining that prize. Slothfulness in the service of God in His professed servants is as damning as open rebellion; for the slothful servant is a wicked servant, and shall be cast into outer darkness among God's open enemies, Matt. xxv. 26, 30. They that are slothful are not "followers of them who through faith and patience inherit the promises." Heb. vi. 11, 12, "And we desire that every one of you do show the same diligence, to the full assurance of hope unto the end; that ye be not slothful, but followers of them who through faith and patience inherit the promises." And all they who follow that cloud of witnesses that are gone before to heaven, "lay aside every weight, and the sin that easily besets them, and run with patience the race that is set before them," Heb. xii 1. That true faith, by which persons rely on the righteousness of Christ, and the work that He hath done for them, and truly feed and live upon Him, is evermore accompanied with a spirit of earnestness in the Christian work and course. This was typi-

fied of old, by the manner of the children of Israel's feeding on
the paschal lamb; they were directed to eat it, as those that were
in haste, with their loins girded, their shoes on their feet, and
their staff in their hand, Exod. vii. 11.

3. Every true Christian perseveres in this way of universal
obedience, and diligent and earnest service of God, through all
the various kinds of trials that he meets with, to the end of life.
That all true saints, all those that obtain eternal life, do thus
persevere in the practice of religion and the service of God, is a
doctrine so abundantly taught in the Scripture, that particularly
to rehearse all the texts which imply it would be endless; I shall
content myself with referring to some given below.*

But that perseverance in obedience, which is chiefly insisted
on in the Scripture as a special note of the truth of grace, is the
continuance of professors in the practice of their duty, and being
steadfast in a holy walk, through the various trials that they
meet with.

By trials here, I mean those things that a professor meets with
in his course, that especially render his continuance in his duty
and faithfulness to God, difficult to nature. These things are
from time to time called in Scripture by the name of trials, or
temptations (which are words of the same signification). These
are of various kinds: there are many things that render continuance in the way of duty difficult by their tendency to cherish and
foment, or to stir up and provoke, their lusts and corruptions.
Many things make it hard to continue in the way of duty, by
their being of an alluring nature, and having a tendency to
entice persons to sin, or by their tendency to take off restraints
and embolden them in iniquity. Other things are trials of the
soundness and steadfastness of professors, by their tendency to
make their duty appear terrible to them, and so to affright and
drive them from it; such as the sufferings which their duty will
expose them to—pain, ill will, contempt, reproach and loss of

---

* Deut. v. 29; Deut. xxxii. 18, 19, 20; 1 Chron. xxviii. 9; Psal. lxxviii.
7, 8, 10, 11, 35, 36, 37, 41, 42, 56, &c.; Psal. cvi. 3, 12-15; Psal. cxxv. 4, 5;
Prov. xxvi. 11; Isa. lxiv. 5; Jer. xvii. 13; Ezek. iii. 20, and xviii. 24, and
xxxiii. 12, 13; Matt. x. 22, and xiii. 4-8, with verses 19-23, and xxv. 8, and
xxiv. 12, 13, Luke ix. 62, and xii. 35, &c., and xxii. 28, and xvii. 32; John
viii. 30, 31, and xv. 6, 7, 8, 10, 16; Rom. ii. 7, and xi. 22; Col. i. 22, 23;
Heb. iii. 6, 12, 14, and vi. 11, 12, and x. 35, &c.; James i. 25; Rev. ii. 13,
26, and ii. 10; 2 Tim. ii. 15; 2 Tim. iv. 4-8.

outward possessions and comforts. If persons, after they have made a profession of religion, live any considerable time in this world, which is so full of changes and so full of evil, it cannot be otherwise than that they should meet with many trials of their sincerity and steadfastness. And besides, it is God's manner in His providence, to bring trials on His professing friends and servants designedly, that He may manifest them, and may exhibit sufficient matter of conviction of the state which they are in, to their own consciences, and oftentimes to the world; as appears by innumerable Scriptures.

True saints may be guilty of some kinds and degrees of backsliding, may be foiled by particular temptations, and may fall into sin, yea great sins. But they never can fall away so as to grow weary of religion and the service of God, and habitually to dislike it and neglect it, either on its own account, or on account of the difficulties that attend it; as is evident by Gal. vi. 9, Rom. ii. 7, Heb. x. 36, Isa. xliii. 22, Mal. i. 13. They can never backslide so as to continue no longer in a way of universal obedience; or so that it shall cease to be their manner to observe all the rules of Christianity, and do all duties required, even in the most difficult circumstances. This is abundantly manifest by the things that have been observed already. Nor can they ever fall away so as habitually to be more engaged in other things than in the business of religion; or so that it should become their way and manner to serve something else more than God; or so as statedly to cease to serve God with such earnestness and diligence, as still to be habitually devoted and given up to the business of religion; unless those words of Christ can fall to the ground, " Ye cannot serve two masters," and those of the apostle, " He that will be a friend of the world is the enemy of God;" and unless a saint can change his God and yet be a true saint. Nor can a true saint ever fall away so that it shall come to this, that ordinarily there shall be no remarkable difference in his walk and behaviour since his conversion, from what was before. They that are truly converted are new men, new creatures; new not only within, but without; they are sanctified throughout, in spirit, soul and body; old things are passed away, all things are become new; they have new hearts, and new eyes, new ears, new tongues, new hands, new feet; i.e., a new conversation and practice; and they walk in newness of life, and continue to do so to the end of life. And they that fall away show visibly that they never were risen with Christ. And especially when men's opinion of their being converted, and so in a safe estate, is the very cause of their failure, it is a most evident sign of their hypocrisy. And this is the case, whether their falling away be into their former sins or into some new kind of wickedness, having the corruption of nature only turned into a new channel instead of its being mortified. As when persons that think themselves converted, though they do not return to former profaneness and lewdness, yet from the high opinion they have of their experiences, graces, and privileges, gradually settle more and more and more in a self–righteous and spiritually proud temper of mind, and in such a manner of behaviour as naturally arises therefrom. When it is thus with men, however far they may seem to be from their former evil practices, this alone is enough to condemn them, and may render their last state far worse than the first. For this seems to be the very case of the Jews of that generation that Christ speaks of, Matt. xii. 43-45. They had been awakened by John the Baptist's preaching, and brought to a reformation of their former licentious courses, whereby the unclean spirit was as it were turned out, and the house swept and garnished; yet, being empty of God and of grace, full of themselves, and exalted in an exceeding high opinion of their own righteousness and eminent holiness, they became habituated to an answerably self-exalting behaviour. They changed the sins of publicans and harlots for those of the Pharisees; and in issue, had seven devils and were worse than at the first.

Thus I have explained what exercise and fruit I mean, when I say, that gracious affections have their exercise and fruit in Christian practice.

The reason why gracious affections have such a tendency and effect appears from many things that have already been observed in the preceding parts of this discourse.

The reason of it appears particularly from this, that gracious affections arise from those operations and influences which are spiritual, and that the inward principle from whence they flow is something divine, a communication of God, a participation of the divine nature, Christ living in the heart, the Holy Spirit dwelling there in union with the faculties of the soul, as an internal vital principle, exerting His own proper nature in the exercise of those faculties. This is sufficient to show us why true grace should have such activity, power, and efficacy. No wonder that that which is divine is powerful and effectual; for it has omnipotence on its side. If God dwells in the heart, and is vitally united to it, He will show that He is a God, by the efficacy of His operation. Christ is not in the heart of a saint as in a sepulchre, or as a dead Saviour that does nothing; but as in His temple, and as One that is alive from the dead. For in the heart where Christ savingly is, there He lives and exerts Himself after the power of that endless life that He received at His resurrection. Thus every saint who is the subject of the benefit of Christ's sufferings, is made to know and experience the power of His resurrection. The Spirit of Christ which is the immediate spring of grace in the heart, is all life, all power, all act: 1 Cor. ii. 4, "In demonstration of the Spirit and of power." 1 Thess. i. 5, "Our gospel came not unto you in word only, but also in power, and in the Holy Ghost." 1 Cor. iv. 20, "The kingdom of God is not in word, but in power." Hence saving affections, though oftentimes they do not make so great a noise and show as others, yet have in them a secret solidity, life, and strength, whereby they take hold of and carry away the heart, leading it into a kind of captivity, 2 Cor. x. 5, gaining a full and steadfast determination of the will for God and holiness. Psal. cx. 3, "Thy people shall be willing in the day of thy power." And thus it is that holy affections have a governing power in the course of a man's life. A statue may look very much like a real man, and a beautiful man; yea, it may have, in its appearance to the eye, the resemblance of a very lively, strong, and active man; but yet an inward principle of life and strength is wanting; and therefore it does nothing, it brings nothing to pass; there is no action or operation to answer the show. False discoveries and affections do not go deep enough to reach and govern the spring of men's actions and practice. The seed in stony ground had not deepness of earth, and the root did not go deep enough to bring forth fruit. But gracious affections go to the very bottom of the heart, and take hold of the very inmost springs of life and activity.

Herein chiefly appears the power of true godliness, viz., in its being effectual in practice. And the efficacy of godliness in this respect is what the apostle has respect to when he speaks of the power of godliness, 2 Tim. iii. 5, as is very plain; for he there is particularly declaring how some professors of religion would notoriously fail in the practice of it, and then in the 5th verse observes, that in being thus of an unholy practice, they deny the power of godliness though they have the form of it. Indeed the power of godliness is exerted in the first place within the soul, in the sensible, lively exercise of gracious affections there. Yet the principal evidence of this power of godliness is in those exercises of holy affections that are practical, in conquering the will, the lusts and the corruptions of men, and carrying men on in the way of holiness, through all temptation, difficulty and opposition.

Again, the reason why gracious affections have their exercise and effect in Christian practice appears from this (which has also been before observed), that "the first objective ground of gracious affections is the transcendently excellent and amiable nature of divine things, as they are in themselves, and not any conceived relation they bear to self or self-interest." This shows why holy affections will cause men to be holy in their practice universally. What makes men partial in religion is that they seek themselves, and not God, in their religion; and close with religion, not for its own excellent nature, but only to serve a turn. He that closes with religion only to serve a turn, will close with no more of it than he imagines serves that turn; but he that closes with religion for its own excellent and lovely nature, closes with all that has that nature: he that embraces religion for its own sake embraces the whole of religion. This also shows why gracious affections will cause men to practise religion perseveringly, and at all times. Religion may alter greatly in process of time, as to its consistence with men's private interest, in many respects; and therefore he that complies with it only for selfish views, is liable, in change of times, to forsake it; but the excellent nature of religion, as it is in itself, is invariable; it its always the same, at all times and through all changes; it never alters in any respect.

The reason why gracious affections issue in holy practice also further appears from the kind of excellency of divine things, that is the foundation of all holy affections, viz., "their moral excellency, or the beauty of their holiness." No wonder that a love to holiness, for holiness' sake, inclines persons to practise holiness, and to practise everything that is holy. Since holiness is the main thing that excites, draws, and governs all gracious affections, it is no wonder that all such affections tend to holiness. That which men love, they desire to have and to be united to, and possessed of. That beauty which men delight in, they desire to be adorned with. Those acts which men delight in, they necessarily incline to do.

And what has been observed of that divine teaching and leading of the Spirit of God which there is in gracious affections, shows the reason of this tendency of such affections to a universally holy practice. For, as has been said, the Spirit of God in this His divine teaching and leading gives the soul a natural relish of the sweetness of that which is holy, and of everything that is holy, so far as it comes in view, and excites a disrelish and disgust of everything that is unholy.

The same also appears from what has been observed of the nature of that spiritual knowledge which is the foundation of all holy affection, as consisting in a sense and view of that excellency in divine things which is supreme and transcendent. For hereby these things appear, above all others, worthy to be chosen and adhered to. By the sight of the transcendent glory of Christ, true Christians see Him worthy to be followed, and so are powerfully drawn after Him. They see Him worthy that they should forsake all for Him. By the sight of that superlative amiableness, they are thoroughly disposed to be subject to Him, and engaged to labour with earnestness and activity in His service, and made willing to go through all difficulties for His sake. And it is the discovery of this divine excellency of Christ that makes them constant to Him: for it makes so deep an impression upon their minds that they cannot forget Him; they will follow Him whithersoever He goes, and it is in vain for any endeavour to draw them away from Him.

The reason of this practical tendency and issue of gracious affections further appears from what has been observed of such affections being " attended with a thorough conviction of the judgment of the reality and certainty of divine things." No wonder that they who were never thoroughly convinced that there is any reality in the things of religion, will never be at the labour and trouble of such an earnest, universal, and persevering practice of religion, through all difficulties, self- denials, and sufferings in a dependence on that, of which they are not truly convinced. But on the other hand, they who are thoroughly convinced of the certain truth of those things must needs be governed by them in their practice; for the things revealed in the Word of God are so great, and so infinitely more important than all other things, that it is inconsistent with human nature, that a man should fully believe the truth of them, and not be influenced by them above all things in his practice.

Again, the reason of this expression and effect of holy affections in the practice appears from what has been observed of " a change of nature, accompanying such affections." Without a change of nature, men's practice will not be thoroughly changed. Until the tree be made good, the fruit will not be good. Men do not gather grapes of thorns, nor figs of thistles. The swine may be washed and appear clean for a little while, but yet, without a change of nature, he will still wallow in the mire. Nature is a more powerful principle of action than anything that opposes it: though it may be violently restrained for a while, it will finally overcome that which restrains it: it is like the stream of a river, it may be stopped a while with a dam, but if nothing be done to dry the fountain, it will not be stopped always; it will have a course, either in its old channel or a new one. Nature is a thing more constant and permanent than any of those things that are the foundation of carnal men's reformation and righteousness. When a natural man denies his lust, and lives a strict, religious life, and seems humble, painful, and earnest in religion, it is not natural; it is all a force against nature; as when a stone is violently thrown upwards; but that force will be gradually spent; yet nature will remain in its full strength, and so prevails again, and the stone returns downwards. As long as corrupt nature is not mortified, but the principle left whole in a man, it is a vain thing to expect that it should not govern. But if the old nature be indeed mortified, and a new and heavenly nature infused, then may it well be expected that men will walk in newness of life, and continue to do so to the end of their days.

The reason of this practical exercise and effect of holy affections may also be partly seen from what has been said of that spirit of humility which attends them. Humility is that wherein a spirit of obedience does much consist. A proud spirit is a rebellious spirit, but a humble spirit is a yieldable, subject, obediential spirit. We see among men that the servant who is of a haughty spirit is not apt in everything to be submissive and obedient to the will of his master; but it is otherwise with that servant who is of a lowly spirit.

And that lamb-like, dove-like spirit that has been spoken of, which accompanies all gracious affections, fulfils (as the apostle observes, Rom. xiii. 8, 9, 10, and Gal. v. 14) all the duties of the second table of the law; wherein Christian practice does very much consist, and wherein the external practice of Christianity chiefly consists.

The reason why gracious affections are attended with strict, universal and constant obedience, further appears from what has been observed of that tenderness of spirit which accompanies the affections of true saints, causing in them so quick and lively a sense of pain through the presence of moral evil, and such a dread of the appearance of evil.

And one great reason why the Christian practice which flows from gracious affections is universal, constant, and persevering, appears from what has been observed of those affections themselves, from whence this practice flows, being universal and constant in all kinds of holy exercises, and towards all objects, and in all circumstances, and at all seasons, in a beautiful symmetry and proportion.

And much of the reason why holy affections are expressed and manifested in such an earnestness, activity, and engagedness and perseverance in holy practice, appears from what has been observed of the spiritual appetite and longing after further attainments in religion, which evermore attends true affection, and does not decay but increases as those affections increase.

Thus we see how the tendency of holy affections to such a Christian practice as has been explained, appears from each of those characteristics of holy affection that have been before spoken of.

And this point may be further illustrated and confirmed, if it be considered that the holy Scriptures do abundantly place sincerity and soundness in religion in making a full choice of God as our only Lord and portion, forsaking all for him, and, in a full determination of the will for God and Christ, on counting the cost; in our heart's closing and complying with the religion of Jesus Christ, with all that belongs to it, embracing it with all its difficulties, as it were hating our dearest earthly enjoyments and even our own lives, for Christ; giving up ourselves, with all that we have, wholly and for ever, unto Christ, without keeping back anything, or making any reserve; or, in one word, in the great duty of self-denial for Christ; or in denying, *i.e.*, as it were, disowning and renouncing ourselves for Him, making ourselves nothing that He may be all.   See the texts to this purpose referred to below.* Now, surely, having a heart to forsake all for Christ, tends to actually forsaking all for Him, so far as there is occasion, and we have the trial. A having a heart to deny ourselves for Christ tends to a denying ourselves indeed, when Christ and self-interest stand in competition. A giving up of ourselves, with all that we have, in our hearts, without making any reserve there, tends to our behaving ourselves universally as His, as subject to His will, and devoted to His ends. Our heart's entirely closing with the religion of Jesus, with all that belongs to it, and as attended with all its difficulties, upon a deliberate counting the cost, tends to a universal closing with the same in act and deed, and actually going through all the difficulties that we meet with in the way of religion, and so holding out with patience and perseverance.

The tendency of grace in the heart to holy practice, is very direct, and the connection most natural, close, and necessary. True grace is not an inactive thing; there is nothing in heaven or earth of a more active nature; for it is life itself, and the most active kind of life, even spiritual and divine life. It is no barren thing; there is nothing in the universe that in its nature has a greater tendency to fruit. Godliness in the heart has as direct a relation to practice, as a fountain has to a stream, or as the luminous nature of the sun has to beams sent forth, or as life has to breathing or the beating of the pulse or any other vital act; or as a habit or principle of action has to action; for it is the very nature and notion of grace, that it is a principle of holy action or practice. Regeneration, which is that work of God in

* Matt. v. 29, 30; chap. vi. 24; chap. viii. 19-22; chap. iv. 18-22; chap. x. 37, 38, 39; chap. xiii. 44, 45, 46; chap. xvi. 24, 25, 26; chap. xviii. 8, 9; chap. xix. 21, 27, 28, 29; Luke v. 27, 28; chap. x. 42; chap. xii. 33, 34; chap. xiv. 16-20, 25-33; chap. xvi. 13; Acts iv. 34, 35; chap. v. 1-11; Rom. vi. 3-8; Gal. ii. 20; chap. vi. 14; Philip. iii. 7.

which grace is infused, has a direct relation to practice; for it is the very end of it, with a view to which the whole work is wrought. All is calculated and framed, in this mighty and manifold change wrought in the soul, so as directly to tend to this end. Yea, it is the very end of the redemption of Christ: Tit. ii. 14, " Who gave himself for us, that he might redeem us from all iniquity, and purify unto himself a peculiar people, zealous of good works." Eph. i. 4, " According as he hath chosen us in him before the foundation of the world, that we should be holy and without blame before him in love." Chap. ii. 10, " Created unto good works, which God hath foreordained that we should walk in them." Holy practice is as much the end of all that God does about his saints, as fruit is the end of all the husbandman does about the growth of his field or vineyard; as the matter is often represented in Scripture, Matt. iii. 10, chapter xiii. 8, 23, 30-38, chapter xxi. 19, 33, 34, Luke xiii. 6, John xv. 1-8, 1 Cor. iii. 9, Heb. vi. 7, 8, Isa. v. 1-8, Cant. viii. 11, 12, Isa. xxvii. 2, 3.* And therefore everything in a true Christian is calculated to reach this end. This fruit of holy practice is what every grace, and every discovery, and every individual thing which belongs to Christian experience, has a direct tendency to.

The constant and indissoluble connection that there is between a Christian principle and profession in the true saints, and the fruit of holy practice in their lives, was typified of old in the frame of the golden candlestick in the temple. It is beyond doubt that that golden candlestick, with its seven branches and seven lamps, was a type of the church of Christ. The Holy Ghost Himself has been pleased to put that matter out of doubt, by representing his church by such a golden candlestick, with seven lamps, in the fourth chapter of Zechariah, and representing the

* " To profess to know much is easy; but to bring your affections into subjection, to wrestle with lusts, to cross your wills and yourselves, upon every occasion, this is hard. The Lord looketh that in our lives we should be serviceable to Him, and useful to men. That which is within, the Lord and our brethren are never the better for it: but the outward obedience, flowing thence glorifieth God, and does good to men. The Lord will have this done. What else is the end of our planting and watering, but that the trees may be filled with sap? And what is the end of that sap, but that the trees may bring forth fruit? What careth the husbandman for leaves and barren trees?" (Dr. John Preston, 1587-1628: *Sermon on the Church's Duty in her Carriage.*)

seven churches of Asia by seven golden candlesticks, in the first
chapter of the Revelation.   That golden candlestick in the
temple was everywhere, throughout its whole frame, made with
knops and flowers: Exod. xxv. 31-40, and chapter xxxviii. 17-24.
The word translated knop, in the original, signifies apple or
pomegranate.   There was a knop and a flower, a knop and a flower:
wherever there was a flower, there was an apple or pomegranate
with it: the flower and the fruit were constantly connected,
without fail.   The flower contained the principle of the fruit,
and a beautiful promising appearance of it; and it never was a
deceitful appearance; the principle or show of fruit, had evermore real fruit attending it, or succeeding it. So it is in the
church of Christ: there is the principle of fruit in grace in the
heart; and there is an amiable profession, signified by the open
flowers of the candlestick; and there is answerable fruit, in holy
practice, constantly attending this principle and profession.
Every branch of the golden candlestick, thus composed of
golden apples and flowers, was crowned with a burning, shining
lamp on the top of it.   For it is by this means that the saints
shine as lights in the world, by making a fair and good profession of religion, and having their profession evermore joined
with answerable fruit in practice: agreeable to that of our
Saviour, Matt. v. 15, 16, " Neither do men light a candle, and
put it under a bushel, but on a candlestick, and it giveth light
unto all that are in the house. Let your light so shine before
men, that they may see your good works, and glorify your
Father which is in heaven."   A fair and beautiful profession,
and golden fruits accompanying one another, are the amiable
ornaments of the true church of Christ.   Therefore we find that
apples and flowers were not only the ornaments of the candlestick in the temple, but of the temple itself, which is a type of
the church; which the apostle tells us " is the temple of the
living God."   See 1 Kings vi. 18: " And the cedar of the house
within was carved with knops and open flowers."   The ornaments and crown of the pillars, at the entrance of the temple,
were of the same sort: they were lilies and pomegranates, or
flowers and fruits mixed together, 1 Kings vii. 18, 19.   So it is
with all these that are " as pillars in the temple of God, who
shall go no more out," or never be ejected as intruders; as it is
with all true saints: Rev. iii. 12, " Him that overcometh will I

make a pillar in the temple of my God, and he shall go no more out."

Much the same thing seems to be signified by the ornaments on the skirt of the ephod, the garment of Aaron the high priest; which were golden bells and pomegranates. That these skirts of Aaron's garment represent the church, or the saints (that are as it were the garment of Christ), is manifest; for they are evidently so spoken of, Psal. cxxxiii. 1, 2: "Behold, how good and how pleasant it is for brethren to dwell together in unity! It is like the precious ointment upon the head, that ran down upon the beard, even Aaron's beard, that went down to the skirts of his garments." That ephod of Aaron signified the same with the seamless coat of Christ our great High Priest. As Christ's coat had no seam, but was woven from the top throughout, so it was with the ephod, Exod. xxxix. 22. As God took care in His providence that Christ's coat should not be rent; so God took special care that the ephod should not be rent, Exod. xxviii. 32, and chap. xxxix. 23. The golden bells on this ephod by their precious matter and pleasant sound, well represent the good profession that the saints make; and the pomegranates, the fruit they bring forth. And as in the hem of the ephod, bells and pomegranates were constantly connected, as is once and again observed, there was a golden bell and a pomegranate, a golden bell and a pomegranate, Exod. xxviii. 34, and chap. xxxix. 26, so it is in the true saints; their good profession and their good fruit, do constantly accompany one another: the fruit they bring forth in life evermore answers the pleasant sound of their profession.

Again, the very same thing is represented by Christ, in His description of his spouse, Cant. vii. 2: "Thy belly is like a heap of wheat, set about with lilies." Here again are beautiful flowers and good fruit accompanying one another. The lilies were fair and beautiful flowers, and the wheat was good fruit.

As this fruit of Christian practice is evermore found in true saints, according as they have opportunity and trial, so it is found in them only; none but true Christians do live such an obedient life, so universally devoted to their duty, and given up to the business of a Christian. All unsanctified men are workers of iniquity: they are of their father the devil, and the lusts of their father they will do. There is no hypocrite that will go through with the business of religion, and both begin and finish the tour. They will not endure the trials God is wont to bring on the professors of religion, but will turn aside to their crooked ways; they will not be thoroughly faithful to Christ in their practice, and follow Him whithersoever He goes. Whatever lengths they may go in religion in some instances, and though they may appear exceeding strict, and mightily engaged in the service of God for a season, yet they are servants to sin; the chains of their old taskmasters are not broken: their lusts have yet a reigning power in their hearts; and therefore to these masters they will bow down again.* Daniel xii. 10, " Many shall be purified and made white, and tried: but the wicked will do wickedly, and none of the wicked shall understand." Isa. xxvi. 10, " Let favour be showed to the wicked, yet will he not learn righteousness; in the land of uprightness will he deal unjustly." Isa. xxxv. 8, " And a highway shall be there, and a way, and it shall be called the way of holiness; the unclean shall not pass over it. Hos. xiv. 9, " The ways of the Lord are right, and the just shall walk in them: but the transgressors shall fall therein." Job xxvii. 8, 10, " What is the hope of the hypocrite? Will he delight himself in the Almighty? Will he always call upon God?" An unsanctified man may hide his sin, and may in many things, and for a season refrain from sin; but he will not be brought finally to renounce his sin, and give it a bill of divorce; sin is too dear to him, for him to be willing for that: " Wickedness is sweet in his mouth; and therefore he hides it under his tongue; he spares it, and forsakes it not; but keeps it still within his mouth," Job xx. 12, 13. Herein chiefly consists the straitness of the gate, and the narrowness of the way that leads to life; upon the account of which, carnal men will not go in thereat, viz., that it is a way of utterly denying and finally renouncing all ungodliness, and so a way of self-denial or self-renunciation.

Many natural men, under the means that are used with them, and God's strivings with them to bring them to forsake their sins, do by their sins as Pharaoh did by his pride and covetousness, which he gratified by keeping the children of Israel in

* " No unregenerate man, though he go never so far, let him do never so much, but he lives in some one sin or other, secret or open, little or great. Judas went far, but he was covetous; Herod went far, but he loved his Herodias. Every dog hath his kennel; every swine hath his·swill; and every wicked man his lust." *Shepard's Sincere Convert*, p. 62.

bondage, when God strove with him to bring him to let the people go. When God's hand pressed Pharaoh sore, and he was exercised with fears of God's future wrath, he entertained some thoughts of letting the people go, and promised he would do it; but from time to time he broke his promises, when he saw there was respite. When God filled Egypt with thunder and lightning, and the fire ran along the ground, then Pharaoh was brought to confess his sin with seeming humility, and to show a great resolution to let the people go. Exod. ix. 27, 28, "And Pharaoh sent, and called for Moses and Aaron, and said unto them, I have sinned this time: the Lord is righteous, and I and my people are wicked: entreat the Lord (for it is enough) that there be no more mighty thunderings and hail; and I will let you go, and ye shall stay no longer." So sinners are sometimes, by thunders and lightnings and great terrors of the law, brought to a seeming work of humiliation, and to an appearance of parting with their sins; but are no more thoroughly brought to a disposition to dismiss them, than Pharaoh was to let the people go. Pharaoh, in the struggle that was between his conscience and his lusts, was for contriving that God might be served, while at the same time he enjoyed his lusts that were gratified by the slavery of the people. Moses insisted that Israel's God should be served and sacrificed to: Pharaoh was willing to consent to that, but would have it done without his parting with the people; "Go ye, sacrifice to your God in the land," says he, Exod. viii. 25. So, many sinners are for contriving to serve God and enjoy their lusts too. Moses objected against complying with Pharaoh's proposal, that serving God and yet continuing in Egypt under their task-masters, did not agree together and were inconsistent one with another (there is no serving God, and continuing slaves to such enemies of God at the same time). After this Pharaoh consented to let the people go, provided they did not go far away: he was not willing to part with them finally, and therefore would have them within reach. So do many hypocrites with respect to their sins. Afterwards Pharaoh consented to let the men go, if they would leave the women and children, Exod. x. 8, 9, 10. And then after that, when God's hand was yet harder upon him, he consented that they should go, even women and children, as well as men, provided they would leave their cattle behind! But he was not willing to let them go and all that they had, Exod. x. 24.

So it sometimes is with sinners; they are willing to part with some of their sins, but not all; they are brought to part with the more gross acts of sin, but not to part with their lusts in lesser indulgencies of them. Whereas we must part with all our sins, little and great; and all that belongs to them, men, women, children, and cattle; they must be let go, with "their young, and with their old, with their sons, and with their daughters, with their flocks, and with their herds, there must not be a hoof left behind;" as Moses told Pharaoh, with respect to the children of Israel. At last, when it came to extremity, Pharaoh consented to let the people all go, and all that they had; but he was not steadfastly of that mind; he soon repented and pursued after them again, and the reason was, that those lusts of pride and covetousness that were gratified by Pharaoh's dominion over the people, and the gains of their service, were never really mortified in him, but only violently restrained. And thus, being guilty of backsliding, after his seeming compliance with God's commands, he was destroyed without remedy. Thus there may be a forced parting with ways of disobedience to the commands of God, that may seem to be universal, as to what appears for a little season; but because it is a mere force, without the mortification of the inward principle of sin, sinners will not persevere in it; but will return as the dog to his vomit; and so bring on themselves dreadful and remediless destruction. There were many false disciples in Christ's time, that followed Him for a while; but none of them followed Him to the end; but some on one occasion, and some on another, went back and walked no more with Him.*

From what has been said, it is manifest that Christian practice,

---

* "The counterfeit and common grace of foolish virgins, after some time of glorious profession, wilt certainly go out and be quite spent. It consumes in the using and shining and burning.—Men that have been most forward, decay: their gifts decay, life decays. It is so, after some time of profession: for at first, it rather grows than decays and withers; but afterwards they have enough of it, it withers and dies. The Spirit of God comes upon many hypocrites, in abundant and plentiful measure of awakening grace: it comes upon them, as it did upon Balaam, and as it were in overflowing waters, which spread far, and grow very deep, and fill many empty places. Though it doth come upon them so, yet it doth never rest within, so as to dwell there, to take up an eternal mansion for himself.—Hence it doth decay by little and little, until at last it is quite gone. As ponds filled with rain water, which comes upon them; not spring water, that riseth up within them; it dries up by little and little, until quite dry." *Shepard's Parable of the Ten Virgins*, p. 451, 452.

or a holy life, is a great and distinguishing sign of true and saving grace. But I may go further and assert that it is the chief of all the signs of grace, both as an evidence of the sincerity of professors unto others, and also to their own consciences.

But then it is necessary that this be rightly taken, and that it be well understood and observed in what sense and manner Christian practice is the greatest sign of grace. Therefore to set this matter in a clear light, I will endeavour particularly and distinctly to prove that Christian practice is the principal sign by which Christians are to judge both of their own and others' sincerity of godliness; withal observing some things that are needful to be particularly noted in order to a right understanding of this matter.

I. *I shall consider Christian practice and holy life, as a manifestation and sign of the sincerity of a professing Christian to the eye of his neighbours and brethren.*

And that this is the chief sign of grace in this respect is very evident from the Word of God. Christ, who knew best how to give us rules to judge of others, has repeated it and inculcated it, that we should know them by their fruits: Matt. vii. 16, "Ye shall know them by their fruits." And then, after arguing the point, and giving clear reasons why it must needs be, that men's fruits must be the chief evidence of what sort they are, in the following verses he closes by repeating the assertion, verse 20, "Wherefore by their fruits ye shall know them." Again, chap. xii. 33, "Either make the tree good, and his fruit good; or else make the tree corrupt, and his fruit corrupt." As much as to say, it is a very absurd thing for any to suppose that the tree is good and yet the fruit bad, that the tree is of one sort and the fruit of another; for the proper evidence of the nature of the tree is its fruit. Nothing else can be intended by that last clause in the verse, "For the tree is known by its fruit," than that the tree is chiefly known by its fruit, that this is the main and most proper diagnostic by which one tree is distinguished from another. So Luke vi. 44, "Every tree is known by his own fruit." Christ nowhere says, Ye shall know the tree by its leaves or flowers, or ye shall know men by their talk, or ye shall know them by the good story they tell of their experiences, or ye shall know them by the manner and air of their speaking, and emphasis and pathos of expression, or by their speaking feelingly, or by making a very great show by abundance of talk, or by many tears and affectionate expressions, or by the affections ye feel in your hearts towards them; but by their fruits shall ye know them; the tree is known by its fruit; every tree is known by its own fruit. And as this is the evidence that Christ has directed us mainly to look at in others, in judging of them, so it is the evidence that Christ has mainly directed us to give to others, whereby they may judge of us: Matt. v. 16, "Let your light so shine before men, that they (others) seeing your good works, may glorify your Father which is in heaven." Here Christ directs us to manifest our godliness to others. Godliness is as it were a light that shines in the soul. Christ directs that this light not only shine within, but that it should shine out before men, that they may see it. But which way shall this be? It is by our good works. Christ doth not say, that others hearing your good works, your good story, or your pathetical expressions; but "that others, *seeing* your good works, may glorify your Father which is in heaven." Doubtless, when Christ gives us a rule how to make our light shine that others may have evidence of it, His rule is the best that is to be found. And the apostles mention a Christian practice as the principal ground of their esteem of persons as true Christians. As the Apostle Paul, in the 6th chapter of Hebrews. There the apostle, in the beginning of the chapter, speaks of them that have great common illuminations, that have "been enlightened, and have tasted of the heavenly gift, and were made partakers of the Holy Ghost, and have tasted the good word of God, and the powers of the world to come, that afterwards fall away, and are like barren ground, that is nigh unto cursing, whose end is to be burned;" and then immediately adds in the 9th verse (expressing his charity for the Christian Hebrews, as having that saving grace, which is better than all these common illuminations), "But, beloved, we are persuaded better things of you, and things that accompany salvation, though we thus speak." And then, in the next verse, he tells them what was the reason he had such good thoughts of them: he does not say that it was because they had given him a good account of a work of God upon their souls, and talked very experimentally; but it was their work and labour of love; "for God is not unrighteous, to forget your work and labour of love, which ye have showed towards his name, in that ye have ministered to the saints, and do minister." And the same apostle speaks of a faithful serving of God in practice, as the proper proof to others of men's loving Christ above all, and preferring his honour to their private interest: Phil. ii. 21, 22, "For all seek their own, not the things which are Jesus Christ's; but ye know the proof of him, that as a son with the father, he hath served with me in the gospel." So the Apostle John expresses the same as the ground of his good opinion of Gaius, 3 John 3-6, "For I rejoiced greatly when the brethren came and testified of the truth that is in thee." But how did the brethren testify of the truth that was in Gaius? And how did the apostle judge of the truth that was in him? It was not because they testified that he had given them a good account of the steps of his experiences and talked like one that felt what he said, and had the very language of a Christian but they testified that he walked in the truth; as it follows, "even as thou walkest in the truth. I have no greater joy than to hear that my children walk in the truth. Beloved, thou doest faithfully whatsoever thou doest to the brethren and to strangers; which have borne witness of thy charity before the church." Thus the apostle explains what the brethren had borne witness of, when they came and testified of his walking in the truth. And the apostle seems in this same place to give it as a rule to Gaius how he should judge of others; in verse 10, he mentions one Diotrephes, that did not carry himself well, and led away others after him; and then in the 11th verse, he directs Gaius to beware of such, and not to follow them; and gives him a rule whereby he may know them, exactly agreeable to that rule Christ had given before, "by their fruits ye shall know them." Says the apostle, "Beloved, follow not that which is evil, but that which is good. He that doeth good is of God; but he that doeth evil hath not seen God." And I would further observe, that the Apostle James, expressly comparing that way of showing others our faith and Christianity by our practice or works, with other ways of showing our faith without works, or not by works, does plainly and abundantly prefer the former: James ii. 18, "Yea, a man may say, Thou hast faith, and I have works; show me thy faith without thy works, and I will not show thee my faith by my works." A manifestation of our faith without works, or in a way diverse from works, is a manifestation of it in words, whereby a man professes faith. As the apostle says, verse 14, " What doth it profit, my brethren, though a man say he hath faith?" Therefore, here are two ways of manifesting to our neighbour what is in our hearts; one by what we say, and the other by what we do. But the apostle abundantly prefers the latter as the best evidence. Now certainly all accounts we give of ourselves in words, our saying that we have faith, and that we are converted, and telling the manner how we came to have faith, and the steps by which it was wrought, and the discoveries and experiences that accompany it, are still but manifesting our faith by what we say; it is but showing our faith by our words; which the apostle speaks of as falling vastly short of manifesting of it by what we do, and showing our faith by our works.

And as the Scripture plainly teaches that practice is the best evidence of the sincerity of professing Christians, so reason teaches the same thing. Reason shows that men's deeds are better and more faithful interpreters of their minds than their words. The common sense of all mankind, through all ages and nations, teaches them to judge of men's hearts in other matters chiefly by their practice; as, whether a man be a loyal subject, a true lover, a dutiful child, or a faithful servant. If a man profess a great deal of love and friendship to another, reason teaches all men that such a profession is not so great an evidence of his being a real and hearty friend, as his appearing a friend in deeds; being faithful and constant to his friend in prosperity and adversity, ready to lay out himself, and deny himself, and suffer in his personal interest, to do him a kindness. A wise man will trust to such evidences of the sincerity of friendship further than a thousand earnest professions and solemn declarations and most affectionate expressions of friendship in words. And there is equal reason why practice should also be looked upon as the best evidence of friendship towards Christ. Reason says the same that Christ said, in John xiv. 21, " He that hath my commandments, and keepeth them, he it is that loveth me." Thus, if we see a man who in the course of his life seems to follow and imitate Christ, and greatly to exert and deny himself for the honour of Christ, and to promote His kingdom and interest in the world; reason teaches that this is an evidence of love to Christ, more to be depended on than if a man only says he has love to Christ, and tells of the inward experiences he has had of love to Him, what strong love he felt, and how his heart was drawn out in love at such and such a time, when it may be there appears but little imitation of Christ in his behaviour, and he seems backward to do any great matter for Him, or to put himself out of his way for the promoting of His kingdom, but seems to be apt to excuse himself whenever he is called to deny himself for Christ. A man, in declaring his experiences, may tell how he found his heart weaned from the world, and how he saw the vanity of it, so that all looked as nothing to him at such and such times, and he may profess that he gives up all to God, and calls heaven and earth to witness to it; yet in his practice he is violent in pursuing the world; what he gets he keeps close; he is exceeding loth to part with much of it to charitable and pious uses; it comes from him almost like his heart's blood. But there is another professing Christian that says not a great deal, yet in his behaviour appears ready at all times to forsake the world, whenever it stands in the way of his duty, and is free to part with it at any time to promote religion and the good of his fellow creatures. Reason teaches that the latter gives far the more credible manifestation of a heart weaned from the world. And if a man appears to walk humbly before God and men, and to be of a conversation that savours of a broken heart, appearing patient and resigned to God under affliction, and meek in his behaviour amongst men, this is a better evidence of humiliation than if a person only tells how great a sense he had of his own unworthiness, how he was brought to lie in the dust, and was quite emptied of himself, and saw himself nothing and all over filthy and abominable, &c. &c.; yet if he acts as if he looks upon himself as one of the first and best of saints, and by just right the head of all the Christians in the town; if he is assuming, self-willed, and impatient of the least contradiction or opposition; we may be assured in such a case, that a man's practice comes from a lower place in his heart than his profession. So (to mention no more instances) if a professor of Christianity manifests in his behaviour a pitiful tender spirit towards others in calamity, if he is ready to bear their burdens with them, willing to spend his substance for them, and to suffer many inconveniences in his worldly interest to promote the good of others' souls and bodies; is not this a more credible manifestation of a spirit of love to men, than only a man's telling what love he felt to others at certain times, how he pitied their souls, how his soul was in travail for them, and how he felt hearty love and pity to his enemies; when in his behaviour he seems to be of a very selfish spirit, close and niggardly, all for himself, and none for his neighbours, and perhaps envious and contentious? Persons in a pang of affection may think they have a willingness of heart for great things, to do much and to suffer much, and so may profess it very earnestly and confidently, when really their hearts are far from it. Thus many in their affectionate pangs have thought themselves willing to be damned eternally for the glory of God. Passing affections easily produce words; and words are cheap; and godliness is more easily feigned in words than in actions. Christian practice is a costly, laborious thing. The self-denial that is required of Christians, and the narrowness of the way that leads to life, does not consist in words, but in practice. Hypocrites may much more easily be brought to talk like saints, than to act like saints.

Thus it is plain, that Christian practice is the best sign or manifestation of the true godliness of a professing Christian, to the eye of his neighbours.

But then the following things should be well observed, that this matter may be rightly understood.

First, it must be observed that when the Scripture speaks of Christian practice as the best evidence to others of sincerity and truth of grace, a profession of Christianity is not excluded but supposed. The rules mentioned were rules given to the followers of Christ, to guide them in their thoughts of professing Christians, and those that offered themselves as members of their society, whereby they might judge of the truth of their pretences, and the sincerity of the profession they made; and not for the trial of heathens, or those that made no pretence to Christianity, and that Christians had nothing to do with. This is as plain as is possible in that great rule which Christ gives in the 7th of Matthew, "By their fruits ye shall know them." He there gives a rule how to judge of those that professed to be Christians, yea, that made a very high profession, false prophets, "who came in sheep's clothing," as ver. 15. So also says the Apostle James, chap. ii. 18, "Show me thy faith without thy works, and I will show thee my faith by my works." It is evident that both these sorts of persons, offering to give these diverse evidences of their faith, are professors of faith: this is implied in each offering to give evidences of the faith professed. And it is evident by the preceding verses that the apostle is speaking of professors of faith in Jesus Christ. So it is very plain that the Apostle John, in those passages that have been observed in his third epistle, is speaking of professing Christians. Though in these rules the Christian practice of professors be spoken of as the greatest and most distinguishing sign of their sincerity in their profession, and much more evidential than their profession itself, yet a profession of Christianity is plainly presupposed. It is not the main thing in the evidence, nor anything distinguishing in it, yet it is a thing requisite and necessary in it. As having an animal body is not anything distinguishing of a man from other creatures, and is not the main thing in the evidence of human nature, yet it is a thing requisite and necessary in the evidence. If any man should say plainly that he was not a Christian, and did not believe that Jesus was the Son of God or a Person sent of God, these rules of Christ and his apostles do not at all oblige us to look upon him as a sincere Christian, let his visible practice and virtues be what they will. And not only do these rules take no place with respect to a man that explicitly denies Christianity, and is a professed deist, Jew, heathen, or open infidel; but also with respect to a man that only forbears to make a profession of Christianity; because these rules were given us to judge of professing Christians only. Fruits must be joined with open flowers; bells and pomegranates go together.

But here will naturally arise this inquiry, viz., When may a man be said to profess Christianity, or what profession may properly be called a profession of Christianity?

I answer, in two things.

1. In order to a man's being properly said to make a profession of Christianity, there must undoubtedly be a profession of all that is necessary to his being a Christian, or of so much as belongs to the essence of Christianity. Whatsoever is essential in Christianity itself, the profession of that is essential in the profession of Christianity. The profession must be of the thing professed. For a man to profess Christianity is for him to declare that he has it. And therefore so much as belongs to the true denomination of a thing, so much is essential to a true declaration of that thing. If we take only a part of Christianity,

and leave out a part that is essential to it, what we take is not Christianity; because something of the essence of it is wanting. So if we profess only a part, and leave out a part that is essential, that which we profess is not Christianity. Thus, in order to a profession of Christianity, we must profess that we believe that Jesus is the Messiah; for this reason, that such a belief is essential to Christianity. And so we must profess, either expressly or implicitly, that Jesus satisfied for our sins, and other essential doctrines of the gospel, because a belief of these things also is essential to Christianity. But there are other things as essential to religion as an orthodox belief; which it is therefore as necessary that we should profess, in order to our being truly said to profess Christianity. Thus it is essential to Christianity that we repent of our sins, that we be convinced of our own sinfulness, and that we are sensible we have justly exposed ourselves to God's wrath, and that our hearts do renounce all sin, and that we do with our whole hearts embrace Christ as our only Saviour; and that we love Him above all, and are willing for His sake to forsake all, and that we do give up ourselves to be entirely and forever His, &c. Such things as these do as much belong to the essence of Christianity as the belief of any of the doctrines of the gospel: and therefore the profession of them does as much belong to a Christian profession. Not that in order to being professing Christians, it is necessary that there should be an explicit profession of every individual thing that belongs to Christian grace or virtue: but certainly, there must be a profession, either express or implicit, of what is of the essence of religion. And as to those things that Christians should express in their profession, we ought to be guided by the precepts of God's word, or by Scripture examples of public professions of religion which God's people have made from time to time. Thus they ought to profess their repentance of sin: as of old, when persons were initiated as professors, they came confessing their sins, manifesting their humiliation for sin, Matt. iii. 6. And the baptism they were baptized with was called the baptism of repentance, Mark i. 4. And John, when he had baptized them, exhorted them to bring forth fruits meet for repentance, Matt. iii. 8, *i.e.*, agreeable to that repentance which they had professed; encouraging them that, if they did so, they should escape the wrath to come, and be gathered as wheat into God's garner, Matt. iii. 7-12. So the

Apostle Peter says to the Jews, Acts ii. 38, "Repent, and be baptized;" which shows that repentance is a qualification that must
be visible in order to baptism; and therefore ought to be publicly
professed. So when the Jews that returned from captivity
entered publicly into covenant, it was with confession, or public
confession of repentance of their sins, Neh. ix. 2. This profession of repentance should include or imply a profession of conviction, that God would be just in our damnation: see Neh. ix.
33-35, and chapter x. They should profess their faith in Jesus
Christ, and that they embrace Christ, and rely upon Him as their
Saviour with their whole hearts, and that they do joyfully entertain the gospel of Christ. Thus Philip, in order to baptize the
eunuch, required that he should profess that he believed with all
his heart: and they that were received as visible Christians, at
that great outpouring of the Spirit which began at the day of
Pentecost, appeared gladly to receive the gospel: Acts ii. 41,
"Then they that gladly received his word were baptized; and
the same day there were added unto them about three thousand
souls." They should profess that they rely on Christ's righteousness only, and on His strength; and that they are devoted to
Him, as their only Lord and Saviour, and that they rejoice in
Him as their only righteousness and portion. It is foretold that
all nations shall be brought publicly to make this profession, Isa.
xlv. 22-25: "Look unto me, and be ye saved, all the ends of the
earth; for I am God, and there is none else. I have sworn by
myself, the word is gone out of my mouth in righteousness, and
shall not return, that unto me every knee shall bow, every tongue
shall swear. Surely, shall one say, In the Lord have I righteousness and strength; even to him shall men come, and all that are
incensed against him shall be ashamed. In the Lord shall all
the seed of Israel be justified, and shall glory." They should
profess to give up themselves entirely to Christ, and to God
through Him; as the children of Israel, when they publicly recog-
nised their covenant with God: Deut. xxvi. 17, "Thou hast
avouched the Lord this day to be thy God, and to walk in his
ways, and to keep his statutes, and his commandments, and his
judgments, and to hearken unto his voice." They ought to profess a willingness of heart to embrace religion with all its difficulties, and to walk in a way of obedience to God universally and
perseveringly, Exod. xix. 8, and xxiv. 3, 7, Deut. xxvi. 16-19,

2 Kings xxiii. 3, Neh. x. 28-39, Psal. cxix. 57, 106. They ought to profess that all their hearts and souls are in these engagements to be the Lord's and forever to serve Him, 2 Chron. xv. God's people swearing to God, and swearing by His Name, or to His Name, as it might be rendered (by which seems to be signified their solemnly giving up themselves to Him in covenant, and vowing to receive Him as their God, and to be entirely His, to obey and serve Him), is spoken of as a duty to be performed by all God's visible Israel, Deut. vi. 13, and x. 20, Psal. lxiii. 11, Isa. xix. 18, chap. xlv. 23, 24, compared with Rom. xiv. 11, and Phil. ii. 10, 11, Isa. xlviii. 1, 2, and lxv. 15, 16, Jer. iv. 2, and v. 7, and xii. 16, Hos. iv. 15, and x. 4. Therefore, in order to persons being entitled to full esteem and charity with their neighbours, as being sincere professors of Christianity; by those forementioned rules of Christ and His apostles, there must be a visibly holy life, with a profession either expressing or plainly implying such things as those which have been now mentioned. We are to know them by their fruits, that is, we are by their fruits to know whether they are what they profess to be; not that we are to know by their fruits that they have something in them they do not so much as pretend to.

And moreover,

2. That profession of these things which is properly called a Christian profession, and which must be joined with Christian practice, in order to persons being entitled to the benefit of those rules, must be made (as to what appears) understandingly: that is, they must be persons that appear to have been so far instructed in the principles of religion, as to be in an ordinary capacity to understand the proper import of what is expressed in their profession. For sounds are no significations or declarations of anything, any further than men understand the meaning of their own sounds.

But in order to persons making a proper profession of Christianity, such as the Scripture directs to, and such as the followers of Christ should require, for the acceptance of the professors, with full charity, as members of their society; it is not necessary they should give an account of the particular steps and method by which the Holy Spirit, sensibly to them, wrought and brought about those great essential things of Christianity in their hearts. There is no footstep in the Scripture of any such

way of the apostles or primitive ministers and Christians requir-
ing any such relation, in order to their receiving and treating
others as their Christian brethren, to all intents and purposes,
or of their first examining them concerning the particular
method and order of their experiences. They required of them
a profession of the things wrought; but no account of the manner of working was required of them. Nor is there the least
shadow in the Scripture of any such custom in the church of
God from Adam to the death of the Apostle John.

I am far from saying that it is not requisite that persons
should give any sort of account of their experiences to their
brethren. For persons to profess those things wherein the
essence of Christianity lies, is the same thing as to profess that
they experience those things. Thus for persons solemnly to profess that, in a full conviction of their own utter sinfulness, misery,
and impotence, and totally undone state as in themselves, and
their just desert of God's utter rejection and eternal wrath, and
the utter insufficiency of their own righteousness, or anything
in them, to satisfy divine justice, or recommend them to God's
favour, they do entirely depend on the Lord Jesus Christ, and
His satisfaction and righteousness; that they do with all their
hearts believe the truth of the gospel of Christ; and that in a full
conviction of His sufficiency and perfect excellency as a Saviour,
as exhibited in the gospel, they do with their whole souls cleave
to Him, and acquiesce in Him, as the refuge and rest of their
souls, and fountain of their comfort; that they repent of their
sins, and utterly renounce all sin, and give up themselves wholly
to Christ, willingly subjecting themselves to Him as their King;
that they give Him their hearts and their whole man; and are
willing and resolved to have God for their whole and everlasting
portion; and in a dependence on His promises of a future eternal
enjoyment of Him in heaven, to renounce all the enjoyment of
this vain world, selling all for this great treasure and future
inheritance, and to comply with every command of God, even
the most difficult and self-denying, and devote their whole lives
to God's service; and that in forgiveness of those that have
injured them, and a general benevolence to mankind, their
hearts are united to the people of Jesus Christ as their people, to
cleave to them and love them as their brethren, and worship and
serve God, and follow Christ in union and fellowship with them,

being willing and resolved to perform all those duties that belong
to them, as members of the same family of God and mystical
body of Christ : I say, for persons solemnly to profess such things
as these, as in the presence of God, is the same thing as to profess
that they are conscious of, or do experience such things in their
hearts.

Nor do I suppose that persons giving an account of their experience of particular exercises of grace, with the times and circumstances, give no advantage to others in forming a judgment
of their state; or that persons may not fitly be inquired of concerning these in some cases, especially cases of great importance,
where all possible satisfaction concerning persons' piety is especially to be desired and sought after, as in the case of ordination
or approbation of a minister. It may give advantage in forming
a judgment, in several respects; and among others, in this, that
hereby we may be better satisfied that the professor speaks
honestly and understandingly in what he professes; and that he
does not make the profession in mere formality.

In order to a profession of Christianity being accepted to any
purpose, there ought to be good reason, from the circumstances
of the profession, to think that the professor does not make such
a profession out of a mere customary compliance with a prescribed form, using words without any distinct meaning, or in a
very lax and ambiguous manner, as confessions of faith are often
subscribed; but that the professor understandingly and honestly
signifies what he is conscious of in his own heart; otherwise his
profession can be of no significance, and no more to be regarded
than the sound of things without life. But indeed (whatever
advantage an account of particular exercises may give in judging
of this) it must be owned that the professor having been previously thoroughly instructed by his teachers, and given good
proof of his sufficient knowledge, together with a practice agreeable to his profession, is himself the best evidence of this.

Nor do I suppose but that, if a person that is inquired of about
particular passages, times, and circumstances of his Christian
experience, among other things, seems to be able to give a distinct account of the manner of his first conversion, in such a
method as has been frequently observable in true conversion,
so that things seem sensibly and distinctly to follow one another
in the order of time, according to the order of nature, it adds

lustre to the evidence he gives his brethren of the truth of his experiences.

But the thing that I speak of as unscriptural is the insisting on a particular account of the distinct method and steps, wherein the Spirit of God did sensibly proceed, in first bringing the soul into a state of salvation, as a thing requisite in order to receiving a professor into full charity as a real Christian; or, for the want of such relation, to disregard other things in the evidence persons give to their neighbours of their Christianity, that are vastly more important and essential.

Secondly, That we may rightly understand how Christian practice is the greatest evidence that others can have of the sincerity of a professing Christian, it is needful that what was said before, showing what Christian practice is, should be borne in mind; and that it should be considered how far this may be visible to others. Merely that a professor of Christianity is what is commonly called an honest man, and a moral man (*i.e.*, we have no special transgression or iniquity to charge him with, that might bring a blot on his character), is no great evidence of the sincerity of his profession. This is not making his light shine before men. This is not that work and labour of love showed towards Christ's name, which gave the apostle such persuasion of the sincerity of the professing Hebrews, Heb. vi. 9, 10. We may see nothing in a man, but he may be a good man; there may appear nothing in his life and conversation inconsistent with his being godly, and yet neither may there be any great positive evidence that he is so. But there may be great positive appearance of holiness in men's visible behaviour. Their life may appear to be a life devoted to the service of God: they may appear to follow the example of Jesus Christ, and come up in a great measure to those excellent rules in the 5th, 6th, and 7th chapters of Matthew, and 12th of Romans, and many other parts of the New Testament: there may be a great appearance of their being universal in their obedience to Christ's commands and the rules of the gospel. They may appear to be universal in the performance of the duties of the first table, manifesting the fear and love of God; and also universal in fulfilling rules of love to men, love to saints, and love to enemies: rules of meekness and forgiveness, rules of mercy and charity, and looking not only at our own things but also at the things of others; rules of doing good to men's souls

and bodies, to particular persons and to the public; rules of temperance and mortification, and of a humble conversation; rules
of bridling the tongue, and improving it to glorify God and
bless men, showing that in their tongues is the law of kindness.
They may appear to walk as Christians, in all places, and at all
seasons, in the house of God, and in their families, and among
their neighbours, on Sabbath days and every day, in business
and in conversation, towards friends and enemies, towards
superiors, inferiors, and equals. Persons in their visible walk
may appear to be very earnestly engaged in the service of God
and mankind. They may appear to lay out themselves in the
work of a Christian, and to be very constant and steadfast in it
under all circumstances and temptations. There may be great
manifestations of a spirit to deny themselves, and suffer for God
and Christ, and the interest of religion, and the benefit of their
brethren. There may be great appearances in a man's walk of
a disposition to forsake anything, rather than to forsake Christ,
and to make everything give place to His honour. There may
be great manifestations in a man's behaviour of such religion as
this being his element, and of his placing the delight and happiness of his life in it; and his conversation may be such that
he may carry with him a sweet odour of Christian graces and
heavenly dispositions wherever he goes. And when it is thus in
the professors of Christianity, here is an evidence to others of
their sincerity in their profession, to which all other manifestations are not worthy to be compared.

There is doubtless a great variety in the degrees of evidence
that professors exhibit of their sincerity, in their life and practice; as there is a variety in the fairness and clearness of accounts
persons give of the manner and method of their experiences:
but undoubtedly such a manifestation as has been described of
a Christian spirit in practice, is vastly beyond the fairest and
brightest story of particular steps and passages of experience that
ever was told. And in general, a manifestation of the sincerity
of a Christian profession in practice is far better than a relation
of experiences. But yet,

Thirdly, It must be noted, agreeable to what was formerly
observed, that no external manifestations and outward appearances whatsoever, that are visible to the world, are infallible evidences of grace. These manifestations that have been mentioned

are the best that mankind can have; and they are such as oblige Christians entirely to embrace professors as saints, and love them and rejoice in them as the children of God, and are sufficient to give them as great satisfaction concerning them, as ever is needful to guide them in their conduct, or for any purpose that needs to be answered in this world. But nothing that appears to them in their neighbour can be sufficient to beget an absolute certainty concerning the state of his soul: for they see not his heart, nor can they see all his external behaviour. Much of it is in secret, and hid from the eye of the world; and it is impossible certainly to determine how far a man may go in many external appearances and imitations of grace, from other principles. Though undoubtedly, if others could see so much of what belongs to men's practice as their own consciences may see of it, it might be an infallible evidence of their state, as will appear from what follows.

Having thus considered Christian practice as the best evidence of the sincerity of professors to others, I now proceed,

3. To observe that the Scripture also speaks of Christian practice as a distinguishing and sure evidence of grace to persons' own consciences. This is very plain in 1 John ii. 3: "Hereby we do know that we know him, if we keep his commandments." And the testimony of our consciences, with respect to our good deeds, is spoken of as that which may give us assurance of our own godliness, 1 John iii. 18, 19: "My little children, let us not live in word, neither in tongue, but in deed and in truth. And hereby we know that we are of the truth, and shall assure our hearts before him." And the Apostle Paul, in Heb. vi., speaks of the work and labour of love of the Christian Hebrews as that which both gave him a persuasion that they had something above the highest common illuminations, and also as that evidence which tended to give them the highest assurance of hope concerning themselves, verse 9, &c.: "But, beloved, we are persuaded better things of you, and things that accompany salvation, though we thus speak. For God is not unrighteous, to forget your work and labour of love, which ye have showed toward his name, in that ye have ministered to his saints, and do minister. And we desire that every one of you do show the same diligence, to the full assurance of hope unto the end." So the apostle directs the Galatians to examine their behaviour or

practice, that they might have rejoicing in themselves in their own happy state, Gal. vi. 4: "Let every man prove his own work, so shall he have rejoicing in himself alone, and not in another." And the psalmist says, Psal. cxix. 6, "Then shall I not be ashamed, when I have respect unto all thy commandments;" *i.e.,* then I shall be bold, and assured, and steadfast in my hope. And in that of our Saviour, Matt. vii. 19, 20: "Every tree that bringeth not forth good fruit, is hewn down and cast into the fire. Wherefore by their fruits ye shall know them." Though Christ gives this, firstly, as a rule by which we should judge of others, yet in the words that next follow He plainly shows, that He intends it also as a rule by which we should judge ourselves: "Not every one that saith unto me, Lord, Lord, shall enter into the kingdom of heaven; but he that doeth the will of my Father which is in heaven. Many will say to me in that day, Lord, Lord, &c.—— And then will I profess unto them, I never knew you: depart from me, ye that work iniquity. Therefore, whosoever heareth these sayings of mine, and doeth them, I will liken him unto a wise man, which built his house upon a rock. —— And everyone that heareth these sayings of mine, and doeth them not, shall be likened unto a foolish man, which built his house upon the sand." I shall have occasion to mention other texts to show the same thing, hereafter.

But for the greater clearness in this matter, I would, first, show how Christian practice, doing good works, or keeping Christ's commandments, is to be taken, when the Scripture represents it as a sure sign to our own consciences, that we are real Christians. And secondly, will prove that this is the chief of all evidences that men can have of their own sincere godliness.

First, I would show how Christian practice, or keeping Christ's commandments, is to be taken, when the Scripture represents it as a sure evidence to our own consciences, that we are sincere Christians.

And here I would observe, that we cannot reasonably suppose that when the Scripture in this case speaks of good works, good fruit, and keeping Christ's commandments, it has respect merely to what is external, or the motion and action of the body without including anything else, having no respect to any aim or intention of the agent, or any act of his understanding or will. For consider men's actions so, and they are no more good works or acts of obedience, than the regular motions of a clock; nor are they considered as the actions of the man, nor any human actions at all. The actions of the body, taken thus, are neither acts of obedience nor disobedience, any more than the motions of the body in a convulsion. But the obedience and fruit that is spoken of is the obedience and fruit of the man; and therefore not only the acts of the body, but the obedience of the soul, consisting in the acts and practice of the soul. Not that I suppose when the Scripture speaks in this case of gracious works and fruit and practice, that in these expressions are included all inward piety and holiness of heart, both principle and exercise, both spirit and practice: because then, in these things being given as signs of a gracious principle in the heart, the same thing would be given as a sign of itself, and there would be no distinction between root and fruit. But only the gracious exercise, and holy act of the soul is meant, and given as the sign of the holy principle and good estate. Neither is every kind of inward exercise of grace meant; but the practical exercise, that exercise of the soul and exertion of inward holiness, which there is in an obediential act; or that exertion of the mind and act of grace, which issues and terminates in what they call the imperate acts of the will; in which something is directed and commanded by the soul to be done, and brought to pass in practice.

Here, for a clearer understanding, I would observe, that there are two kinds of exercise of grace. 1. There are those that some call immanent acts, that is, those exercises of grace that remain within the soul, that begin and are terminated there, without any immediate relation to anything to be done outwardly, or to be brought to pass in practice. Such are the exercises of grace which the saints often have in contemplation; when the exercise that is in the heart, does not directly proceed to, or terminate in, anything beyond the thoughts of the mind, however they may tend to practice (as all exercises of grace do) more remotely. 2. There is another kind of acts of grace, that are more strictly called practical, or effective exercises, because they immediately respect something to be done. They are the exertions of grace in the commanding acts of the will, directing the outward actions. As when a saint gives a cup of cold water to a disciple in and from the exercise of the grace of charity, or voluntarily

endures persecution in the way of his duty, immediately from
the exercise of a supreme love to Christ. Here is the exertion
of grace producing its effect in outward actions. These exercises
of grace are practical and productive of good works, not only
because they are of a productive nature (for so are all exercises
of true grace), but because they are the producing acts. This is
properly the exercise of grace in the act of the will; and this is
properly the practice of the soul. And the soul is the immediate
actor of no other practice but this; the motions of the body follow from the laws of union between the soul and body, which
God, and not the soul, has fixed and maintains. The act of the
soul and the exercise of grace that is exerted in the performance
of a good work, is the good work itself, so far as the soul is concerned in it, or so far as it is the soul's good work. The determinations of the will are indeed our very actions, so far as they are
properly ours, as Dr. Doddridge observes.* In this practice of
the soul is included the aim and intention of the soul, which is
the agent. For not only should we not look on the motions of
a statue, doing justice or distributing alms by clockwork, as any
acts of obedience to Christ in that statue; but neither would any
body call the voluntary actions of a man, externally and materi-
ally agreeable to a command of Christ, by the name of obedience
to Christ, if he had never heard of Christ, or any of His commands, or had no thought of His commands in what he did. If
the acts of obedience and good fruit spoken of, be looked upon,
not as mere motions of the body, but as acts of the soul, the
whole exercise of the spirit of the mind in the action must be
taken in, with the end acted for, and the respect the soul then
has to God, &c., otherwise they are no acts of denial of ourselves,
or obedience to God, or service done to Him, but something else.
Such effective exercises of grace as these many of the martyrs
have experienced in a high degree. And all true saints live a life
of such acts of grace as these, as they all live a life of gracious
works, of which these operative exertions of grace are the life
and soul. And this is the obedience and fruit that God mainly
looks at. He looks at the soul more than at the body, as much as
the soul, in the constitution of the human nature, is the superior
part. As God looks at the obedience and practice of the man, He
looks at the practice of the soul; for the soul is the man in God's

* *Scripture Doctrine of Salvation by Grace through Faith*, Sermon I.

sight, "for the Lord seeth not as man seeth, for he looketh on the heart."

And thus it is that obedience, good works, good fruits, are to be taken, when given in Scripture as a sure evidence to our own consciences of a true principle of grace: even as including the obedience and practice of the soul, as preceding and governing the actions of the body. When practice is given in Scripture as the main evidence to others of our true Christianity, then is meant *that* in our practice which is visible to them, even our outward actions: but when practice is given as a sure evidence of our real Christianity to our own consciences, then is meant *that* in our practice which is visible to our own consciences; which is not only the motion of our bodies, but the exertion of the soul, which directs and commands that motion; which is more directly and immediately under the view of our own consciences, than the acts of the body. And that this is the intent of the Scripture, not only does the nature and reason of the thing show, but it is plain by the Scripture itself. Thus it is evident that when Christ, at the conclusion of His Sermon on the Mount, speaks of doing or practising those sayings of His as the grand sign of professors being true disciples, without which He likens them to a man that built his house upon the sand, and with which, to a man that built his house upon a rock; He has a respect, not only to the outward behaviour, but to the inward exercise of the mind in that behaviour: as is evident by observing what those preceding sayings of His are that He refers to, when He speaks of our doing or practising them; and we shall find they are such as these: "Blessed are the poor in spirit; blessed are they that mourn; blessed are the meek; blessed are they that do hunger and thirst after righteousness; blessed are the merciful; blessed are the pure in heart; whosoever is angry with his brother without a cause, &c.; whosoever looketh on a woman to lust after her, &c.; love your enemies; take no thought for your life," and others of the like nature, which imply inward exercises: and when Christ says, John xiv. 21, "He that hath my commandments, and keepeth them, he it is that loveth me;" He has evidently a special respect to that command several times repeated in the same discourse (which He calls, by way of eminence, His commandment), that they should love one another as He had loved them (see chap. xiii. 34, 35, and chap. xv. 10-14).

But this command respects chiefly an exercise of the mind or heart, though exerted in practice. So when the Apostle John says, 1 John ii. 3, "Hereby we do know that we know him, if we keep his commandments;" he has plainly a principal respect to the same command, as appears by what follows, ver. 7-11, and 2nd Epist, ver. 5, 6. When we are told in Scripture that men shall at the last day be judged according to their works, and all shall receive according to the things done in the body, it is not to be understood only of outward acts; for, if so, why is God so often spoken of as searching the hearts and trying the reins, "that he may render to every one according to his works?" As Rev. ii. 23, "And all the churches shall know that I am he which searcheth the reins and hearts; and I will give unto every one of you according to your works." Jer. xvii. 10, "I the Lord search the heart, I try the reins, even to give every man according to his ways, and according to the fruit of his doings." But if by his ways, and the fruit of his doings, is meant only the actions of his body, what need of searching the heart and reins in order to know them? Hezekiah in his sickness pleads his practice as an evidence of his title to God's favour, as including not only his outward actions, but what was in his heart: Isa. xxxviii. 3, "Remember now, O Lord, I beseech thee, how I have walked before thee in truth, and with a perfect heart."

Though in this great evidence of sincerity that the Scripture gives us, what is inward is of greatest importance, yet what is outward is included and intended, as connected with the practical exertion of grace in the will, directing and commanding the actions of the body. And hereby are effectually cut off all pretensions that any man can have to evidences of godliness, who externally lives wickedly; because the great evidence lies in that inward exercise and practice of the soul, which consists in the acts of the will, commanding outward acts. But it is known that these commanding acts of the will are not one way, and the actions of the bodily organs another: for the unalterable law of nature is that they should be united as long as soul and body are united, and the organs are not so destroyed as to be incapable of those motions that the soul commands. Thus it would be ridiculous for a man to plead that the commanding act of his will was to go to the public worship, while his feet carry him to a tavern or brothel-house; or that the commanding

act of his will was to give such a piece of money he had in his
hand to a poor beggar, while his hand at the same instant kept
it back and held it fast.

Secondly, *I proceed to show, that Christian practice, taken in
the sense that has been explained, is the chief of all the evidences
of a saving sincerity in religion, to the consciences of the professors of it;* much to be preferred to the method of the first convictions, enlightenings, and comforts in conversion, or any
immanent discoveries or exercises of grace whatsoever, that begin
and end in contemplation.* The evidence of this appears by
the following arguments.

ARGUMENT I.—Reason plainly shows that those things which
put it to the proof what men will actually cleave to and prefer
in their practice, when left to follow their own choice and inclinations, are the proper trial what they do really prefer in their
hearts. Sincerity in religion, as has been observed already, consists in setting God highest in the heart, in choosing Him before
other things, in having a heart to sell all for Christ, &c. But a
man's actions are the proper trial what a man's heart prefers. As
for instance, when it is so that God and other things come to
stand in competition, God is as it were set before a man on one
hand, and his worldly interest or pleasure on the other (as it
often is so in the course of a man's life); his behaviour in such
case, in actually cleaving to the one and forsaking the other, is
the proper trial showing which he prefers. Sincerity consists in
forsaking all for Christ in heart; but to forsake all for Christ in
heart is the very same thing as to have a heart to forsake all for
Christ; but certainly the proper trial whether a man has a heart
to forsake all for Christ, is his being actually put to it, the having
Christ and other things coming in competition, that he must
actually or practically cleave to one and forsake the other. To
forsake all for Christ in heart, is the same thing as to have a
heart to forsake all for Christ when called to it: but the highest
proof to ourselves and others that we have a heart to forsake all

* " Look upon John, Christ's beloved disciple and bosom companion!
He had received the anointing to know Him that is true, and he knew
that he knew Him, 1 John ii. 3. But how did he know that? He might
be deceived; (as it is strange to see what a melancholy fancy will do) what
is his last proof? 'Because we keep his commandments.' " *Shepard's
Parable of the Ten Virgins,* p. 210.

for Christ when called to it, is actually doing it when called to it, or so far as called to it. To follow Christ in heart is to have a heart to follow Him. To deny ourselves in heart for Christ is the same thing as to have a heart to deny ourselves for Him in fact. The main and most proper proof of a man's having an heart to anything, concerning which he is at liberty to follow his own inclinations, and either to do or not to do as he pleases, is his doing of it. When a man is at liberty whether to speak or keep silence, the most proper evidence of his having a heart to speak, is his speaking. When a man is at liberty whether to walk or sit still, the proper proof of his having a heart to walk, is his walking. Godliness consists not in a heart which intends to do the will of God, but in a heart which does it. The children of Israel in the wilderness had the former, of whom we read, Deut. v. 27-29, "Go thou near, and hear all that the Lord our God shall say; and speak thou unto us all that the Lord our God shall speak unto thee, and we will hear it, and do it. And the Lord heard the voice of your words, when ye spake unto me; and the Lord said unto me, I have heard the voice of the words of this people, which they have spoken unto thee; they have well said all that they have spoken. O that there were such an heart in them, that they would fear me and keep all my commandments always, that it might be well with them, and with their children for ever!" The people manifested that they had a heart to intend to keep God's commandments, and to be very forward in those intentions; but God manifests, that this was far from being the thing that He desired, wherein true godliness consists, even a heart actually to keep them.

It is therefore exceedingly absurd, and even ridiculous, for any to pretend that they have a good heart, while they live a wicked life, or do not bring forth the fruit of universal holiness in their practice. For it is proved in fact that such men do not love God above all. It is foolish to dispute against plain fact and ex-perience. Men that live in ways of sin, and yet flatter themselves that they shall go to heaven, or expect to be received hereafter as holy persons without a holy life and practice, act as though they expected to make a fool of their Judge. Which is implied in what the apostle says (speaking of men's doing good works and living a holy life, thereby exhibiting evidence of their title to everlasting life), Gal. vi. 7: "Be not deceived; God is not

mocked; for whatsoever a man soweth, that shall he also reap."
As much as to say, "Do not deceive yourself with an expectation
of reaping life everlasting hereafter, if you do not sow to the
Spirit here; it is in vain to think that God will be made a fool of
by you, that He will be shammed and baffled with shadows instead of substances, and with vain pretence instead of that good
fruit which He expects, when the contrary to what you pretend
appears plainly in your life before His face." In this manner the
word *mock* is sometimes used in Scripture. Thus Delilah says to
Samson, "Behold thou hast mocked me, and told me lies."
Judges xvi. 10, 13; *i.e.*, "Thou hast baffled me, intending to
make a fool of me, as if I might be easily turned off with any
vain pretence instead of the truth." So it is said that Lot, when
he told his sons-in-law that God would destroy that place,
"seemed as one that mocked, to his sons-in-law," Gen. xix. 14;
i.e., he seemed as one that would make a game of them, as though
they were such credulous fools as to regard such bugbears. But
the great Judge, whose eyes are as a flame of fire, will not be
mocked or baffled with any pretences, without a holy life. If in
his name men have prophesied and wrought miracles, and have
had faith so that they could remove mountains and cast out devils,
and however high their religious affections have been, however
great resemblances they have had of grace, and though their
hiding-place has been so dark and deep that no human skill nor
search could find them out; yet if they are workers or practisers
of iniquity, they cannot hide their hypocrisy from their Judge:
Job xxxiv. 22, "There is no darkness, nor shadow of death,
where the workers of iniquity may hide themselves." Would
a wise prince suffer himself to be fooled and baffled by a subject,
who should pretend that he was a loyal subject, and should tell
his prince that he had an entire affection to him, and that at
such and such a time he had experience of it, and felt his
affections strongly working towards him, and should come expecting to be accepted and rewarded by his prince, as one of
his best friends on that account, though he lived in rebellion
against him, following some pretender to his crown, and from
time to time stirring up sedition against him? Or would a
master suffer himself to be shammed and gulled by a servant,
that should pretend to great experiences of love and honour
towards him in his heart, and a great sense of his worthiness

and kindness, when at the same time he refused to obey him, and he could get no service done by him?

ARGUMENT II.—As reason shows that those things which occur in the course of life, which put it to the proof whether men will prefer God to other things in practice, are the proper trial of the uprightness and sincerity of their hearts; so the same are represented as the proper trial of the sincerity of professors in the Scripture. There we find that such things are called by that very name, trials or temptations (which I before observed are both words of the same signification). The things that put it to the proof whether men will prefer God to other things in practice, are the difficulties of religion, or those things which occur that make the practice of duty difficult and cross to other principles beside the love of God; because in them God and other things are both set before men together, for their actual and practical choice; and it comes to this, that we cannot hold to both, but one or the other must be forsaken. And these things are all over the Scripture called by the name of trials or proofs.* And they are called by this name, because hereby professors are tried and proved of what sort they be, whether they be really what they profess and appear to be; and because in them, the reality of a supreme love to God is brought to the test of experiment and fact; they are the proper proofs in which it is truly determined by experience whether men have a thorough disposition of heart to cleave to God or no: Deut. viii. 2, "And thou shalt remember all the way which the Lord thy God led thee these forty years in the wilderness, to humble thee, and to prove thee, whether thou wouldest keep his commandments or no:" Judges ii. 21, 22, "I also will not henceforth drive out any from before them of the nations which Joshua left when he died; that through them I may prove Israel, whether they will keep the way of the Lord." So chap. iii. 1, 4, and Exod. xvi. 4.

The Scripture, when it calls these difficulties of religion by the name of temptations or trials, explains itself to mean thereby the trial or experiment of their faith: James i. 2, 3, "My brethren, count it all joy when ye fall into divers temptations;

* 2 Cor. viii. 2; Heb. xi. 36; 1 Pet. i. 7; chap. iv. 12; Gen. xxii. 1; Deut. viii. 2, 16; chap. xiii. 3; Exod. xv. 25; chap. xvi. 4; Judges ii. 22; chap. iii, 1, 4; Psal. lxvi. 10, 11; Dan. xii. 10; Rev. iii. 10; Job xxiii. 10; Zech. xiii. 9; James i. 12; Rev. ii. 10; Luke viii. 13; Acts xx. 19; James i. 2, 3; 1 Pet. i. 6-7.

knowing this, that the trying of your faith worketh patience:"
1 Pet. i. 6, 7, "Now for a season ye are in heaviness through
manifold temptations; that the trial of your faith being much
more precious than of gold," &c. So the Apostle Paul speaks of
that expensive duty of parting with our substance to the poor,
as the proof of the sincerity of the love of Christians: 2 Cor. viii.
8. And the difficulties of religion are often represented in
Scripture as being the trial of professors, in the same manner
that the furnace is the proper trial of gold and silver: Psal. lxvi.
10, 11, "Thou, O God, hast proved us: thou hast tried us as silver
is tried: thou broughtest us into the net, thou laidst affliction
upon our loins." Zech. xiii. 9, "And I will bring the third part
through the fire; and will refine them as silver is refined; and
will try them as gold is tried." That which has the colour and
appearance of gold, is put into the furnace to try whether it be
what it seems to be, real gold or no. So the difficulties of religion
are called trials, because they try those that have the profession
and appearance of saints, whether they are what they appear to
be, real saints.

If we put true gold into the furnace, we shall find its great
value and preciousness: so the truth and inestimable value of
the virtues of a true Christian appear when under these trials:
1 Pet. i. 7, "That the trial of your faith, being much more precious than of gold that perisheth, might be found unto praise,
and honour, and glory." True and pure gold will come out of
the furnace in full weight: so true saints, when tried, come forth
as gold, Job xxiii. 10. Christ distinguishes true grace from
counterfeit by this, that it is gold tried in the fire, Rev. iii. 17, 18.
So that it is evident that these things are called trials in Scripture,
principally as they try or prove the sincerity of professors. And,
from what has now been observed, it is evident that they are the
most proper trial or proof of their sincerity; inasmuch as the very
meaning of the word trial, as it is ordinarily used in Scripture,
is the difficulty occurring in the way of a professor's duty, as the
trial or experiment of his sincerity. If trial of sincerity be the
proper name of these difficulties of religion, then, doubtless,
these difficulties of religion are properly and eminently the trial
of sincerity; for they are doubtless eminently what they are
called by the Holy Ghost: God gives things their name from
that which is eminently their nature. And, if it be so that these

things are the proper and eminent trial, proof, or experiment of the sincerity of professors, then certainly the result of the trial or experiment (that is, persons' behaviour or practice under such trials) is the proper and eminent evidence of their sincerity; for they are called trials or proofs, only with regard to the result, and because the effect is eminently the proof or evidence. And this is the most proper proof and evidence to the conscience of those that are the subjects of these trials. For when God is said by these things to try men and prove them, to see what is in their hearts and whether they will keep His commandments or no, we are not to understand, that it is for His own information, or that He may obtain evidence Himself of their sincerity (for he needs no trials for His information); but chiefly for their conviction, and to exhibit evidence to their consciences.*

Thus, when God is said to prove Israel by the difficulties they met with in the wilderness, and by the difficulties they met with from their enemies in Canaan, to know what was in their hearts, whether they would keep His commandments or no; it must be understood, that it was to discover them to themselves, that they might know what was in their own hearts. So when God tempted or tried Abraham with that difficult command of offering up his son, it was not for His satisfaction, whether he feared God or no, but for Abraham's own greater satisfaction and comfort, and the more clear manifestation of the favour of God to him. When Abraham had proved faithful under this trial, God says to him, " Now I know that thou fearest God, seeing thou hast not withheld thy son, thine only son, from me." Which plainly implies, that in this practical exercise of Abraham's grace under this trial, was a clearer evidence of the truth of his grace than ever was before; and the greatest evidence to Abraham's conscience; because God Himself gives it to Abraham as such, for his comfort and rejoicing; and speaks of it to him as what might be the greatest evidence to his conscience of his being upright in the sight of his Judge. Which proves what I say, that holy practice, under trials, is the highest evidence of the sincerity of professors

---

* " I am persuaded, as Calvin is, that all the several trials of men are to show them to themselves, and to the world, that they be but counterfeits; and to make saints known to themselves the better, Rom. v. 5. Tribulation works trial, and that hope, Prov. xvii. 3. If you will know whether it will hold weight, the trial will tell you." *Shepard's Parable of the Ten Virgins*, p. 302.

to their own consciences.   And we find that Christ from time to
time used the same method to convince the consciences of those
that pretended friendship to Him, and to show them what they
were.   This was the method he took with the rich young man,
Matt. xix. 16, &c.   He seemed to show a great respect to Christ;
he came kneeling to Him, and called Him "good Master," and
made a great profession of obedience to the commandments; but
Christ tried him, by bidding him go and sell all that he had, and
give to the poor, and come and take up his cross and follow Him,
telling him that then he should have treasure in heaven.   Similarly he tried another that we read of, Matt. viii. 20.   He made a
great profession of respect to Christ: says he, Lord, I will follow
thee whithersoever thou goest.   Christ immediately puts his
friendship to the proof, telling him that the foxes had holes,
and the birds of the air had nests, but that the Son of Man had
not where to lay His head.   And thus Christ is wont still to try
professed disciples in general, in His providence.   So the seed
sown in every kind of ground, stony ground, thorny ground, and
good ground, which in all appears alike when it first springs up,
yet is tried, and the difference made to appear, by the burning
heat of the sun.

Seeing therefore, that these are the things that God makes use
of to try us, it is undoubtedly the surest way for us to pass a right
judgment on ourselves, to try ourselves by the same things. These
trials of His are not for His information, but for ours; therefore
we ought to receive our information from thence.   The surest
way to know our gold is to look upon it and examine it in God's
furnace, where He tries it for that end, that we may see what it
is.   If we have a mind to know whether a building stands strong
or no, we must look upon it when the wind blows.   If we would
know whether that which appears in the form of wheat, has the
real substance of wheat, or is only chaff, we must observe it when
it is winnowed.   If we would know whether a staff be strong, or a
rotten broken reed, we must observe it when it is leaned on and
weight is borne upon it.   If we would weigh ourselves justly, we
must weigh ourselves in the scales that God makes use of to
weigh us.*   These trials in the course of our practice are as it

* Dr. Richard Sibbes (1577-1635), in his *Bruised Reed*, says, "When
Christ's will cometh in competition with any earthly loss or gain, yet if
then, in that particular case, the heart will stoop to Christ, it is a true

were the balances in which our hearts are weighed, or in which
Christ and the world, or Christ and His competitors, as to the
esteem and regard they have in our hearts, are weighed or are
put into opposite scales, by which there is opportunity to see
which preponderates. When a man is brought to the dividing
of paths, the one of which leads to Christ, and the other to the
object of his lusts, to see which way he will go, or is brought,
and as it were set between Christ and the world, Christ on the
right hand, and the world on the left, so that, if he goes to one,
he must leave the other, to see which his heart inclines most to,
or which preponderates in his heart; this is just the same thing
as laying Christ and the world in two opposing scales; and his
going to the one, and leaving the other, is just the same thing
as the sinking of one scale, and rising of the other. A man's practice, therefore, under the trials of God's providence, is as much
the proper evidence of the superior inclination of his heart as the
motion of the balance, with different weights in opposite scales,
is the proper experiment of the superior weight.

ARGUMENT III.—Another argument that holy practice, in the
sense which has been explained, is the highest kind of evidence
of the truth of grace to the consciences of Christians, is, that in
practice, grace, in Scripture style, is said to be made perfect, or
to be finished. So the Apostle James says, James ii. 22, "Seest
thou how faith wrought with his works, and by works was faith
made perfect?" (or finished, as the word in the original properly
signifies). So the love of God is said to be made perfect, or
finished, in the keeping of His commandments. 1 John ii. 4, 5,
"He that saith, I know him, and keepeth not his commandments, is a liar, and the truth is not in him: but, whoso keepeth
his word, in him verily is the love of God perfected." The commandment of Christ, which the apostle has especially respect to,
when he here speaks of our keeping His commandments, is (as I
observed before) that great commandment of His which respects
deeds of love to our brethren, as appears by the following verses.
Again, the love of God is said to be perfected in the same sense,

---

sign. For the truest trial of the power of grace is in such particular cases
as touch us the nearest; for there our corruption maketh the greatest
head. When Christ came near home to the young man in the gospel
(Matt. xix. 22), he lost a disciple of him." Sibbes' Works, Nicol's Puritan
Divines, Vol. I, p. 87.)

chapter iv. 12: "If we love one another, God dwelleth in us, and his love is perfected in us." Here, doubtless, the apostle has still respect to loving one another, in the same manner that he had explained in the preceding chapter, speaking of loving one another as a sign of the love of God, verses 17, 18: "Whoso hath this world's good, and shutteth up his bowels, &c., how dwelleth the love of God in him? My little children, let us not love in word, neither in tongue, but in deed (or in work) and in truth." By thus loving in work, the apostle says, "The love of God is perfected in us." Grace is said to be perfected or finished in holy practice, as therein it is brought to its proper effect, and to that exercise which is the end of the principle; the tendency and design of grace herein is reached, and its operation completed and crowned. The tree is made perfect in the fruit; it is not perfected in the seed's being planted in the ground; it is not perfected in the first quickening of the seed, and in its putting forth root and sprout; nor is it perfected when it comes up out of the ground; nor is it perfected in bringing forth leaves; nor yet in putting forth blossoms: but, when it has brought forth good ripe fruit, then it is perfected, therein it reaches its end, the design of the tree is finished: all that belongs to the tree is completed and brought to its proper effect in the fruit. So is grace in its practical exercises. Grace is said to be made perfect or finished in its work or fruit, in the same manner as it is said of sin, James i. 15, "When lust hath conceived, it bringeth forth sin; and sin, when it is finished, bringeth forth death." Here are three steps; first, sin in its principle or habit, in the being of lust in the heart; and nextly, here is its conceiving, consisting in the immanent exercises of it in the mind; and lastly, here is the fruit that was conceived, actually brought forth in the wicked work and practice. And this the apostle calls the finishing or perfecting of sin: for the word, in the original, is the same that is translated perfected in those forementioned places.

Now certainly if grace be in this manner made perfect in its fruit, if these practical exercises of grace are those exercises wherein grace is brought to its proper effect and end, and the exercises wherein whatsoever belongs to its design, tendency and operation, is completed and crowned; then these exercises must be the highest evidences of grace, above all other exercises. Certainly the proper nature and tendency of every principle must appear best and most fully in its most perfect exercises, or in those exercises wherein its nature is most completely exerted, and its tendency most fully answered and crowned, in its proper effect and end. If we would see the proper nature of anything whatsoever, and see it in its full distinction from other things, let us look upon it in the finishing of it. The Apostle James says, by works is faith made perfect; and introduces this as an argument to prove, that works are the chief evidence of faith, whereby the sincerity of the professors of faith is justified, James ii. And the Apostle John, after he had once and again told us that love was made perfect in keeping Christ's commandments, observes, 1 John iv. 18, that "perfect love casteth out fear," meaning (at least in part) love made perfect in this sense; agreeably to what he had said in the foregoing chapter, that, by loving in deed or work, we know that we are of the truth and shall assure our hearts, verses 18, 19.

ARGUMENT IV.—Another thing which makes it evident that holy practice is the principal evidence that we ought to make use of in judging both of our own and others' sincerity, is, that this evidence is above all others insisted on in Scripture. A common acquaintance with the Scripture, together with a little attention and observation, will be sufficient to show to any one that this is ten times more insisted on as a note of true piety throughout the Scripture, from the beginning of Genesis to the end of Revelation, than anything else. And, in the New Testament, where Christ and His apostles do expressly and of declared purpose lay down signs of true godliness, this is almost wholly insisted on. It may be observed that Christ and His apostles do not only often say those things, in their discoursing on the great doctrines of religion, which do show what the nature of true godliness must be, or from whence the nature and signs of it may be inferred by just consequence—often occasionally mentioning many things which appertain to godliness—but they do also often of set purpose give signs and marks for the trial of professors, putting them upon trying themselves by the signs they give, introducing what they say with such like expressions as these: "By this you shall know that you know God: by this are manifest the children of God and the children of the devil: he that hath this builds on a good foundation, he that hath it not, builds on the sand:

hereby we shall assure our hearts: he is the man that loveth Christ," &c.   But I can find no place where either Christ or His apostles in this manner give signs of godliness (though the places are many), but where Christian practice is almost the only thing insisted on.   Indeed in many of these places, love to the brethren is spoken of as a sign of godliness; and, as I have observed before, there is no one virtuous affection or disposition so often expressly spoken of as a sign of true grace, as our having love one to another: but then the Scriptures explain themselves to intend chiefly this love as exercised and expressed in practice, or in deeds of love.   So does the Apostle John, who, above all others, insists on love to the brethren as a sign of godliness, most expressly explain himself, in that way, 1 John iii. 14, &c. "We know that we have passed from death unto life, because we love the brethren: he that loveth not his brother abideth in death. Whoso hath this world's good, and seeth his brother have need, and shutteth up his bowels of compassion from him, how dwelleth the love of God in him?   My little children, let us love, not in word, neither in tongue, but in deed (*i.e.*, in deeds of love) and in truth.   And hereby we know that we are of the truth, and shall assure our hearts before him." So that when the Scripture so much insists on our loving one another as a great sign of godliness, we are not thereby to understand the immanent workings of affection which men feel one to another, so much as the soul's practising all the duties of the second table of the law; all which the New Testament tells us again and again a true love one to another comprehends, Rom. xiii. 8-10, Gal. v. 14, Matt. xxii. 39, 40. So that, really, there is no place in the New Testament where the declared design is to give signs of godliness, but that holy practice, and keeping Christ's commandments, is the mark chosen out from all others to be insisted on. Which is an invincible argument that it is the chief of all the evidences of godliness: unless we suppose that when Christ and His apostles, on design, set themselves about this business of giving signs by which professing Christians in all ages might determine their state, they did not know how to choose signs so well as we could have chosen for them. But, if we make the Word of Christ our rule, then undoubtedly those marks which Christ and His apostles did chiefly lay down and give to us that we might try ourselves by them, those same marks we ought especially to receive, and chiefly to make use of, in the trial of ourselves.* And surely those things which Christ and His apostles chiefly insisted on in the rules they gave, ministers ought chiefly to insist on in the rules they give. To insist much on those things that the Scripture insists little on, and to insist very little on those things on which the Scripture insists much, is a dangerous thing; because it is going out of God's way, and is to judge ourselves and guide others in an unscriptural manner. God knew which way of leading and guiding souls was safest and best for them: He insisted so much on some things, because He knew it to be needful that they should be insisted on; and let other things more alone as a wise God, because He knew it was not best for us so much to lay the weight of the trial there. As the Sabbath was made for man, so the Scriptures were made for man; and they are, by infinite wisdom, fitted for our use and benefit. We should, therefore, make them our guide in all things, in our thoughts of religion and of ourselves. And for us to make that great which the Scripture makes little, and that little which the Scripture makes great, tends to give us a monstrous idea of religion; and (at least indirectly and gradually) to lead us wholly away from the right rule, and from a right opinion of ourselves, and to establish delusion and hypocrisy.

ARGUMENT V.—Christian practice is plainly spoken of in the Word of God as the main evidence of the truth of grace, not only to others, but to men's own consciences. It is not only more spoken of and insisted on than other signs but in many places where it is spoken of, it is represented as the chief of all evidences. This is plain in the manner of expression from time to time. If God were now to speak from heaven to resolve our doubts concerning signs of godliness, and should give some particular sign, that by it all might know whether they were sincerely godly or not, with such emphatical expressions as these, " The man that has such a qualification or mark, that is the man that is a true saint; That is the very man; By this you may know; This is the thing by which it is manifest who are saints and who are sinners; Such men as these are saints indeed;" —should not we look upon it as a thing beyond doubt, that this

* " It is a sure rule, says Dr. Preston, that, what the Scriptures bestow much words on, we should have much thoughts on: and what the Holy Ghost urgeth most, we should prize most." *The Church's Carriage.*

was given as a special and eminently distinguishing note of true godliness? But this is the very case with respect to the sign of grace I am speaking of. God has again and again uttered Himself in His Word in this very manner concerning Christian practice, as John xiv., "He that hath my commandments, and keepeth them, he it is that loveth me." This Christ gives to the disciples, not so much to guide them in judging of others, as to apply to themselves for their own comfort after His departure, as appears by every word of the context. And by the way I would observe that not only the emphasis with which Christ utters Himself is remarkable, but also His so much insisting on and repeating the matter, as He does in the context: verse 15, "If ye love me, keep my commandments." Verse 23, "If a man love me, he will keep my words." And verse 24, "He that loveth me not, keepeth not my sayings." And in chapter xv. over and over: verse 2, "Every branch in me that beareth not fruit, he taketh away; and every branch that beareth fruit; he purgeth it." Verse 8, "Herein is my Father glorified, that ye bear much fruit; so shall ye be my disciples." Verse 14, "Ye are my friends, if ye do whatsoever I command you." We have this mark laid down with the same emphasis again, John viii. 31 : "If ye continue in my word, then are ye my disciples indeed." And again, 1 John ii. 3, "Hereby do we know that we know him, if we keep his commandments." And verse 5, "Whoso keepeth his word, in him verily is the love of God perfected; hereby know we that we are in him." And chapter iii. 18, 19, "Let us love in deed, and in truth; hereby we know that we are of the truth." What is translated *hereby* would have been a little more emphatical if it had been rendered more literally from the original, BY THIS we do know. And how evidently is holy practice spoken of as the grand note of distinction between the children of God and the children of the devil, in verse 10 of the same chapter? "In this the children of God are manifest, and the children of the devil." He is speaking of a holy, and a wicked practice, as may be seen in all the context; as verse 3, "Every man that hath this hope in him, purifieth himself, even as he is pure." Verses 6-10, "Whosoever abideth in him, sinneth not; whosoever sinneth, hath not seen him, neither known him. Little children, let no man deceive you; he that doeth righteousness, is righteous, even as he is righteous : he that committeth sin is of the devil. Whosoever is

born of God, sinneth not. Whosoever doeth not righteousness,
is not of God." So we have the like emphasis, 2 John 6: "This
is love, that we walk after his commandments;" that is (as we
must understand it), this is the proper evidence of love. So
1 John v. 3, "This is the love of God; that we keep his commandments." So the Apostle James, speaking of the proper evidences
of true and pure religion, says, James i. 27, "Pure religion and
undefiled before God and the Father, is this, to visit the fatherless
and widows in their affliction, and to keep himself unspotted
from the world." We have the like emphatical expressions used
about the same thing in the Old Testament, Job xxviii. 28:
"And unto man he said, Behold, the fear of the Lord, that is
wisdom; and to depart from evil is understanding." Jer. xxii. 15,
16, "Did not thy father eat and drink, and do judgment and
justice? He judged the cause of the poor and needy—was not
this to know me? saith the Lord." Psal. xxxiv. 11, &c., "Come,
ye children, hearken unto me; I will teach you the fear of the
Lord.—Keep thy tongue from evil, and thy lips from speaking
guile; depart from evil, and do good; seek peace and pursue it."
Psal. xv. 1-2, "Who shall abide in thy tabernacle? Who shall
dwell in thy holy hill? He that walketh uprightly," &c. Psal.
xxiv. 3, 4, "Who shall ascend into the hill of the Lord? or who
shall stand in his holy place? He that hath clean hands, and a
pure heart," &c. Psal. cxix. 1, "Blessed are the undefiled in the
way, who walk in the law of the Lord." Verse 6, "Then shall I
not be ashamed, when I have respect to all thy commandments."
Prov. viii. 13, "The fear of the Lord is to hate evil."

The Scripture never uses such emphatical expressions concerning any other signs of hypocrisy, and unsoundness of heart, as
concerning an unholy practice. So Gal. vi. 7, "Be not deceived;
God is not mocked; for whatsoever a man soweth, that shall he
also reap." 1 Cor. vi. 9, 10, "Be not deceived; neither fornicators,
nor idolaters, &c., shall inherit the kingdom of God." Eph. v. 5,
6, "For this ye know, that no whoremonger nor unclean person,
&c., hath any inheritance in the kingdom of Christ and of God.
Let no man deceive you with vain words." 1 John iii. 7, 8,
"Little children, let no man deceive you; he that doeth righteousness is righteous, even as he is righteous; he that committeth sin
is of the devil." Chap. ii. 4, "He that saith, I know him, and
keepeth not his commandments, is a liar and the truth is not

in him." And chap. i. 6, "If we say that we have fellowship with
him, and walk in darkness, we lie, and do not the truth." James
i. 26, "If any man among you seem to be religious, and bridleth
not his tongue, but deceiveth his own heart, this man's religion
is vain." Chap..iii. 14, 15, "If ye have bitter envying and strife
in your hearts, glory not, and lie not against the truth. This
wisdom descendeth not from above, but is earthly, sensual,
devilish." Psal. cxxv. 5, "As for such as turn aside unto their
crooked ways, the Lord shall lead them forth with the workers of
iniquity." Isa. xxxv. 8, "An highway shall be there, and it shall
be called the way of holiness; the unclean shall not pass over it."
Rev. xxi. 27, "And there shall in no wise enter into it whatsoever worketh abomination, or maketh a lie." And in many places,
"Depart from me, I know you not, ye that work iniquity."

ARGUMENT VI.—Another thing which makes it evident that
holy practice is the chief of all the signs of the sincerity of professors, not only to the world, but to their own consciences, is,
that this is the grand evidence which will hereafter be made use
of, before the judgment seat of God, according to which His
judgment will be regulated, and the state of every professor of
religion unalterably determined. In the future judgment there
will be an open trial of professors, and evidences will be made use
of in the judgment. For God's future judging of men in order
to their eternal retribution, will not be His trying, and finding
out, and passing a judgment upon the state of men's hearts, in
His own mind; but it will be a declarative judgment; and the
end of it will be not God's forming a judgment within Himself,
but the manifestation of His judgment and the righteousness of
it to men's own consciences, and to the world. And therefore
the day of judgment is called the day of the revelation of the
righteous judgment of God, Rom. ii. 5. And the end of God's
future trial and judgment of men, as to the part that each one
in particular is to have in the judgment, will be especially the
clear manifestation of God's righteous judgment to his conscience; as is manifest by Matt. xviii. 31-35; chap. xx. 8-15, chap.
xxii. 11-13, chap. xxv. 19-35, Luke xix. 15-26. And therefore,
though God needs no medium whereby to make the truth evident to Himself, yet evidences will be made use of in His future
judging of men. And doubtless the evidences will be such as
will be best fitted to serve the ends of the judgment; viz., the

manifestation of the righteous judgment of God, not only to the world, but to men's own consciences. But the Scriptures do abundantly teach us that the grand evidences which the Judge will make use of in the trial, for these ends, according to which the judgment of every one shall be regulated and the irreversible sentence passed, will be men's works or practice here in this world: Rev. xx. 12, "And I saw the dead, small and great, stand before God; and the books were opened;—and the dead were judged out of those things which were written in the books, according to their works." So verse 13, "And the sea gave up the dead which were in it; and death and hell gave up the dead which were in them; and they were judged every man according to their works." 2 Cor. v. 10, "For we must all appear before the judgment seat of Christ; that every one may receive the things done in his body, whether it be good or bad." Men's practice is the only evidence that Christ represents the future judgment as regulated by in that most particular description of the day of judgment which we have in the Holy Bible, Matt. xxv. 31-46. See also Rom. ii. 6-13, Jer. xvii. 10 and xxxii. 19, Job xxxiv. 11, Prov. xxiv. 12, Rev. xxii. 12, Matt. xvi. 27, Rev. ii. 23, Ezek. xxxiii. 20, 1 Pet. i. 17. The Judge, at the day of judgment, will not (for the conviction of men's own consciences, and to manifest them to the world) go about to examine men as to the method of their experiences, or set every man to tell his story of the manner of his conversion; but his works will be brought forth, as evidences of what he is, what he has done in darkness and in light: Eccl. xii. 14, "For God shall bring every work into judgment, with every secret thing, whether it be good, or whether it be evil." In the trial that professors shall be the subjects of in the future judgment, God will make use of the same evidences, to manifest them to themselves and to the world, which He makes use of to manifest them in the temptations or trials of His providence here, viz., their practice, in cases wherein Christ and other things come into actual and immediate competition. At the day of judgment, God, for the manifestation of his righteous judgment, will weigh professors in a balance that is visible. And the balance will be the same that He weighs men in now, which has been already described.

Hence we may undoubtedly infer that men's works (taken in the sense that has been explained) are the highest evidences by which they ought to try themselves. Certainly that which our supreme Judge will chiefly make use of to judge us by when we come to stand before Him, we should chiefly make use of to judge ourselves by.* If it had not been revealed in what manner and by what evidence the Judge would proceed with us hereafter, how natural would it be for one to say, "O that I knew what token God will chiefly look for and insist upon in the last and decisive judgment, and which he expects that all should be able to produce who would then be accepted of Him, and according to which sentence shall be passed; that I might know what token or evidence especially to look at and seek after now, as I would be sure not to fail then!" And seeing God has so plainly and abundantly revealed what this token or evidence is, surely, if we act wisely, we shall regard it as of the greatest importance.

Now from all that has been said, I think it to be abundantly manifest that Christian practice is the most proper evidence of the gracious sincerity of professors, to themselves and others; and the chief of all the marks of grace, the sign of signs, and evidence of evidences, that which seals and crowns all other signs.——I had rather have the testimony of my conscience, that I have such a saying of my Supreme Judge on my side as that, John xiv. 21, "He that hath my commandments, and keepeth them, he it is that loveth me," than the judgment and fullest approbation of all the wise, sound, and experienced divines, that have lived this thousand years, on the most exact and critical examination of my experiences as to the manner of my conversion. Not that there are no other good evidences of a state of grace but this. There may be other exercises of grace besides these efficient exercises, which the saints may have in contemplation, that may be very satisfying to them, but yet this is the chief and most proper evidence. There may be several good evidences that a tree is a fig-tree; but the highest and most proper evidence of it is that it actually bears figs. It is possible that a man may have a good assurance of a state of grace at his first conversion, before he has had opportunity to gain assurance by this great evidence I am

* "That which God maketh a rule of His own judgment, as that by which He judgeth of every man, that is a sure rule for every man to judge himself by. That which we shall be judged by at the last day is a sure rule to apply to ourselves for the present. Now by our obedience and works He judgeth us. 'He will give to every man according to his works.'" Dr. Preston's The Church's Carriage.

speaking of.—If a man hears that a great treasure is offered him, in a distant place, on condition that he will prize it so much as to be willing to leave what he possesses at home, and go a journey for it, over the rocks and mountains that are in the way, to the place where it is; it is possible the man may be well assured that he values the treasure to the degree spoken of as soon as the offer is made him : he may feel within him a willingness to go for the treasure, beyond all doubt; but yet, this does not hinder but that his actual going for it is the highest and most proper evidence of his being willing, not only to others, but to himself. But then as an evidence to himself, his outward actions and the motions of his body in his journey are not considered alone, exclusive of the action of his mind, and a consciousness within himself of the thing that moves him and the end he goes for; otherwise his bodily motion is no evidence to him of his prizing the treasure. In such a manner is Christian practice the most proper evidence of a saving value of the pearl of great price, and treasure hid in the field.

Christian practice is the sign of signs, in this sense that it is the great evidence which confirms and crowns all other signs of godliness. There is no one grace of the Spirit of God but that Christian practice is the most proper evidence of the truth of it. As it is with the members of our bodies, and all our utensils, the proper proof of the soundness and goodness of them is in the use of them : so it is with our graces (which are given to be used in practice, as much as our hands and feet, or the tools with which we work, or the arms with which we fight), the proper trial and proof of them is in their exercise in practice. Most of the things we use are serviceable to us, and so have their serviceableness proved, in some pressure, straining, agitation, or collision. So it is with a bow, a sword, an axe, a saw, a cord, a chain, a staff, a foot, a tooth, &c. And they that are so weak as not to bear the strain or pressure we need to put them to, are good for nothing. So it is with all the virtues of the mind. The proper trial and proof of them is in being exercised under those temptations and trials that God brings us under, in the course of His providence, and in being put to such service as strains hard upon the principles of nature.

Practice is the proper proof of the true and saving knowledge of God; as appears by that of the apostle already mentioned,

"Hereby we know that we know him, that we keep his commandments." It is in vain for us to profess that we know God if in works we deny Him, i. 16. And if we know God, but glorify Him not as God, our knowledge will only condemn us, and not save us, Rom. i. 21. The great note of that knowledge which saves and makes happy, is that it is practical: John xiii. 17, "If ye know these things, happy are ye if ye do them." Job xxviii. 28, "To depart from evil is understanding."

Holy practice is the proper evidence of repentance. When the Jews professed repentance, when they came confessing their sins to John as he preached the baptism of repentance for the remission of sins, he directed them to the right way of getting and exhibiting proper evidences of the truth of their repentance when he said to them, "Bring forth fruits meet for repentance," Matt. iii. 8. Which was agreeable to the practice of the Apostle Paul; see Acts xxvi. 20. Pardon and mercy are from time to time promised to him who has this evidence of true repentance, that he forsakes his sin, Prov. xxviii. 13, Isa. lv. 7, and many other places.

Holy practice is the proper evidence of a saving faith. It is evident that the Apostle James speaks of works, as what eminently justify faith, or (which is the same thing) justify the professors of faith, and vindicate and manifest the sincerity of their profession, not only to the world but to their own consciences; as is evident by the instance he gives of Abraham, James ii. 21-24. And in verses 20 and 26, he speaks of the practical and working nature of faith, as the very life and soul of it; in the same manner that the active nature and substance which is in the body of a man, is the life and soul of that. And if so, doubtless practice is the proper evidence of the life and soul of true faith, by which it is distinguished from a dead faith. For doubtless, practice is the most proper evidence of a practical nature, and operation the most proper evidence of an operative nature.

Practice is the best evidence of a saving belief of the truth. That is spoken of as the proper evidence of the truth's being in a professing Christian, that he walks in the truth, 3 John 3: "I rejoiced greatly when the brethren came and testified of the truth that is in thee, even as thou walkest in the truth."

Practice is the most proper evidence of a true coming to Christ, and accepting of and closing with Him. A true and saving coming to Christ, is (as Christ often teaches) a coming so as to forsake all for Him. And, as was observed before, to forsake all for Christ in heart is the same thing as to have a heart actually to forsake all; but the proper evidence of having a heart actually to forsake all, is, indeed, actually to forsake all so far as called to it. If a prince make suit to a woman in a far country, that she would forsake her own people and father's house and come to him to be his bride, the proper evidence of the compliance of her heart with the king's suit is her actually forsaking her own people and father's house and coming to him. By this her compliance with the king's suit is made perfect, in the same sense that the Apostle James says, " By works is faith made perfect."* Christ promises us eternal life on condition of our coming to Him: but it is such a coming as He directed the young man to, who came to inquire what he should do that he might have eternal life; Christ bade him go and sell all that he had, and come to Him, and follow Him. If he had consented in his heart to the proposal, and had therein come to Christ in his heart, the proper evidence of it would have been his doing of it; and therein his coming to Christ would have been made perfect. When Christ called Levi the publican, sitting at the receipt of custom and in the midst of his worldly gains, the closing of Levi's heart with this invitation of His Saviour to come to him was manifested and made perfect by his actually rising up, leaving all, and following Him, Luke v. 27, 28. Christ and other things are set before us together, for us particularly to cleave to one and forsake the other; in such a case, a practical cleaving to Christ is a practical acceptance of Christ; as much as a beggar's reaching out his hand and taking a gift that is offered is his practical acceptance of the gift. Yea, that act of the soul which cleaves to Christ in practice is itself the most perfect coming of the soul to Christ.

* " Our real taking of Christ appears in our actions and works: Isa. i. 19, ' If ye consent and obey, ye shall eat the good things of the land.' That is, if ye will consent to take JEHOVAH for your Lord and King: if ye give consent, there is the first thing; but that is not enough, but if ye also obey. The consent that standeth in the inward act of the mind, the truth of it will be seen in your obedience, in the acts of your lives. ' If ye consent and obey, ye shall eat the good things of the land;' that is, you shall take of all that He hath that is convenient for you; for then you are married to Him in truth, and have an interest in all His goods." *Dr. Preston's The Church's Carriage.*

Practice is the most proper evidence of trusting in Christ for salvation. The proper signification of the word *trust* both in common speech and in the Holy Scriptures, is the emboldening and encouragement of a person's mind to run some venture in practice, or in something that he does on the credit of another's sufficiency and faithfulness. And, therefore, the proper evidence of his trusting is the venture he runs in what he does. He is not properly said to run any venture, in a dependence on anything, who does nothing on that dependence, or whose practice is no otherwise than if he had no dependence. For a man to run a venture on a dependence on another is for him to do something from that dependence by which he seems to expose himself, and which he would not do were it not for that dependence. And, therefore, it is in complying with the difficulties and seeming dangers of Christian practice, in a dependence on Christ's sufficiency and faithfulness to bestow eternal life, that persons are said to venture themselves upon Christ, and trust in Him for happiness and life. They depend on such promises as that, Matt. x. 39, "He that loseth his life for my sake, shall find it." And so they part with all, and venture their all, in a dependence on Christ's sufficiency and truth. And this is the Scripture notion of trusting in Christ, in the exercise of a saving faith in Him. Thus Abraham, the father of believers, trusted in Christ, and by faith forsook his own country, in a reliance on the covenant of grace God established with him, Heb. xi. 8, 9. Thus also, "Moses by faith refused to be called the son of Pharaoh's daughter, choosing rather to suffer affliction with the people of God, than to enjoy the pleasures of sin for a season," Heb. xi. 24, &c. By faith, others exposed themselves to be stoned and sawn asunder, or slain with the sword; they "endured the trial of cruel mockings and scourgings, bonds and imprisonments, and wandered about in sheep-skins, and goat-skins, being destitute, afflicted, tormented." And in this sense the Apostle Paul by faith trusted in Christ, and committed himself to Him, venturing himself and his whole interest in a dependence on the ability and faithfulness of his Redeemer, under great persecutions and in suffering the loss of all things: 2 Tim. i. 12, "For the which cause I also suffer these things; nevertheless I am not ashamed, for I know whom I have believed, and am persuaded that he is able to keep that which I have committed unto him against that day."

If a man should have word brought him from the king of a distant island that he intended to make him his heir; if, upon receiving the tidings, he immediately leaves his native land and friends and all that he has in the world, to go to that country, in a dependence on what he hears, then he may be said to venture himself, and all that he has in the world upon it. But if he only sits still and hopes for the promised benefit, inwardly pleasing himself with the thoughts of it, he cannot properly be said to venture himself upon it; he runs no venture in the case; he does nothing by which he would be exposed to any suffering in case all should fail. So he that, on the credit of what he hears of a future world, and in a dependence on the report of the gospel concerning life and immortality, forsakes all, or does so at least so far as there is occasion, making everything entirely give place to his eternal interest; he, and he only, may properly be said to venture himself on the report of the gospel. And this is the proper evidence of a true trust in Christ for salvation.

Practice is the proper evidence of a gracious love, both to God and men. The texts that plainly teach this have been so often mentioned already that it is needless to repeat them.

Practice is the proper evidence of humility. That expression and manifestation of humility of heart which God insists on, we should regard as the proper expression and manifestation of it: but this is walking humbly. Micah vi. 8, " He hath showed thee O man, what is good; and what doth the Lord require of thee, but to do justly, to love mercy, and to walk humbly with thy God?"

This is also the proper evidence of the true fear of God: Prov. viii. 13, " The fear of the Lord is to hate evil." Psal. xxxiv. 11, &c., " Come, ye children, hearken unto me; I will teach you the fear of the Lord. Keep thy tongue from evil, and thy lips from speaking guile: depart from evil, and do good; seek peace and pursue it." Prov. iii. 7, " Fear the Lord, and depart from evil." Prov. xvi. 6, " By the fear of the Lord, men depart from evil." Job i. 8, " Hast thou considered my servant Job—a perfect and an upright man, one that feareth God, and escheweth evil?" Chap. ii. 3, " Hast thou considered my servant Job—a perfect and an upright man, one that feareth God, and escheweth evil? And still he holdeth fast his integrity, although thou movedst me against him." Psal. xxxvi. 1, " The transgression of the wicked saith within my heart, There is no fear of God before his eyes."

Similarly, in rendering again according to benefits received, is the proper evidence of true thankfulness. Psal. cxvi. 12, "What shall I render unto the Lord for all his benefits towards me?" 2 Chron. xxxii. 25, "But Hezekiah rendered not again according to the benefit done unto him." Paying our vows unto God, and ordering our conversation aright, seem to be spoken of as the proper expression and evidence of true thankfulness, Psal. l. 14, "Offer unto God thanksgiving, and pay thy vows unto the Most High." Verse 23, "Whoso offereth praise, glorifieth me: and to him that ordereth his conversation aright will I show the salvation of God."

The proper evidence of gracious desires and longings, and that which distinguishes them from those that are false and vain, is, that they are not idle wishes and wouldings like Balaam's, but effectual in practice to stir up persons earnestly and thoroughly to seek the things they long for. Psalm xxvii. 4, "One thing have I desired of the Lord, that will I seek after." Psal. lxiii. 1, 2, "O God, thou art my God, early will I seek thee: my soul thirsteth for thee, my flesh longeth for thee in a dry and thirsty land, where no water is; to see thy power and thy glory." Verse 8, "My soul followeth hard after thee." Cant. i. 4, "Draw me, we will run after thee."

Practice is the proper evidence of a gracious hope: 1 John iii. 3, "Every man that hath this hope in him purifieth himself even as he is pure." Patient continuance in well-doing, through the difficulties and trials of the Christian course, is often mentioned as the proper expression and fruit of a Christian hope: 1 Thess. i. 3, "Remembering without ceasing your work of faith, and labour of love, and patience of hope." 1 Pet. i. 13, 14, "Wherefore gird up the loins of your mind, be sober, and hope to the end for the grace that is to be brought unto you at the revelation of Jesus Christ, as obedient children," &c. Psal. cxix. 166, "Lord, I have hoped in thy salvation, and done thy commandments." Psal. lxxviii. 7, "That they might set their hope in God, and not forget the works of the Lord, but keep his commandments."

A cheerful practice of our duty, and doing the will of God, is the proper evidence of a truly holy joy. Isa. lxiv. 5, "Thou meetest him that rejoiceth and worketh righteousness." Psal. cxix. 111, 112, "Thy testimonies have I taken as an heritage for ever; for they are the rejoicing of my heart. I have inclined mine heart to perform thy statutes alway, even unto the end." Verse 14, "I have rejoiced in the way of thy testimonies as much as in all riches." 1 Cor. xiii. 6, "Charity rejoiceth not in iniquity, but rejoiceth in the truth." 2 Cor. viii. 2, "The abundance of their joy abounded unto the riches of their liberality."

Practice also is the proper evidence of Christian fortitude. The trial of a good soldier is not in his chimney corner, but in the field of battle, 1 Cor. ix. 25-27, 2 Tim. ii. 3-5.

And, as the fruit of holy practice is the chief evidence of the truth of grace, so the degree in which experiences have influence on a person's practice, is the surest evidence of the degree of that which is spiritual and divine in his experiences. Whatever pretences persons may make to great discoveries, great love and joys, they are no further to be regarded than they have influence on their practice. Not but that allowances must be made for the natural temper. But that does not hinder but that the degree of grace is justly measured by the degree of the effect in practice. For the effect of grace is as great, and the alteration as remarkable, in a very ill natural temper, as another. Although a person of such a temper will not behave himself so well, with the same degree of grace as another, the diversity from what was before conversion, may be as great; because a person of a good natural temper did not behave himself so ill before conversion.

Thus I have endeavoured to represent the evidence there is that Christian practice is the chief of all the signs of saving grace. And, before I conclude this discourse, I would say something briefly in answer to two objections that may possibly be made by some against what has been said upon this head.

OBJECTION I.—Some may be ready to say: this seems to be contrary to that opinion, so much received among good people, that professors should judge of their state chiefly by their inward experience, and that spiritual experiences are the main evidences of true grace.

I answer, it is doubtless a true opinion, and justly much received among good people, that professors should chiefly judge of their state by their experience. But it is a great mistake that what has been said is at all contrary to that opinion. The chief sign of grace to the consciences of Christians being Christian practice, in the sense that has been explained and according to what has been shown to be the true notion of Christian practice, is not at all inconsistent with Christian experience being the chief evidence of grace. Christian or holy practice is spiritual practice; and that is not the motion of a body that knows not how, nor when, nor wherefore it moves: but spiritual practice in man is the practice of a spirit and body jointly, or the practice of a spirit animating, commanding, and actuating a body to which it is united, and over which it has power given it by the Creator. And, therefore, the main thing in this holy practice is the holy action of the mind, directing and governing the motions of the body. And the motions of the body are to be looked upon as belonging to Christian practice, only secondarily, and as they are dependent and consequent on the acts of the soul. The exercises of grace that Christians find, or are conscious to within themselves, are what they experience within themselves. Herein therefore lies Christian experience: and this Christian experience consists as much in those operative exercises of grace in the will, that are immediately concerned in the management of the behaviour of the body, as in other exercises. These inward exercises are not the less a part of Christian experience because they have outward behaviour immediately connected with them. A strong act of love to God is not the less a part of spiritual experience because it immediately produces and effects some self-denying and expensive outward action, which is much to the honour and glory of God.

To speak of Christian experience and practice as if they were two things properly and entirely distinct, is to make a distinction without consideration or reason. Indeed, all Christian experience is not properly called practice, but all Christian practice is properly experience. And the distinction that is made between them is not only an unreasonable but an unscriptural distinction. Holy practice is one kind or part of Christian experience; and both reason and Scripture represent it as the chief and most important and most distinguishing part of it. So it is represented in Jer. xxii. 15, 16: "Did not thy father eat and drink, and do justice and judgment?—He judged the cause of the poor and needy—Was not this to know me, saith the Lord?" Our inward acquaintance with God surely belongs to the head of experimental religion: but this, God represents as consisting chiefly in that experience which there is in holy practice. So the exercises of those graces of the love of God, and the fear of God, are a part of experimental religion: but these the Scripture represents as consisting chiefly in practice, in those forementioned texts: 1 John v. 3, "This is the love of God, that we keep his commandments." 2 John 6, "This is love, that we walk after his commandments." Psal. xxxiv. 11, &c., "Come, ye children, and I will teach you the fear of the Lord: depart from evil, and do good." Such experiences as these Hezekiah took comfort in, chiefly on his sick bed, when he said, "Remember, O Lord, I beseech thee, how I have walked before thee in truth, and with a perfect heart." And such experiences as these, the Psalmist chiefly insists upon, in the 119th Psalm, and elsewhere.

Such experiences as these the Apostle Paul mainly insists upon, when he speaks of his experiences in his epistles; as Rom. i. 9, "God is my witness, whom I serve with my spirit in the gospel of his Son." 2 Cor. i. 12, "For our rejoicing is this, the testimony of our conscience, that—by the grace of God, we have had our conversation in the world." Chap. iv. 13, "We having the same spirit of faith, according as it is written, I have believed, and therefore hath I spoken; we also believe, and therefore speak." Chap. v. 7, "We walk by faith, not by sight." Ver. 14, "The love of Christ constraineth us." Chap. vi. 4-7, "In all things approving ourselves as the ministers of God, in much patience, in afflictions, in necessities, in distresses, in labours, in watchings, in fastings. By pureness, by knowledge, by long-suffering, by kindness, by the Holy Ghost, by love unfeigned—by the power of God." Gal. ii. 20, "I am crucified with Christ: nevertheless I live; yet not I, but Christ liveth in me: and the life, which I now live in the flesh, I live by the faith of the Son of God." Phil. iii. 7, 8, "But what things were gain to me, those I counted loss for Christ. Yea, doubtless, and I count all things but loss, for the excellency of the knowledge of Christ Jesus my Lord, and do count them but dung that I may win Christ." Col. i. 29, "Whereunto I also labour, striving according to his working, which worketh in me mightily." 1 Thess. ii. 2, "We were bold in our God, to speak unto you the gospel of God with much contention." Ver. 8-10, "Being affectionately desirous of you, we were willing to have imparted unto you, not the gospel of God only, but also our own souls, because ye were dear unto us. For ye remember, brethren, our labour and travail, labouring night and day. Ye are witnesses, and God also, how holily, and justly, and unblameably, we behaved ourselves among you." And such experiences as these they were that this blessed apostle chiefly comforted himself in the consideration of, when he was going to martyrdom: 2 Tim. iv. 6, 7, "For I am now ready to be offered, and the time of my departure is at hand. I have fought a good fight, I have finished my course, I have kept the faith."

And not only does the most important and distinguishing part of Christian experience lie in spiritual practice; but such is the nature of those exercises of grace wherein spiritual practice consists, that nothing is so properly called by the name of experimental religion. This is properly Christian experience, wherein the saints have opportunity to see, by actual experience and trial, whether they have a heart to do the will of God, and to forsake other things for Christ, or no. As that is called experimental philosophy which brings opinions and notions to the test of fact, so is that properly called experimental religion, which brings religious affections and intentions to the like test.

There is a sort of external religious practice, without inward experience, which in the sight of God is esteemed good for nothing. And there is what is called experience, that is without practice, being neither accompanied nor followed with a Christian behaviour; and this is worse than nothing. Many persons seem to have very wrong notions of Christian experience and spiritual light and discoveries. Whenever a person finds within him a heart to treat God as God, at the time that he has the trial, and finds his disposition effectual in the experiment, that is the most proper and most distinguishing experience. And to have at such a time that sense of divine things, that apprehension of the truth, importance and excellency of the things of religion, which then sways and prevails and governs his heart and hands; this is the most excellent spiritual light, and these are the most distinguishing discoveries. Religion consists much in holy affection; but those exercises of affection which are most distinguishing of true religion are these practical exercises. Friendship between earthly friends consists much in affection; but those strong exercises of affection that actually carry them through fire and

water for each other are the highest evidences of true friendship.

There is nothing in what has been said contrary to what is
asserted by some sound divines, when they say that there are no
sure evidences of grace, but the acts of grace. For that doth not
hinder but that these operative, productive acts, those exercises
of grace that are effectual in practice, may be the highest evidences above all other kinds of acts of grace. Nor does it hinder
but that, when there are many of these acts and exercises following one another in a course, under a variety of trials, the evidence
is still heightened, as one act confirms another. A man, by once
seeing his neighbour, may have good evidence of his presence;
but by seeing him from day to day, and conversing with him in
various circumstances, the evidence is established. The disciples
when they first saw Christ, after His resurrection, had good evidence that He was alive; but, by conversing with Him for forty
days, and His showing Himself alive to them by many infallible
proofs, they had yet higher evidence.*

The witness or seal of the Spirit that we read of doubtless consists in the effect of the Spirit of God on the heart, in the im-
plantation and exercises of grace there, and so consists in
experience. And it is also beyond doubt, that this seal of the
Spirit is the highest kind of evidence of the saints' adoption that
ever they obtain. But in these exercises of grace in practice,
that have been spoken of, God gives witness, and sets to His seal,
in the most conspicuous, eminent, and evident manner. It has
been abundantly found to be true in fact, by the experience of
the Christian church, that Christ commonly gives, by His Spirit,

* " The more these visible exercises of grace are renewed, the more certain you will be. The more frequently these actings are renewed, the
more abiding and confirmed your assurance will be. A man that has been
assured of such visible exercises of grace, may quickly after be in doubt
whether he was not mistaken. But when such actings are renewed again
and again, he grows more settled and established about his good estate.
If a man see a thing once, that makes him sure; but, if afterwards, he
fear he was deceived, when he comes to see it again, he is more sure he
was not mistaken. If a man read such passages in a book, he is sure it
is so. Some months after, some may bear him down that he was mistaken, so as to make him question it himself; but when he looks, and
reads it again, he is abundantly confirmed. The more men's grace·is
multiplied, the more their peace is multiplied:" 2 Pet. i. 2, " Grace and
peace be multiplied unto you through the knowledge of God, and of Jesus
our Lord." *Stoddard's Way to know Sincerity and Hypocrisy.*

the greatest and most joyful evidences to His saints of their son-ship in those effectual exercises of grace under trials, which have been spoken of; as is manifest in the full assurance and unspeak-able joys of many of the martyrs. Agreeable to 1 Pet. iv. 14, " If ye be reproached for the name of Christ, happy are ye; for the spirit of glory and of God resteth upon you." And that in Rom. v. 2, 3, " We rejoice in hope of the glory of God, and glory in tribulations." And agreeable to what the Apostle Paul often declares of what he experienced in his trials. And when the Apostle Peter, in my text, speaks of the joy unspeakable and full of glory, which the Christians to whom he wrote, experi-enced, he has respect to what they found under persecution, as appears by the context. Christ manifested Himself as the Friend and Saviour of His saints, to Shadrach, Meshach and Abednego in the furnace. And when the apostle speaks of the witness of the Spirit, in Rom. viii. 15-17, he has a more immediate respect to what the Christians experienced, in their exercises of love to God, in suffering persecution; as is plain by the context. He is, in the foregoing verses, encouraging the Christians of Rome under their sufferings, that though their bodies be dead, because of sin, yet they should be raised to life again. But it is more especially plain by the verse immediately following, verse 18, " For I reckon that the sufferings of this present time, are not worthy to be compared with the glory that shall be revealed in us." So the apostle has evidently respect to their persecutions in all that he says to the end of the chapter. When the apostle speaks of the earnest of the Spirit, which God had given to him, in 2 Cor. v. 5, the context shows plainly that he has respect to what was given him in his great trials and sufferings. And in that promise of the white stone and new name to him that overcomes, Rev. ii. 17, it is evident Christ has a special respect to a benefit that Christians should obtain, by overcoming in the trial they had in that day of persecution. This appears by verse 13, and many other passages in the epistles to the seven churches of Asia.

Objection II.—Some also may be ready to object against what has been said of Christian practice being the chief evidence of the truth of grace, that this is a legal doctrine; and that this making practice a thing of too great importance in religion, magnifies works, and tends to lead men to make too much of their own doings, to the diminution of the glory of free grace,

and does not seem well to consist with the great gospel doctrine
of justification by faith alone.

But this objection is altogether without reason. Which way
is it inconsistent with the freeness of God's grace that holy practice should be a sign of God's grace? It is our works being the
price of God's favour, and not their being the sign of it, that is
the thing which is inconsistent with the freeness of that favour.
Surely the beggar's looking on the money he has in his hands,
as a sign of the kindness of him who gave it to him, is in no
respect inconsistent with the freeness of that kindness. It is his
having money in his hands as the price of a benefit, that is the
thing which is inconsistent with the free kindness of the giver.
The notion of the freeness of the grace of God to sinners, as that
is revealed and taught in the gospel, is not that no holy and
amiable qualifications or actions in us shall be a fruit, and so a
sign of that grace; but that it is not the worthiness or loveliness
of any qualification or action of ours which recommends us to
that grace. Free grace implies that kindness is shown to the
unworthy and unlovely; that there is great excellency in the
benefit bestowed, and no excellency in the subject as the price of
it; that goodness goes forth and flows out, from the fulness of
God's nature, the fulness of the Fountain of good, without any
amiableness in the object to draw it. And this is the notion of
justification without works (as this doctrine is taught in the
Scripture), that it is not the worthiness or loveliness of our works,
or anything in us, which is in anywise accepted with God, as a
balance for the guilt of sin, or a recommendation of sinners to
His acceptance as heirs of life. Thus we are justified only by the
righteousness of Christ, and not by our righteousness. And when
works are opposed to faith in this affair, and it is said that we
are justified by faith and not by works, thereby is meant that it is
not the worthiness or amiableness of our works, or anything in
us, which recommends us to an interest in Christ and His benefits; but that we have this interest only by faith, or by our
souls receiving Christ, or adhering to and closing with Him. But
that the worthiness or amiableness of nothing in us recommends
and brings us to an interest in Christ, is no argument that
nothing in us is a sign of an interest in Christ.

If the doctrines of free grace, and justification by faith alone,
be inconsistent with the importance of holy practice as a sign of

grace, then they are equally inconsistent with the importance of
anything whatsoever in us as a sign of grace, any holiness, or
any grace that is in us, or any of our experiences or religion. For
it is as contrary to the doctrines of free grace and justification by
faith alone, that any of these should be the righteousness by
which we are justified, as that holy practice should be so. It is
with holy works as it is with holy qualifications; it is inconsistent
with the freeness of gospel grace, that a title to salvation should
be given to men for the loveliness of any of their holy qualifications, as much as that it should be given for the holiness of their
works. It is inconsistent with the gospel doctrine of free grace
that an interest in Christ and His benefits should be given for
the loveliness of a man's true holiness, for the amiableness of his
renewed, sanctified, heavenly heart, his love to God and being
like God, or his experience of joy in the Holy Ghost, self-empti-
ness, a spirit to exalt Christ above all, and to give all glory to
Him, and a heart devoted unto Him. It is, I say, inconsistent
with the gospel doctrine of free grace that a title to Christ's
benefits should be given out of regard to the loveliness of any
of these, or that any of these should be our righteousness in the
affair of justification. And yet this does not hinder the importance of these things as evidences of an interest in Christ.
Just so it is with respect to holy actions and works. To make
light of works because we are not justified by works, is the same
thing in effect as to make light of all religion, all grace and
holiness, yea, true evangelical holiness, and all gracious experience; for all is included, when the Scripture says, we are not
justified by works; for by works in this case, is meant all our own
righteousness, religion, or holiness, and every thing that is in us,
all the good we do, and all the good which we are conscious of,
all external acts, and all internal acts and exercises of grace, and
all experiences, and all those holy and heavenly things wherein
the life and power and the very essence of religion do consist,
all those great things which Christ and His apostles mainly
insisted on in their preaching, and endeavoured to promote, as
of the greatest consequence in the hearts and lives of men, and
all good dispositions, exercises and qualifications of every kind
whatsoever; and even faith itself, considered as a part of our
holiness. We are justified by none of these things; and if we
were, we should, in a Scripture sense, be justified by works. And

therefore if it be not legal, and contrary to the evangelical doctrine of justification without works, to insist on any of these as of great importance, as evidences of an interest in Christ; then no more is it thus, to insist on the importance of holy practice. It would be legal to suppose that holy practice justifies by bringing us to a title to Christ's benefits as the price of it, or as recommending to it by its preciousness or excellence; but it is not legal to suppose, that holy practice justifies the sincerity of a believer, as the proper evidence of it. The Apostle James did not think it legal to say that Abraham our father was justified by works in this sense. The Spirit that indited the Scripture did not think the great importance and absolute necessity of holy practice to be inconsistent with the freeness of grace. He commonly teaches them both together; as in Rev. xxi. 6, 7, God says, "I will give unto him that is athirst of the fountain of the water of life freely;" and then adds, in the very next words, "He that overcometh shall inherit all things," as though behaving well in the Christian race and warfare were the condition of the promise. So in the next chapter, in the 14th and 15th verses, Christ says, "Blessed are they that do his commandments, that they may have right to the tree of life, and may enter in through the gates into the city." He then declares in the 15th verse how they that are of a wicked practice shall be excluded; and yet, in the two verses next following, does with very great solemnity give forth an invitation to all to come and take of the water of life freely: "I am the root and the offspring of David, and the bright and morning star. And the Spirit and the bride say, Come. And let him that heareth, say, Come. And let him that is athirst, Come; and whosoever will, let him come and take the water of life freely." So chapter iii. 20, 21, "Behold I stand at the door and knock; if any man hear my voice, and open the door, I will come in to him, and sup with him, and he with me." But then it is added in the next words, "To him that overcometh will I grant to sit with me in my throne." And in that great invitation of Christ, Matt. xi. 28-30, "Come unto me, all ye that labour and are heavy laden, and I will give you rest," Christ adds in the next words, "Take my yoke upon you, and learn of me, for I am meek and lowly in heart; and ye shall find rest unto your souls; for my yoke is easy, and my burden is light": as though taking the burden of Christ's service, and imitating His example, were necessary in order to the promised rest. So in that great invitation to sinners to accept of free grace, Isa. lv., "Ho, every one that thirsteth, come ye to the waters, and he that hath no money; come ye, buy and eat; yea, come, buy wine and milk without money and without price"; even there, in the continuation of the same invitation, the sinner's forsaking his wicked practice is spoken of as necessary to the obtaining mercy: verse 7, "Let the wicked forsake his way, and the unrighteous man his thoughts; and let him return unto the Lord, and he will have mercy upon him, and to our God, for he will abundantly pardon." So the riches of divine grace in the justification of sinners, is set forth with the necessity of holy practice, Isa. i. 16, &c.: "Wash you, make you clean, put away the evil of your doings from before mine eyes, cease to do evil, learn to do well, seek judgment, relieve the oppressed, judge the fatherless, plead for the widow. Come now, and let us reason together; saith the Lord; though your sins be as scarlet, they shall be as white as snow; though they be red like crimson, they shall be as wool."

And in that most solemn invitation of wisdom, Prov. ix., after it is represented what great provision is made, and how all things were ready, the house built, the beasts killed, the wine mingled, the table furnished, and the messengers sent forth to invite the guests; then we have the free invitation, verses 4-6: "Whoso is simple, let him turn in hither; as for him that wanteth understanding (i.e., has no righteousness), she saith to him, Come, eat of my bread, and drink of the wine which I have mingled." But then in the next breath it follows, "Forsake the foolish, and live; and go in the way of understanding," as though forsaking sin, and going in the way of holiness, were necessary in order to live. So that the freeness of grace, and the necessity of holy practice, which are thus from time to time joined together in Scripture, are not inconsistent one with another. Nor does it at all diminish the honour and importance of faith, that the exercises and effects of faith in practice should be esteemed the chief signs of it; any more than it lessens the importance of life, that action and motion are esteemed the chief signs of that.

So that in what has been said of the importance of holy practice as the main sign of sincerity, there is nothing legal, nothing derogatory to the freedom and sovereignty of gospel grace, nothing in the least clashing with the gospel doctrine of justi-

fication by faith alone without the works of the law, nothing in
the least tending to lessen the glory of the Mediator and our
dependence on His righteousness, nothing infringing on the
special prerogatives of faith in the affair of our salvation, nothing
in any wise detracting from the glory of God and His mercy, or
exalting man, or diminishing his dependence and obligation. So
that if any are against such an importance of holy practice as
has been spoken of, it must be only from a senseless aversion to
the letters and sound of the word *works*, when there is no reason
in the world to be given for it, but what may be given with equal
force, why they should have an aversion to the words *holiness*,
godliness, grace, religion, experience, and even *faith* itself; for
to make a righteousness of any of these is as legal, and as inconsistent with the way of the new covenant, as to make a righteousness of holy practice.

It is greatly to the hurt of religion for persons to make light
of, and insist little on, those things which the Scripture insists
most upon as of most importance in the evidence of our interest
in Christ, under a notion that to lay weight on these things is
legal, and an old covenant way; and so, to neglect the exercises
and effectual operations of grace in practice, and insist almost
wholly on discoveries, and the method and manner of the immanent exercises of conscience and grace in contemplation; de-
pending on an ability to make nice distinctions in these matters,
and a faculty of accurate discerning in them, from philosophy or
experience. It is in vain to seek for any better or any further
signs than those that the Scriptures have most expressly mentioned, and most frequently insisted on, as signs of godliness.
They who pretend to a greater accuracy in giving signs, or by
their extraordinary experience or insight into the nature of
things, to give more distinguishing marks which shall more
thoroughly search out and detect the hypocrite, are but certain
to darken their own minds, and the minds of others; their re-
finings and nice discerning are in God's sight, but refined foolishness and a sagacious delusion. Here are applicable those words
of Agur, Prov. xxx. 5, 6, " Every word of God is pure; he is a
shield unto them that put their trust in him : add thou not unto
his words, lest he reprove thee, and thou be found a liar." Our
discerning, with regard to the hearts of men, is not much to be
trusted. We can see but a little way into the nature of the soul,

and the depths of man's heart. The ways are so many whereby persons' affections may be moved without any supernatural influence, the natural springs of the affections are so various and so secret, so many things have oftentimes a joint influence on the affections, the imagination, and that in ways innumerable and unsearchable, natural temper, education, the common influences of the Spirit of God, a surprising concourse of affecting circumstances, an extraordinary coincidence of things in the course of men's thoughts, together with the subtle management of invisible malicious spirits, the ways are so many, I say, that no philosophy or experience will ever be sufficient to guide us safely through this labyrinth and maze, without our closely following the clue which God has given us in His Word. God knows His own reasons why He insists on some things, and plainly sets them forth as the things that we should try ourselves by rather than others. It may be it is because He knows that these things are attended with less perplexity, and that we are less liable to be deceived by them than others. He best knows our nature; He knows the nature and manner of His own operations; He best knows the way of our safety; He knows what allowances to make for different states of His church, and different tempers of particular persons, and varieties in the manner of His own operations, how far nature may resemble grace, and how far nature may be mixed with grace, what affections may rise from imagination, and how far imagination may be mixed with spiritual illumination. And therefore it is our wisdom not to take His work out of His hands, but to follow Him, and lay the stress of the judgment of ourselves there where He has directed us. If we do otherwise, no wonder if we are bewildered, confounded, and fatally deluded. But if we had got into the way of looking chiefly at those things which Christ and His apostles and prophets chiefly insisted on, and so in judging of ourselves and others, chiefly regarding practical exercises and effects of grace, not neglecting other things, it would be of manifold happy consequence. It would above all things tend to the conviction of deluded hypocrites, and to prevent the delusion of those whose hearts were never brought to a thorough compliance with the straight and narrow way which leads to life. It would tend to deliver us from innumerable perplexities, arising from the various inconsistent schemes there are about methods and steps of experience. It would greatly tend to prevent professors neglecting strictness of life and tend to promote their engagedness and earnestness in their Christian walk. It would become fashionable for men to show their Christianity, more by an amiable distinguished behaviour, than by an abundant and excessive declaring their experiences. We should get into the way of appearing lively in religion, more by being lively in the service of God and our generation than by the liveliness and forwardness of our tongues, and making a business of proclaiming on the house tops with our mouths the holy and eminent acts and exercises of our own hearts. Christians that are intimate friends would talk together of their experiences and comforts in a manner better becoming Christian humility and modesty, and more to each other's profit: their tongues not running before, but rather going behind their hands and feet, after the prudent example of the blessed apostle, 2 Cor. xii. 6. Many occasions of spiritual pride would thus be cut off, and so a great door shut against the devil. A great many of the main stumbling-blocks against experimental and powerful religion would be removed, and religion would be declared and manifested in such a way that, instead of hardening spectators, and exceedingly promoting infidelity and atheism, it would, above all things, tend to convince men that there is a reality in religion, and greatly awaken them, and win them, by convincing their consciences of the importance and excellency of religion. Thus the light of professors would so shine before men, that others, seeing their good works, would glorify their Father which is in heaven.